# What in the World Is Going On?

## Living with Confidence in a Chaotic World

# What in the World Is Going On?

10 Prophetic Clues You Cannot Afford to Ignore

---

# Living with Confidence in a Chaotic World

What on Earth Should We Do Now?

## Dr. David Jeremiah

THOMAS NELSON
Since 1798

NASHVILLE   DALLAS   MEXICO CITY   RIO DE JANEIRO

Published in Nashville, Tennessee, by Thomas Nelson. Thomas Nelson is a registered trademark of Thomas Nelson, Inc.

Published in association with Yates & Yates, LLP, www.yates2.com.

Thomas Nelson, Inc. titles may be purchased in bulk for educational, business, fund-raising, or sales promotional use. For information, please e-mail SpecialMarkets@ThomasNelson.com.

In *What in the World Is Going On?* "Battle of Armageddon" © 1944 Sony/ATV Music Publishing LLC. All rights administered by Sony/ATV Music Publishing LLC, 8 Music Square West, Nashville, TN 37203. All rights reserved. Used by permission.

Unless otherwise noted, Scripture quotations are taken from the New King James Version˚. © 1982 by Thomas Nelson, Inc. Used by permission. All rights reserved.

Scripture quotations marked ASV are from the American Standard Version.

Scripture quotations marked KJV are from the King James Version of the Bible.

Scripture quotations marked NASB are from the New American Standard Bible˚, © The Lockman Foundation 1960, 1962, 1963, 1968, 1971, 1972, 1973, 1975, 1977. Used by permission.

Scripture quotations marked NIV are from the Holy Bible, New International Version˚, NIV˚. © 1973, 1978, 1984 by Biblica, Inc.™ Used by permission of Zondervan. All rights reserved worldwide. www.zondervan.com.

Scripture quotations marked NLT are from the Holy Bible, New Living Translation. © 1996. Used by permission of Tyndale House Publishers, Inc., Wheaton, Illinois 60189. All rights reserved.

Scripture quotations marked MSG are from *The Message* by Eugene H. Peterson. © 1993, 1994, 1995, 1996, 2000. Used by permission of NavPress Publishing Group. All rights reserved.

ISBN 978-0-8499-4909-8

*Printed in the United States of America*

11 12 13 14 15 QG 5 4 3 2 1

# Contents

*What in the World Is Going On?*

# *Living with Confidence in a Chaotic World*

# What in the World
# Is Going On?

"Blessing and honor and glory and power

Be to Him who sits on the throne,

And to the Lamb, forever and ever!" (Revelation 5:13*b*)

# Acknowledgments

LAST FALL, WHEN I BEGAN TO TEACH THE TRUTHS OF THIS BOOK TO the church I pastor in Southern California, I was taken aback by the number of people who came to me each week and said, "You are going to put this information in a book, aren't you?" Here's my answer! Thanks for your encouragement!

Barbara Boucher is my administrative assistant at Shadow Mountain Community Church. Her servant-hearted willingness to serve where she is needed reflects the spirit of this church family.

I owe a great deal to the team of people who surround me at Turning Point Ministries. Diane Sutherland understands the pressures that descend upon our office when a book is in the making. During those days especially, she guards my time and organizes my life. I dare not think of the chaos of my existence without her dedicated ministry.

Since this book seeks to shine the light of the Scriptures on twenty-first-century world events, the burden of research has been huge. Cathy Lord excels at this task. She never rests until she has found the exact quote, statistic, or source we are looking for. Cathy, your commitment to detail amazes me. Thank you for your hard work!

Paul Joiner is the creative services director at Turning Point. He is an integral part of all that we do around the world through radio, television, and print media. Paul, your creativity is infectious, and your fingerprints are all over this project.

Rob Morgan and William Kruidenier read each chapter and added their suggestions. Rob and William, thank you for your thoughtful contributions. Thanks also to my friend Chuck Emert for his valuable input.

Thomas Nelson editor Joey Paul has been encouraging me to write another book on prophecy for several years. When I sent him the preliminary notes for this book, he called back immediately and said, "David, this is it!" Joey, your friendship is a blessing in my life.

This was my first opportunity to work with writer and editor Tom Williams. He has been a gracious addition to our publication team. Tom, I hope we get to work together again soon.

On the first pages of all my books, you will see the name of Yates and Yates, the literary agency founded by Sealy Yates. Thank you, Sealy, for believing in this book and for coordinating the efforts between the Turning Point team and the Thomas Nelson team.

I want to express my gratitude to my son David, whose leadership at Turning Point makes it possible for me to invest my time in studying and writing.

Finally, I give thanks to Almighty God for my wife, Donna. When I first started talking about *What in the World Is Going On?*, I told her that my plans were to teach this material in our Sunday night services. She looked at me and said, "David, that needs to be taught in the morning services so everyone can hear it." I always do what she tells me to do!

Most of all, I want to express my hope that God will be glorified as we tell the story of His plans for our future!

# Knowing the Signs

WHAT IN THE WORLD IS GOING ON? NEVER BEFORE IN MY lifetime have I read such jarring headlines, distressing news analyses, or dire predictions for America and the world. Things are getting so chaotic that many pundits are using the term *perfect storm* to explain the confluence of wide-ranging food shortages, record-high fuel prices, and natural disasters.

In a recent twenty-four-hour period, major newswires carried the following disturbing reports: A cyclone in Myanmar caused upwards of eighty-four thousand deaths, along with the loss of primary rice fields in a time of severe global rice shortages. A powerful volcano that had been considered dormant for nine thousand years erupted in Chile. A virulent new virus infected tens of thousands of China's children, causing mounting fears of a widespread epidemic. Longtime antagonists China and Japan announced a pledge of "peace, friendship and cooperation as neighbors," including a joint venture in oil refining. In resurgent Russia, newly installed president Dmitri Medvedev promptly named Vladimir Putin as prime minister, calling it "the most important position in the executive power."[1]

Within that same time frame, housing defaults and foreclosures continued to fuel America's economic tailspin. As if that weren't enough bad news, oil soared to its highest closing price on the New York Mercantile Exchange since oil trading began twenty-five years ago, and the dollar continued to sputter against most foreign currencies. When stories like these pile one on top of the other, we can't help but wonder . . . what in the world is going on?

As we look out at the world of the early twenty-first century, food shortages are producing widespread hunger in places that have previously known plenty. Outright starvation is replacing hunger in regions that have known want. Among the poorest, it has become a struggle just to survive. In Thailand, the world's leading rice exporter, prices doubled in the first quarter of this year. Food prices have fueled riots in Haiti, Cameroon, Egypt, Mexico, Philippines, Indonesia, Ivory Coast, and several other African nations. Desperation is so high in Thailand, Philippines, and Pakistan that armed personnel have been called in to protect food harvesters, supervise grain sales, and guard warehouses. A UN observer warned, "A hungry man is an angry man, and as food gets more and more difficult to access . . . we can expect to see more incidents of civil unrest."[2]

While natural disasters cannot be prevented, the wise remain alert to signs of their approach so they can take protective measures. This was done when the volcano erupted in Chile. Despite being perceived as benign or even extinct, the Chaitén volcano gave off dozens of warning signs, in the form of earthquakes. Surprised by the first eruption, wise government officials recognized the continuing danger. They ordered mandatory evacuations as the volcano again turned violent and spewed deadly ash and lava into the air. As a result, not one death was directly attributed to the eruption.[3] When signs are recognized and appropriate warnings are issued, disaster can often be avoided.

On the other hand, the disaster in Myanmar shows what happens when the signs are ignored. As early as six days before Cyclone Nargis made landfall, Myanmar officials were notified of the potential for a large-scale storm. Throughout the next several days, as the storm intensified and took direct aim at the country's heavily populated delta, the ruling military junta received regular weather updates and warnings. Even with the increasing urgency of these warnings and the obvious signs in the intensely churning sky, the government issued no warnings and ordered no evacuations. Their failure left the people at the mercy of the 160-mile-per-hour winds and twelve-foot storm surges. The result? Several weeks later, with the number of dead and missing already totaling more than 78,000, and with more than 2.5 million left homeless, global relief teams remained poised to deliver food and supplies but, for political reasons, were denied entry into the country.

Within days, before the world could absorb the events in Myanmar, a 7.9 earthquake decimated southern China. Seven thousand schoolchildren and their teachers were buried beneath the rubble of their schools. Upwards of 70,000 died, and 5 million were left homeless. Scores of powerful aftershocks continued to threaten further destruction and hampered rescue efforts. China tested her new friendship agreement with Japan by requesting that they send their crack rescue teams to supplement the 130,000 military personnel already mobilized by China. One aftershock that no one anticipated was China's request for aid from Taiwan, long considered a renegade, if not an enemy. China also accepted help from Russia and North Korea.

Are we seeing signs today that should warn us of anything? What in the world is going on when enemies of Israel bestow posthumous honors to the headmaster of a UN school in Gaza for his work as chief engineer of the Islamic Jihad's bomb squad?[4] What about that parade of tankers, fighter jets, and missiles in Moscow on May Day, reminiscent of the Cold War era? What about the doubling of millions of dollars of investments in Iraqi stocks, currently traded by scribbles on a dry-erase board? Or what about the largest US embassy complex ever built now ready for occupancy in Baghdad, formerly the infamous ancient Babylon, the city that throughout the Bible stands as the antithesis of everything good? What about the planned restoration of Babylon to its fabled glory? What about the increased use of biometrics, those scans of fingerprints, irises, and faces used for personal identification in Iraq and other "places of global conflict"? Currently such forms of ID are used to bar people from markets or certain neighborhoods, and they are ready to be implemented worldwide in the name of security. When you hear these reports, do you find yourself thinking, *What in the world is going on?*

The events unfolding in today's world are ominously threatening to unsettle institutions, reorder national political alignments, change the balance of world power, and destabilize the equitable distribution of resources. People everywhere are beginning to live in a state of fear and anxiety. Serious people are asking, "If these things are happening today, what will the future be like for my children and grandchildren? Do current headlines give us any signs about what is coming next?"

There is one reliable source of information about the future—one that has an astounding record of accuracy. The Bible! But, strangely, many who purport to preach God's Word shy away from teaching prophecy. A preacher friend tells of "a pastor who once boasted that he didn't preach about prophecy because, in his words, 'Prophecy only distracts people from the present.' An astute colleague deftly retorted, 'Well, then, there's certainly a lot of distraction in the Scripture!' Fulfilling prophecy is one of God's calling cards."[5]

Indeed, one of the most convincing evidences of biblical inspiration is the staggering number of prophecies that have been fulfilled with pinpoint accuracy. Perhaps the most familiar examples are the fulfillments of more than three hundred prophecies relating to Christ's first coming to earth. In his book *The Rapture*, Dr. Tim LaHaye remarked, "No scholar of academic substance denies that Jesus lived almost 2,000 years ago. And we find three times as many prophecies in the Bible relating to His second coming as to His first. Thus, the second advent of our Lord is three times as certain as His first coming, which can be verified as historical fact."[6]

The Bible has proven to be absolutely dependable. Therefore we can trust it as the one source of reliable information about the meaning of the events of our day and what those events tell us about our hope for the future as we look toward the return of Christ. The Lord Jesus Himself spoke of the wisdom of discerning the signs of the times and of taking appropriate action as we wait for His return (Matthew 24, Mark 16). The Bible gives us clues conveying crucial information for interpreting the signs as the days of man's rule on earth wind toward their end. In each of the ten chapters of this book, we will apply these clues and point out these signs, viewing current events from the perspective of God's wonderful Word. We will be warned and challenged, but we will also be encouraged and comforted. Our purpose is not to make you fearful, but to make you aware so you can be prepared.

Popular radio personality Clifton Fadiman was a certifiable bookworm. Not only was he the book editor for a national magazine and a published author, but his love of books and his sense of what made a book good landed him the position of an editor for the Book of the Month Club, a post he held for fifty years. He once explained how he went about deciding what kind of book the reading public wanted: "What do our members, in the depths of their being, hanker for? They want books that explain our terrifying age honestly . . . Our age is so scary and fractionated that we need this kind of help more than people did in the [last] century. We thirst for books that put together pieces of the jigsaw puzzle."[7]

I am sure there have never been any times more "scary and fraction-ated" than these early days of the twenty-first century. In this book, I want to help you find the truth about what is going on. I want to show you that while our age is certainly "fractionated," it need not be scary—not for Christians who trust the Lord and know how to read the signs and understand coming events. As you read this book, I trust you will begin to put together the pieces of the puzzle, that you will recognize the clues that God has given us to find peace in "our terrifying age," and that you will come to an understanding of what in the world is going on. But mostly, I hope this book will help to "Let not your heart be troubled, neither let it be afraid" (John 14:27).

—David Jeremiah
San Diego, California
July 2008

# ONE

# The Israel Connection

MAY 14, 1948, WAS A PIVOTAL DAY IN HUMAN HISTORY. ON THAT afternoon, a car carrying prominent Jewish leader David Ben-Gurion rushed down Rothschild Boulevard in Tel Aviv and stopped in front of the Tel Aviv Art Museum. Four o'clock was only minutes away, and inside, more than four hundred people—Jewish religious and political leaders and press representatives from all over the world—were assembled in an auditorium, anxiously awaiting his arrival. Ben-Gurion quickly bounded up the steps. Precisely at four o'clock, local time, he stepped to the podium, called the meeting to order, and read these historic words:[1]

> This right is the natural right of the Jewish people to be masters of their own fate, like all other nations, in their own sovereign State. Accordingly, we . . . are here assembled . . . and by virtue of our natural and historic right, and on the strength of the resolution of the General Assembly of the United Nations, hereby declare the establishment of the Jewish State in Eretz-Israel, to be known as the State of Israel.[2]

Six thousand miles away, President Truman sat in the Oval Office, reading a forty-word statement about to be released to the press. He penciled in a few added words, then signed his approval and noted the time. It was 6:10 p.m. One minute later, the White House press secretary read the release to the world. The United States had officially recognized the birth of the modern nation of Israel.

Isaiah's prophecy, written 740 years before the birth of Jesus, declared: "Who has heard such a thing? Who has seen such things? Shall the earth be made to give birth in one day? Or shall a nation be born at once?" (Isaiah 66:8). Secular Israel was born that day.

As I write this chapter, Israel is about to celebrate her sixtieth anniversary as a nation. What amazes many people is that in those six decades, this tiny nation with a population of slightly more than 7 million has become the geopolitical center of the world. Why is this so? Why is a fledgling country with a total land space smaller than New Jersey mentioned in the nightly news more than any other nation except the United States?

To answer these questions, we must understand what happened on that day in 1948, what is happening today in Israel, and how these events affect the entire world. For answers, we must turn not to the evening news or the front page of the newspaper, but to the Bible. As Rabbi Binyamin Elon, a member of the Israeli Knesset, wrote:

> I believe that if you do not know how to read the Bible, you cannot
> understand the daily newspaper. If you do not know the biblical story
> of Abraham, Isaac, and Jacob, you cannot possibly understand the
> miracle of the modern state of Israel.[3]

The story of Israel begins at the very beginning of the Bible, in the book of Genesis. The very proportion of the coverage tells us something about the importance of Israel. Only two chapters are given to the whole story of creation. One chapter records the fall of man. Eight chapters cover the thousands of years from creation to the time of Abram. Then we find that fully thirty-eight chapters deal with the life stories of Abraham, Isaac, and Jacob—the progenitors of the Jewish race. Apparently God finds Abraham and his descendants to be of enormous importance.

## The Abrahamic Covenant

The Almighty God of heaven and earth made a binding covenant with Abraham, who was to be the father of the Jewish nation. The provisions of that covenant are recorded in Genesis 12:1–3:

> Now the LORD had said to Abram:
> "Get out of your country,
> From your family
> And from your father's house,
> To a land that I will show you.
> I will make you a great nation;
> I will bless you
> And make your name great;
> And you shall be a blessing.
> I will bless those who bless you,
> And I will curse him who curses you;
> And in you all the families of the earth shall be blessed."

Notice that God's covenant with Abraham consists of four unconditional promises. First, God promised to bless Abraham. That promise has been lavishly kept; Abraham has been blessed in many ways. For thousands of years, the very name of Abraham has been revered by Jews, Christians, and Muslims alike—a significant portion of the world's population. Abraham has also been blessed through the gifts God gave to his descendants, the Jews. Mark Twain once wrote:

Jews constitute but one percent of the human race. It suggests a nebulous dim puff of star dust in the blaze of the Milky Way. Properly the Jew ought hardly to be heard of; but he is heard of. He is as prominent on this planet as any other people. His commercial importance is extravagantly out of proportion to the smallness of his bulk. His contributions to the world's list of great names in literature, science, art, music, finance, medicine, and abstruse learning are also altogether out of proportion to the weakness of his numbers. He has made a marvelous fight in the world in all ages and he has done it with his hands tied behind him.[4]

One astounding fact that dramatically illustrates Twain's point is the disproportionate number of Nobel Prizes awarded to Jews. From 1901 to 2007, a total of 777 Nobel Prizes have been given to individuals in recognition of significant contributions to mankind. Of that total, 176 have been awarded to Jews. Of the 6 billion inhabitants of the world, only slightly more than 13 million are Jewish—less than two-thirds of 1 percent of the total world population. That miniscule percentage of the population has won 22.6 percent of all the Nobel Prizes awarded to date.[5]

Second, God promised to bring out of Abraham a great nation. Currently, nearly 5.4 million Jews live in Israel alone. Another 5 million live in the United States, and a significant Jewish population remains scattered throughout the world.[6] Add to these present figures all the descendants of Abraham who have lived throughout history and you truly have a population as uncountable as the nighttime stars (see appendix A for a chart of Jewish population statistics).

Third, God promised to make Abraham a blessing to many. That promise has been spectacularly kept. Just think what the world would be missing had it not been for the Jews. Without the Jews, we would have no Bible. Without the Jews, there would have been no Jesus. Without the Jewish Jesus, there would be no Christianity. Without the Jews, there would be no Ten Commandments, the Law that has largely been the basis of jurisprudence and statutory proceedings among most of the civilized nations of the world.

Fourth, God promised to bless those who blessed Israel and curse those who cursed her. He has kept that promise faithfully. No nation has blessed Israel like the United States of America, and no nation has been as blessed as the United States. In one of my previous books, I elaborated on this fact:

I believe one of the reasons America has been blessed as a nation is that she has become a homeland for the Jewish people. Here the Jews can retain their religion. Here they have economic, social, and educational opportunities. Today the Christian church in America stands firmly between the Jew and the repetition of any further anti-Semitism.[7]

Throughout history, the judgments of God have fallen heavily upon Israel's oppressors—Egypt, Assyria, Babylon, Rome, and in more modern times, Spain, Germany, and Russia. Today, as forces less friendly to Israel gain influence in the United States, there are many who believe that America is dangerously close to being added to this hit list. Hal Lindsey wrote:

Although America continues to be Israel's principal protector, and continues to enjoy the concomitant blessings that come with it, America's good fortunes began to wane about the time the White House forced Israel into the Oslo Agreement. The "land for peace" formula called for Israel to give up some of the land of Promise in exchange for peace. In other words, it was a form of blackmail whose terms were drawn up in Washington and forced upon Israel for the express purpose of undoing what God had already done, including dividing Jerusalem and taking part of it from the Jews.[8]

God has certainly kept his promise to Abraham. He has blessed him and the nation that has come from him; He has multiplied his seed as the sands of the earth and stars of the sky; He has made him a blessing to the whole world; those who have blessed him have been blessed, and those who have cursed him have been cursed.

Of all God's covenant promises to Abraham, I believe the most amazing is His promise concerning the land. God told Abraham to leave his country, his family, and his father's house and go "to a land that I will show you" (Genesis 12:1). God then led Abraham to the land that would belong to his descendants forever. You can feel the awe and sense the meaning this promise has to Jews in this passage from Rabbi Binyamin Elon's book, *God's Covenant with Israel*:

I travel to my home in Beth El from Jerusalem on the same route that Abraham and others traveled in Biblical times, from Shechem to Hebron and places in between. Today we pass many other beautiful flourishing Jewish communities along the way . . . When I reach the Givat Assaf intersection, I am always inspired by the large sign posted there, sponsored by our local grocer: "Here, in Beth El, 3800 years ago, the Creator of the World promised the Land of Israel to the people of Israel. It is by virtue of this promise that we dwell today in Haifa, Tel Aviv, Shilo, and Hebron."[9]

## The Record of Israel's Land

To this very day, the issue of who controls the Promised Land is the most volatile in international politics. But we need not worry; the right to the Promised Land has already been determined by the only One who has the authority to determine it. The land is called holy because it belongs to God. The Bible tells us that the earth is the Lord's to do with as He wills (Psalm 24:1; Exodus 19:5). In His covenant with Abraham, God designated who would control this land: He gave it to Abraham and his descendants, the people of Israel.

We read of God's choice of the Jews in Deuteronomy 7:6, where He declared the people of Israel holy, chosen to be "a people for Himself, a special treasure above all the peoples on the face of the earth." When I first began studying prophecy, I remember reading an offbeat little rhyme about Israel by British journalist William Norman Ewer: "How odd of God to choose the Jews." And when you think about it, this poetic quip expresses a valid observation. Doesn't it seem a little odd that of all the people on earth, God selected these particular people to be His chosen nation? Why would God choose the Jews?

The Bible tells us that His choice of Israel had nothing to do with merit. It was not because she was more numerous than other people in the world; she was the least (Deuteronomy 7:7). It was not because Israel was more sensitive to God than other nations. Although God called her by name, Israel did not know Him (Isaiah 45:4). It was not because Israel was more righteous than other nations. When God later confirmed His promise of land to the Jews, He reminded them that they were a rebellious, stiff-necked people (Deuteronomy 9:6–7).

If God chose to bless the nation of Israel not because she was more populous or spiritually responsive or righteous than other nations, just why did He choose the Jews? The answer: because *it was His sovereign purpose to do so.* His sovereign purpose means He cares what happens to His people and their land. He is not merely a passive observer to all that is taking place in Israel. As He told the people through Moses, theirs was "a land for which the LORD your God cares; the eyes of the LORD your God are always on it, from the beginning of the year to the very end of the year" (Deuteronomy 11:12).

## God's Covenant and the Land of Israel

The people of Israel today are the beneficiaries of God's covenant with Abraham. And to those who are sensitive to the historical nature of the covenant, their possession of the land God promised to Abraham thousands of years ago has great meaning. The deep feeling Jews have for their land is powerfully expressed in this passage by Rabbi Binyamin Elon:

> I walk the streets of the Promised Land where Abram walked. I drive through the roads and plains where Isaac tended his flocks. I hike to the hilltops from where Jacob peered expectantly in all directions . . . I see these things and remember clearly the biblical truth. God gave the Promised Land, all of it, to our Patriarchs: Abraham, Isaac, and Jacob.[10]

Another rabbi, Abraham Joshua Heschel, attributes the Jews' strong connection with their land to the power of God's covenant with

Abraham to hold the Jewish people together throughout the ages with a common, bonding love for the land:

> The love of this land was due to an imperative, not an instinct, not to a sentiment. There is a covenant, an engagement of the people to the land. We live by covenants. We could not betray our pledge or discard the promise. When Israel was driven into exile, the pledge became a prayer; the prayer a dream; the dream a passion, a duty, a dedication . . . It is a commitment we must not betray . . . To abandon the land would make a mockery of all our longings, prayers, and commitments. To abandon the land would be to repudiate the Bible.[11]

## An Exact Covenant

Some have suggested that the promise of land to Abraham's descendants is not to be taken literally. They say it is merely a symbol that indicates a general blessing, or perhaps the promise of heaven. But the Bible is too specific to let us get by with such ephemeral vagueness. It describes the land in definite terms and outlines it with clear geographical boundaries. Dr. John Walvoord stressed this point when he wrote:

> The term *land* . . . used in the Bible, means exactly what it says. It is not talking about heaven. It is talking about a piece of real estate in the Middle East. After all, if all God was promising Abraham was heaven, he could have stayed in Ur of the Chaldees. Why go on the long journey? Why be a pilgrim and a wanderer? No, God meant *land*.[12]

The land promised to Abraham takes in much more area than what the present nation of Israel occupies. Genesis 15:18 tells us that it stretches all the way from the Mediterranean Sea on the west to the

Euphrates River on the east. Ezekiel fixes the northern boundary of Palestine at Hamath, one hundred miles north of Damascus (Ezekiel 48:1), and the southern boundary at Kadesh, about one hundred miles south of Jerusalem (Ezekiel 48:28).

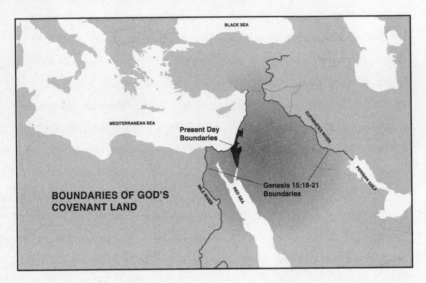

## An Everlasting Covenant

And I will establish My covenant between Me and you and your descendants after you . . . Also I give to you and your descendants after you the land in which you are a stranger, all the land of Canaan, as an everlasting possession; and I will be their God. (Genesis 17:7–8)

In this remarkable prophecy God promised Abraham and his descendants the land of Canaan as their possession in perpetuity. When you look at a map and locate that tiny strip of land Israel now claims as hers, you can see that she does not now, nor has she ever fully occupied the land that was described to Abraham in God's covenant promise. If Israel were currently occupying all the land promised to her, she would control all the holdings of present day Israel, Lebanon, the West Bank of Jordan, and substantial portions of Syria, Iraq, and Saudi Arabia. Not until the Millennium will Israel occupy all the land the Lord gave her in His promise to Abraham.

## The Relocation of the People of Israel

### The Scattering of the Jews

Just as the people of Israel were about to enter the land of promise, Moses told them that a time was coming when their idolatry would cause them to be driven from the land: "And the LORD will scatter you among the peoples, and you will be left few in number among the nations where the LORD will drive you" (Deuteronomy 4:27). God reiterated this prophecy through Ezekiel and Hosea (Ezekiel 12:15; Hosea 9:17). Israel had no excuse. Her people had been warned again and again that God was a jealous God and would not tolerate His people worshipping false gods (Exodus 34:14).

Centuries before the Roman emperor Titus destroyed Jerusalem in AD 70, Jews had been scattered into the world by the Assyrians and Babylonians. Describing the prevalence of Jews throughout the known world, the historian and philosopher Strabo wrote:

> This people has already made its way into every city, and it is not easy to find any place in the habitable world which has not received this nation and in which it has not made its power felt.[13]

After the fall of Jerusalem to the Romans, this dispersion intensified, and Jews were scattered like chaff in the wind to the four corners of the earth.

## The Suffering of the Exiled Jews

No doubt you remember the poor Jewish milkman Tevye in the classic movie *Fiddler on the Roof*. Burdened with poverty and trying to maintain traditions while coping with oppression from the Jew-hating Russians, he cries out to God, "I know, I know, we are Your chosen people. But, once in a while, can't You choose someone else?"[14] Tevye is a picture of the quintessential displaced Jew. What he experienced was exactly what Moses prophesied:

And among those nations you shall find no rest, nor shall the sole of your foot have a resting place; but there the LORD will give you a trembling heart, failing eyes, and anguish of soul. (Deuteronomy 28:65)

Tevye illustrated this prophecy by providing a vivid picture of what scattered Jews have endured throughout the centuries since their dispersions from their promised land. Like Tevye, Jews in many lands have faced persecution in the form of pogroms, discrimination, exclusion from certain occupations, isolation in ghettos, and forced evacuation when the space they occupied was wanted for other purposes.

To appreciate the broad scope and magnitude of Jewish dispersion and persecution, consider the following historical facts:

Before and during World War II, Jews throughout Europe were the target of merciless state-sponsored persecution. In 1933, nine million Jews lived in twenty-one European countries. By 1945, two out of three European Jews had been murdered. When the smoke finally cleared, the terrible truth came out. The Holocaust brought about the extermination of one-third of the worldwide Jewish population at the time. Following the German invasion of the Soviet Union in 1941, mobile killing units following the German army began shooting massive numbers of Jews on the outskirts of conquered cities and towns. Seeking more efficient means to accomplish their obsession, the Nazis created a private and organized method of killing huge numbers of Jewish civilians. Extermination centers were established in Poland. Millions died in the ghettos and concentration camps through starvation, execution, brutality and disease. Of the six million Jews murdered during the Second World War, more than half were exterminated in the Nazi death camps. And the names Treblinka, Auschwitz, and Dachau became synonymous with the horrors of the Holocaust.[15]

Yes, God chose the Jews. He singled them out to be the recipients of His great and unique covenant blessings. But the greater the blessing, the greater the burden they bore for failing God. So the question is, was it worth it? How should Tevye's question be answered—would the Jews have been better off if God had chosen someone else? Rabbi Leo Baeck (1873–1956) weighed the sufferings of the Jewish people against their covenant blessings and drew a helpful conclusion:

> No people is heir to such a revelation as the Jew possesses; no people has had such a weight of divine commandment laid upon it; and for this reason no people has been so exposed to difficult and exacting times. The inheritance has not always been realized, but it is one that will endure, awaiting its hour.[16]

Baeck tells us that the story of the Jews is not over yet. It may seem that their sufferings outstrip their blessings, but that's because the fullness of their inheritance is yet to come. It is *awaiting its hour*. In other words, if you think the Jews have not yet been sufficiently blessed, just wait; you ain't seen nothing yet. God's promise in its fullness is yet to be kept.

## The Rebirth of the Nation of Israel

Do we have reason to believe that God's promise to Israel will be kept? Will the Jews ever realize the fulfillment of the covenant to possess that particular tract of land with clear geographic boundaries promised as an everlasting possession? The prophet Isaiah asserted that it would happen in the Millennium. He prophesied that the Lord would "set His hand again the second time to recover the remnant of His people who are left" (Isaiah 11:11). God also addressed the issue through Ezekiel when He said, "I will take you from among the nations, gather you out of all countries, and bring you into your own land" (Ezekiel 36:24).

The fulfillment of those prophecies was set in motion on that day in 1948 when the United States recognized the new state of Israel. On the evening of that announcement, popular radio commentator Lowell Thomas said in his evening broadcast that Americans in every part of the country would be turning to their Bibles for historical background, enabling them to understand "this day in history."[17] And indeed, as the prophecies found in Isaiah, Ezekiel, Matthew, and Revelation show, both the Old Testament and the New Testament pointed to this day when the Jews would return to the land promised them and initiate fulfillment of the ancient prophecies.

To comprehend what an incredible act of God it is to preserve the beleaguered Jews throughout history and then return them to their land, consider this observation by Gary Frazier:

You cannot find the ancient neighbors of the Jews anywhere. Have you ever met a Moabite? Do you know any Hittites? Are there any tours to visit the Ammonites? Can you find the postal code of a single Edomite? No! These ancient peoples disappeared from history and from the face of the earth. Yet the Jews, just as God promised, returned to their land.[18]

While the complete fulfillment is yet to come, the return of the Jews to Israel in 1948 was an astounding event unprecedented in world history. Never had a decimated ancient people managed to retain their individual identity through almost twenty centuries and reestablish their nation in their original homeland. The event was specifically prophesied, and it happened exactly as foretold. It was clearly a miraculous act of God.

Many events had to dovetail perfectly to bring about the fulfillment of God's promise to Israel, but I want to point out two events in particular that serve to illustrate the miraculous nature of the rebirth of the nation of Israel. You will be amazed at the mysterious workings of God's providence.

The single most influential event that triggered the return of the scattered Jews to their homeland began with Chaim Weizmann. Weizmann was a Russian Jew, a brilliant chemist and a leader in the Zionist movement, who immigrated to England in 1904. During World War I, English armies used gunpowder made of cordite, which produced little smoke and thus did not blind gunners to their targets or reveal their positions. But since the manufacture of cordite required acetone made from a compound imported from their enemy, Germany, the English government was desperate to find another source. Prime Minister Lloyd George and Winston Churchill turned to Weizmann and set him up in a gin distillery, where he quickly developed a biochemical process for producing synthetic acetone.

The success of his ingenious process for creating acetone contributed to the ultimate Allied victory. The minimal salary and token reward that Weizmann received from the government earned him significant leverage when he pressed his persistent petitions for a Jewish homeland in Israel.[19]

As it happened, by the war's end, England gained possession of the land of Palestine—the very land promised in God's covenant with Abraham—from the defeated Ottoman Empire. As an act of a grateful nation and through Weizmann's influence within the government, England officially issued the Balfour Declaration of 1917, which declared:

> His Majesty's Government views with favor the establishment in Palestine of a national home for the Jewish people, and will use their best endeavors to facilitate the achievement of this object . . .[20]

The second influential event that brought the scattered Jews back to Palestine was the liberation of Jewish prisoners from Auschwitz, Dachau, and other Nazi concentration camps. When Germany collapsed at the end of World War II, the liberation of these Jewish prisoners caused worldwide shock at the grossly inhumane treatment inflicted by the Nazis. This generated sympathy that drew Jewish wealth from around the world and enabled the relocation of more than a million displaced Jews to Palestine.

That brings us all the way back to May 14, 1948. On this day, the United Nations officially recognized the State of Israel, with US president Harry Truman determining the deciding vote. The Israeli government established the State of Israel, thus fulfilling the twenty-five-hundred-year-old prophecy recorded in the Bible. Great Britain ended its mandate in Palestine and removed its troops, leaving more than 650,000 Jews to govern themselves in their own land.

## The Return to the God of Israel

I am often asked if Israel's presence in her own land today is the final fulfillment of God's promise to regather His people. Many assume that it is, but I have to tell them that the answer is no! What is happening in Israel today is primarily the result of a secular Zionist movement, whereas Ezekiel wrote about a spiritual return of God's people to Him when he said:

> For I will take you from the nations, gather you from all the lands and bring you into your own land . . . Moreover, I will give you a new heart and put a new spirit within you . . . I will put My Spirit within you and cause you to walk in My statutes, and you will be careful to observe My ordinances. You will live in the land that I gave to your forefathers; so you will be My people, and I will be your God. (Ezekiel 36:24–28 NASB)

The return of Jews to the refounded nation of Israel is the first stage of that regathering, but it certainly does not fulfill the requirements of a spiritual return to the Lord. Secularist Israeli Yossi Beilin makes this point abundantly clear. Beilin is an agnostic and proponent of "secular conversion to Judaism," who has served in many roles in Israel's government. He speaks for many Israelis when he says that "secular Jews are not a marginal group in Jewish life. We are the mainstream. We are people in the government, we are people in the Parliament."[21] To him,

Judaism is "a people, a culture, an existence" as well as a religion; there-fore, the Jewishness of its atheists and agnostics goes unquestioned.[22]

From the moment of God's promise to Abraham to this present hour, the prophecies concerning Israel's total possession and blessing in the land remain unfulfilled. The most dramatic events lie ahead of us. Israel today is an island of a few million immigrants surrounded by a sea of three hundred million enemies, many of them militant and eager to wipe the tiny nation off the map. From a purely human point of view, it would seem inevitable that, sooner or later, Israel will be destroyed.

Indeed, Israel has been attacked over and over since its founding, sometimes in all-out wars and incessantly by terrorists. The Jewish people have survived by remaining vigilant, but they long for peace. According to the Bible, a future leader will fulfill this longing by bro-kering a seven-year peace deal with Israel's enemies. But Scripture also tells us that this peace plan will be broken, and Israel will be attacked once again, this time as never before. Countless armies will amass against the boxed-in nation, leaving it with no human hope of victory. Only Christ's return, His judgment, and His reign will finally bring true peace to Israel.

It is then that God's covenant with Abraham will reach its ultimate fulfillment. The Jews will return to the Lord, and as Ezekiel and Jeremiah prophesied, they will be His people, and He will be their God. The bor-ders of the land will expand to the dimensions described in Genesis 15 and Ezekiel 48. Christ's return will also fulfill the prophecy of Jeremiah that God would gather the Jews. "Behold, I will gather them out of all countries where I have driven them . . . I will bring them back to this place, and I will cause them to dwell safely. They shall be My people, and I will be their God" (Jeremiah 32:37–38).

Ezekiel makes it clear that this gathering means He will return every single living Jew back to the land. For he wrote that the Lord said He would gather them again to their own land "and . . . none of them [will be] captive any longer" (Ezekiel 39:28).

Today we see this prophecy being fulfilled right before our eyes. In 2006, for the first time in nineteen hundred years, Israel became home to the largest Jewish community in the world, surpassing the Jewish population in the United States. From the 650,000 who returned when the Jewish state was founded in 1948, the population of Israel has swelled to approximately 5.4 million, and it is expected to exceed 6 million by 2020.[23]

The significance of Israel's reemergence in her ancient homeland is that this had to occur in order to set the stage for the final fulfillment of biblical prophecies. Israel had to be a nation in her own land before the predictions previously noted could come about. The return of the Jews to their homeland is also significant in another way: it pinpoints where we are on history's timeline. As author Milton B. Lindberg pointed out:

> Without the existence of the nation of Israel, we would not be able to say with certainty that we are in the last days. That single event, more than any other, is the most prominent sign that we are living in the final moments before the coming of Jesus! The Hebrew People have been called God's timepiece of the ages.[24]

## God's Providence in Action: The Story Behind the Story

Clark Clifford (1906–1998), an influential Washington lawyer, became a political advisor to President Harry Truman. He also became one of Truman's most trusted personal counselors and friends. Clifford opened his memoirs, *Counsel to the President,* by describing a meeting in the president's office on a Wednesday afternoon in the spring of 1948.

"Of all the meetings I ever had with the Presidents," wrote Clifford, "this one remains the most vivid." President Truman was meeting with Secretary of State General George C. Marshall, whom Truman regarded as "the greatest living American," about whether or not to recognize the state of Israel. British control of Palestine would run out in two days, and when it did, the Jewish Agency intended to announce the creation of a new state, still unnamed at that time. Most observers thought it would be named Judea.[25]

Marshall, mastermind of America's victory in World War II and author of the Marshall Plan, inspired a respect bordering on awe. He was adamantly opposed to recognizing Israel and not at all hesitant to express his opinion forcefully. His view was shared by almost every member of Truman's White House—except Clifford—and by virtually everyone in the State Department and Defense Department.

Several months before that meeting, James Forrestal, Truman's secretary of defense, had bluntly told Clifford, "You fellows over at the White House are just not facing up to the realities in the Middle East. There are thirty million Arabs on one side and about six hundred thousand Jews on the other. It is clear that in any contest, the Arabs are going to overwhelm the Jews. Why don't you face up to the realities? Just look at the numbers!"[26]

Clifford, however, knew that Truman had strong reasons for wanting to help the Jews, reasons that would not register on the scale of values at the departments of State or Defense. Truman detested intolerance and discrimination and had been deeply moved by the plight of the Jews during World War II. More to the point, Clifford wrote, Truman was "a student and believer in the Bible from his youth. From his reading of the Old Testament he felt the Jews derived a legitimate historical right to Palestine, and he sometimes cited such biblical lines as Deuteronomy 1:8, 'Behold, I have given up the land before you; go in and take possession of the land which the Lord hath sworn unto your fathers, to Abraham, to Isaac, and to Jacob.'"[27]

So at 4:00 p.m. on that Wednesday, May 12, the president met with his advisors in the Oval Office. Truman sat at his desk facing his famous plaque that read, *The Buck Stops Here*. Around the desk sat General Marshall and his deputy, officials from the State Department, and a handful of Truman's counselors, including Clark Clifford. They were exactly fifty hours away from the birth of the new, unnamed nation.

One by one, the president's advisors gave reasons for deferring any decision on the recognition of Israel. Finally it was Clifford's turn. Bucking the overwhelming consensus in the room, he boldly presented reasons for recognizing the new state. He barely finished before General Marshall erupted in a torrent of anger, and the officials from the State Department backed his opposition unanimously and vigorously. After the heated discussion, Marshall glared icily at the president and said, "If you follow Clifford's advice and if I were to vote in the election, I would vote against you!"[28]

Everyone in the room was stunned. The meeting came to an abrupt end with the question unresolved. Truman himself was greatly shaken by the fierceness of the general's opposition. The president, running for reelection, was on thin ice politically, and he could not afford to lose the support of such a towering figure as Marshall. Clifford left the meeting thinking the case was lost.

But over the next two days, Clifford, Truman, and a handful of others worked toward reaching a compromise within the administration. They succeeded when General Marshall finally said bitterly that while he could not support the president's position, he would not oppose it. So at 6:11 p.m. on May 14, 1948, Truman's press secretary, Charlie Ross, stepped out to meet an awaiting press and read these words:

> The government has been informed that a Jewish state has been pro-claimed in Palestine . . . The United States recognizes the provisional government as de facto authority of the new State of Israel.[29]

Another biographer wrote that "he [Truman] felt great satisfaction in what he had been able to do for the Jewish people, and was deeply moved by their expressions of gratitude, then and for years to come. When the Chief Rabbi of Israel, Isaac Halevi Herzog, called at the White House, he told Truman, 'God put you in your mother's womb so that you would be the instrument to bring about the rebirth of Israel after two thousand years.'" Another witness to the scene, Truman's administrative assistant David Niles, reported the president's reaction to Herzog's generous assertion: "I thought he was overdoing things," remembered Niles, "but when I looked over at the President, tears were running down his cheeks."[30]

## What Does All this Mean to Me?

Let's return to the questions we posed at the beginning of this chapter. Why has this tiny nation with a population of less than six million become the geopolitical center of the world? Why is a fledgling country with a total land space hardly larger than New Jersey mentioned in the nightly news more than any other nation except the United States? Or, to sum it up, why is Israel so important? I hope this chapter has helped you answer that question. Israel is important because the fulfillment of

God's covenant with its founder, Abraham, greatly affects every one of us. We have shown why it's important for our nation to continue to support and protect Israel. Nations who befriend Israel will be blessed; those that do not will be cursed.

We have shown how the playing out of prophetic events concerning Israel places us in the last days of history's timeline. We have shown how the miraculous survival of God's covenant people, the Jews, demonstrates God's providence and His ability to accomplish His purpose in the face of what seems to human minds impossible odds. The existence of Israel today is exhibit A in the lineup of convincing evidences that the Bible's prophecies concerning the future ahead of us will be fulfilled. This means the future not only of Israel, but also of our world, our nation, as well as your future and mine. This, perhaps, is the most important blessing we can receive from the astounding history of the Jews. It reveals the reality of God—His overwhelming power, the authenticity of His promises, the certainty of His existence, the urgency of His call to us, and His claim on our very being.

When we consider all this, perhaps we can see that it's not so odd of God to choose the Jews.

# TWO

# The Crude Awakening

WHO DOESN'T KNOW THE WORDS TO THE THEME SONG OF *The Beverly Hillbillies* by heart? If you're not old enough to have heard this ditty in the original episodes of the popular sixties sitcom, you've no doubt seen reruns. The series features a dirt-poor hillbilly family that strikes it rich in oil and moves to the upscale Hollywood neighborhood of Beverly Hills. The sitcom plays on the fact that discovering oil on one's property means becoming instantly wealthy, a phenomenon that occurs because oil has become vital to running our highly industrialized society.

America's quest for oil began forty years before Spindletop ever spouted its first Texas oil, when "the most important oil well ever drilled was [bored] in the middle of quiet farm country in northwestern Pennsylvania in 1859." Oil had actually been found and used on our continent much earlier: centuries before, Native Americans had noticed oil seeping out of the rocks and had used it for medicine and in trade with neighboring tribes. Almost thirty years before the signing of the American Declaration of Independence, a map had already been printed showing known oil springs in Pennsylvania.[1]

But on August 27, 1859, Edwin Drake launched the modern petroleum industry by drilling a 69.5-foot well near Titusville, Pennsylvania. It was the first well purposely drilled to find oil, and thus began a search for petroleum that quickly became international and changed the way we live . . . *forever!*

Now, fast-forward to the twenty-first century and observe what has happened in the decades since the drilling of Edwin Drake's little well:

- Mankind's thirst for oil has passed 86 million barrels per day and is expected to rise to 98.5 million barrels a day in 2015.[2]

- The psychological barrier of one hundred dollars a barrel was finally breached in early 2008.

- Oil prices have quintupled in the past six years.[3]

- As I write this, surplus oil production has doubled over recent years, and demand is somewhat reduced,[4] but new, unsettling record highs have been registered so far this year in all gasoline products: home heating fuels, automobile fuel, and, especially, diesel fuel.[5]

Oil is the new gold in the world economy, and more than any factor other than the nation of Israel, oil holds the key to the prophetic events of the future. Oil explains why the Bible focuses its end-time attention on the Middle East. The demand for oil in America has outstripped its capacity to produce the black gold, and the same holds true for much of the rest of the world. Therefore, since the discovery of huge supplies of oil in the Middle Eastern countries, world attention has focused on that area. In an article entitled "The Power of Oil," Dilip Hiro wrote:

The overarching fact is that political leaders all over the world are committed to raising living standards through economic growth, heavily dependent on energy in the form of gas and oil. That includes the United States. Ever since 1932, when American oil companies acquired a stake in the oil resources of Saudi Arabia, Washington's policies have been geared to securing Middle East oil at the expense of all else.[6]

Few would question the fact that oil has become the new basis for our world economy. It is now the stuff of life, the resource most highly valued by the industrialized and emerging nations of the world, the blood that flows through their economic veins and gives life to prosperity in today's global economy. The greatest source of that lifeblood is now in the Middle East, so that is where the eyes of the world are focused.

What does this tell us about coming events? In Luke's gospel, Jesus contrasts our ability to discern weather signs with our inability to understand the more important signs of the time: "You can discern the face of the sky and of the earth, but how is it you do not discern this time?" (Luke 12:56). Surely the world's fascination with oil—a hot commodity with a source in lands hostile or borderline hostile to Israel and to us—qualifies as a "sign."

# The Control of the World's Oil Supply

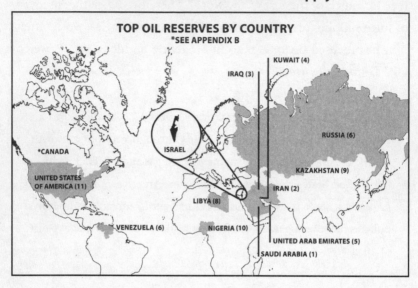

To get a clear picture of the primary sources for oil, here is a 2007 list of the world's greatest conventional oil reserves by country:[7]

| Rank | Country | Billions of Barrels |
|---|---|---|
| 1 | Saudi Arabia | 264.3 |
| 2 | Iran | 137.5 |
| 3 | Iraq | 115.0 |
| 4 | Kuwait | 101.5 |
| 5 | United Arab Emirates | 97.8 |
| 6 | Venezuela | 80.0 |
| 6 | Russia | 79.5 |
| 8 | Libya | 41.5 |

The United States is ranked eleventh with a mere 29.9 billion barrels!

The five top countries with the greatest known oil reserves are Arab nations, and the reserves in those countries total almost *716 billion barrels.* The Middle East/Persian Gulf area has about 60 percent of the world's known oil reserves lying beneath its desert sands. The sophisticated handling and processing facilities developed in those countries by the major Western oil companies have been nationalized. They are now controlled by a few Arab leaders.

Furthermore, Arab control of oil goes beyond the realities of supply and demand. Historically, all of the world's oil has been traded in US dollars, which has assured stability for the dollar and the US economy. The dollar had always been backed by the gold standard until President Nixon took it off in 1971. But then in 1973, oil prices rose sharply, threatening to throw the dollar into free fall around the world. In order to stabilize the dollar, the US government entered into a relationship with Saudi Arabia, the world's largest oil supplier. According to the agreement, the United States would back the Saudi government as an ally if the Saudis would demand that all purchases of its oil be in US dollars. This would ensure the primacy of the dollar in the world economy. The net effect of this agreement was that the US dollar was, in effect, backed by oil instead of gold. Then on February 17, 2008, Iran opened its own trading exchange in which oil is brokered in euros instead of dollars, further threatening the stability of the US dollar.

The Middle Eastern countries are not the only ones giving the United States trouble in the global oil market. You probably noticed that Venezuela, tied for number six on the oil reserve list, is another primary source of America's oil. But Hugo Chavez, the president of Venezuela, is no friend of America. During the 2006 United Nations sessions in New York City, Chavez verbally assaulted the American government and called our president a devil. Chavez has met several times with Iranian president Mahmoud Ahmadinejad and has vowed to "unite the Persian Gulf and the Caribbean, giving Iran entrée into Latin America."[8] This could bring even more insecurity to United States oil sources, giving powerful influence over South American oil to a Middle Eastern country. So as you can see, control of the lion's share of the world's oil is centralized in the Middle East.

No doubt you've heard preachers assert that civilization as we know it will face a gargantuan, final showdown in the Middle East. In the not-too-distant past you may have wondered, *Why the Middle East? Why would this handful of relatively small countries become so important to world powers?* Perhaps you figured the showdown would more likely be brought on by the population masses in China, the wealth and global power of the United States, the ingenuity of Japan, or the rising up of poverty-oppressed multitudes in India. Why, of all places, would things come to a head in the Middle East? Today, after considering the source of the world's oil and all the global hands reaching out to grasp it, we don't ask that question nearly as often!

Here's an interesting sidelight about world oil reserves. My friend Robert Morgan flew into New Orleans several years ago, and the man who met him at the airport was a geophysicist for a major oil company. Driving to the hotel, he explained to Robert that oil deposits result from the decomposition of plant and animal life now buried by eons of time. Oil is found all over the world, he said, even under the ice of the Arctic and Antarctic. That means forests and abundant vegetation once covered the world until destroyed in a vast global cataclysm (such as a worldwide flood).

The geophysicist went on to say that the earth's richest, deepest, and largest deposits of petroleum lie under the sands of countries just to the east of Israel, in the location pinpointed in the Bible as the garden of Eden. Eden was a teeming expanse of forests, foliage, and gardens with rich fertility unparalleled in human history.[9]

Barren sand and blazing desert now exist where once grew a garden flourishing with dense, lush flora, the likes of which the world has not seen since. It was destroyed in some disastrous upheaval and has decayed into the largest deposits of oil in the world. I had never before imagined that the gasoline I pump into my car might be the ruined remains of the rich, vast foliage of the garden of Eden.

It's ironic to think that Satan may finance the Battle of Armageddon at the end of human history with revenues generated from the garden he spoiled at the beginning of human history.

## The Consumers of the World's Oil Supply

The vast majority of the world's oil is consumed by four entities. Russia ranks fourth with 2.92 million barrels used per day. Japan is third, consuming 5.16 million barrels per day. China, the world's largest country in terms of population, is now number two in oil consumption at 7.27 million barrels per day. At a rate of 20.7 million barrels per day, the United States ranks first in oil consumption.[10]

China continues to increase her thirst for oil. In 2005, China had a total of twenty million cars on the road.[11] One well-known investment firm now estimates that China will have 1.1 billion cars on the road by 2050.

The European Union, once the number-two consumer of oil, now burns 1.83 million barrels per day and has fallen to thirteenth place among the top oil-consuming nations, an overall usage reduction despite growth in the number of member nations.[12] Last year when we visited London, our hosts told us how Brits had handled the oil situation in their country. Responding to the energy crisis in 1973, they reduced consumption and imposed taxes on gasoline to raise significant revenue to import high-priced oil. By 2007, conservation had become a way of life in England, even as the price per gallon of gas more than doubled its cost in the United States. I later discovered that the same thing had happened all over Europe.

It probably comes as no surprise to anyone that the world's number-one consumer of oil is America, guzzling almost 21 million barrels of crude oil per day, or 25 percent of all the oil produced in the world. If present trends continue, US consumption will rise to 27 million barrels a day by 2020, and demand will expand to 34 percent by 2030. Added to this is the fact that the United States consumes 43 percent of the world's motor gasoline, and no new gasoline refinery has been built in the United States since 1976. Stop for a moment and ponder the meaning of all this: the United States is number eleven in oil reserves and number one in oil consumption, with the demand growing by leaps and bounds. It doesn't take a rocket scientist to see that a crisis is looming in our future.

Many forward-looking statesmen worldwide, aware of the coming crisis, have mandated the development and use of alternative energy sources such as solar and wind power and alternative fuels for motor vehicles. However, recent studies have shown that despite such mandates for biofuels use, the "law of unintended consequences" is at work. Rather than saving the planet from oil dependence and global warming, biofuels are raising food prices, endangering the hungry, and only slightly reducing the need for oil. Even if all the corn and soybean crops produced in the United States were converted for fuel, it would only be enough to meet 20 percent of consumption demands.[13]

At this point in time, no alternative energy source shows promise of solving the problem. And until that solution surfaces, the United States will continue to be heavily dependent on foreign sources to maintain its vital influx of oil.

## The Conflicts over the World's Oil Supply

In 1973 a group of Arab nations launched an attack on Israel, initiating the Yom Kippur War. One result of this war was the uniting of Arab nations in a common cause as never before. This new show of unity was manifest partly in the military conflict and partly in a less obvious way. On October 17, 1973, the Arab nations conspired to reduce their oil production below the previous norm and attempted to embargo nations that favored Israel, principally the United States and the Netherlands. This hostile act made it increasingly evident that the Arab world would use their control of major oil reserves to leverage their bid for world power.

Some US citizens will remember the effect of that Arab embargo. The price of oil quadrupled to twelve dollars a barrel. Cars formed long, winding lines at gas stations. Conservation measures were put into effect, including a national highway speed limit of 55 mph. We were being attacked in a new kind of war—an economic war with ominous implications. The price of oil did not go down after the Arab oil blackmail of 1973–74, and that crisis precipitated the fastest transfer of money in history, sucking dollars out of the United States and stashing them in swelling Arab treasuries. The ultimate price of the war, however, would not be exacted in money alone, but in the political and economic reshaping of the world. For the first time in centuries, the Middle East became a major consideration in every international event.

The first acknowledgment of this new political reality came from President Jimmy Carter in his State of the Union address on January 23, 1980. In that address Carter announced an important policy change concerning the Middle East:

> Let our position be absolutely clear: An attempt by any outside force to gain control of the Persian Gulf region will be regarded as an assault on the vital interests of the United States of America, and such an assault will be repelled by any means necessary including military force.[14]

This became known as the Carter Doctrine: the determination to protect the Persian Gulf even at the expense of our own troops. This paradigm shift in foreign policy would soon be tested.

In August 1990, Iraqi dictator Saddam Hussein sent troops into Kuwait to take over that nation's oil fields. President George H. W. Bush and his defense secretary, Dick Cheney, put the Carter Doctrine into action, sending US troops to Kuwait to repel the Iraqi invasion. President Bush defended his action to the nation, saying, "Our country now imports nearly half the oil it consumes and could face a major threat to its economic independence . . . The sovereign independence of Saudi Arabia is of vital interest to the United States."[15]

While other justifications for the war were given, experts agree that the Gulf War in 1990–91 was the first in world history fought almost entirely over oil. And make no mistake: while the war in Iraq is about terrorism, it is also about oil—oil that is sold to finance the Muslim terrorist regime and oil that is necessary for the West to function economically.

# The Concerns About the World's Oil Supply

## Are We Running Out of Oil?

It was Saturday morning, and I was on my way to my office to put the final touches on the message for the weekend. I was scheduled to preach on the importance of oil in the prophetic program of the end times. When I stopped to get a cup of coffee, I spotted the weekend edition of the *Wall Street Journal*. The headline read, "Where Has All The Oil Gone?" The article, written by Ann Davis, was about the huge oil tanks in Cushing, Oklahoma, where many of our reserves are stored. According to the article, a run on oil futures has depleted the tanks to their lowest level ever.[16]

So where *has* all the oil gone? Do these near-empty tanks mean we are running out of it? This is a difficult question to answer. According to the CEO and president of the Saudi Aramco, we have tapped "only 18 percent of [global] conventional and non-conventional producible potential." In his words, "we are looking at more than 4.5 trillion barrels of potentially recoverable oil"—enough to power the globe at current levels of consumption for "more than 140 years."[17] On the other hand, we do not have access to all of that oil, nor do we have the present-day capacity to harvest it all if we knew where it was.

The rate of oil discovery has been falling ever since the 1960s when 47 billion barrels a year were discovered, mostly in the Middle East. In the '70s the rate dropped to about 35 billion barrels while the industry concentrated on the North Sea. In the '80s it was Russia's turn, and the discovery rate dropped to 24 billion. It dropped even further in the '90s as the industry concentrated on West Africa but only found some 14 billion barrels.[18]

To say that we are running out of oil might be untrue but to say that we are consuming at the level of our current ability to produce oil is true. The oil shortage is real and will continue to have an enormous effect upon our culture. According to the official energy statistics posted by the U.S. government, last updated in July of 2007, the total world oil supply in 2006 was exceeded by the total world petroleum consumption in 2005.[19]

Did you catch the sobering point in this quote? Let me repeat it: in 2005 the world used more oil than was even produced in the following year. And there is one energy rule that even I can understand: energy use cannot exceed available supply.

## Can We Protect Our Sources of Oil?

Our dependence on foreign oil has become a major concern—especially since the oil lies under the control of nations with which we have tenuous or hostile relationships. Paul Roberts addressed this concern in his book, *The End of Oil: On the Edge of a Perilous New World*. Perhaps the greatest casualty of the Iraq war may be the very idea of energy security:

But with the continuing fiasco in Iraq, it is now clear that even the most powerful military entity in world history cannot stabilize a country at will or "make it" produce oil simply by sending in soldiers and tanks. In other words, since the Iraqi invasion, the oil market now understands that the United States cannot guarantee the security of oil supplies—for itself or for anyone else. That new and chilling knowledge, as much as anything else, explains the high price of oil.[20]

According to Roberts, our ability to protect our foreign oil inflow is limited at best. Even if we commit to using brute military force, as the Carter Doctrine says we are ready to do, we cannot ensure an endless supply of oil from hostile countries.

## Is There Any Oil in Israel?

It would help, of course, if we could depend on oil from our one staunch Middle Eastern ally, Israel. But as former prime minister Golda Meir ruefully quipped, "Let me tell you something we Israelis have against Moses. He took us forty years into the desert in order to bring us to the one place in the Middle East that has no oil."[21]

While little oil has ever been discovered in Israel, today there is a growing belief that there may be significant oil deposits under its surface. Two major oil companies have been formed to explore oblique references to oil found in the Bible. Ezekiel speaks of a time when God would do better for Israel than at her beginnings (36:11). How could Israel ever be more prosperous than she was in the days of King Solomon? During his reign the wealth of Israel was the wonder and envy of the known world. Yet here is God telling Israel that at some time in the future she will be wealthier still.

In his book *The Coming Peace in the Middle East*, Dr. Tim LaHaye suggests one way that this coming wealth could be explained:

> Suppose that a pool of oil, greater than anything in Arabia . . . were discovered by the Jews . . . This would change the course of history. Before long, Israel would be able independently to solve its economic woes, finance the resettlement of the Palestinians, and supply housing for Jews and Arabs in the West Bank, East Bank, or anywhere else they might choose to live.[22]

In an article written for WorldNet Daily, Aaron Klein asked this question: "Is Israel sitting on an enormous oil reserve mapped out in the Old Testament that when found will immediately change the geopolitical structure of the Middle East and confirm the validity of the Bible to people around the world?"[23] John Brown, an evangelical Christian and founder and chairman of Zion Oil and Gas, believes that there is indeed oil in Israel. He is certain that several biblical passages indicate where rich deposits might be found. As examples, he cites two passages: "Let Asher be blessed . . . and let him dip his foot in oil" (Deuteronomy 33:24 KJV). "Joseph is . . . a fruitful bough by a well . . . Blessings of heaven above, blessings of the deep that lies beneath . . . shall be on the head of Joseph, and on the crown of the head" (Genesis 49:22–26 NKJV).

Brown's explanation of why these passages indicate the presence of oil is fascinating. He says that maps of the territory allotted to the twelve tribes when they entered Palestine show that the shape of Asher's area resembles a giant foot. That foot is "dipped" into the top, or "crown" area belonging to the land given to the tribe of Joseph's son Manasseh. "The oil is there," Brown asserts, "where Joseph's head is met by Asher's foot."[24] And Brown is willing to put his money where his mouth is. In 2007, his company was granted two extended licenses for approximately 162,100 acres that include the Joseph and Asher-Menashe areas, which Brown believes contain oil.[25]

The discovery of oil on Israeli soil would greatly reduce the threat against Israel from her hostile allies, taking the oil weapon out of their hands. "Finding oil will give Israel a huge strategic advantage" over its Arab enemies, Brown said. "It will change the political and economic structure of the region overnight."[26]

But in spite of the tantalizing possibilities of oil in Israel, it has not yet been found. This means we must continue to deal with the reality of a world in which oil remains in the control of countries essentially hostile to us or at best only tenuously allied.

## How Does the Oil Situation Affect Our Future?

### The Emergence of Prophetic Alliances

Ezekiel foretold a time when Russia would attack Israel. In detailing how the military aggression would take place, the prophet listed a coalition of some of the nations that would join with Russia in the attack. "I will turn you around, put hooks into your jaws, and lead you out, with all your army, horses, and horsemen, all splendidly clothed, a great company with bucklers and shields, all of them handling swords. Persia, Ethiopia, and Libya are with them, all of them with shield and helmet" (38: 4–5).

Until March 21, 1935, Persia was the official name of the country we now call Iran. Not once in the past twenty-five hundred years has Russia formed a military connection with Persia/Iran, until now.[27] But now these two nations have formed a military alliance that continues to be strengthened by the political situation in our world. Russia recently signed a billion-dollar deal to sell missiles and other weaponry to Iran. And the connection is even broader, as Joel C. Rosenberg, former aid to Israeli prime minister Benjamin Netanyahu, points out: "Over 1000 Iranian nuclear scientists have been trained in Russia by senior Russian scientists."[28] Here is an end-time alliance that was prophesied twenty-five hundred years ago, and in the last five years it has become a reality. Obviously, the stage is being set!

### The Emergence of Petroleum Alliances

Omer Selah, with Israel's Fuel Authority, was recently quoted in the *Jerusalem Post*:

The issue of oil becomes more and more critical with each passing year, for Western democracies in general, and for Israel in particular. What we are seeing is a confluence of several negative factors and processes in this region . . . A huge percentage of the world's oil reserves . . . is found in the possession of powers not friendly to the West or to Israel.[29]

And the wealth of these few oil-producing nations is growing at such an exponential rate that they are struggling to find ways to invest their exploding resources. The magnitude of their investment "problem" was reported in a *New York Times* article. Between 2000 and 2007, oil revenues for the OPEC nations went from $243 billion to $688 billion, not including the price spikes that occurred in November and December of 2007. It's estimated that these countries have $4 trillion invested around the world from the money earned in oil exports.[30]

Our enemies consider this kind of wealth to be a gigantic weapon with the blessing of Allah. As author Don Richardson puts it: "Muslim strategists ask their followers, *Why do we find in these modern times that Allah has entrusted most of the world's oil wealth primarily to Muslim nations?* Their answer: Allah foresaw Islam's need for funds to finance a final politico-religious victory over what Islam perceives as its ultimate enemy: Christianized Euro-American civilization."[31]

Another *New York Times* article headlined in the spring of 2002, "Iranian Urges Muslims to Use Oil as a Weapon." In this article, Ayatollah Ali Khamenei is quoted as having said:

The oil belongs to the people and can be used as a weapon against the West and those who support the savage regime of Israel . . . If Islamic and Arab countries . . . for only one month suspend the export of oil to Israel and its supporter, the world would be shaken.[32]

It should be clear to us that America's ride on the crest of wealth and power faces unprecedented threats from newly rich, newly united Middle Eastern countries that have no love for us. Indeed, many of them would love to see us reduced to the ashes of history. And it should be just as clear that they are feeling the newfound power that control of most of the world's oil has given them. These factors do not bode well for the United States, Israel, and their Western allies.

## What Are We to Do?

So far this chapter has given you very little good news and little reason to be optimistic—that is, if your outlook is entirely earthly. As we look back on where we have been as a nation and where we find ourselves today, we could easily become discouraged. The secret, however, is to look beyond both the past and the present and focus on the future. We are, in fact, unusually blessed. We are being given the opportunity to be firsthand observers to the staging of events that will precede the ultimate coming of Christ to this earth. Events written about centuries ago are now unfolding right before our eyes and are telling us that our patient anticipation will soon be rewarded. In the meantime, we must . . .

### *Keep on Waiting*

Jesus told His disciples that just as you can tell that summer is near when the fig tree puts forth leaves, you can also tell that the Son of Man is returning by recognizing the signs given by the prophets

(Matthew 24:32). As we see these signs appearing, our question is, what shall we do?

First of all, we wait. There is nothing we can do to hasten His coming, so we have been called to be patient. "Therefore be patient, brethren, until the coming of the Lord. The farmer waits for the precious produce of the soil, being patient about it, until it gets the early and late rains. You too be patient; strengthen your hearts, for the coming of the Lord is near" (James 5:7–8 NASB). No man knows exactly when the Lord will return (Matthew 24:36), but by the signs we can discern the season of His coming. And I am not alone in believing we are in that season. We do not, however, know exactly how long that season will be, so our duty as faithful servants is to wait patiently.

### Keep on Working

Some modern believers seem to have concluded that the coming of Christ is a call to passivity. Their attitude seems to be, *Well, since He's coming soon, there's no point in making any big plans or working to fulfill them. It's all about to come to an end anyway.* Over the years we've seen extreme examples of passive waiting. People who believed they had pinpointed the time of His coming to the day got rid of their earthly goods, gathered on a mountaintop or in a compound, and simply waited passively. That is emphatically not what is meant by waiting. The Lord Himself set the example while He was on this earth. He said, "I must work the works of Him who sent Me while it is day; the night is coming when no one can work" (John 9:4 NKJV). In one of His parables, He also said, "Blessed is that servant whom his master, when he comes, will find so doing [serving]" (Matthew 24:46 NKJV).

That is the key to pleasing the Lord in these last days—continue to

work diligently at what God has called you to do. Believing in the imminent return of Jesus involves more than simply waiting, as important as
that may be. It is rather a matter of *working* while we wait. Working
hard. Working faithfully. Working in the power and joy and filling of
the Holy Spirit.

Someone once asked me what I would like to be doing when the
Lord comes back. That's easy. I would like to be standing behind my
pulpit before my flock, declaring and explaining and applying the
Word of God. For me there is nothing better. There is no greater joy.

What would you like to be doing when He returns? Where would
you like to be when the trumpet sounds, when the archangel shouts,
and when, in the twinkling of an eye, we are changed and rise into the
clouds to meet Him?

## Keep on Watching

On numerous occasions Jesus told His followers to watch. He
exhorted them to be full of anticipation, to look up and lift their
heads up and realize that their redemption was drawing near (Luke
21:28). The apostle Paul continued the theme of watchfulness, telling
the Roman believers to awake out of their sleep, for their salvation
was nearer than when they first believed (Romans 13:11).

Wait, work, and watch: these are the three things Christians are
exhorted to do when they see the signs of Christ's imminent coming.
What does this look like for Christians today? How can we gear up
our wills and our emotions to keep on going in this era of church
history when the future looks so ominous?

C. S. Lewis answered that question almost seventy years ago in another
time when extreme danger loomed on the horizon. In an address to

Oxford University students shortly after the English declared war with Germany, Lewis stated well the attitude Christians should have in times like his and ours:

> This impending war has taught us some important things. Life is short. The world is fragile. All of us are vulnerable, but we are here because this is our calling. Our lives are rooted not only in time, but also in eternity, and the life of learning, humbly offered to God, is its own reward.[33]

In his speech, Lewis asserted that an impending crisis makes no difference to the nature of our duty and our calling. The truth is that danger is always part of our environment in this fallen world; the presence of an obvious and immediate danger merely intensifies our awareness of this reality that we tend to ignore. Any one of us could meet death at any moment through an accident, an invisible blood clot, or by an act of a deranged gunman. An impending war such as that which Lewis and his students faced, or an impending battle that may be in our own future changes nothing. Our task as faithful stewards to God's calling is to keep to our duty—to be patient and watch, but also to keep on working.

We need not despair. As children of the living God, we live with continual hope. We work, we love, and we laugh and find joy because we always know that an end is coming. Whether the battle does or doesn't come in our lifetime changes nothing about the way we should live. Our own "end time" will come, and it could arrive at any moment. So our task is to keep on plugging along, faithfully fitting into the place where God put us as productive members of society.

I am convinced that God puts each one of us exactly where He wants us and gives each of us a task that advances His eternal plan in a particular way. Remember the words of Queen Esther's guardian Mordecai when she was afraid to face the deadly danger of appearing uninvited before the king to plead for her people: ". . . If you remain silent at this time, relief and deliverance will arise for the Jews from another place . . . And who knows whether you have not attained royalty for such a time as this?" (Esther 4:14 NASB). God raised up Esther at a particular time for a particular purpose. Today is the time God has ordained for you and me to be alive, and we are placed in our time and place with no less purpose than Esther. Your task may not be as grandiose as hers; you may not be called on to save your nation. But as Lewis said elsewhere in his speech to the Oxford undergraduates, "The work of a Beethoven and the work of a charwoman become spiritual on precisely the same condition, that of being offered to God, of being done humbly 'as to the Lord.'"[34]

You may wonder, *What's the point in keeping on doing my little insignificant job when such doom hangs over the world?* The point is that you are filling your role as an agent of God in this particular time, and your work may have a greater effect than you imagine. Few of us see the ultimate result of our actions. But by the power of the ripple effect, what you do either as a CEO or a salesclerk may join the current of God's intent and bring about His will in enormous ways you would never dream of. So it is vital that each of us takes our God-given tasks seriously. We must stick to our work, remain watchful, and patiently wait on the timing of the Lord.

Southern evangelist Vance Havner gives us the real key to keeping to our task and finding joy in the face of impending doom: "We are not just looking for something to happen, we are looking for Someone to come! And when these things begin to come to pass, we are not to drop our heads in discouragement, or shake our heads in despair, but we are to lift our heads in delight."[35]

# THREE

# Modern Europe . . . Ancient Rome

THE RED, STAMPED WORDS *TOP SECRET* GLARED OMINOUSLY from the manila envelope on the president's desk. The top government officials had been ordered to the Oval Office promptly at 8:00 a.m. Security was at its highest level; word must not leak out that the president of the United States, the vice president, the joint chiefs of staff, the National Security Council, congressional leaders, and selected members of the cabinet had been called for this executive briefing.

The president had never looked more serious. As the high officials and advisors assembled—men entrusted with decisions that could affect millions of lives—the president's face was ashen and grim. With his fingers pressed together under his chin, he looked as if he were praying. Considering the news he was about to share, his attitude was perfectly appropriate. When the group was assembled, he signaled to an armed guard, who opened a door to allow one more man to enter.

The man hesitated for a moment until the president pointed to a chair directly in front of the polished executive desk. The man took his seat before the leadership advisers of the most powerful nation on earth and awaited the president's signal.

"Gentlemen," the president said soberly, "prepare yourself to hear stunning news that will profoundly affect our nation and the future of the world as we know it. Listen carefully, for your very lives are at stake."[1]

This scene has not occurred exactly as described, yet it is not altogether fiction. It did occur at a different time in a different place with different players. And it may easily occur again in the near future. Let's begin by examining the time when it did occur—when one man, divinely moved to write the inspired words, accurately prophesied the rise and fall of empires and their rulers.

## The Vision of the King

More than two thousand years ago, God gave His servant Daniel a vision of the future that we recognize as the most comprehensive prophetic insight ever given to man. While it was not uncommon for God to communicate to His own people through dreams and visions, it is astounding to realize that He gave this greatest vision of all time not only to Daniel, but also to a Babylonian king named Nebuchadnezzar, one of history's most wicked Gentile rulers.

Here is how that message came about. It was the second year of Nebuchadnezzar's rule over Babylon. Although the king was secure on his throne with all of his enemies subdued or in captivity, he nevertheless found himself in great anxiety about the future. His anxiety stemmed from a recurring dream sent to him by Almighty God—a vivid, nightmarish dream, and one he could not understand, though he sensed ominous implications within it. So the king called in his counselors. But since he had forgotten important details of the dream, he demanded that his brain trust not only interpret the nightmare, but that they also give him a vivid description of it.

The king's demand was unprecedented and, as you can imagine, his counselors thought it a bit unfair. When they could not meet his demand, Nebuchadnezzar, in a fit of pique, ordered the execution of all the wise men of Babylon (Daniel 2:12–13).

When the Jewish captive Daniel heard of the king's edict, he and his friends prayed to God for a vision of Nebuchadnezzar's dream and its interpretation. Then he went to the executioner and said, "Do not destroy the wise men of Babylon; take me before the king, and I will tell the king the interpretation" (v. 24).

Daniel soon found himself standing before Nebuchadnezzar, who asked him if he could reveal the meaning of his dream. Daniel explained that he could not, but he had connections with Someone who could: "The secret which the king has demanded, the wise men, the astrologers, the magicians, and the soothsayers cannot declare to the king. But there is a God in heaven who reveals secrets, and He has made known to King Nebuchadnezzar what will be in the latter days. Your dream, and the visions of your head upon your bed were these" (vv. 27–28).

As Daniel explained, just as God had sent the dream to Nebuchadnezzar, God had also revealed the dream and its interpretation to Daniel (v. 19). Then came the scene in Nebuchadnezzar's "oval office" as the Jewish prophet stood before the king and unfolded for him the future of his nation.

First Daniel described the king's vision:

"As for you, O king, thoughts came to your mind while on your bed, about what would come to pass after this; and He who reveals secrets has made known to you what will be . . . You, O king, were watching; and behold, a great image! This great image, whose splendor was excellent, stood before you; and its form was awesome. This image's head was of fine gold, its chest and arms of silver, its belly and thighs of bronze, its legs of iron, its feet partly of iron and partly of clay." (Daniel 2:29, 31–33)

The overarching purpose of this image was to teach Nebuchadnezzar, Daniel, and everyone else on the planet what happens when man puts himself in control. This vision gives us the history of human civilization, written not by Will Durant or Edward Gibbon, but by God Himself.

While the events Daniel unfolded may seem to come about by the power of kings and armies, he understood that the collapse and rise of empires is all God's doing: "*He* changes the times and the seasons; *He* removes kings and raises up kings; *He* gives wisdom to the wise and knowledge to those who have understanding" (Daniel 2:21, *emphasis added*).

Daniel then began to explain to Nebuchadnezzar that his dream was about the kingdoms of this world—his own kingdom and those that would succeed it. He told the king that the colossal metallic image represents four successive gentile world powers that would rule over Israel in the days ahead. The word *kingdom* is used ten times in these verses (vv. 36–45). Exactly what is a kingdom? It is the dominion that a king rules, or a "*king-dom*inion." It designates the people and territory under the rule of a single government. As Daniel was about to explain, the varied components of this statue represent the worldwide dominions that would follow and replace one another in the future.

## The Four World Empires

Through Daniel, God gave King Nebuchadnezzar a composite history of the remaining days of the world. We know this because he spoke specifically of "days to come" and "things to come" (Daniel 2:28, 29 NIV).

He began to reveal the meaning of the dream of the statue in five sections: the head of gold, the breast and arms of silver, the belly and thighs of copper and brass, the legs of iron, and the feet . . . part iron, part clay.

The first world empire, represented by the statue's head of gold, was Nebuchadnezzar's own kingdom of Babylon. Daniel's words to the king are clear. "You, O king, are a king of kings. For the God of heaven has given you a kingdom, power, strength, and glory; and wherever the children of men dwell, or the beasts of the field and the birds of the heaven, He has given them into your hand, and has made you ruler over them all—you are this head of gold" (Daniel 2:37–38 NKJV).

Nebuchadnezzar would not have doubted that the head of gold referred to his kingdom since the chief deity of Babylon was Marduk, known as "the god of gold." The historian Herodotus described the image of Marduk as a dazzling sight—a golden statue seated upon a golden throne before a golden table and a golden altar. Pliny tells us that the robes of Marduk's priests were interlaced with gold.[2]

The second world empire revealed in the king's dream is represented by the image's chest of silver, from which two silver arms emerge (Daniel 2:32). This is the Medo-Persian Empire that conquered Babylon in 539 BC and remained in power for approximately two hundred years. We need feel no uncertainty about that interpretation because later, when Daniel reported the events surrounding the end of the Babylonian empire, he stated clearly that it would be the dual monarchy of the Medes and the Persians that would take control of Nebuchadnezzar's empire (Daniel 5:28). The two nations are again confirmed as Babylon's successor in Daniel 8:20.

The third world empire revealed within the image is represented by its belly and thighs of bronze. Daniel told the king it will be a "kingdom of bronze, which shall rule over all the earth" (Daniel 2:39). This is the empire of Greece, the kingdom of Phillip of Macedon and his famous son, Alexander the Great. Not only does history confirm Greece as the empire that succeeded the Medo-Persians, but Daniel himself affirmed it by naming Greece specifically in Daniel 8:21. Under Alexander, the Greek empire was unified and encompassed more territory than either of the previous empires. Alexander had such a lust for conquest that after subduing virtually all of the known world, he sat down and wept, fearing there were no more territories left to conquer. It is appropriate that this third kingdom is characterized by the bronze midsection of the massive image. Alexander's soldiers armored themselves in bronze and brass helmets and breastplates, and carried bronze and brass shields and swords.

The fourth empire displayed in the image is symbolized by its legs of iron. Daniel describes this empire as "strong as iron, inasmuch as iron breaks in pieces and shatters everything; and like iron that crushes, that kingdom will break in pieces and crush all the others" (2:40). History shows us clearly that Rome is the fourth kingdom. Not only was Rome the successor to the Greek empire, but the iron legs of the image provide a powerful symbol that characterizes the nature of the Romans. The word *iron* is used fourteen times in the text describing Rome in Daniel 2. Historians often use *iron* as an adjective when characterizing the Roman Empire: Rome's *iron hand*. Rome's *iron grip.* Rome's *iron rule.* Rome's *iron fist.* Rome's *iron heel.* Rome's *iron legions.*

History confirms the progression of Daniel's explanation of Nebuchadnezzar's dream. The Babylonians were overthrown by the Medo-Persians; the Medo-Persians were conquered by the Greeks; and when the Grecian empire was conquered by Rome, all of the lands and peoples of the previous kingdoms were assimilated into one kingdom known as the Roman Empire. This empire came into existence fifty years before Jesus was born, and it continued in power throughout the Lord's earthly ministry and beyond. It was Roman rule that put Jesus on the cross. It was the imperialistic Romans who ruled ruthlessly throughout the world during the early days of the church.

The fact that Rome is represented in the statue by its two iron legs is also significant, as the following quote explains:

By A.D. 395 the Roman Empire had split into two political areas of rule: the [Latin-speaking] West with its capital in Rome, and the [Greek-speaking] East with its capital in Constantinople (modern Istanbul, Turkey), which included the land of Israel. This division of the empire is depicted in the statue's two legs.[3]

But this splitting of the mighty Roman Empire into two political units was not to be the last division that kingdom would suffer as Daniel explained to Nebuchadnezzar when he turned his attention to the statue's feet and toes. He noted that in the king's dream, the feet and toes were composed of a mixture of iron and clay. Though positioned at the bottom of the image, these extremities are apparently highly important, for Daniel said as much about the feet and toes as he had said about all the other parts of the image combined.

Here are Daniel's words as he explained to the king the meaning of the material composing the image's feet:

> "Whereas you saw the feet and toes, partly of potter's clay and partly of iron, the kingdom shall be divided; yet the strength of iron shall be in it, just as you saw the iron mixed with ceramic clay. And as the toes of the feet were partly of iron and partly of clay, so the kingdom shall be partly strong and partly fragile. As you saw iron mixed with ceramic clay, they will mingle with the seed of men; but they will not adhere to one another, just as iron does not mix with clay." (Daniel 2:41–43)

According to Daniel, there is to be yet another division in the Roman Empire. Not a division of two, as indicated by the image's two legs, but of ten, as symbolized by its ten toes. Daniel foretells a time when the Roman Empire will consist of ten kingdoms or leaders. Since the downward movement from one section of the statue to the next represents the passage of time, the "feet and toes" stage must follow the "legs" stage. But when we look back at the history that followed Daniel's prediction, we find nothing in history that even remotely corresponds to a tenfold Roman coalition. That shows us that this fifth and final feet-and-toes-stage kingdom is yet to come and is yet to perform its prescribed role in human history.

Daniel gives us one other piece of information that enables us to understand the timing of the events conveyed in Nebuchadnezzar's dream. He tells us that this final form of the Roman Empire will be on the earth when God sets up His earthly kingdom. "And in the days of these kings [the rulers of the ten segments of the Roman kingdom], the God of heaven will set up a kingdom which shall never be destroyed; and the kingdom shall not be left to other people; it shall break in pieces and consume all these kingdoms, and it shall stand forever" (Daniel 2:44).

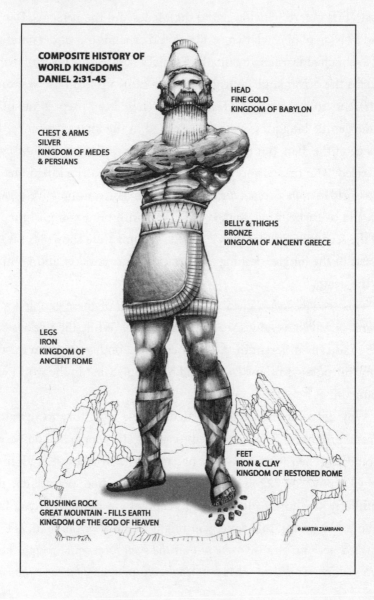

**COMPOSITE HISTORY OF WORLD KINGDOMS DANIEL 2:31-45**

HEAD
FINE GOLD
KINGDOM OF BABYLON

CHEST & ARMS
SILVER
KINGDOM OF MEDES & PERSIANS

BELLY & THIGHS
BRONZE
KINGDOM OF ANCIENT GREECE

LEGS
IRON
KINGDOM OF ANCIENT ROME

FEET
IRON & CLAY
KINGDOM OF RESTORED ROME

CRUSHING ROCK
GREAT MOUNTAIN - FILLS EARTH
KINGDOM OF THE GOD OF HEAVEN

© MARTIN ZAMBRANO

## Daniel's Corroborating Dream

Years after Nebuchadnezzar's dream of the towering image and four-teen years before Babylon fell to the Medes and the Persians, Daniel had a vision of his own that confirms and expands our understanding of Nebuchadnezzar's dream. In Daniel's vision, a powerful wind stirred the ocean, and "four great beasts came up from the sea, each different from the other" (Daniel 7:3). These beasts represented the same gentile kingdoms as those depicted in the king's dream of the image of the man, but this time the character of those kingdoms was revealed. The first vision (Daniel 2) characterized the kingdoms of the world *as man assessed them*—majestic, massive, impressive, gigantic, and overwhelming. Man is impressed with his accomplishments. In the second vision (Daniel 7), the kingdoms were shown as savage beasts of the jungle, slashing and attacking one another and fighting to the death.

This second vision gives us *God's appraisal* of these gentile kingdoms—destructive, divisive, angry, and cruel. While the two visions were radically different in their presentation, both were given for the same purpose—to show Daniel and his people what in the world was going on!

Why did God choose this particular time in history to reveal so great a prophecy? It was designed to assure His people in a desperate moment of their history. Assyria had taken the Northern Kingdom of Israel captive in 722 BC, and now, two hundred years later, the Southern Kingdom of Judah was in captivity in Babylon. If you had been a Jew during that time, you might well have wondered, *Is God finished with us? Are we to be put on the shelf forever?* Through these two visions, God assured His beleaguered people: *This isn't the end.*

*There is a time in the future when I will once again be involved with you as a nation. But I want you to know what is going to happen between now and then.*

Much of what was revealed to Daniel in these dreams has already happened. But not all of it. The three prophesied kingdoms have come and gone, and the fourth kingdom has also made its appearance in history. But Daniel's later vision included additional information about the future of the fourth kingdom not given to the Babylonian monarch—information about events that are yet in the future. Let's look at how Daniel describes it: "After this I saw in the night visions, and behold, a fourth beast, dreadful and terrible, exceedingly strong. It had huge iron teeth; it was devouring, breaking in pieces, and trampling the residue with its feet. It was different from all the beasts that were before it, and it had ten horns" (Daniel 7:7). Daniel is careful to explain that the ten horns are ten kings who shall arise from this kingdom (v. 24).

We know that this ten-kingdom prophecy of Daniel's remains in the future because not only has the ten-leader form of the Roman Empire never existed in history, but neither has such a kingdom been suddenly crushed as prophecy indicates it will be. According to Daniel 2, the Roman Empire in its final form will experience sudden destruction. The Roman Empire of Jesus' day did not end suddenly. It gradually deteriorated and declined over many centuries until the western part, the Holy Roman Empire, fell in AD 476, and the eastern part, the Byzantine Empire, fell in AD 1453. You can hardly imagine a more gradual slide from glory to oblivion! We must conclude, then, that some form of the Roman Empire must emerge in the end times, and according to Daniel, it will be in place prior to the coming of Christ to rule and reign over the earth.

## The Rebirth of the Roman Empire

The future manifestation of the Roman Empire that Daniel prophesied twenty-five hundred years ago will take the form of a coalition or
confederation of ten world leaders and will encompass the same territory as the historic Roman Empire. And today we can see that
coalition taking shape right before our eyes! It began as early as 1930,
when the French statesman Aristide Briand attempted to enlist twenty-
six nations in what he first called "the United States of Europe" and
modified to "the European Union." In his proposal he said, "The
nations of Europe today must unite in order to live and prosper." The
European press gave Briand's novel idea little attention, and nothing
came of it.[4]

That is, nothing came of it *at that time*. But Briand's call for European
unity was merely one world war ahead of the curve. Fewer than
twenty years later, one of the world's most respected leaders issued
the same call:

> In 1946, following the devastation of Europe during the Second
> World War, Winston Churchill forcefully asserted that "the tragedy of
> Europe" could only be solved if the issues of ancient nationalism and
> sovereignty could give way to a sense of European "national group-
> ing." He said that the path to European peace and prosperity on the
> world stage was clear: "We must build a United States of Europe."[5]

Churchill's call initiated a series of steps toward unification; some
were faltering, but others gained traction. The Benelux Conference of
1948, held in Brussels, Belgium, would lay the foundation for a new

organization "to unite European countries economically and politically to secure a lasting peace."[6] Only three tiny nations attended the meeting—the Netherlands, Luxembourg, and Belgium. These nations came together because they saw unity as their only hope of survival in the postwar world.

Another step was taken in April 1951, when these three nations signed the Treaty of Paris with three additional nations, Germany, France, and Italy, forming a common market for coal and steel in an environment of peace and equality.

March 25, 1957, saw a major step toward European unification when the Treaty of Rome was signed on Capitoline Hill, one of the famous Seven Hills of Rome. On this occasion, Italy, France, and Germany joined the Netherlands, Luxembourg, and Belgium, creating the European Economic Community—the Common Market.

In 1973, the United Kingdom, Ireland, and Denmark joined the EEC, and Greece was added in 1981, making it a ten-nation confederation. On January 1, 1986, Spain and Portugal came into the union, and the agenda expanded beyond economics when the EEC officially adopted the goal of a politically unified Europe. In 1987 the Single European Act was implemented. With the fall of the Berlin Wall in 1989, Germany was reunified, and East Germany was integrated into the membership. In December 1992, the economic borders between the nations of the European community were removed, and a common passport was issued to travelers. Study in universities within the nations was also permitted without any restrictions. Austria, Finland, and Sweden joined the Union in 1995.

In 2002, eighty billion coins were produced for use in the twelve participating nations of the Eurozone, thus introducing the new monetary unit, the euro. Despite expected fluctuations, the rise in euro value has been steady and observable. The dollar is declining against the euro, and many experts believe that within five years the euro may actually replace the US dollar as the standard world currency. As we learned in the previous chapter, the Iranians have recently refused to accept the American dollar as payment for oil, requiring payment to be made in euro.

The march toward European unification continued on May 1, 2004, when Cyprus, the Czech Republic, Estonia, Hungary, Latvia, Lithuania, Malta, Poland, Slovakia, and Slovenia were added, bringing the total to twenty-five nations. These nations brought 75 million people into the European Union, expanding its population to 450 million people and surpassing North America as the world's biggest economic zone. In January 2007, Romania and Bulgaria were admitted to the EU, bringing the total number of nations to twenty-seven.[7]

While Israel was part of the original Roman Empire, it is not currently a part of the European Union. The EU considers Israel ineligible for membership due to human rights violations, based on its occupation of the West Bank, Gaza Strip, Golan Heights, and East Jerusalem. It has been proposed, however, that if Israel would sign a peace treaty with its hostile neighbors, it would be offered membership in the EU.[8]

Gradually yet steadily, the nations of Europe have come together, creating a modern replica of the ancient Roman Empire. Europe is more integrated today than at any time since the days of ancient Rome. The United States of Europe is considered by many to be the second most powerful political force in our world.

## ROMAN EMPIRE THEN & NOW

Old Roman Empire Outlined in Black
European Union Nations in Gray

FINLAND

SWEDEN

ESTONIA

DENMARK

LATVIA

LITHUANIA

IRELAND   ENGLAND   NETHERLANDS
LUXEMBOURG
BELGIUM   POLAND

GERMANY   CZECH

SLOVAKIA

AUSTRIA   HUNGARY
SLOVENIA

FRANCE   ITALY   ROMANIA

BULGARIA

SPAIN

PORTUGAL

NORTHERN AFRICA   GREECE
MALTA   CYPRUS

LIBYA   EGYPT

## Consolidation of the European Government

Currently the EU government is organized into three bodies: a Parliament, the Council of European Union, and the European Commission. The Parliament is considered "the Voice of the People" because citizens of the EU directly elect its 785 members. The Parliament passes European laws in conjunction with the Council. Its president is elected to serve a five-year term.

The Council, "the Voice of the Member States," consists of twenty-seven members who are also the heads of their national governments. This body participates with Parliament in the passing of laws and also establishes common foreign policy and security policies. As I write this book, a Reform Treaty is currently in the ratification process. This treaty contains proposals for two major changes to the structure of the Council. First, it will reduce the membership of the Council from twenty-seven to seventeen and elect a full-time president for a two and a half-year extendable term, replacing the current rotating presidency, which changes every six months. These steps toward power consolidation may have very serious implications for the future.

The third body of EU government, the European Commission, consists of twenty-seven commissioners whose tasks are to draft new laws and implement policies and funding. Its president is nominated by the Council of European Union for a five-year term.[9]

Other EU governmental entities include: the Court of Justice, the Court of Auditors, the European Central Bank, and the European Investment Bank.[10]

Former British prime minister Tony Blair is rumored to be the likely candidate for Europe's first president of the Council. These rumors circulated as far back as 2002 and gained momentum in 2007 after Blair stepped down from his position as prime minister of Great Britain. French president Nicolas Sarkozy was the first leader to propose Blair for Europe's first president. In a speech given in January 2008, Sarkozy said this about Tony Blair:

He is intelligent, he is brave and he is a friend. We need him in Europe. How can we govern a continent of 450 million people if the President changes every six months and has to run his own country at the same time? I want a President chosen from the top—not a compromise candidate—who will serve for two-and-a-half years.[11]

As we track these developments toward ever-increasing unity and more centralized power among the European nations, we can see a new empire in the making—an empire that occupies the same territory as the ancient Roman Empire. Turning back to Daniel for further insight into the nature of this rising coalition, we are intrigued by his description of it as a mixture of two noncohering materials. We already know that iron represented the strength of the old Roman Empire. In the newly constituted empire, however, the prophecy tells us that iron will be mixed with ceramic clay. Clay is nothing like the other materials that composed the image of Nebuchadnezzar's dream. Clay speaks of weakness and instability.

The best interpretation of this unstable mix is that the combination of clay and iron represents the diverse racial, religious, and political elements that will comprise this final form of the Roman Empire. That is, in fact, what we see today in the early manifestation of the European coalition. While the EU has great economic and political clout, the cultures and languages of its various countries are so incredibly diverse that it cannot hold together any more than iron

and clay unless unity is imposed and enforced by an extremely powerful leader. As the EU prepares to elect a strong president for a longer
term, we can see how an uneasy unity could come about.

## The Need for Renewed Vigilance

From this brief study of modern Europe and ancient Rome, we can
begin to understand the meaning of what is going on in the world
today. Three things in particular emerge from our study that should
increase our vigilance.

### The Consolidation of World Power

Since the time of the Roman Empire, there has been no nation or
empire with the power to govern or dominate the known world. But
it is coming. In the future there will be a short period of time when
the world will be unified under one dominant leader.

We saw in Daniel's second vision that the fourth beast had ten horns
growing from its head. We need not wonder at the meaning of the beast
and the ten horns, for the meaning of Daniel's dream was given directly
to him: "The fourth beast shall be a fourth kingdom on earth, which
shall . . . devour the whole earth, trample it and break it in pieces. The
ten horns are ten kings who shall arise from this kingdom" (Daniel
7:23–24). The fourth beast represents the fourth successive kingdom
after Babylon, which history identifies as the Roman Empire. But since
Rome was never ruled simultaneously by ten kings, we know that those
kings are yet to arrive on the stage of world history to rule a newly
formed empire that overlays the territory of the ancient Roman Empire.
Today the concentration of power in the European Union signals the
beginning of this new world order.

## The Coming of One World Leader

According to Daniel's prophecy, a supreme leader will rise from among the ten-leader confederacy in Europe. "And another shall rise after them; he shall be different from the first ones, and shall subdue three kings. He shall speak pompous words against the Most High, shall persecute the saints of the Most High, and shall intend to change times and law. Then the saints shall be given into his hand for a time and times and half a time" (Daniel 7:24–25). This leader will emerge from the group of ten to take control of the new European Union. He will become the final world dictator. We know him as the Antichrist, and we will have more to say about him in chapter 7. But the point we must not miss now is this: the new European Union is one of the conditional preludes to the coming of the Antichrist. As Arno Froese, executive director of Midnight Call Ministries, wrote:

The new European power structure will fulfill the prophetic predictions which tell us that a one world system will be implemented. When established, it will fall into the hands of the Antichrist.[12]

And we can have little doubt that such a thing could easily happen when we see how glibly statesmen and politicians can gravitate to power. Paul-Henri Spaak, the first president of the UN General Assembly, first president of the European Parliament, and onetime secretary general of NATO, is credited with making this stunning statement:

We do not need another committee. We have too many already. What we want is a man of sufficient stature to hold the allegiance of all people, and to lift us out of the economic morass into which we are sinking. Send us such a man and be he god or devil, we will receive him.[13]

Statements such as this should chill us to the bone. It shows that the world as a whole in its ignorance will actually embrace the power that will seek to enslave it. The European Union is the kindling awaiting the spark of the Antichrist to inflame the world with unprecedented evil. It is certainly a time to be vigilant.

### The Condition for the Treaty with Israel

In the ninth chapter of Daniel's prophecy, he tells us of a treaty that will be signed between his people and the world leader who will head the realigned Roman Empire: "Then he shall confirm a covenant with many for one week; but in the middle of the week he shall bring an end to sacrifice and offering" (Daniel 9:27). Daniel tells us here that Israel will sign a treaty with the Antichrist, and that this treaty will be forged to last for a "week," literally in prophetic language, a "week of years," or seven years. This treaty will be an attempt to settle the Arab-Israeli controversy that today focuses the world's attention on the Middle East. After three and one-half years, that treaty will be broken, and the countdown to Armageddon will begin.

## Heeding the Warning

The stage is now set in Europe for these events to occur. Israel is back in her land, oil is concentrating world focus on the Middle East, and the nations of the ancient Roman Empire are reunifying. Prophecies of events long predicted are coming to pass. I think any honest person must admit that something big is going on in the world. The prophecies of Daniel show us what it is: the hands on the prophetic clock are moving toward midnight. The warning has been sounded, and we will do well to heed it.

I live in San Diego, and these days the people of my area get a bit edgy as the end of October approaches. While most of the country is gathering frost on pumpkins, we are experiencing extreme heat, low humidity, and powerful winds—perfect conditions for devastating wildfires that devour everything in their path.

In 2003 we lived through the firestorm that consumed more than 390,000 acres of land, destroyed 2,430 homes, and inflicted $2.2 billion in property damage.[14] In October 2007, the National Weather Service issued a Red Flag Warning, indicating that conditions were ripe for another major wildfire. On Sunday, October 21, while we were worshipping in our first morning service, ominous billows of smoke began to rise from the backcountry, thirty-three miles away. When I walked out of church that morning, I could see the smoke, and the frightening images of 2003 returned to my mind.

The San Diego Fire Department, using a sophisticated new warning system called Reverse 9-1-1, sent phone messages to homes that were in harm's way. The messages were short and to the point: "This area, get out! This area, get out!" Thousands of San Diegans evacuated their homes, but as is always the case, some refused to leave.

In an attempt to protect their home, one father and his fifteen-year-old son chose to remain behind when the rest of their family evacuated. Two and a half hours into the fire, Capt. Ray Rapue of Cal Fire ordered them to evacuate the area immediately. The father got into his pickup truck, his son got on an ATV, and they started to leave their property. But for reasons unknown, when Fire Engine 3387 drove onto their property, both the father and his son turned around and went back to the house.

The captain again warned them to evacuate because of the dense smoke. The father jumped on the ATV with his son, but lack of oxygen caused the ATV to stall out. Then they both climbed into the fire engine and were warned to stay in the cab while the firefighters continued their work. Soon, depleted oxygen, intense heat, and choking smoke drove the firefighters to attempt their own escape. But the now-overloaded fire engine also stalled.

What happened next is called a *burnover*. Before the firefighters could deploy their tentlike emergency shelters inside the cab, the windows exploded from the heat of the fire advancing from the double-wide home. Fireman Brooke Linman was trying to comfort the panicked young man when voracious flames leapt into the cab. The boy let out a terrible scream as nearly half his body was severely burned. "He kept asking me if we were going to die," reported the fireman later. "I said, 'No, we're not going to die.'" The captain ordered the firefighters and the young man out of the burning cab, and they sought refuge behind large rocks on the property.

Overhead in a command airplane, CAL FIRE chief Ray Chaney reported hearing over his radio a primal scream from the ground below. "Ahhhh! Ahhhh! Ahhhh!" came the wrenching sound in plaintive, agonized spurts. Chief Chaney was able to guide a helicopter through the dense smoke to within a few feet of the trapped group. Two minutes later the helicopter lifted off with its cargo of the injured and quickly returned for the two others. All the rescued were then transported to a trauma center. The father died in that blaze. The son and four heroic fire personnel were severely burned. As I write this chapter five months later, the young man remains hospitalized.[15]

## The Importance of Warnings

We will never know why this man and his son chose to disregard the repeated warnings, but the point came when all warnings were futile.

There was no longer any time to run. Living in the fire zone of Southern California has made me aware of the importance of warnings.

As I look at world events through the lens of God's prophetic Word, I have become acutely aware of the warning signs. But warnings are useful only if we heed them. As the prophetic clock moves toward its final strike, we must not wait until it's too late to move out of harm's way. The admonition of Paul to the Roman believers should spur us to action: "Knowing the time, that now it is high time to awake out of sleep: for now our salvation is nearer than when we first believed" (Romans 13:11).

Knowing the meaning behind the events we see in the daily news helps us to understand what is going on in the world. Today's headlines show the wisdom of Paul's warning—it is high time for us to awake out of sleep and realize that things will not continue to go on indefinitely as they are now. Indeed, as the signs from Daniel's prophecies show us, things are coming to a head. Events are moving us toward the moment when warnings will be too late, and we will be caught in the firestorm of a great evil that will trouble the world before Christ finally returns to set things right.

The question for you is, are you heeding the warnings? Are you prepared to stand before God? Have you accepted His offer of salvation? He is telling us by the events that surround us that the window of opportunity will soon be gone. Please do not wait until it is too late!

# FOUR

# Islamic Terrorism

GEORGES SADA WAS AN AIR FORCE GENERAL UNDER SADDAM Hussein. Though ethnically an Iraqi, he was not a Muslim but an Assyrian Christian. He refused to join the Baathist Party under Saddam, which blocked his ascent into the ranks of power. But he was a military hero, Iraq's top air force pilot, and the man Saddam called on to hear the truth about military matters because Saddam knew his yes-men would tell him only whatever he wanted to hear.

In his book, *Saddam's Secrets: How an Iraqi General Defied and Survived Saddam Hussein,* Sada speaks about the spreading impact of Islam around the world:

I'm often asked about militant Islam and the threat of global terrorism. More than once I've been asked about the meaning of the Arabic words *Fatah* and *Jihad.* What I normally tell them is that to followers of the militant brand of Islam, these doctrines express the belief that Allah has commanded them to conquer the nations of the world both by cultural invasion and by the sword. In some cases this means moving thousands of Muslim families into a foreign land—by building mosques and changing the culture from the inside out, and by refusing to assimilate or adopt the beliefs or values of that nation—to conquer the land for Islam. This is an invidious doctrine, but it's . . . being carried out in some places today by followers of this type of Islam.[1]

Sada went on to warn Americans not to think that the Islamic revolution is a Middle Eastern or European problem. Their ultimate goal is conquest of the West and America:

[They] won't be stopped by appeasement. They are not interested in political solutions. They don't want welfare—their animosity is not caused by hunger or poverty or anything of the sort. They understand only one thing: total and complete conquest of the West and of anyone who does not bow to them and their dangerous and out-of-date ideology of hate and revenge.[2]

Americans do not seem to take the threat of Islam seriously. In fact, the Pew Research Center tells us that US citizens are essentially oblivious to the potential danger of radical Muslims. "According to poll results issued recently, 58 percent of Americans indicated that they knew either 'not very much' or 'nothing' about the Muslim religion, Islam . . . the fastest growing religion in America."[3]

According to Sada, Americans are particularly vulnerable to the spread of militant Islam because our enemies take advantage of traits that we consider socially positive:

What I want to say next is not easy for me to say but I think I must say it anyway. One of the nicest things about the American people is that you are generous and friendly people, and because of this you are sometimes naïve and overly trusting. You want to be friendly, so you open up to people and then you're surprised when they stab you in the back. Many brave young soldiers have died in Iraq for this reason, but I think this is also a big part of the problem with the State Department and others in government who fail to understand the true nature of this enemy.[4]

General Sada's book addresses a major phenomenon that is going on in our world today, and one that we all should want to know more about. The rise of radical Islam has changed the lives of everyone, especially since 9-11. We experience it every time we wait in an airport security line, every time we hear news reports of another terrorist bombing, and indeed, every time we turn on the news and hear reporters and commentators speak of how Islamic culture is growing in our own land. Most of us don't know how to respond. We hear on the one hand that Islam is a major threat to our world, and on the other that Muslims are greatly misunderstood and want nothing more than to be at peace with us. In this chapter I hope to show you what is going on in the world behind the headlines and give you information on how to understand and deal with the new rise of Islam.

## Is Islam Militant or Peaceful?

Last year Fox News aired a special called "Radical Islam: Terror in Its Own Words," which revealed "the evil aims of radical Islam." The documentary included shocking clips from Islamic television, showing clerics and political leaders openly advocating attacks on the United States and Israel. The documentary also included programs shown on

Islamic TV in which young children sing of their desire to participate in violent *jihad* or to become suicide bombers. The program went on to show never-before-aired footage from a radical Islamic rally in California where the audience was told, "One day you will see the flag of Islam over the White House."[5]

More recently, al-Aqsa, the Hamas-owned television station in Gaza, aired a children's program in which a boy puppet sneaks into the White House, kills President George W. Bush with "the sword of Islam," and vows "the White House would be turned into a mosque."[6]

In the face of such reports as these, one of the most baffling and unsettling puzzles about Islam is the constant contention on the part of some Muslim leaders that they are a peace-loving people. Yet even as they make the claim, Islamic terrorists continue to brutally murder any person or group with whom they find fault. In his foreword to Don Richardson's book *The Secrets of the Koran*, former radical Shi'ite Muslim Reza F. Safa asked:

> If Islam is a peaceful religion, then why did Mohammed engage in 47 battles? Why, in every campaign the Muslim armies have fought throughout history, have they slaughtered men, women and children who did not bow their knees to the lordship of Islam? The reign of terror of men such as Saddam, Khomeini, Ghadafi, Idi Amin and many other Muslim dictators are modern examples. If Islam is so peaceful, why are there so many verses in the Koran about killing the infidels and those who resist Islam? If Islam is peaceful, why isn't there even one Muslim country that will allow freedom of religion and speech? Not one! If Islam is peaceful, who is imparting this awful violence to hundreds of Islamic groups throughout the world who kill innocent people in the name of Allah?

But since the statehood of Israel . . . men such as Ghadafi and Osama bin Laden have been blowing the dust off the sword of a forceful world-invading religion.[7]

To get a handle on these two contradictory sides of Islam, it will help us to delve briefly into the history of how the religion came to be and what beliefs it holds today.

## The History of Islam

In his book *The Age of Faith*, Will Durant wrote:

In the year 565 Justinian died, master of a great empire. Five years later Mohammed was born into a poor family in a country three quarters desert, sparsely peopled by nomad tribes whose total wealth could hardly have furnished the sanctuary of St. Sophia. No one in those years would have dreamed that within a century these nomads would conquer half of Byzantine Asia, all of Persia and Egypt, most of North Africa, and be on their way to Spain. The explosion of the Arabian peninsula into the conquest and conversion of half the Mediterranean world is the most extraordinary phenomenon of medieval history.[8]

The name *Islam* literally means *submission*. A Muslim is "one who submits to God." According to conservative estimates, there are about 1.5 billion Muslims in our world today. Approximately 1.4 million live in the United States, which is about 6 percent of the US adult population. While we usually associate Islam with the Middle East, the largest Muslim populations are actually in Asia.[9]

According to Islamic tradition, the founder of Islam, Mohammad, was born in Mecca (in present-day Saudi Arabia) in AD 570. Mecca was a thriving center of religious pilgrimage, filled with numerous temples and statues dedicated to the many gods the Arabian people worshipped at the time.

Mohammad's father died before the prophet was born, and his mother died when he was six years old. He was raised by his paternal grandfather, grew up to become a camel driver and then a merchant, and at the age of twenty-six, married a wealthy caravan owner named Khadija. Khadija was forty years old and had been divorced four times. In spite of her age, she and Mohammad had six children together.

Durant further noted, "Mohammad's son-in-law, Ali, described his father-in-law as being "of middle stature, neither tall nor short. His complexion was rosy white; his eyes black; his hair, thick, brilliant, and beautiful, fell to his shoulders. His profuse beard fell to his breast . . . There was such sweetness in his visage that no one, once in his presence, could leave him. If I hungered, a single look at the Prophet's face dispelled the hunger. Before him, all forgot their griefs and pains."[10]

Mohammad worked in professions that brought him into contact with a number of Christians and Jews who caused him to question the religion of his own people. He was forty years old and meditating in a cave outside Mecca when he received his first revelation. From that moment on, according to his testimony, God occasionally revealed messages to him, which he declared to the people. These messages, which Muhammad received throughout his life, form the verses of the Qu'ran, which Muslims regard as the divine word of God.

In the seventh-century Arabian world of Mohammad, the people worshipped more than 360 different gods, one for each day of the lunar year. One of these was the moon god, the male counterpart to the female sun god. The moon god was called by various names, one of which was Allah, and it was the favorite god of Mohammad's family. As Dr. Robert Morey explains, "The literal Arabic name of Muhammad's father was Abd-Allah. His uncle's name was literally Obied-Allah. These names . . . reveal the personal devotion that Muhammed's pagan family had to the worship of Allah, the moon god."[11]

As Mohammad began to promote his new religion, it was only natural that he would choose to elevate the moon god, Allah, and declare him to be the one true God. His devotion to Allah was single-minded and fierce, and in establishing and spreading his religion of Islam, Mohammad slaughtered thousands of people who resisted conversion. As his instructions to his followers show, there was no subtlety in his evangelistic technique. Abd El Schafi, an expert on ancient Muslim scholarship, informs us: "One of Muhammad's popular claims is that God commanded him to fight people until they became Muslims . . . All Muslim scholars without exception agree on this."[12]

Opposition in Mecca forced Mohammad and his followers to flee to Medina in AD 620, where he became the head of the first Muslim community. In AD 631 he returned to Mecca, where he died the following year. At his death, the Islamic community became bitterly divided over the question of who would be Mohammad's successor. Even today that division survives in the two Islamic sects, now known as Shi'ite and Sunni. Conflict between these sects is one of the major stress points in Iraq and throughout the Islamic world.

At the death of Mohammad, the group we know as the Sunni followed the leadership of Abu Bakr, Mohammad's personally chosen successor. The Sunni now comprise about 90 percent of the Islamic world. They believe that Muhammad's spiritual gifts died with him and that their only authority today is the Qu'ran. The Baath party of Saddam Hussein was part of the Sunni sect.

The Shi'ites maintained that Mohammad passed on a legacy of personal authority in addition to the Qu'ran, called the Hadith, as author Winfried Corduan explains:

> The Shi'ites, on the other hand, identified with Muhammad's son-in-law Ali, whom they saw as possessing a spiritual endowment directly from the prophet. The Shi'ites believe that their leaders, the imams, have authority on par with the Qu'ran. It is the Shi'ites that believe that the Twelfth Imam went into concealment hundreds of years ago and continues to live there until he returns as the Mahdi . . . the Muslim Messiah![13]

When Abu Bakr succeeded Mohammad, he and his successors launched *jihads* (or holy wars) that spread the religion of Islam from northern Spain to India and threatened Christian Europe. Christians resisted the threat, and a series of wars followed that drove the Islamic invaders back into the Middle Eastern countries, where they still dominate. Their zeal to have their religion dominate the world has not diminished, however, and it remains a threat to all who do not maintain vigilance.

## The Habits of Islam

Sunni Muslims mandate five acts of worship, which are frequently referred to as the five pillars of Islam. Shi'ite Muslim worship comprises eight ritual practices, but these overlap and encompass the same five pillars of Islam as practiced by the Sunni. The five pillars are as follows:[14]

1. *To recite the* Shahadah: The *Shahadah* is the Islamic creed, "There is no god but Allah, and Muhammad is his messenger." Its recitation is the duty of every Muslim.

2. *To pray (salat)*: Muslims pray while bowing toward Mecca five times each day: in the early morning, in the early and late afternoon, at sunset, and an hour after sunset.

3. *To fast (sawm)*: Muslims refrain from food during the daylight hours throughout the lunar month of Ramadan. This month is to be given over to meditation and reflection, and it ends with a joyous celebration.

4. *To give alms (zakat)*: Muslims are required to give 2.5 percent (one-fortieth) of their income to the poor and those in need. They may give more as a means of gaining further divine reward, but the 2.5 percent is an obligatory minimum. The percentage is based on the amount of accumulated wealth or income held for a lunar year above a minimum of three ounces of gold.

5. *To make the pilgrimage (hajj)*: Those physically and financially able must visit Mecca at least once during their lifetime. The journey usually takes at least a week and includes many stops at other holy sites along the way.

## The Hatred of Islam

No doubt the most frightening word associated with Islam is *jihad*. Sometimes called the "sixth pillar" of Islam, *jihad* actually means "struggle." The "Greater Jihad" is the inner struggle of each Muslim to submit to Allah. The "Lesser Jihad" is the outward struggle to defend the Islamic community. This is the jihad that strikes fear in the hearts of any who reject radical Islam. These Muslims take jihad to mean violent defense of Islam; to them it authorizes the expansion of the Islamic religion even by means of deadly aggression.

The overt hatred for the West expressed in jihad has already spawned many mortal attacks, and the fanaticism that produced them has not diminished. In her book, completed days before her assassination, former prime minister of Pakistan Benazir Bhutto wrote that one of the primary aims of the militants is:

> . . . to provoke a clash of civilizations between the West and . . . Islam. The great hope of the militants is a collision, an explosion between the values of the West and what the extremists claim to be the values of Islam . . . The attacks on September 11, 2001, heralded the . . . dream of bloody confrontation . . . if the fanatics and extremists prevail . . . then a great *fitna* (disorder through schism or division) would sweep the world. Here lies their ultimate goal: chaos.[15]

The hatred that the Muslims have for the Jews needs no documentation. But the settlement of Israel into her homeland in 1948 took this hatred to a level of murderous fury. The militants and radicals refer to Israel as "little Satan," and the United States as "big Satan," and they are determined to wipe both countries off the map.

While the majority of the world's 1.5 billion Muslims want no part of this deadly violence and attempt to live in peace with their neighbors, the number of radicals who preach violence and terror is mushrooming around the world. Experts say that 15 to 20 percent of Muslims are radical enough to strap a bomb on their bodies in order to kill Christians and Jews. If this number is accurate, it means about three hundred million Muslims are willing to die in order to take you and me down.

To get a picture of how bitterly Islam hates Jews and Christians, one has only to listen to the speeches of their clerics and leaders. Recently, Sheikh Ibrahim Mdaires delivered a sermon at a mosque in the Gaza Strip that was broadcast live to the Arab world. The text of that sermon has circulated around the globe. It represents the alarming doctrines and attitudes being taught and preached in many mosques and Islamic schools.

> With the establishment of the state of Israel, the entire Islamic nation was lost, because Israel is a cancer . . . The Jews are a virus resembling AIDS, from which the entire world suffers. You will find that the Jews were behind all the civil strife in this world. The Jews are behind the suffering of the nations . . . We [the Muslims] have ruled the world before, and by Allah, the day will come when we will rule the entire world again. The day will come when we will rule America. The day will come when we will rule Britain and the entire world—except the Jews. The Jews will not enjoy a life of tranquility under our rule, because they are treacherous by nature, as they have been throughout history. The day will come when everything will be relieved of the Jews . . . Listen to the Prophet Muhammad, who tells you about the evil that awaits the Jews. The stones and trees will want the Muslims to finish off every Jew.[16]

If this diatribe does not give you reason enough to believe that Islam is the enemy of America and Christianity, consider that today, as I write these words, there is not a single one of the fifty-five predominately Muslim nations on earth today where Christians are not persecuted. As General Sada warned, we cannot afford to relax our vigilance in the name of naïve tolerance and multiculturalism.

# The Hopes of Islam

Speeches like that of Mdaires show us that radical Islam has a vision of its future that does not bode well for those who stand in the way. To get a better understanding of this vision, we will now look briefly at some of the goals the Islamic world hopes to achieve.

## Islam Hopes to Rule the World

In his book *Secrets of the Koran,* Don Richardson tells the chilling story of Islam's plan to gain political and religious control of the entire world:

> The world needs to be warned. At least 40 million Muslim youth in the Muslim world's religious schools, called madrasas, are avidly memorizing the entire Koran plus a generally extremist body of related traditions—the hadiths . . . These schools are breeding grounds for potential terrorists . . . Hatred for Jews and Christians (largely synonymous with Israel and America) and general disdain for all non-Muslims . . . are deeply instilled . . . Simply put, 40 million trainees in Muslim madrasas are a societal nuclear bomb.
>
> Consider this from professor Mochtar Buchori, a member of the Indonesian Parliament: If we add all the universities, colleges, high schools, junior high schools, and elementary schools in the United States, we find that the total is about 24,000 institutions. Yet Buchori counts 37,362 Muslim madrassas in Indonesia, alone! Of these only 8 percent have any input from Indonesia's government. In 92 percent, the teaching agenda is controlled by Muslim clerics.[17]

Traditionally in the United States, Arabic language courses have been taught only at universities, mosques, and Islamic schools. But that has recently changed. In September 2006, Carver Elementary School, a publicly financed K–8 school in San Diego, absorbed into its enrollment about one hundred students from a defunct charter school serving mostly Somali Muslims. To accommodate the special religious customs of the Muslim children, the administration formed, in effect, an Islamic school within an American school. Accommodations included adding courses in the Arabic language, modifying the cafeteria menu in accordance with Islamic dietary restrictions, providing gender-separated classes, and establishing an afternoon recess allowing for the Islamic prayer specified for that time of the day—all at an additional cost to the school district of $450,000!

Just when Carver was becoming comfortable with this arrangement, a substitute teacher observed that the afternoon Muslim prayer was being led by an employee of the school district. The sub reported the apparent "indoctrination" of students to Islam at a public session of the school board. Investigations began into the accommodations and the apparent double standard that bans Christianity from public institutions and yet accommodates "an organized attempt to push public conformance with Islamic law."[18]

Here we see General Sada's warning played out in tangible form. We Americans want to be nice. We want to accommodate. We want to believe that if we are tolerant of others, they will reciprocate. We tend to forget the general's warning that militant Muslims don't think that way, and each inch we give in the name of accommodation, they will take in the name of conquest.

It is one thing to read about Muslim determination to take over the world; it is quite another to watch it happening right before our eyes, as it is in Europe. The most startling and underreported social migration of our age is the Islamification of Europe, which has great bearing on the territories of the old Roman Empire that we discussed in the previous chapter. Tony Blankley of the *Washington Times* devoted his book, *The West's Last Chance*, to sounding an alarm about this Islamic infiltration. This is how he sees this threat to Western culture:

> In much of the West, and particularly in Europe, there is blind denial that radical Islam is transforming the world. Most Europe elites and far too many American politicians and journalists believe that our challenges are business and politics as usual. They are sheep who cannot sense the wolf pack in the woods . . . The threat of the radical Islamists taking over Europe is every bit as great to the United States as was the threat of the Nazis taking over Europe in the 1940s. We cannot afford to lose Europe. We cannot afford to see Europe transformed into a launching pad for Islamist jihad . . .
>
> The moral threat we face comes not merely from Osama bin Laden and a few thousand terrorists. Rather, we are confronted with the Islamic world—a fifth of mankind—in turmoil, and insurgent as it has not been in at least five hundred years, if not fifteen hundred years. The magnitude of this cultural upheaval cannot yet be measured . . . To point out the obvious, the resurgence of a militant Islam drove America to fight two wars in Muslim countries in two years, disrupted America's alliance with Europe, caused the largest reorganization of the American government in half a century (with the creation of the Department of Homeland Security), changed election results in Europe, and threatened the stability of most of the governments in the Middle East.[19]

We can easily see and resist the effects of jihad in militant terrorism, but we have trouble seeing and resisting the more subtle strategy that the Muslims call *fatah*. *Fatah* is infiltration, moving into a country in numbers large enough to affect the culture. It means taking advantage of tolerant laws and accommodative policies to insert the influence of Islam. In places where a military invasion will not succeed, the slow, systematic, and unrelenting methods of *fatah* are conquering whole nations. Two illustrations are instructive, the first concerning France:

What we're seeing in many places is a "demographic revolution." Some experts are projecting that by the year 2040, 80 percent of the population of France will be Muslim. At that point the Muslim majority will control commerce, industry, education, and religion in that country. They will also, of course, control the government, as well, and occupy all the key positions in the French Parliament. And a Muslim will be president.[20]

Islamification is also happening in England, but the Muslims there are not waiting for further population growth to institute *fatah*. They are advancing their goal of dominance by taking advantage of the British policy of pluralistic tolerance. An example occurred in September 2006 when the British home secretary, John Reid, gave a speech to Muslim parents in east London, encouraging them to protect their children from pressure to become suicide bombers. A robed and turbaned fundamentalist Muslim leader who had lavishly praised the suicide bombers of the horrific attack on London's transportation system was in the audience. He got up and shouted the speaker down. He ranted at the home secretary for five minutes, shouting, "How dare you come to a Muslim area? . . . I am furious. I am absolutely furious—John Reid should not come to a Muslim area." Muslims are not only immigrating massively to western countries but also claiming entitlement to keep their settlements off-limits to native citizens. The "ghettoization" of London into "non-Muslim no-go zones" is an ongoing controversy in the British press.[21]

Earlier this year in the city of Oxford—where Hugh Latimer, Nicholas Ridley, and Thomas Cranmer were martyred for their Christian faith and the famous Oxford Movement began—the seven hundred members of a mosque, which is valued at two million British pounds, petitioned "for their right as British citizens to practice their faith." What right did they demand? The right to broadcast a two-minute *adhan*—the Muslim call to prayer—from the mosque minaret three times a day. The amplified call would be heard a mile or more away, meaning the volume would disrupt the lives of countless non-Muslims. One Oxford University professor summed up the controversy in this way: "It's not a matter of people's right to religious freedom, it's about making Islam the religion of public space."[22]

In early 2008, England's archbishop of Canterbury, Rowan Williams, gave the world a stunning example of General Sada's claim of Western naiveté concerning Islamic intentions. Williams told a BBC correspondent that the growing Islamic population in Britain made it expedient to be accommodative. He said "the UK had to face up to the fact" that it "seems unavoidable" that Islam's legal system, *sharia* law, will be "incorporated into British law." His term for this blending of laws was "constructive accommodation."[23] *Sharia* law, derived from the Qu'ran and teachings of Muhammad, is the legal system by which Muslims are to live. In the West, the law is fairly benign and deals mainly with family and business. But in Muslim countries it can include such things as "honor killings" in cases of suspected immorality.

Some foresee the incorporation of *sharia* into English law as a fatal blow to the historic Christianity of England. A recent Church of England General Synod survey reported that "63 percent fear that the Church will be disestablished within a generation, breaking a bond that has existed between the Church and State since the Reformation."[24] The controversy is not merely about allowing religious freedom, but rather about how intrusive a tolerant nation should allow an immigrant religion to be.

You may hear other terms used to describe the Islamic goal of world domination. For example, "biological jihad" or "demographic jihad" describes the nonviolent strategy of Muslims moving into Europe and the West and having more babies than their hosts. Within several generations they hope to repopulate traditionally Christian cultures with their own people, and they are certainly on track to reach that goal. According to a Vatican report issued recently, the Roman Catholic Church understands this: "For the first time in history, we are no longer at the top: Muslims have overtaken us."[25]

## Islam Hopes to Return Its Messiah

This Islamic hope surfaced in a speech by Iranian president Mahmoud Ahmadinejad, a disciple of Ayatollah Khomeini, the cleric who launched the successful 1979 revolution that turned Iran into a strict Islamic state. In 2005, Ahmadinejad was called before the United Nations Security Council to explain his continued determination to develop nuclear weapons. He began his speech by declaring: "In the Name of the God of Mercy, Compassion, Peace, Freedom and Justice . . ." and ended his speech with this prayer: "I pray to you to hasten the emergence of your last repository, the promised one, that perfect and pure human being, the one that will fill this world with justice and peace."[26] The "promised one" in Ahmadinejad's prayer was a reference to the Twelfth Imam, a figure in Shi'ite teaching that parallels the figure of Al-Mahdi in Sunni teaching. In essence, both of these titles refer to the Islamic messiah who is yet to come.

Shi'ia Islam believes that the Twelfth Imam can appear only during a time of worldwide chaos. This explains many of Ahmadinejad's defiant actions—why he presses forward with his nuclear program in spite of world censure and why he is adamant about destroying Israel. In an infamous speech in Tehran on October 25, 2005, he said, "Israel must be wiped off the map," and he warned leaders of Muslim nations who recognized the state of Israel that they would "face the wrath of their own people."[27] With these defiant and divisive actions, Ahmadinejad is fomenting the chaotic environment that he believes will induce the Islamic messiah to come. In a televised speech in January 2008, Ahmadinejad reiterated: "What we have right now is the last chapter . . . Accept that the life of Zionists will sooner or later come to an end."[28] On March 14, 2008, Ahmadinejad "swept the nationwide ballot with about 70 percent support."[29]

The world as a whole seems to be starting to take Ahmadinejad seriously, but the people of Israel are totally convinced. They understand that he is determined to destroy them. And the prophet Ezekiel backs up that understanding. He tells us that the hatred Iran bears (Iran being the current name of the biblical Persia) toward the Jewish nation will play an important role in a major end-time battle. John Walvoord summarizes the scenario:

> The rise of Islamic terror is setting the stage for the events in Ezekiel 38–39. These chapters prophesy an invasion of Israel in the end times by a vast coalition of nations, all of whom are Islamic today except Russia. Israel has said that a new "axis of terror"—Iran, Syria,

and the Hamas-run Palestinian government—is sowing the seeds of the first world war of the twenty-first century. The rise of Islam, and especially radical Islamic terrorism, strikingly foreshadows Ezekiel's great prophecy.[30]

Even though the hope for an Islamic messiah is surely futile, the chaos radical Islamic leaders are creating to bring about that hope is all too real and deadly. So deadly that much of the biblical prophecies concerning the end times will be brought about by the beliefs and actions of radical Islam. And we are beginning to feel the pressure of those impending events in the rise and rapid spread of Islamic radicalism in our own time.

## Responding to the Islamic Threat

How are we responding to the rise of Islamic radicalism? Not too well, I fear. On the whole, those who shape our culture and policies seem to bear out General Sada's observation that we "fail to understand the true nature of this enemy." In our rush to be democratic, tolerant, and inclusive, we are inadvertently accommodating the radical agenda of Islamic conquest. We must stop being deceived about this threat. We must stand our ground and affirm truths that many seem all too willing to give up in the name of tolerance and accommodation. If you are looking for a beginning place, here are two truths on which I see much confusion today. It is critical that we affirm these truths to maintain a clear understanding of the vast chasm between Christianity and Islam.

### "Allah" Is Not Another Name for the God of the Bible

In mid-August 2007, Fox News instigated a blogger's field day when it reported that seventy-one-year-old Dutch Catholic Bishop

Muskens of Breda "wants everyone to call God 'Allah.'" Fox quoted from Muskens's interview on a Dutch TV program in which he said, "Allah is a very beautiful word for God. Shouldn't we all say that from now on, we will call God 'Allah'?" The bishop further added, "What does God care what we call him?" Fox's Roman Catholic news analyst disagreed with the bishop, stating, "Words and names mean things. Referring to God as Allah means something."[31]

Indeed they do! As journalist Stan Goodenough reminded his *Jerusalem Newswire* readers, in the name of Allah, people hijack planes and use them to wreak unspeakable devastation, blow themselves up in crowded public venues to annihilate innocent people, and in the name of Allah, "millions of people pray for the destruction of Israel and the United States." Goodenough observed that when God introduced Himself to Moses, He gave His name as YHWH—Jehovah. He went on to say, "He also has many other names describing aspects of His nature and character. 'Allah' is not one of them."[32]

Bishop Muskens surely knows the biblical names for God, so what was he thinking when he urged Christians to call God Allah? As he explained, "If Muslims and Christians address God with the same name, this contributes to harmonious living between both religions."[33] When Islamic leaders heard this, their mosques must have rung with the slaps of high fives. Their policy of *fatah* was working beautifully. And they must have ascended into unspeakable ecstasies when the spokesman for the Council on American-Islamic Relations immediately embraced Muskens's proposal, saying, "It reinforces the fact that Muslims, Christians and Jews all worship the same God."[34]

We hear this appalling claim often these days, but nothing could be farther from the truth. Allah and God are emphatically not the same! To claim otherwise is nothing short of a slander against the one true God. As Hal Lindsey explains:

The doctrine of Satan is that all religions are equally valid, that all paths lead to God, that God is impersonal, unknowable, and it is therefore irrelevant to Him what we call Him or how we worship Him. If Allah and God are one and the same, then wouldn't the worship of the Hindu chief gods, Vishnu and Shiva, also be the worship of Allah and God, only by a different name? Pretty soon, everybody is God . . . Which is the same as saying that nobody is.[35]

The God of the Bible and the Allah of the Qu'ran are nothing alike. The differences are vast and allow no possibility of synthesis. The God of the Bible is knowable. According to the Qu'ran, Allah is so exalted that he cannot be known. The God of the Bible is a personal being with intellect, emotion, and will. Muslim theology tells us Allah is not to be understood as a person. The God of the Bible is a spirit. To Muslims, such a thought is blasphemous and demeaning to Allah. The God of the Bible is one God in three persons. The Qu'ran denies the Trinity and views it as a major heresy. The God of the Bible is a God of love. Allah does not have emotional feelings toward man. The God of the Bible is a God of grace. According to the Qu'ran, there is no savior or intercessor. Clearly the God of the Bible and Allah are not at all the same and should never be equated with one another![36]

## The Qu'ran Is Not a Divine Book on Par with the Bible

Just as many say the God of the Bible and Allah are the same, many also say that we should consider the Qu'ran to be on the same level as the Bible. Actually, the Muslims believe the Qu'ran to be the mother of all books and the Bible as subservient to it. A comparison of the two books will show the absurdity of such a claim. The Bible is a masterpiece of cohesion, depth, literate quality, and consistency. God inspired more than 40 men over a period of 1,400 years to write the God-breathed words that carry His unified message from Genesis to Revelation (2 Timothy 3:16).

The Qu'ran, on the other hand, is a self-contradicting book supposedly given by the angel Gabriel to Mohammad. Since Mohammad could neither read nor write, the sayings were translated and collected from the memories of those who had heard him.

Objective readers who have read both the Bible and the Qu'ran are immediately able to tell the difference between the quality and comprehensibility of the two books. Historian Edward Gibbon (1737–1794) is an example of such a reader. He could hardly be accused of being a Christian, yet he described the Qu'ran as "an incoherent rhapsody of fable, and precept, and declamation, which sometimes crawls in the dust, and sometimes is lost in the clouds."[37]

## Muslims Are Not Beyond the Reach of God's Grace

Recently I saw a bumper sticker that made me stop and consider. It read, "Have You Prayed for Osama Bin Laden Today." I must admit I had not. Yet Peter reminds us that "the Lord is . . . not willing that any should perish but that all should come to repentance" (2 Peter 3:9). I am absolutely certain that the "any" of this verse includes Muslims. We may find it hard to pray for avowed enemies who threaten our destruction, but one of the characteristics of Christlikeness given by Jesus Himself is to "love your enemies, bless those who curse you, do good to those who hate you, and pray for those who spitefully use you and persecute you" (Matthew 5:44). I believe that includes Osama bin Laden and his radical Islamic counterparts.

We have good evidence that such prayers are effective. Through the miracle of satellite delivery, our weekly television program, *Turning*

*Point,* is now available in almost every Arab country. We routinely get e-mail and letters from individuals who have come to Christ through the ministry of God's Word beamed into their lives via satellite TV. Recently we received a letter from an Arab country. The writer told us that he had accepted Christ into his heart and expressed great gratitude for the encouragement of God's truth. A note at the bottom of the letter pleaded with us not to send any materials to his address. That postscript made us vividly aware of the courage it takes for a Muslim in an Islamic country to confess Christ as Savior.

God is at work in the Islamic world. We have reports that many Muslims are being confronted with the gospel in their dreams. Here is the testimony of one Saudi Arabian who was born close to Mecca and grew up going to the mosque five times a day. For many nights he had a terrifying nightmare in which he was being taken down into hell. This dream, always vivid and horrifying, destroyed the man's peace night after night. Suddenly one evening, Jesus appeared in his dream and said, "Son, I am the way, the truth, and the life. And if you would give your life to Me, I would save you from the hell that you have seen."

This young man knew something of Jesus from the distorted teachings of the Qu'ran, but he didn't know the Jesus of the New Testament. So he began searching for a Christian who could help him. Since Christianity is banned in Saudi Arabia, and a Christian caught witnessing to a Muslim could be beheaded, the young man's search took time. But the Lord eventually led him to an Egyptian Christian who gave him a Bible. He began reading, and when he got into the New Testament, he was moved to give his life totally to Jesus Christ.

Soon afterward, an opponent of the young man discovered his conversion and accused him of being a Christian. The authorities arrested and imprisoned him. In jail, he was tortured and eventually sentenced to death by beheading. But on the morning of his scheduled execution, no one showed up to escort him from the cell. Two days later the authorities threw open his cell door and screamed at him: "You demon! Get out of this place!"[38]

The man learned later that his execution had not taken place because on the very day he was to be beheaded, the son of his accuser had mysteriously died. The new Christian is now quietly working to bring other Muslims to faith in Christ.

In this chapter we have explored one of the unsettling events that is going on in today's world—the rising threat of radical Islam. In the true story I related above, we have the key to the Christian response to this threat. As Abraham Lincoln said, "The best way to destroy an enemy is to make him a friend." The best way to counter the threat of Islam is to make Christians out of Muslims. I don't claim that this will turn away prophecies of events sure to come, but it does give you a role in the drama to be played. Our prayers, our testimonies, our love and care for our Islamic neighbors may not turn the inevitable tide for the world, but they can turn the tide for individuals and allow them to escape the wrath to come. And that is definitely worth doing.

# FIVE

# Vanished Without a Trace

ONE OF THE MORE POPULAR CBS TV SHOWS IS THE FICTIONAL drama *Without a Trace*. It is set in New York City's special FBI missing persons unit. Each episode is devoted to finding one missing person, and, usually, one of the agents assigned to the case develops a strong emotional interest that carries the story along. In reality, the FBI has no dedicated missing persons unit; investigations into disappearances are assigned to agents on a case-by-case basis. At the end of each episode, however, the show does touch on reality by providing public service information to help the FBI locate real-life missing persons.

Another TV show built on the theme of missing persons was the Fox Broadcasting drama *Vanished*. The plotline centered on a Georgia senator whose wife apparently vanished into thin air. That series failed to attract enough viewers to survive the season, provoking anger among those who had become hooked when the thirteen aired episodes never resolved the mystery.

And mystery is exactly what the word *vanished* implies. Headlines about people who vanish rivet our attention: "Relatives Wait for Word of Vanished Sailors"; "Man Vanishes After Concert"; "Search Continues for Woman Who Vanished"; "Police Say Man Vanished Without a Trace." We read such headlines with eerie wonder: *What could have happened to the missing person? How could he have simply been there one moment and not the next?*

According to the Bible, a time is coming when this very thing will happen on a massive, global scale. A day is coming when a billion people will suddenly vanish from the face of the earth without a trace! And when that event occurs, calling in the FBI will be of no use. A TV series based on the mystery would never have a conclusion, for these vanished people will never again be seen until the Lord Himself returns. What will this worldwide phenomenon be like? That is a question in the minds of many who—through popular novels, sermons, or religious writings— have heard of this event but don't understand it. They know that Christians call it the Rapture, yet they have little idea what it means or what in the world is going on that could bring it about. In this chapter I will seek to resolve this common confusion.

## The Great Disappearance

Some of us are familiar with massive evacuations, which leave large areas empty and desolate, as if their inhabitants had simply vanished. As I mentioned in a previous chapter, I pastor a church located in the fire zone of Southern California. In October 2007, we witnessed the largest evacuation of homes in California history, and the largest evacuation for fire in United States history. Emergency personnel evacuated 350,000 homes, displacing 1 million Californians as sixteen simultaneous fires swept through our community.[1]

Imagine a person who missed the call to evacuate, waking up after everyone was gone and stumbling through the acrid smoke and empty streets, confused and amazed, wondering why he had been left behind. That person's reaction would be nothing compared to the shock of those who witness the coming worldwide evacuation.

The Bible tells us that on that day, millions of people will disappear from the face of the earth in less than a millisecond. And the purpose of that evacuation is similar to that of the emergency evacuation of Southern Californians: to avoid horrific devastation. This evacuation will remove God's people from the disastrous effects of coming earthquakes, fire, and global chaos. As Bruce Bickel and Stan Jantz explain, the evacuation itself will create considerable chaos and destruction:

> Jumbo jets plummet to earth as they no longer have a pilot at the controls. Driverless buses, trains, subways, and cars will cause unimaginable disaster. Classrooms will suddenly be without teachers . . . Doctors and nurses seem to abandon their patients in the middle of surgical operations, and patients will vanish from operating tables. Children disappear from their beds. People run through the streets looking for missing family members who were there just moments ago. Panic grips every household, city and country.[2]

Attempting to put realism into this event for my first youth group as a fledgling pastor, I utilized the idea of an imaginary newspaper covering the recent Rapture. The lead article read:

> At 12:05 last night a telephone operator reported three frantic calls regarding missing relatives. Within fifteen minutes all communications were jammed with similar inquiries. A spot check around the

nation found the same situation in every city. Sobbing husbands sought information about the mysterious disappearance of wives. One husband reported, "I turned on the light to ask my wife if she remembered to set the clock, but she was gone. Her bedclothes were there, her watch was on the floor . . . she had vanished!" An alarmed woman calling from Brooklyn tearfully reported, "My husband just returned from the late shift . . . I kissed him . . . he just disappeared in my arms."

These two descriptions of the coming disappearance are quite disturbing. Considering the devastation, loss, grief, and confusion the event will cause, it may seem strange that it is called the Rapture. According to my online dictionary, the word *rapture* means "an expression or manifestation of ecstasy or passion," and "being carried away by overwhelming emotion."[3] Everyone wants that kind of euphoric delight, which is why marketing experts have made *rapture* a popular term in today's culture.

There's a perfume called Rapture, and also a well-known New York City-based rock band. Many novels and movies carry the word *rapture* in their titles. A concert-promoting agency calls itself Planet Rapture. One sporting goods company even sells a set of golf clubs called Rapture! The world is looking for rapture, so marketers offer it everywhere.

So why would Christians use *Rapture*, of all terms, to denote a chaotic event when a billion people will suddenly disappear from the earth? The word *Rapture* is the Latin version of a phrase the Bible uses to describe the catching away of all Christians before the end times.

The focus is on looking at the event not from the viewpoint of those who remain, but from that of those who are evacuated. All true Christians will be caught up from the earth and raptured into the presence of the Lord before the seven-year period of evil, the Tribulation, breaks throughout the earth. This will fulfill the promise He made to His disciples in John 14:1–3:

> Let not your heart be troubled; you believe in God, believe also in Me. In My Father's house are many mansions; if it were not so, I would have told you. I go to prepare a place for you. And if I go and prepare a place for you, I will come again and receive you to Myself; that where I am, there you may be also.

Followers of Christ who are raptured will be spared the trauma of death and the coming disasters that will occur when the Tribulation breaks out upon the earth. That is indeed a cause for true rapture on the part of those who love the Lord and long to be with Him.

One morning recently I spoke about the Rapture during a series of messages on prophecy. Later I was told that on the way out of church, a girl expressed confusion to her mother about something I had said. "Dr. Jeremiah keeps talking about all the signs that are developing concerning the Lord's return. And then in the next breath he says that nothing needs to happen before Jesus comes back to take us home to be with Him. I don't understand!" It seemed to this girl that I had contradicted myself. First, I seemed to say that certain prophesied signs would occur before the coming of Christ; then I seemed to say that nothing needed to occur before Jesus comes to claim His own. The girl's honest confusion deserves to be addressed because I believe she speaks for many who are similarly puzzled about events relating to the Rapture.

Most of the misunderstanding comes from confusing two events: the Rapture and the Second Coming. When we talk about the signs that signal the return of Christ, we speak not of the Rapture but of the Lord's ultimate return to the earth with all His saints. According to the book of Revelation, this coming of Christ occurs after the Rapture and differs from it in at least two ways: First, the Rapture will be a "stealth event" in which Christ will be witnessed by believers only. His second coming, on the other hand, will be a public event. Everyone will see Him. "Behold, He is coming with clouds, and every eye will see Him, even they who pierced Him. And all the tribes of the earth will mourn because of Him" (Revelation 1:7; see also Zechariah 14:1, 3–5; Revelation 19:11–21).

Second, all believers are raptured. He will immediately take them back into heaven with Him. But when Christ returns to earth seven years later in the Second Coming, He is coming to stay. This return, usually referred to as "the Second Advent," will take place at the end of the Tribulation period and usher in the Millennium—a thousand-year reign of Christ on this earth. So, first, the Rapture will occur seven years before the Second Advent. At that time Christ will take us to be with Him in heaven, immediately before the seven-year tribulation period. Then second, we will return to earth with Him at His Second Advent.

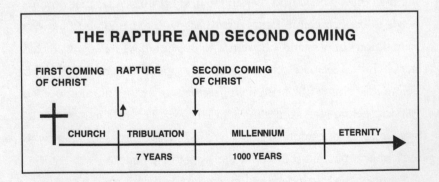

There is another important difference. There are no events that must take place before the Rapture occurs. It's all a matter of God's perfect timing. When I preached that signs are developing concerning the Lord's return, I referred to events that must yet occur before the return of Christ in the Second Advent.

The prophecies I spoke of concern the Second Advent, but that does not mean that the Rapture doesn't figure into prophecy. Future events cast shadows that are precursors to their coming. Since the Rapture takes place seven years before the Second Advent, the signs that point to the Second Advent cast shadows that clue us in to the imminent Rapture. The fact that the Rapture precedes the Second Advent makes the signs portending the Advent all the more immediate and ominous. For those who are left behind, the Rapture will give irrefutable confirmation of end-time events, seven years before they come to pass.

The New Testament indicates that the Rapture of those who have put their trust in Christ is the next major event on the prophetic calendar. In other words, the Rapture awaits us on the horizon—it could happen at any moment. This is the clear message of the Bible, and it is a truth I have taught consistently for more than thirty years.

## Unraveling the Rapture

The apostle Paul was the first to reveal the details of the Rapture. He wrote of it in his first letter to the Corinthians, but it was in his first letter to the church in Thessalonica that he presented his most concise teaching on the subject.

Like many today, the Christians in that city were confused about the events that would take place in the future. They, too, wondered what in the world was going on. While they believed that Jesus was coming back someday, they could not figure out what would happen to their Christian parents and loved ones who had already died. So Paul wrote to instruct them concerning God's plan for both the living and the dead in the Rapture. In this writing, he explained in detail exactly what the Rapture is all about.

> But I do not want you to be ignorant, brethren, concerning those who have fallen asleep, lest you sorrow as others who have no hope. For if we believe that Jesus died and rose again, even so God will bring with Him those who sleep in Jesus.
>
> For this we say to you by the word of the Lord, that we who are alive and remain until the coming of the Lord will by no means precede those who are asleep. For the Lord Himself will descend from heaven with a shout, with the voice of an archangel, and with the trumpet of God. And the dead in Christ will rise first. Then we who are alive and remain shall be caught up together with them in the clouds to meet the Lord in the air. And thus we shall always be with the Lord. Therefore comfort one another with these words. (1 Thessalonians 4:13–18)

This passage tells us all we need to know about the Rapture. Let's look more deeply into what Paul said, point by point. First, he wrote: "But I do not want you to be ignorant, brethren, concerning those who have fallen asleep, lest you sorrow as others who have no hope" (1 Thessalonians 4:13). In this statement, the apostle addressed the ignorance of the Thessalonians concerning the state of those who had died believing in Christ. The word he used to describe that state has great significance for every believer today. Paul said that they had fallen asleep. For the word translated *asleep*, he used the Greek word *koimao*, which has as one of its meanings, "to sleep in death." The same word is used to describe the deaths of Lazarus, Stephen, David, and Jesus Christ (*emphasis added in the following examples*):

Lazarus: "These things He said, and after that He said to them, 'Our friend Lazarus *sleeps*, but I go that I may wake him up.'" (John 11:11)

Stephen: "Then he [Stephen] knelt down and cried out with a loud voice, 'Lord, do not charge them with this sin.' And when he had said this, he *fell asleep*." (Acts 7:60)

David: "For David, after he had served his own generation by the will of God, *fell asleep*, was buried with his fathers, and saw corruption." (Acts 13:36)

Jesus Christ: "But now Christ is risen from the dead, and has become the firstfruits of those who have *fallen asleep*." (1 Corinthians 15:20)

This concept of death is emphasized in the wonderful word early Christians adopted for the burying places of their loved ones. It was the Greek word *koimeterion,* which means "a rest house for strangers, a sleeping place." It is the word from which we get our English word *cemetery.* In Paul's day, this word was used for inns or what we would call a hotel or motel. We check in at a Hilton Hotel or a Ramada Inn, expecting to spend the night in sleep before we wake up in the morning refreshed and raring to go. That is exactly the thought Paul expressed in words such as *koimao* and *koimeterion.* When Christians die, it's as if they are slumbering peacefully in a place of rest, ready to be awakened at the return of the Lord. The words have great import, for they convey the Christian concept of death, not as a tragic finality, but as a temporary sleep.

In the next part of the Thessalonian passage, we find Paul affirming their hopes that their loved ones will live again. He did this by tying that hope to the Resurrection and the Rapture: "lest you sorrow as others who have no hope. For if we believe that Jesus died and rose again, even so God will bring with Him those who sleep in Jesus" (1 Thessalonians 4:13c–14). Here Paul tells the Thessalonians (and us) that God's plan for our future gives us such a new perspective on death that when someone we love dies, we are not overcome with sorrow and despair, for on that day when those who are alive in Christ are raptured, those who died in Christ will be raised to be with Him.

Paul reasoned that Christians can believe this promise of resurrection because it is backed up by the resurrection of Christ Himself. The logic is simple: if we believe that Jesus died and rose again, is it hard to believe His promise that He can perform the same miracle for us and those we love?

Paul did not forbid us to grieve; it is natural to feel sorrow when a loved one passes away, even when that loved one is a Christian. We miss the person terribly, and as Tennyson put it, we long for "the touch of a vanished hand and the sound of a voice that is still."[4] Jesus Himself wept by the tomb of Lazarus. But because of our Lord's promise of resurrection, we are not to grieve the way non-Christians do—as people to whom death is the ultimate tragedy—for they have no grounds for hope.

Tim LaHaye is the coauthor of the famous Left Behind series, which at last count had sold more than sixty-five million books. He became fascinated with the doctrine of the Rapture as a nine-year-old boy at his father's grave. He wrote:

My love for second-coming teachings, particularly the Rapture of the church, was sparked as I stood at my father's grave at the age of nine. His sudden death of a heart attack left me devastated. My pastor, who also was my uncle, pointed his finger toward heaven and proclaimed, "This is not the last of Frank LaHaye. Because of his personal faith in Christ, one day he will be resurrected by the shout of the Lord; we will be translated to meet him and our other loved ones in the clouds and be with them and our Lord forever." That promise from Scripture was the only hope for my broken heart that day. And that same promise has comforted millions of others through the years.[5]

As Dr. LaHaye said, the promise of the Rapture has comforted millions, and it is right that it should, for it is a promise we can depend on to be utterly sound.

## The Chronological Program of the Rapture

As Paul continued in his letter to the Thessalonians, he wrote: "For this we say to you by the word of the Lord" (1 Thessalonians 4:15a).

Here Paul affirms that what he is about to say is by divine authority. He is authorized to say it "by the word of the Lord." This bold assertion suggests that what followed was not to be taken lightly because it was a revelation given directly to the apostle by God himself. In 1 Corinthians, Paul referred to the Rapture as a "mystery" (15:51). And the biblical definition of a mystery is "a truth that has not been revealed before."

Having established his authority to reveal what had formerly been a mystery, Paul went on to explain the first of the sequence of events that make up the Rapture.

### There Will Be an Order of Priority

Paul then told the Thessalonians, "we who are alive and remain until the coming of the Lord will by no means precede those who are asleep" (1 Thessalonians 4:15*b*). Here Paul was saying that not only will those who have died in Christ be present at the return of the Lord, but they will actually have a place of priority. He said that those who are alive at the Rapture will not be taken up to Christ ahead of "those who are asleep," which means all believers who have died prior to the Rapture.

There is a linguistic root we need to examine here. The Greek word *phthano* in this verse means "come before, precede." When the Greek was translated into the English of the King James era, the word "prevent" was used because it then carried the meaning "to go or arrive before." Over many years, *prevent* has come to mean "to keep from happening." The emphatic point of this verse is that we will "by no means precede those who are asleep" in Christ. Those who have died believing in Christ will take precedence over us in the Rapture.

## There Will Be a Return

Paul continued by saying, "For the Lord Himself will descend from heaven with a shout, with the voice of an archangel, and with the trumpet of God" (1 Thessalonians 4:16*a*).

As you read these words, the Lord Jesus Christ is seated in the heavens at the right hand of the Almighty Father. But when the right moment comes, He will initiate the Rapture by literally and physically rising from the throne, stepping into the corridors of light, and actually descending into the atmosphere of planet Earth from which He rose into the heavens over the Mount of Olives two thousand years ago. It is not the angels or the Holy Spirit but the Lord Himself who is coming to draw believers into the heavens in the Rapture.

The details of this passage paint an amazingly complete sensory picture of the Rapture. Paul even gave the sounds that will be heard—a shout, the voice of an archangel, and the trumpet of God. The purpose and relationship of these three sounds have generated considerable discussion. Some have claimed that the shout is for the church, the archangel's voice is for the Jews, and the trumpet is for all gentile believers. But these claims are mistaken. The three allusions to sounds are not to be taken as coordinate but rather as subordinate. Paul was not describing three separate sounds; he was describing only one sound in three different ways.

This sound will be like a shout, ringing with command authority like the voice of an archangel. It will also be like the blare of a trumpet in its volume and clarity. And the sound will be exclusively directed— heard only by those who have placed their trust in Christ. When Jesus raised Lazarus from the dead, he shouted "Lazarus, come forth!" (John 11:43). I've heard Bible students speculate as to what might have happened had Jesus forgotten to mention Lazarus's name. Would all the dead within the range of His voice have emerged from their graves? At the Rapture that is exactly what will happen. His shout of "Come forth!" will not name a single individual, but it will be heard by every believer in every grave around the world. All those tombs will empty, and the resurrected believers will fly skyward.

This arising from the grave was the hope that Winston Churchill movingly expressed in the planning of his own funeral. Following the prayer by the archbishop of Canterbury and the singing of "God Save the Queen," a trumpeter perched in the highest reaches of the dome of St. Paul's Cathedral sounded "The Last Post" (or "Taps" as we know it). As the last sorrowful note faded, "high in another gallery, sounded the stronger blaring 'Reveille.'"[6] The call to sleep was followed by a call to arise.

## There Will Be a Resurrection

As Paul continued his writing to the Thessalonians, he asserted that the expectation expressed by believers such as Churchill is not vain. The coming resurrection is a reality. Paul wrote, "And the dead in Christ will rise first" (1 Thessalonians 4:16b). As he indicates here, the call to resurrection at the Rapture will not summon all the dead, but believers only. A time will come much later when *all* the dead will be raised to stand before the white throne in judgment. But at this first call, our believing loved ones who have already died will arise to take first place in the program of the Rapture.

## There Will Be a Rapture

Paul explained the next event in the Rapture sequence: "Then we who are alive and remain shall be caught up" (1 Thessalonians 4:17a). The words *caught up* are translated from a Greek word that has as one of its meanings "to snatch out or away speedily." This word emphasizes the sudden nature of the Rapture. Paul described this suddenness in his letter to the Corinthians: ". . . in a moment, in the twinkling of an eye, at the last trumpet. For the trumpet will sound, and the dead will be raised incorruptible, and we shall be changed" (1 Corinthians 15:52).

In a split second the Lord will call all believers to Himself to share in His glory; not one will remain behind. It is hard to imagine just what that will be like, but I read a paragraph recently that created this vivid picture:

Millions of people from all parts of the earth feel a tingling sensation pulsating throughout their bodies. They are all suddenly energized. Those with physical deformities are healed. The blind suddenly see.

Wrinkles disappear on the elderly as their youth is restored. As these people marvel at their physical transformation, they are lifted skyward. Those in buildings pass right through the ceiling and roof without pain or damage. Their flesh and bones seem to dematerialize, defying all known laws of physics and biology. As they travel heavenward, some of them see and greet those who have risen from their graves. After a brief mystical union . . . they all vanish from sight.[7]

Lest such pictures as this lead us to think the Rapture is a fanciful, futuristic dream, we find such experiences validated historically. Throughout the Bible, we have records of several people who had actual experiences very similar to the Rapture:

Enoch: "By faith Enoch was taken away so that he did not see death, 'and was not found, because God had taken him'; for before he was taken he had this testimony, that he pleased God." (Hebrews 11:5)

Elijah: "Then it happened, as they continued on and talked, that suddenly a chariot of fire appeared with horses of fire, and separated the two of them; and Elijah went up by a whirlwind into heaven." (2 Kings 2:11)

Paul: "I know a man in Christ who fourteen years ago—whether in the body I do not know, or whether out of the body I do not know, God knows—such a one, was *caught up* to the third heaven. And I know such a man—whether in the body or out of the body I do not know, God knows—how he was *caught up* into Paradise and heard inexpressible words, which it is not lawful for a man to utter." (2 Corinthians 12:2–4, *emphasis added*)

I find it significant that twice in this passage Paul used the words *caught up*, which are translated from the word meaning "rapture" in the Greek language.

> Jesus Christ: "And while they looked steadfastly toward heaven as He went up, behold, two men stood by them in white apparel, who also said, 'Men of Galilee, why do you stand gazing up into heaven? This same Jesus, who was taken up from you into heaven, will so come in like manner as you saw Him go into heaven.'" (Acts 1:10–11)

These records affirm the utter reality of the Rapture by providing us with prototypes of sorts to show that God can accomplish this coming event He promises to His people.

## There Will Be a Reunion

Paul continued his explanation of the Rapture: "Then we who are alive and remain shall be caught up together with them [the believing dead who have arisen] in the clouds to meet the Lord in the air. And thus we shall always be with the Lord" (1 Thessalonians 4:17). Note that Paul began here with the word *then*, which is an adverb indicating sequence. It connects the previous events of the Rapture that we have already considered with this final event in a definite order of sequential reunions as follows:

1. Dead bodies reunited with their spirits
2. Resurrected believers reunited with living believers
3. Resurrected believers and raptured believers meet the Lord

As Paul pointed out, the ultimate consequence of this reunion with the Lord is that there will be no subsequent parting. After His return, our union and communion with Him will be uninterrupted and eternal. This glorious fact alone shows us why the word *rapture* is an altogether appropriate term for this event.

## The Comforting Purpose of the Rapture

After completing his description of the Rapture to the Thessalonians, Paul wrapped up the passage with this practical admonition: "Therefore comfort one another with these words" (1 Thessalonians 4:18).

Here the apostle was telling both the Thessalonians and believers today that it's not enough simply to passively understand what was just explained about the Rapture, Christian death, and the Resurrection. Our understanding should spur us toward a certain action—to "comfort one another." And in the preceding verses he gave exactly the kind of information that makes true comfort possible. When believers suffer the loss of family members or dearly loved friends, we have in Paul's descriptions of Christian death and resurrection all that is needed to comfort each other in these losses. Christian death is not permanent; it is merely a sleep. A time is coming when we and our loved ones will be reunited in a rapturous meeting, when Christ Himself calls us out of this world or out of our graves to be with Him forever in an ecstatic relationship of eternal love. Nineteenth-century Bible teacher A. T. Pierson made this interesting observation about these things:

It is a remarkable fact that in the New Testament, so far as I remember, it is never once said, after Christ's resurrection, that a disciple died—that is, without some qualification: Stephen *fell asleep*. David, after he had served his own generation by the will of God *fell asleep and was laid with his father*. Peter says, "Knowing that I must shortly *put off this my tabernacle* as the Lord showed me." Paul says, "*the time of my departure is at hand."* (The figure here is taken from a vessel that, as she leaves a dock, throws the cables off the fastenings, and opens her sails to the wind to depart for the haven) . . . The only time where the word "dead" is used, it is with qualification: "the *dead in Christ,"* "the *dead which die in the Lord."*[8]

As Pierson implies, Christ abolished death so completely that even the term *death* is no longer appropriate for believers. That is why Paul wrote that we should comfort one another with reminders that for Christians, what we call death is nothing more than a temporary sleep before we are called into our uninterrupted relationship with Christ forever.

Today as never before, we are beginning to see the signs of our Lord's impending return. Some of these signs we have already covered—the rebirth of Israel as a nation, the growing crises over oil, the reformation of Europe in accordance with Daniel's prophecy, and the growth of militant, radical Islam. All these developments point toward that day when our Lord will come to rapture His followers out of this world.

I believe it is the Rapture that will trigger the cataclysmic upheavals that will ravage the earth for the seven years that follow it. The Tribulation will come about by the law of natural consequences. According to Jesus, Christians are the salt and light of the world (Matthew 5:13–14). Salt prevents decay; light proclaims truth. When all the Christians in the entire world are removed from the earth in one day, all the salt and all the light will suddenly be gone. The result is predictable. You may think the world today is degenerating into rampant greed and immorality, and indeed it is. But as bad as things are becoming, we can hardly overstate the horror that will occur when society loses the tempering influence of Christians.

As the Bible teaches, every believer in Christ is indwelt by the Holy Spirit. This means the Holy Spirit ministers to today's world through followers of Christ. When all Christians are removed from the earth, the restraining ministry of the Holy Spirit will be completely absent. No salt! No light! No indwelling Spirit of God! The result will be horrific. Jesus himself described what will happen next: "For then there will be great tribulation, such as has not been since the beginning of the world until this time, no, nor ever shall be. And unless those days were shortened, no flesh would be saved" (Matthew 24:21–22).

As these dire words are being fulfilled during the Tribulation period, we who are followers of Christ will have already been raptured to heaven. This is another source of great comfort for Christians. No promise has been more precious to believers than the one made to the church of Philadelphia in Revelation: "Because you have kept My command to persevere, I also will keep you from the hour of trial which shall come upon the whole world, to test those who dwell on the earth" (Revelation 3:10).

Please note that our Lord's promise is not merely to keep us *in* the hour of trial, but rather *from* the hour of trial. As Paul wrote, "God did not appoint us to wrath, but to obtain salvation through our Lord Jesus Christ" (1 Thessalonians 5:9). The promise is that we who are believers will not experience the horrors of the Tribulation, and this is an enormous source of comfort.

## How Shall We then Live?

We have been given two directives as to how we should live as we anticipate Christ's return. We should be looking for Him and living for Him.

## We Should Be Looking for the Lord

Paul warned us in three of his letters to be alert and watchful for the Lord's return:

> Looking for the blessed hope and glorious appearing of our great God and Savior Jesus Christ. (Titus 2:13)

> For our citizenship is in heaven, from which we also eagerly wait for the Savior, the Lord Jesus Christ. (Philippians 3:20)

> And to wait for His Son from heaven, whom He raised from the dead, even Jesus who delivers us from the wrath to come. (1 Thessalonians 1:10)

Wayne Grudem suggests that the degree to which we are actually longing for Christ's return is a measure of our spiritual condition. As he explains:

> The more Christians are caught up in enjoying the good things of this life, and the more they neglect genuine Christian fellowship and their personal relationship with Christ, the less they will long for His return. On the other hand, many Christians who are experiencing suffering or persecution, or who are more elderly and infirm, and those whose daily walk with Christ is vital and deep, will have a more intense longing for His return.[9]

As Dr. Grudem suggests, the idea is not merely to watch for Jesus' coming as we might watch for a storm in a black cloud, but rather to anticipate it as something we look forward to and long for.

## We Should Be Living for the Lord

The three great apostles, Paul, Peter, and John, all had something to say about how we should live in the face of Christ's impending return:

> For the grace of God that brings salvation has appeared to all men, teaching us that, denying ungodliness and worldly lusts, we should live soberly, righteously, and godly in the present age, looking for the blessed hope and glorious appearing of our great God and Savior Jesus Christ, who gave Himself for us, that He might redeem us from every lawless deed and purify for Himself His own special people, zealous for good works. (Titus 2:11–14)

> Therefore, since all these things will be dissolved, what manner of persons ought you to be in holy conduct and godliness. (2 Peter 3:11)

> Beloved, now are we children of God; and it has not yet been revealed what we shall be, but we know that when He is revealed, we shall be like Him, for we shall see Him as He is. And everyone who has this hope in Him purifies himself, just as He is pure. (1 John 3:2–3)

You would think it obvious that since signs tell us that Christ is coming soon, people would take extra care to live as God would have them live—lives of purity and holiness. If you know that guests are coming soon to your home but you don't know exactly when they will arrive, you will keep your house swept, picked up, and dusted in anticipation. You don't want them ringing your doorbell with your dishes piled in the sink, beds unmade, and mud prints tracking the carpet. The admonitions of Paul, Peter, and John to stay ready by living pure and holy lives are hardly more than just plain common sense. But common sense does not always prevail in the lives of fallen humans, and that is why these apostles felt it worthwhile to admonish us to live as if Jesus could come at any moment. The fact is He can.

Two years after the wildfires of 2003, San Diego regional authorities installed Reverse 9-1-1. The early warning system was first used to warn residents of the approaching wildfires of 2007. Some home owners, however, did not receive a call or had phone systems that screened out the warning call as an unrecognized number. Others received the call but chose to ignore it. Some of those who did not hear the warning did not vacate their homes and, as a result, lost their lives.[10]

God has sounded the warnings loudly and clearly. They have come through His prophets in the Old Testament, through New Testament writers, and even through Jesus Himself. The firestorm is coming in the form of the seven years of tribulation, when no Christian influence will temper the evil that will plunge the earth into a cauldron of misery and devastation. But you can avoid the destruction and be evacuated. You can enter your name on the list of those who will hear the trumpet call of the Rapture by turning to Christ and beginning to live the pure and holy life that characterizes those who will enter heaven. As the apostle John wrote: "But there shall by no means enter it [the heavenly city of God] anything that defiles, or causes an abomination or a lie, but only those who are written in the Lamb's Book of Life" (Revelation 21:27).

If your name is not in that book, when the Rapture occurs you will be left behind to experience horrors worse than anything the world has yet seen. I hope you will not wait another day; turn to Jesus Christ now, before it is too late, and become one of those who will hear His call on that great and terrible day.

# SIX

# Does America Have a Role in Prophecy?

EVERY DAY WHEN THE SUN RISES OVER WASHINGTON DC, ITS first rays fall on the eastern side of the city's tallest structure, the 555-foot Washington Monument. The first part of that monument to reflect the rising sun is the eastern side of its aluminum capstone, where these words are inscribed: *Laus Deo*, Latin for "Praise be to God." This compact prayer of praise, visible to the eyes of heaven alone, is tacit recognition of our nation's unique acknowledgment of the place of God in its founding and its continuance.[1]

Were these words merely a grandiose but empty claim to national piety, or do they reflect a true reality? In the introduction to the book *The Light and the Glory,* authors Peter Marshall and David Manuel ask a very profound question:

What if Columbus' discovering of America had not been accidental at all? What if it were merely the opening curtain of an extraordinary drama? Did God have a special plan for America? . . . What if He dealt with whole nations like He dealt with individuals? What if in particular He had a plan for those He would bring to America, a plan which saw this continent as a stage for a new era in the drama of mankind's redemption?[2]

President Ronald Reagan believed that God did have a plan for our nation. He wrote, "I have always believed that this anointed land was set apart in an uncommon way, that a divine plan placed this great continent here between the oceans to be found by people from every corner of the earth who had a special love of faith and freedom."[3]

## The Sovereignty of God in the Founding of America

I am convinced that references such as the preceding three are not in vain. It seems clear that God *does* have a plan for America. It is true that we have no direct reference to that plan in the Old or New Testament, but that does not discount the evident fact that God has a sovereign purpose for America in His redemptive plan.

As authors Marshall and Manuel suggest, God's hand on America began with its discoverer. In the rotunda of the Capitol Building is a great painting entitled *The Landing of Columbus,* depicting his arrival on the shores of America. As Marshall asserts, the great explorer discovered the New World "by accident," but yet *not* by accident. God had His hand upon the wheel of the ship and brought it here.

Columbus was not oblivious to God's providence in his discovery. In his journal, Columbus expressed his literal belief that "his voyages were ushering in a millennial age . . . and initiat[ing] a messianic period." He was firmly convinced that Isaiah's words, "so shall they fear the name of the LORD from the west" (Isaiah 59:19), referred to the lands west of Europe that had not yet been discovered. The journal from his first voyage shows that the primary purpose of his explorations was to take the message of salvation through Jesus Christ to the people in this unknown land.[4]

Throughout our nation's history we see America's leaders turning to God for guidance. We see Washington kneeling in the snow of Valley Forge. We see our Founding Fathers on their knees at the first Continental Congress. We see the gaunt Lincoln praying in the hour of national crisis. We see Woodrow Wilson reading his Bible late at night by the White House lights. Washington summarized this national dependence on God, which was evident before his time and continued after him, when he said, "No people can be bound to acknowledge and adore the invisible hand which conducts the affairs of man more than those of the United States."[5]

Clearly America did not become the land of the free and the home of the brave by blind fate or a happy set of coincidences. A benevolent God was hovering over this nation from her very conception so that today, although America has only 5 percent of the world's population, she has more than 50 percent of the modern luxuries that characterize civilization.

Why has God blessed this nation above all other lands? Why has America in her short history outstripped the wealth, power, and influence of all ancient and modern civilizations? Can God have blessed a nation so richly without having for her a pivotal purpose? What is God's plan for America? What is its place in end-time prophecy? These are questions many people are asking today as they watch events coalesce toward world crises. They wonder how America fits into what is going on in the world.

In order to understand America's place in end-time prophecy, we must first answer the question we raised in the previous paragraph: Why has America been blessed above all other lands? Let's explore the reasons for God's favor on America, and then we will show what this means in terms of coming events.

## America Has Been the Force Behind World Missions

"To the United States belongs the distinction of providing three-fourths of the missionaries of the last century and approximately the same amount of money and material aid."[6] This means that 75 per-cent of all missionaries have come from a country boasting only 5 percent of the total world population. God blesses those who make His priorities their priorities. The church I pastor in California is a case in point. More than fifteen years ago that church committed to give to world missions the first 20 percent of every dollar received in offerings. When we started that program back in the early '90s, our missions budget was not quite $250,000 per year. Today it is well over ten times that figure. God loves the world. He loves the people who are yet to hear the gospel. When we love whom He loves, He blesses us. And I believe that principle applies to our nation as well as to our church.

God has blessed America because we have been the launching pad of the world's great missionary movement. In the aftermath of World War II, Americans started 1,800 missions agencies and sent out more than 350,000 missionaries.[7] And as a result, "today, 95 percent of the world's population have access, not only to some portion of Scripture in their language, but also to Christian radio broadcasts, audio recordings, and the *Jesus* film."[8] That achievement is due largely to the missionary zeal of churches in the United States.

## *America Has Been a Friend to the Jewish People*

Ever since the turn of the twentieth century, Jews have made up 3 percent of the total population of the United States, where they have been protected from harassment and anti-Semitism. America has given Jews opportunity for economic, educational, and cultural advancement without fear of losing their religious freedom.

America's historic support of Israel is based not so much on efforts by Jewish lobbyists in Washington or the presence of Jewish groups in our society, but on the Judeo-Christian heritage of our nation. President Truman's determination to recognize Israel as a modern state was fueled by his lifelong belief that in the book of Deuteronomy, God had given the land of Israel to the Jewish people for all time.

At the founding of the modern state of Israel, surrounding Arab nations immediately declared war on the new nation. Few felt Israel could survive, and western nations did not want to become embroiled in the conflict. Truman was under pressure not to intervene. In a dramatic speech to seek support before the United Nations, the Jewish statesman Abba Eban said:

> Israel is the product of the most sustained historic tenacity which the ages recall. The Jewish people have not striven toward this goal for twenty centuries in order that, having once achieved it, it will surrender it in response to an illegitimate and unsuccessful aggression. Whatever else changes, this will not. The state of Israel is an immutable part of the international landscape. To plan the future without it is to build delusions on the sand.[9]

In spite of Eban's eloquent plea, the young nation was in great danger. Both US and UN recognition of Israel were in serious doubt.

Following his speech, Eban flew to Paris to meet with an American delegation regarding recognition. Secretary of State George Marshall, whose support of Israel was tepid at best, had to return home for medical treatment. His deputy, John Foster Dulles, assumed leadership of the delegation.

Eban later wrote that Dulles held the key to the success of the talks. "Behind a dry manner, redolent of oak-paneled courtrooms in the United States, there *was a curious strain of Protestant mysticism* which led him to give the Israel questions a larger importance that its geopolitical weight would indicate"[10] (*emphasis added*).

What Eban called "a curious strain of Protestant mysticism" is actually the historic love that Christians have for the land and people of Israel, based upon their shared religious heritage and scriptures. This, more than anything else, has cemented the friendship between America and Israel for more than sixty years.

As we discovered in the first chapter of this book, God has promised to bless those who bless Israel (Genesis 12:1–3). He has amply fulfilled that promise. America has been abundantly blessed as a nation because we have blessed the Jews.

## America Has Been a Free Nation

In my studies of both the Old and New Testaments, I have observed that the principles of freedom are united with the tenets of Christianity. America today is the laboratory where those blended principles can grow and develop and become an example to all the world. The Bible says, "You shall know the truth, and the truth shall make you free" (John 8:32).

Freedom can never be taken for granted in our world. In early 2007, Freedom House released its annual survey, *Freedom in the World*, which stated that 3 billion people—46 percent of the world's population—live in a free to partly free country. Conversely, 54 percent—or more than half the population of the world—do not live in freedom.[11] In fact, the tendency in a fallen world is always away from freedom and toward despotism and tyranny.

In his 1981 inaugural address, President Ronald Reagan spoke of our freedom in these stirring words: "Above all, we must realize that no arsenal or no weapon in the arsenals of the world is so formidable as the will and moral courage of free men and women. It is a weapon our adversaries in today's world do not have. It is a weapon that we as Americans do have. Let that be understood by those who practice terrorism and prey upon their neighbors."[12]

America has learned what our repressive and terrorist adversaries do not understand: that liberty without law is anarchy, liberty to defy law is rebellion, but liberty limited by law is the cornerstone of civilization. We Americans have tried to share what we have learned by exporting freedom wherever we have gone in the world. We have tried to help people understand that freedom is what creates the life God intended us to have from the very beginning.

America has become the paradise of human liberty—a great oasis in a global desert of trouble, suffering, repression, and tyranny. Our nation is a dramatic exclamation point to the assertion that freedom works!

Today our precious heritage of freedom is being challenged internally by the erosion of our culture. As long-held freedoms come under fire, some Americans, especially those with wealth, are deciding that the United States is no longer the best place to live. According to the book *Getting Out: Your Guide to Leaving America,* some three hundred thousand Americans a year are choosing to leave the country.

This is the first time in history that the number of people exiting this nation has become large enough to be significant, and the emergence of such a trend calls our attention to the degenerating character of America. If our culture continues to jettison the principles that made our nation great, we can hardly expect the blessing of Almighty God to continue.

## America Has Been Founded on God and His Word

It is no mystery why America's founders insisted on the principle of freedom. Their dependence on the God of the Bible led them to subject themselves to Him as the ultimate authority for law rather than set themselves up as autocrats with the audacity to control the lives of their subjects. And because they submitted to God's authority, He has blessed this nation as none has ever been blessed. The Psalmist wrote, "Blessed is the nation whose God is the LORD, the people He has chosen as His own inheritance" (Psalm 33:12). The book of Proverbs adds, "Righteousness exalts a nation, but sin is a reproach to any people" (14:34).

I opened this chapter with a brief look at how America's founders and early leaders exhibited humble reliance on Almighty God. Now I want to show how that godly dependence characterized our governmental philosophy through several generations and resulted in God's blessings on our nation. Our leaders stabilized government with a lifeline between their country and their God, with authority and blessing flowing downward as dependence and thanksgiving flowed upward.

George Washington set the tone for the nation's governmental authority when he said, "It is impossible to rightly govern the world without God and the Bible."[13] That philosophy remained intact through the time of Abraham Lincoln, who is quoted as saying, "God is my witness that it is my constant anxiety and prayer that both myself and this nation should be on the Lord's side."[14]

Benjamin Franklin explained why he requested that each day of the Constitutional Convention be opened in prayer, saying: "The longer I live, the more convincing proofs I see of the truth—that God governs in the affairs of Men. And," he continued, "without His aid, we shall succeed in this political building no better than the builders of Babel."[15]

Henry Wilson (1812–1875) was a US senator and vice president under Ulysses S. Grant from 1873 to 1875. On December 23, 1866, he spoke to a YMCA gathering in Natick, Massachusetts, where he said:

Remember ever, and always, that your country was founded, not by the "most superficial, the lightest, the most irreflective of all European races," but by the stern old Puritans who made the deck of the *Mayflower* an altar of the living God, and whose first act on touching the soil of the new world was to offer on bended knees thanksgiving to Almighty God.[16]

In 1911, President Woodrow Wilson said:

The Bible . . . is the one supreme source of revelation of the meaning of life, the nature of God and spiritual nature and needs of men. It is the only guide of life which really leads the spirit in the way of peace and salvation. America was born a Christian nation. America was born to exemplify that devotion to the elements of righteousness which are derived from the revelations of Holy Scripture.[17]

Today as I write these words, our heritage of national dependence on God is under fire. Forces within our nation threaten its divine lifeline. The attitude of many in our culture today seems symbolized by the powerful legal tides now trying to remove the words *under God* from the Pledge of Allegiance. Those two words were inserted into the pledge in 1954, partly to distinguish our nation from the atheistic communism of the Soviet Union. But while these words came late to the pledge, they certainly reflected what had been a part of America's heritage from the beginning.

For example, on July 2, 1776, General George Washington wrote in the general orders to his men that day, "The fate of unborn millions will now depend, *under God*, on the courage and conduct of this army."[18] Almost a hundred years later, Abraham Lincoln consecrated the military cemetery on the battlefield of Gettysburg, saying: "We here highly resolved that these dead shall not have died in vain; that this nation, *under God,* shall have a new birth of freedom; and that government of the people, by the people, for the people, shall not perish from the earth" (*emphasis added*).[19]

This recognition that our nation was founded on godly principles of freedom and divine authority continued to be the basic assumption of government through the middle of the twentieth century. Our leaders realized that once America failed to acknowledge that we were under God, our basis for freedom and equitable government would come crashing down. President Calvin Coolidge said it well: "The foundation of our society and our government rests so much on the teachings of the Bible that it would be difficult to support them if faith in these teachings would cease to be practically universal in our country."[20] In other words, when America turns from its position of being under God, we can no longer expect His blessings on this nation to continue. We will have broken our lifeline.

As I've been writing this book, two attempts to hack through that lifeline were exposed. At a Dallas-area elementary school, one parent complained that the national motto, "In God We Trust," was painted on a wall in the gym. The school board promptly had the offending words painted over. When several parents complained about its abrupt removal, Texas law and Texas Education Code prevailed, causing a school district representative to admit the district had "made a mistake" and announced, "'In God We Trust' will be repainted on the wall."[21]

Do you remember the capstone of the Washington Monument I wrote about at the beginning of this chapter? Since the actual inscription is not visible at its stately height, the National Park Service has maintained a replica capstone in an exhibit at the 490-foot level. Located near a wall detailing the construction of the monument, the capstone case was positioned such that the public could see the inscription. However, late last year, the display was changed. The case was repositioned against the wall and turned so the east side inscription *Laus Deo* was no longer viewable. A previous reference to that inscription was also omitted from the new description tag on the exhibit. When some citizens complained of the unacceptable modifications, an NPS official responded by saying, "We made a mistake and we are fixing it."[22]

More than a mistake, these removals are an assault. Almost routinely these days, attacks are made on any public reminder of our dependence on God's grace for our national existence. I fear our lifeline is fraying.

## The Silence of the Bible on the Future of America

Dr. Tim LaHaye wrote, "One of the hardest things for American prophecy students to accept is that the United States is not clearly mentioned in Bible prophecy, yet our nation is the only superpower in the world today."[23] Indeed, no specific mention of the United States or any other country in North or South America can be found in the Bible. One reason may be that in the grand scheme of history, the United States is a new kid on the block. As a nation, it is less than 250 years old—much younger than the nations of Bible times that are featured in biblical prophecy. In fact, the Bible makes no mention of most nations in the modern world. The ancient prophets were primarily concerned with the Holy Land and its immediate neighbors. Areas remote from Israel do not figure in prophecy and are not mentioned in the Bible.

Dr. LaHaye went on to raise this question:

> "Does the United States have a place in end time prophecy?" My first response is no, there is nothing about the U.S. in prophecy. At least nothing that is specific. There is an allusion to a group of nations in Ezekiel 38:13 that could apply, but even that is not specific. The question is why? Why would the God of prophecy not refer to the supreme superpower nation in the end times in preparation for the one-world government of the Antichrist?[24]

The question has no one, simple answer, but it will help us understand what is going on in the world today if we look at some of the best thinking that students of prophecy have given us on why America is absent from end-time prophecies.

## America Will Be Incorporated into the European Coalition

Our first answer comes from noted prophecy expert John Walvoord, who wrote:

Although the Scriptures do not give any clear word concerning the role of the United States in relation to the revived Roman Empire, it is clear this will be a consolidation of the power of the West. Unlike the coalitions led by the United States, this coalition will be led by others—the Group of Ten . . . Most citizens of the United States of America have come from Europe, and their sympathies would more naturally be with a European alliance than with Russia, Asia, and Africa . . . Europe and America may be in formal alliance with Israel in opposition to the radical Islamic countries of the Middle East.[25]

According to this theory, though America is not mentioned by name in prophecy, it will be in the mix of the political realignments that foreshadow the end of time. And we can see signs of such realignments taking place today.

With the usual presidential fanfare, President Bush welcomed EU Commission president Jos Barroso and the serving president of the European Council, German chancellor Angela Merkel, in the Rose Garden of the White House in April 2007. The president thanked the two for their part in "the trans-Atlantic economic integration plan that the three of us signed today. It is a statement of the importance of trade. It is a commitment to eliminating barriers to trade. It is a recognition that the closer that the United States and the EU become, the better off our people become. So this is a substantial agreement and I appreciate it."[26] The president went on to say, "I believe it's in this country's interests that we reject isolationism and protectionism and encourage free trade."

The agreement these three leaders signed is called "Framework for Advancing Transatlantic Economic Integration between the United

States of America and the European Union"—an appropriately long title for what one would expect to be a long process. But things moved swiftly. In less than seven months the Transatlantic Economic Council held its first official meeting in Washington DC. In a joint statement it was announced, "Since April, the United States and the European Union have made substantial progress in removing barriers to trade and investment and in easing regulatory burdens."[27]

On the surface there seems to be nothing ominous about such an agreement; it appears to be simply about freeing up economic trade between nations. But a similar, less publicized meeting was held in March 2008 at the State Department, which focused on linking the United States, Mexico, and Canada in a "North American community with the European Union" in anticipation of the "creation of a 'Transatlantic Economic Union' between the European Union and North America."[28] One participant—whose identity is protected by the Chatham House Rule, which permits information to be disseminated without attribution to guarantee confidentiality—made this revealing statement:

> North America should be a premiere platform to establish continental institutions. That's why we need to move the security perimeters to include the whole continent, especially as we open the borders between North American countries for expanding free trade.[29]

Statements such as this reveal an intention toward union that has implications far beyond mere economic trade. And considering the speed at which leaders are pushing union between nations, it appears that it will not be long before we see such a union instituted. What does this mean for America?

## America Will Be Invaded by Outside Forces

Perhaps the silence of Scripture on the future of America indicates that by the time the Tribulation period arrives, America will have lost her influence in the world and will no longer be a major player. As we have noted, America's thirst for oil and our inability to close the gap between supply and demand could cripple our ability to defend our borders and protect our nation. Once again John Walvoord addresses the issue:

> Some maintain that the total absence of any scriptural reference to America in the end time is evidence that the United States will have been crippled by a nuclear attack, weapons of mass destruction, or some other major catastrophe . . . In the post 9/11 world the detonation of a dirty bomb, nuclear device, or biological weapon on U.S. soil is a dreaded yet distinct possibility. Such an attack could kill millions of people and reduce the United States to a second rate power overnight.[30]

Since the deployment of the first atomic bomb on the city of Hiroshima in August 1945, America has enjoyed a certain fear-based aura of invincibility. We now had the big stick, and we were the king of the hill. Both friends and enemies knew that we would use any and all weapons in our formidable arsenal to protect our nation. Even today, according to Ed Timperlake, who served in the Office of the Defense Secretary under Ronald Reagan, "Air Force and Navy personnel continue to stand vigilant 24 hours a day, seven days a week inside the strategic triad of bombers, land-based ICBMs and submarine 'boomers.'"[31]

In today's world, however, such power and vigilance may no longer deter enemies determined to attack the United States. In a truly frightening column in *The Washington Times*, Timperlake went on to observe: "a totally new dimension has emerged regarding a nuclear attack on America. The great tragedy of the murder of Benazir Bhutto brought the world's attention to the possibility of loose nukes falling into the hands of fanatics who would use them." In other words, the political instability in Pakistan could lead to nuclear warheads falling into the hands of radical Islamic jihadists. "It is certain," continued Timperlake, "that a nuclear weapon in the hands of fanatical jihadists will be used. The only current deterrence against its use is a worldwide hunt for the device before Israel, London, New York, or D.C. disappears in a flash."[32]

Timperlake went on to say that jihadists are not our only threat from a rogue nation armed with nuclear weapons. "What about the criminal state of North Korea or the vitriolic anti-Semitic nation of Iran?" he asked. "Either country for many perverse reasons can slip a device to a terrorist group."[33] As if to underscore his point, in late March of 2008, North Korea "test-fired a battery of short-range missiles" only one day after they "expelled South Korean officials from a joint industrial complex north of the border." The three "ship-to-ship missiles [were] launched into the sea."[34]

These enemies have different agendas, but they share a common disregard for human life and a burning hatred for the United States. While we would like to close our ears to predictions of impending disaster, experts such as Timperlake and others see a major attack on our country in the near future as virtually inevitable.

## America Will Be Infected with Moral Decay

The average lifespan of all the world's greatest civilizations from the beginning of history has been about two hundred years. During that two-century span, each of these nations progressed through the following sequence: from bondage to spiritual faith; from spiritual faith to great courage; from courage to liberty; from liberty to abundance; from abundance to complacency; from complacency to apathy; from apathy to dependence; and from dependence back into bondage.[35]

At what point is America in this cycle? Popular blogger La Shawn Barber answered this question in an article titled, "America on the Decline." She wrote:

> In *The Decline and Fall of the Roman Empire*, author Edward Gibbon discusses several reasons for the great civilization's demise, including the undermining of the dignity and sanctity of the home and the decay of religion. America has been compared to the Roman Empire in secular and religious ways. Regardless of its ultimate legacy, America is a civilization on the decline. A couple of centuries from now (or sooner), someone will lament the loss of a once-great civilization that brought prosperity to the world and tried to make it safe for democracy. The glory that was the United States will lay in ruins, brought down not by terrorists but its own debauchery and complacency.[36]

Barber's analysis is right on the money with one exception: given the present situation in our world, another "couple of centuries" for America is not in the equation. Nevertheless, her analysis is perceptive, and she continues it by referencing an expert from decades past. In 1947, forward-looking sociologist Dr. Carle Zimmerman wrote a text called *Family and Civilization*. He identified eleven "symptoms of final decay" observable in the fall of both the Greek and Roman civilizations. See how many characterize our society:

1. No-fault divorce

2. "Birth Dearth"; increased disrespect for parenthood and parents

3. Meaningless marriage rites/ceremonies

4. Defamation of past national heroes

5. Acceptance of alternative marriage forms

6. Widespread attitudes of feminism, narcissism, hedonism

7. Propagation of antifamily sentiment

8. Acceptance of most forms of adultery

9. Rebellious children

10. Increased juvenile delinquency

11. Common acceptance of all forms of sexual perversion[37]

One cannot read lists such as these and doubt that America is throwing away its treasured position as the most blessed nation ever on the face of the earth. Remember, as we noted earlier, God blessed this country for a reason: our nation was founded on submission to Him. But now as the reasons for His blessings upon America are eroding, we can expect the blessings themselves to fade as well. It's a simple matter of cause and effect: remove the cause, and the effect ceases. Once, we invited God into our nation. From the first moments of our existence, we opened our national doors to Him and made Him welcome as our most honored guest. But now our culture seems bent on shutting Him out, as author Mike Evans laments:

Most can remember the classic painting of Jesus standing outside a door waiting to be allowed entry. That poignant portrayal of Christ on the outside, wanting to fellowship with His creation, has never been more powerful than it is today. Prayer has been excised from schools, suits have been filed to force Congress to remove "under God" from the Pledge of Allegiance, displays of the Ten Commandments have been removed from public buildings, and the motto, "In God We Trust," is in danger of extinction. Teachers have been forbidden even to carry a personal Bible in view of students, Christian literature has been removed from library shelves, religious Christmas carols have been banned from school programs, and "spring break" has replaced Easter vacation.[38]

Almost six decades ago, former president Herbert Hoover wrote a warning that I fear America has not heeded. After calling attention to several new programs and concepts, including "New Freedom" and "New Religion," Hoover stated, "We have overworked the word 'new' . . . The practical thing we can do, if we want to make the world over, is to try out the word 'Old' for a while. There are some 'old' things that made this country . . . Some old things are slipping badly in American life and if they slip too far, the lights will go out of America!" Among the old things he listed: "Old Virtues of religious faith, integrity and whole truth . . . honor in public office, economy in government, individual liberty . . . willingness to sacrifice . . . Our greatest danger is not from invasion by foreign armies. Our dangers are that we may commit suicide from within by complaisance with evil."[39]

It saddens me to say it, but I believe the signs make it certain that America is now infected with the deadly disease of moral decay. And as that infection eats away at our foundations, we can expect the law of cause and effect to come into play. Scripture often warns us that even a long-suffering God will not forever strive with men. If we ignore divine directives, we cannot expect God's blessing. A limb that cuts itself off from the trunk will not continue to live.

## America Will Be Impotent Because of the Rapture

If the Rapture were to happen today and all the true believers in Jesus Christ disappeared into heaven in a single moment, America as we know it could be obliterated. It is estimated that at the Rapture, America will lose millions of citizens—all its Christians and their small children.[40] This means that not only would the country lose a minimum of 25 percent of her population, but she would also lose the very best, the "salt" and "light" of the nation. Who can imagine the chaos in our country when all the godly people disappear—enough to populate many vast cities—leaving only those who have rejected God? It is not a pretty picture. We who love Christ will be blessed by the Rapture in more ways than one. We not only will know the joy of being with our beloved Lord but also will be spared the horrors that the world will suffer through the evil of people left in the wake of the Rapture. It's like a reverse surgical operation—one in which all the healthy cells are removed and only the cancerous ones are left to consume one another.

Yet as we look back at all we have been learning, we who will be rescued cannot help but feel a sense of tension in our hearts. Yes, God will save us, but things we've never experienced are about to happen, and changes such as we've never imagined loom on the horizon. It is important to realize that God understands this internal tension. We do not sin by feeling uneasy. Perhaps it's a little like getting married. We anticipate the event with joy but also with butterflies in the stomach. It's not a matter of dread or wanting to draw back; it's merely a matter of our natural discomfort when facing new experiences. But in spite of the uneasiness, we approach with confidence the events we are anticipating because we know they were put into play by the Creator of the universe. He knows the end from the beginning, and because we are His friends, He is letting us in on the eternal secrets of His determined will.

In an article about the United States in prophecy, Herman A. Hoyt made a fine statement that makes a fitting conclusion to this chapter. He wrote:

> Since the promise of Christ's coming for the Church has always been held out to His people as an event that could take place at any moment, surely the events of the present hour in relation to the United States ought to give new stimulus to watch momentarily for His coming. In these days of crisis, our trust should not rest in a nation that may shortly disappear, but in Him who works all things after the counsel of His own will.[41]

Dr. Hoyt is right; what do we have to worry about? Our trust has never been in governments, civilizations, or cultures. By the standards of eternity, these institutions last but a moment, crumbling into dust to be swept away by the winds of history. They are helpful while they are here, but they have never been worthy of our trust. We have always put our trust in the One who stands above institutions, above history, and even above time itself—the One by whose power and permission these things exist, and who knows their times and the ends of their days. Only He is worthy of our ultimate allegiance.

# SEVEN

# When One Man Rules the World

WHEN I FIRST BEGAN STUDYING PROPHECY NEARLY FORTY YEARS ago, I encountered the Bible's prediction that one man would eventually take control of the entire world. Frankly, I could not imagine how such a thing would ever happen. But since the Bible presented this as a major part of the end-time landscape, I believed it, and I preached it even though I could not comprehend it.

Today it is much easier to envision the possibility of such a world ruler. Technology has given us instant global communication. CNN is seen everywhere in the world. The Internet and satellite cell phones reach every country on the face of the earth. Air transportation has shrunk the planet to the point where we can set foot on the soil of any nation in a matter of hours. I am told that there are now missiles that can reach any part of the world in fewer than thirty minutes. Men and nations no longer live in isolation.

There are also other factors that make the ascendance of a global leader more plausible than ever before. The Bible predicts that world-wide chaos, instability, and disorder will increase as we approach the end of this age. Jesus Himself said that there would be wars, rumors of wars, famines, and earthquakes in various places (Matthew 24:6–7). Just before these tensions explode into world chaos, the Rapture of the church will depopulate much of the planet. As many as seventy million people could suddenly disappear from our nation alone.

The devastation wrought by these disasters will spur a worldwide outcry for relief and order at almost any cost. That will set the stage for the emergence of a new world leader who will, like a pied piper, promise a solution to all problems. He will negotiate world peace and promise order and security. This leader, who will emerge out of the newly formed European Union, is commonly referred to in the Bible as the Antichrist.

The very word *antichrist* sends a shudder through the hearts of Christians. All have heard or read of him, and the fear that some feel at the mention of his name comes largely from misunderstandings and confusion about who he is, when he will appear, and what powers he can exercise over God's people. In this chapter I want to dispel those fears and clear up the confusion. I want to show you what is going on in the world as it relates to the biblical predictions and descriptions of the Antichrist and his work.

The word *antichrist* is used four times in the New Testament, each time by the apostle John, and it is found only in his epistles (1 John 2:18, 22; 4:3; and 2 John 7). As the word suggests, the Antichrist is a person who is against Christ. The prefix *anti* can also mean "instead of," and both meanings will apply to this coming world leader. He will overtly oppose Christ and at the same time pass himself off as Christ.

The Antichrist will aggressively live up to his terrible name. He will be Satan's superman, who persecutes, tortures, and kills the people of God and leads the armies of the world into the climactic Battle of Armageddon. He will be the most powerful dictator the world has ever seen, making Caesar, Hitler, Mao, and Saddam seem weak and tame by comparison.

Even though the Antichrist is identified by that name only four times in the Bible, he appears many more times under various aliases. He is also called:

- "the prince who is to come" (Daniel 9:26 NKJV)

- a "fierce" king (Daniel 8:23 NKJV)

- "a master of intrigue" (Daniel 8:23 NIV)

- "a despicable man" (Daniel 11:21 NLT)

- a "worthless shepherd" (Zechariah 11:16–17 NLT)

- "the one who brings destruction" (2 Thessalonians 2:3 NLT)

- "the lawless one" (2 Thessalonians 2:8 NKJV)

- "the evil man" (2 Thessalonians 2:9 NLT)

- the "beast" (Revelation 13:1 NKJV)

As a study of these references shows, the Antichrist is introduced and described in great detail in the Bible, yet his identity is not revealed. That lack of specific identification, however, has not stopped speculation on who he might be and even the outright naming of certain individuals. Many names have been suggested. When you google "Who is Antichrist?" you get about 1.5 million hits. Some of the Web sites post incredibly long and detailed articles—a sign of the extreme fascination generated by this sensational subject.

In the late 1930s and early 1940s, when Hitler was moving through Europe and swallowing up whole nations, many believed that he was the coming Antichrist.

Hitler offered himself as a messiah with a divine mission to save Germany. On one occasion he displayed the whip he often carried to demonstrate that "in driving out the Jews I remind myself of Jesus in the temple." He declared, "Just like Christ, I have a duty to my own people." He even boasted that just as Christ's birth had changed the calendar, so his victory over the Jews would be the beginning of a new age. "What Christ began," he said, "I will complete." . . . At one of the Nuremberg rallies, a giant photo of Hitler carried the caption, "In the beginning was the Word."[1]

I have a pamphlet in my file called *The Beast: The False Prophet and Hitler.* It was published in 1941, the year I was born. This pamphlet presented the formula for identifying Hitler as the Antichrist by showing how the letters in the word *Hitler* link him numerologically with the "number of the beast" given in Revelation 13:16–18:

He causes all, both small and great, rich and poor, free and slave, to receive a mark on their right hand or on their foreheads, and that no one may buy or sell except one who has the mark or the name of the beast, or the number of his name. Here is wisdom. Let him who has understanding calculate the number of the beast, for it is the number of a man: His number is 666.

The pamphlet bases its conclusion on a numerologic formula. Numerologists believe that meaning can be assigned to numbers.

Some biblical numerologists tell us that the number 666, when worked out through a transposition of number assignments to alphabetical letters, will identify the name of a certain man. In the Revelation passage we have only three numerals—666—but according to numerology, through these numbers we can find the man's name. The first step is to numeralize the alphabet: you let 100 stand for A, 101 for B, 102 for C, and so on through the rest of the letters. Then you take Hitler's name and give each letter its numerical value: H=107, I=108, T=119, L=111, E=104, R=117. Now, add up these six numbers, and voilà! The total is 666! So obviously Hitler must be the Antichrist.

Now, to get the most fun out of the game of "Who is the Antichrist?" you must play by these three rules: If the proper name does not reach the necessary total, add a title. If the sum cannot be found in English, try Hebrew, Greek, or Latin. Don't be too particular about the spelling.

And above all, be persistent. If you keep working at it, you can make anybody the Antichrist!

If numerology doesn't work for you, don't despair. There are other ways to identify the Antichrist, as we see by looking at another favorite candidate for the role: President John F. Kennedy. What signs pointed to him? He went through "death" and "resurrection" as a PT boat commander in the South Pacific during World War II. At the Democratic convention in 1956, he received 666 votes. He was also elected president and shot through the head, which is what the Bible says will happen to this future dictator. There were some who expected that as President Kennedy lay in state in the rotunda of the Capitol, he would come out of his casket and assert himself as the ruler of the world . . . which, of course, he failed to do. So, in spite of the elaborate and contrived reasons for believing that these two men and several others in history were to have been the Antichrist, all efforts to identify him have failed.

And they will continue to fail. As I noted above, the Bible does not tell us who the Antichrist will be. In fact, Paul tells us in the second chapter of Thessalonians that this coming world ruler will not be revealed until after the Rapture of the church. "So if you ever reach the point where you think you know who he is, that must mean you have been left behind."[2]

Yet while it is not possible to know the identity of the future world ruler, it is possible to know what kind of a man he will be, for the Bible gives us a wealth of information about him. Let's explore some of that information and learn a little more about the Antichrist.

## The Personality of the Coming World Ruler

### He Will Be a Charismatic Leader

The prophet Daniel described the Antichrist in these graphic terms: "After this I saw in the night visions, and behold, a fourth beast . . . And there . . . were eyes like the eyes of a man, and a mouth speaking pompous words. . . . He shall speak pompous words against the Most High" (Daniel 7:7–8, 25).

In these passages Daniel gives us one of the characteristics of the coming world ruler—his charismatic personality enhanced by his speaking ability, which he will use to sway the masses with spellbinding words of power and promise. We little realize the power of good speaking ability. An actor who is not classically handsome, such as James Earl Jones, can land great parts and charm audiences simply by the power of his resonant and articulate voice. Often Americans are swayed by political candidates who have little to offer, but they offer it in the beautiful package of their smooth intonation and syntax. As Daniel says, the coming world leader will be renowned for this kind of eloquence, which will capture the attention and admiration of the world.

Daniel goes on to tell us that this golden-tongued orator not only will speak in high-blown terms but also will utter pompous words against God. The apostle John described him in a similar fashion in the book of Revelation: "And he was given a mouth speaking great things and blasphemies" (Revelation 13:5).

Considering these and other prophecies, it's not hard to understand why Hitler has often been pegged as the prototype of the Antichrist. Hitler was a man of charisma, great oratory, and pomp. In his now classic book, *Kingdoms in Conflict*, Charles Colson described the well-orchestrated events that were played out in countless crowded halls as Hitler manipulated the German people:

> Solemn symphonic music began the set-up. The music then stopped, a hush prevailed, and a patriotic anthem began and "from the back, walking slowly down the wide central aisle," strutted Hitler. Finally, the Fuhrer himself rises to speak. Beginning in a low, velvet voice, which makes the audience unconsciously lean forward to hear, he speaks his love for Germany . . . and gradually his pitch increases until he reaches a screaming crescendo. But his audience does not think his rasping shouts excessive. They are screaming with him.[3]

Hitler's pomp and charisma were not the only parallels between him and biblical prophecy.

The Bible predicts that a world ruler will arise in Europe who will promise peace while preparing for war. He will mesmerize the world, demanding the worship of the masses in exchange for the right to buy bread. He, like Hitler, will be indwelt by demonic forces, most likely by Satan himself. The parallels are so striking that Robert Van Kampen in his book *The Sign* says that he believes the Antichrist will actually be Hitler raised from the dead. Though this supposition is unlikely, Hitler does provide us a sneak preview showing in miniscule format the kind of man the Antichrist is likely to be.[4]

Daniel continued his description of the Antichrist by telling us he is a man "whose appearance was greater than his fellows" (Daniel 7:20). In terms of his outward appearance, this man will be a strikingly attractive person. The combination of magnetic personality, speaking ability, and extreme good looks will make him virtually irresistible to the masses. When he comes on the scene, people will flock to him like flies to honey, and they will fall over themselves to do anything he asks.

## He Will Be a Cunning Leader

Daniel was given a picture of this world leader in his famous dream recorded in the seventh chapter of his book. Here is what he reported: "I was considering the horns, and there was another horn, a little one, coming up among them, before whom three of the first horns were plucked out by the roots" (Daniel 7:8).

If we read carefully and understand the prophetic symbol of the horns, we learn from this verse that the coming world leader subdues three other kings by plucking them out by their roots. This man will squeeze out the old to make room for the new. He will take over three kingdoms, one by one, not by making war but by clever political manipulation. He begins as the little horn, but then he succeeds in uprooting three of the first horns and thus abrogates their power to himself. Daniel reiterated this event in the eleventh chapter of his prophecy, telling us that this future world leader "shall come in peaceably, and seize the kingdom by intrigue" (Daniel 11:21). The Antichrist will be a political genius, a masterful diplomat, and a clever leader. Arthur W. Pink wrote of him:

> Satan has had full opportunity afforded him to study fallen human nature . . . The devil knows full well how to dazzle people by the attraction of power . . . He knows how to gratify the craving for knowledge . . . He can delight the ear with music and the eye with entrancing beauty . . . He knows how to exalt people to dizzying heights of worldly greatness and fame, and how to control the greatness so that it may be employed against God and His people.[5]

In today's world, every leader wants to be the one who solves the perpetual crisis in the Middle East. American presidents dream of adding that distinction to their legacy. Jimmy Carter thought he had achieved it at Camp David. Bill Clinton tried frantically to eke out a settlement during the final months of his administration. Today, in a renewal of that shuttle diplomacy, President Bush also seeks to broker such a peace agreement. If this attempt fails, and if campaign speeches are any indication, the next US president appears likely to join the pursuit to complete the "road map to world peace."

Perhaps no diplomat worked harder at this goal than secretary of state Henry Kissinger during the Nixon and Ford years. Kissinger was himself a Jew whose family had escaped Germany during the Nazi years and who negotiated the end of the Yom Kippur War. In September 1970, Kissinger managed a Middle Eastern crisis between

Israel, Jordan, and Syria, during which he virtually lived in the White House Situation Room. One top US official who was involved in the sessions was asked if Dr. Kissinger enjoyed the manipulation of American power. "'Enjoy?' exclaimed the official. 'Henry adores power, absolutely adores it. To Henry, diplomacy is nothing without it.'" A Pentagon aid related how Kissinger leaned over large maps, moving toy battleships and aircraft carriers from one end of the Mediterranean to the other, arguing with admirals, expounding on military tactics and then picking up the phone to order the Joint Chiefs of Staff to change the deployment of the Sixth Fleet. The World War II sergeant had become all at once a general and an admiral and, during that crisis, a kind of deputy commander in chief.[6]

Because Kissinger was a European-born Jew of great brilliance who became the most powerful voice in world politics in the 1970s, some people speculated that he might be the Antichrist. He wasn't, of course, nor was he able to resolve the Israeli-Arab conflict. But Kissinger's love for power gives us a snapshot of one characteristic of the coming world ruler. One day a cunning superleader—a man who adores power—will arise and use his manipulative ability to succeed where all other diplomats have failed. He will resolve the Israeli-Arab conflict.

## He Will Be a Cruel Leader

Once again we turn to the writings of Daniel to understand the personality of this coming tyrant.

> Thus he said: "The fourth beast shall be a fourth kingdom on earth, which shall be different from all other kingdoms, and shall devour the whole earth, trample it and break it in pieces . . . He shall speak pompous words against the Most High, shall persecute the saints of

the Most High, and shall intend to change times and law. Then the saints shall be given into his hand for a time and times and half a time." (Daniel 7:23, 25)

Here Daniel tells us that the Antichrist is going to devour the whole world; he will tread the world down. He will break it in pieces. These words hint at something utterly horrific. What will happen to agitate the Antichrist to unleash this immense cruelty? Although all the believers of the present age will be taken to heaven before the reign of this man, new converts will come to Christ during the years of tribulation. This will infuriate the Antichrist, and he will take out his wrath on those new Christians. Many followers of Christ will be martyred for their faith.

The word *persecute* in Daniel 7:25 literally means to "wear out." The same word is used to describe the wearing out of garments. The use of the word here indicates a slow, painful wearing down of the people of God—a torturous, cruel persecution reminiscent of the horrors Nero inflicted on Christians in ancient Rome, but even worse. It would be easier for the saints during the Tribulation if they were simply killed outright, but instead they will be "worn out"—mercilessly tortured by this unthinkably cruel man.

Again, we find a prototype of what is to come in the regime of Hitler. Charles Colson gives us a chilling description of what went on in Nazi concentration camps:

The first Nazi concentration camp opened in 1933. In one camp, hundreds of Jewish prisoners survived in disease-infested barracks on little food and gruesome, backbreaking work. Each day the prisoners were marched to the compound's giant factory, where tons of human waste and garbage were distilled into alcohol to be used as a fuel additive. Even worse than the nauseating smell was the realization that they were fueling the Nazi war machine.[7]

Colson goes on to say that as the result of the humiliation and drudgery of their lives, "dozens of the prisoners went mad and ran from their work, only to be shot by the guards or electrocuted by the fence."[8]

Hitler and the Nazis did not annihilate the Jews all at once; they deliberately and systematically wore down their souls. And that gives us a picture of what will happen in the Tribulation when the Antichrist is in power. He will be a cruel, blood-shedding leader, taking out his wrath on the saints who come to Christ under his regime.

## The Profile of the Coming World Ruler

In the twelfth chapter of Revelation we read of the dragon, or Satan, being thrown out of heaven in a great war. Then in the thirteenth chapter we discover that the dragon comes to earth to begin his program by embodying his agent, the Antichrist. When we link this chapter with verses from Daniel, we get a good profile of this leader by looking at how he comes to power from several different viewpoints. Each of these viewpoints—the political, the national, the spiritual, and the providential—give us a good picture of what he will be like. So let's briefly explore what the Bible tells us about how the Antichrist comes to power.

### He Will Be Politically Inconspicuous

Daniel 7 tells us that the Antichrist will not make a big splash when he arrives on the political scene. He will not enter with a fanfare, announcing, "I am here! I will now take over!" Instead, he will squeeze his way in, little by little, beginning as one among many minor political leaders. In prophetic imagery, he is the little horn who grows to be the big horn. He will attract little attention as he methodically begins to grasp more and more power.

John the apostle emphasized this fact when he wrote that this ominous personality will arise from among the mass of ordinary people. "Then I stood on the sand of the sea. And I saw a beast rising up out of the sea, having seven heads and ten horns, and on his horns ten crowns, and on his heads a blasphemous name" (Revelation 13:1). The *sea* in biblical imagery stands for the general mass of humanity or, more specifically, the gentile nations. We find confirmation of that meaning for the sea in Revelation 17: "Then he said to me, 'The waters which you saw, where the harlot sits, are peoples, multitudes, nations, and tongues'" (v. 15).

What we learn in these passages is that at first the Antichrist will not be obvious. He will not burst onto the scene in all his power and glory, but rather he will rise out of the sea of common humanity, or emerge inauspiciously from among ordinary people, as did Napoleon and Hitler.

## He Will Emerge from a Gentile Nation

From what nation will the coming world ruler emerge? Often we hear that he must come from the Jewish nation. Since he will make a covenant with the nation of Israel, many people reason that perhaps he will be the Jew that Israel anticipates as her messiah. But the Bible gives us no evidence for determining that the Antichrist is a Jew. In fact, we have strong evidence for believing the opposite. Dr. Thomas Ice weighed in on the ethnicity of the Antichrist and concluded:

A widely held belief throughout the history of the church has been the notion that Antichrist will be of Jewish origin. This view is still somewhat popular in our day. However, upon closer examination we find no real Scriptural basis for such a view. In fact, the Bible teaches just the opposite . . . that Antichrist will be of Gentile descent.[9]

As we saw in an earlier chapter, some form of the Roman Empire must be revived before the end times, and this appears to be coming about through the formation of the European Union. The Antichrist will emerge from one of the unified European nations. John's revelation affirms that the world ruler will arise from the masses within a gentile nation.

## He Will Be Spiritually Blasphemous

Daniel said of this world leader, "He shall speak *pompous* words against the Most High, shall persecute the saints of the Most High, and shall intend to change times and law" (Daniel 7:25, *emphasis added*). In his second letter to the Thessalonians, Paul described him as one "who opposes and exalts himself above all that is called God or that is worshiped, so that he sits as God in the temple of God, showing himself that he is God" (2 Thessalonians 2:4).

As Paul wrote in Romans 1, and as the history of ancient Israel warns us over and over, it is a terrible thing to worship a *creature* instead of the *Creator*. Yet as Daniel warned, this man will defy God and demand to be worshipped instead of Him. And his demand will be met. As John wrote, "All who dwell on the earth will worship him, whose names have not been written in the Book of Life of the Lamb slain from the foundation of the world" (Revelation 13:8).

As if declaring himself to be God gives him power over nature and human nature, this ruler will also attempt to change the moral and natural laws of the universe. In the early days of the French Revolution, the new leaders tried to get control of the masses by changing everything that grew out of Christianity or Christian tradition. They set up a new calendar by which years were numbered, not from the birth of Christ but from the date of the revolution. They issued decrees to change all Christian churches to "temples of reason" and to melt down church bells for the metal. They actually tried to replace the seven-day week established by God with a ten-day week.[10] Such extreme actions showing hostility to everything related to God will characterize the coming world leader. No doubt he would even change the length of a year if he could somehow gain control of the earth's rotation!

While the Antichrist is pictured as "the beast rising up out of the *sea*," John wrote that the beast, "that ascends out of the bottomless *pit*," the one who will again be remanded to the bottomless pit until the end of the Millennium, is none other than Satan himself (Revelation 9:11; 11:7; 20:1–3, *emphasis added*). The Antichrist, with his seven heads, ten horns with their ten crowns, and his blasphemous mouth . . . whom all the world marveled at and followed, was given his power by Satan (Revelation 13:1–4).

## He Will Be Limited Providentially

As both Daniel and John show us, the Antichrist is a terrifying person. He is the epitome of evil, the ultimate negation of everything good, the avowed enemy and despiser of God. Every follower of Christ ought to bow before God at this moment and give thanks that he or she will not be on this earth during the reign of the Antichrist. At the same time, we must not forget that this satanic creature is not equal to God. He does not have absolute power or anything close to it. God has him on a chain. In fact, in Revelation 13, we are reminded repeatedly that the Antichrist can only do what he is allowed to do.

Twice in this chapter, we find the little phrase, *and he was given.* "And he was given a mouth speaking great things and blasphemies, and he was given authority to continue for forty-two months" (v. 5). We also find in this chapter, "It was granted to him to make war with the saints and to overcome them. And authority was given him over every tribe, tongue, and nation" (v. 7). As in the story of Job, Satan (and his puppet, the Antichrist) will be able to do only that which God allows. The Antichrist will be able to create terrible havoc and chaos, but ultimately God is still God, and no enemy of His will go beyond the boundaries He sets.

## He Will Have an Intimidating Presence

The four major kingdoms depicted in Daniel's other prophetic vision were likened to certain animals: Babylon was like a lion, Medo-Persia was like a bear, Greece was like a leopard, and Rome was like the ten-horned beast (Daniel 7). In the descriptions of the beast in Revelation, we have all of these characteristics combined into one horrific creature (Revelation 13:2). This likeness of the Antichrist to ferocious beasts is meant to show us the intimidating presence of this satanic creature. He combines in his person all of the threatening characteristics of the kingdoms which have gone before him. Dr. W. A. Criswell wrote:

Think of the golden majesty of Babylon. Of the mighty ponderous massiveness of Cyrus the Persian. Think of the beauty and the elegance and the intellect of the ancient Greek world. Think of the

Roman with his laws and his order and his idea of justice. All of these glories will be summed up in the majesty of this one eventual *Antichrist* who will be like Nebuchadnezzar, like Cyrus, like Tiglath Pileser, like Shalmanezer, like Julius Caesar, like Caesar Augustus, like Alexander the Great, like Napoleon Bonaparte, like Frederick the Great and Charlemagne, all bound up into one.[11]

It's no wonder that people will follow this man and even fall down and worship him. We see in our own political campaigns how quickly people gravitate to charisma and power. Give us a fine-looking candidate with a golden voice, a powerful presence, and the ability to enthrall people with vague rhetoric about an undefined better future, and we follow like sheep as the media bleats the candidate's praises. Completely overlooked is the substance of the man's program. The presence and charisma of the Antichrist will be similar, making his rise to power inevitable.

## The Program of the Coming World Ruler

One of the first acts of this world leader will be to make peace with Israel. And he will keep this covenant during the first three and a half years of his rule. At that point, however, he will change his tactics. He will drop all pretensions of peace and adopt a program of crushing power. He will break his covenant with Israel and subject the Jews to great persecution (Daniel 9:27; Isaiah 28:18).

Then will come the leader's most sensational moment. The Antichrist will actually be killed, but to the astonishment of all the world, he will be raised back to life by the power of Satan in a grotesque counterfeit of the Resurrection of Jesus Christ (Revelation 13:3–4).

After his death and satanic resurrection, the Antichrist will assassinate the leaders of three countries in the European Union, and all other nations will immediately relinquish their power to him. It is then that he will set himself up to be worshipped by all the people of the world. Through his associate, the false prophet, the mark of the beast will be placed upon all those who will follow him. Anyone who does not bear this mark will be unable to buy or sell in the world's economy.

In times past, the idea of a mark that would individually identify everyone in the world for governmental control seemed a far-fetched fantasy possible only in science fiction. No one today, however, questions the possibility of such an identification process. New methods of identification are being invented every day. Recently I became acquainted with RFID, or Radio Frequency Identification. RFID is on the crest of the current wave of technology. The system involves the implantation of a tiny chip (0.05 by 0.05 millimeters) into retail items to thwart shoplifters. They have also been implanted into pets to track them should they stray, and more recently into Alzheimer's patients. These microchips can also be used as personal identity markers surgically implanted under your skin and loaded with tons of recorded information about you.[12] The Antichrist will have available to him this technology and many other options when it comes to implementing the mark of the beast.

In a final act of rebellion against God, this vile person will set himself up in Jerusalem and desecrate the rebuilt temple in what is called the "abomination of desolation." He will then attempt to annihilate every Jew on earth, thus sounding the first ominous note in the prelude to the Battle of Armageddon.

This despot of all despots will be ultimately destroyed when Jesus Christ comes to battle against the Antichrist and his armies. In that climactic war the Antichrist will be killed, and his forces will be destroyed. The victorious Christ will assume His throne as rightful king and ruler of the universe.

More important than speculating about the identity of the Antichrist is remembering that his power broker, Satan, is not the equal opposite of Almighty God. Only God knows the day, the hour, the millisecond that will usher in Satan's reign on earth as Christ raptures the church. Like us, Satan can only look for the signs and wait. Throughout the millennia of his waiting, it is likely that he has been reading scouting reports and evaluating some choice candidates and maybe even issuing a few letters of intent so he will be ready when his hour does come.

Is the Antichrist lurking somewhere out there in the masses of humanity right now? Is his darkened mind already plotting the evils that he will inflict in the last days? I believe it is entirely possible, if not highly probable.

Gary Frazier gives us a possible scenario:

Somewhere at this moment there may be a young man growing to maturity. He is in all likelihood a brooding, thoughtful young man. Inside his heart, however, there is a hellish rage. It boils like a caldron of molten lead. He hates God. He despises Jesus Christ. He detests the Church. In his mind there is taking shape the form of a dream of conquest. He will disingenuously present himself as a friend of Christ and the Church. Yet . . . He will, once empowered, pour out hell itself onto this world. Can the world produce such a prodigy? Hitler was once a little boy. Stalin was a lad. Nero was a child. The tenderness of childhood will be shaped by the devil into the terror of the *antichrist.*[13]

I realize that the picture of the future I've presented in this chapter is not a pretty one. Yet I am so often questioned about the identity of the Antichrist, and there is so much spurious and false information about him floating around, that I felt compelled to address the question. Christians need to know what is going on in the world concerning this dreaded person. But of much greater importance than looking for the Antichrist, we are to be "looking for the blessed hope and glorious appearing of our great God and Savior Jesus Christ" (Titus 2:13).

Jesus told us what to do during this time of waiting. We are to keep our hearts from being unnecessarily troubled. If we believe in Him, He will one day take us to that home He has been preparing for us, and we will be with Him! There is only one way to have that assurance. Jesus said, "I am the way, the truth, and the life. No one comes to the Father except through Me" (John 14:6).

Giving your life to Christ is the only absolute and certain guarantee that when He comes, you will be saved from personally experiencing the evil of the Antichrist by that daring air rescue called the Rapture. You will be taken out of the world into His glorious presence, never to experience the horrors Daniel and John described in their prophecies.

Keep looking up!

# EIGHT

# The New Axis of Evil

ON JANUARY 29, 2002, IN HIS STATE OF THE UNION ADDRESS, President George W. Bush used the term *Axis of Evil* for the first time. He identified Iran, Iraq, and North Korea as "states . . . [who are] arming to threaten the peace of the world . . . These regimes," he said, "pose a grave threat and growing danger. They could provide these arms to terrorists, giving them the means to match their hatred."[1] President Bush was roundly criticized for calling these nations *evil*, but as we will see in this chapter, his description was more than accurate.

On May 6, 2002, US ambassador to the United Nations John Bolton gave a speech titled "Beyond the Axis of Evil," in which he added three more rogue states to the axis: Libya, Syria, and Cuba. Today the term *Axis of Evil* includes all six states.

One nation on this Axis of Evil list is of special interest to us because we find that it is also on God's list. That nation and that list are found in the thirty-eighth and thirty-ninth chapters of Ezekiel. These chapters, written some twenty-six hundred years ago, give us one of the most important and dramatic prophecies in all Scripture.

It is commonly referred to as the prophecy against Gog and Magog, and it is the most detailed prophecy concerning war in the entire Bible. The prophecy predicts an invasion of Israel in the last days—an invasion comprised of enormous masses of troops from a coalition of nations led by Russia and Iran.

It is likely that this invasion will occur shortly after Israel signs a covenant with the new leader of the European Union. Because of this agreement, Israel will be at peace with her Islamic neighbors. The people of Israel will believe that the European powers will protect them from any outside aggressor or invader . . . especially from Russia, which will have joined forces with Iran to develop weapons for the purpose of utterly destroying Israel.

## The Identity of the Nations

Now the word of the Lord came to me, saying, "Son of man, set your face against Gog, of the land of Magog, the prince of Rosh, Meshech, and Tubal, and prophesy against him, and say, 'Thus says the Lord God: "Behold, I am against you, O Gog, the prince of Rosh, Meshech, and Tubal. I will turn you around, put hooks into your jaws, and lead you out, with all your army, horses, and horse-men, all splendidly clothed, a great company with bucklers and shields, all of them handling swords. Persia, Ethiopia, and Libya are with them, all of them with shield and helmet; Gomer and all its troops; the house of Togarmah from the far north and all its troops—many people are with you. Prepare yourself and be ready, you and all your companies that are gathered about you; and be a guard for them."'" (Ezekiel 38:1–7)

Here we see that Ezekiel's prophecy begins with a list of proper names. Many of these names identify certain grandchildren and great-grandchildren of Noah who were the fathers of nations that for a time bore their names (Genesis 10). These nations, which today no longer have those original names, will ultimately form a coalition that will march against Israel. As we identify these nations by their present names and locate them on today's world map, we can see how the stage is being set for this predicted Russian/Islamic invasion of Israel.

*Gog* is an exception on Ezekiel's list. Gog is not one of the descendants of Noah listed in Genesis 10. This name, however, is found twelve times in Ezekiel 38–39. It is not the name of a nation, but rather the title of a ruler. In fact, the word means "ruler," or "the man on top." It is clear that Gog is an individual rather than a nation because God addresses him as such in this prophecy (Ezekiel 38:14; 39:1). Furthermore, Gog is explicitly called "the prince" in Ezekiel 38:2 and 39:1.

The next name in Ezekiel's prophecy is Magog. In his book, *The Nations in Prophecy,* John F. Walvoord wrote, "Magog is best identified with the Scythians . . . The ancient historian Josephus makes that identification and we have no reason to question it. The Scythians apparently lived immediately to the north of . . . Israel, then some of them emigrated north, going all the way to the Asiatic Circle."[2] Interestingly, Herodotus records that these Scythians were of Indo-Aryan heritage and spoke an Iranian language related to Persian.[3] Using these clues, we can identify Magog today as being made up of nations that were formerly parts of the Soviet Union: Kazakhstan, Kyrgyzstan, Uzbekistan, Turkmenistan, Tajikistan, Azerbaijan, Georgia, and possibly Afghanistan.

The next name on Ezekiel's list is Rosh, which is found in the Old Testament more than six hundred times. During Ezekiel's time, the word *Rosh* identified a nation that included people living north of the Black Sea. In the prophecies of Ezekiel, we are told three times (38:6, 15; 39:2) that part of the force that invades Israel will come from the "distant north," or "the remotest parts of the north." The land that is most distantly north and remote to Israel is Russia.

John F. Walvoord wrote:

> If one takes any map of the world and draws a line north of the land of Israel he will inevitably come to the nation of Russia. As soon as the line is drawn to the far north beyond Asia Minor and the Black Sea it is in Russia and continues to be Russia for many hundreds of miles all the way to the Arctic Circle . . . On the basis of geography alone, it seems quite clear that the only nation which could possibly be referred to as coming from the far north would be the nation of Russia.[4]

When the Soviet Union collapsed in the 1990s, many thought that Russia's days of prominence and power were over. But fewer than two decades later we find a resurgent Russia seeking to reclaim the strategic ground she lost. Someone has said that since the days of the collapse of the Soviet Union, the great Russian bear has been like a mother bear robbed of her cubs.[5] If Magog includes the countries of the collapsed Soviet Union, Rosh specifically identifies the nation of Russia, which is presently trying to reassemble its lost empire.

Edward Lucas, a journalist who has covered Eastern Europe for the *Economist* for more than twenty years, has recently written a frightening book titled *The New Cold War*. He warns that Russia is rising again as a hostile power. It is reasserting its military muscle, intensely pursuing global energy markets, coercing neighboring nations back into the old Soviet orbit, silencing journalists and dissidents, and laying the groundwork with modernized weaponry for reestablishing its former power and influence. The West, wrote Lucas, is asleep to the growing danger and is losing the New Cold War. I would have to agree.

His Web site gives some very insightful examples:

> Russia's vengeful, xenophobic, and ruthless rulers have turned the sick man of Europe into a menacing bully. The rise to power of Vladimir Putin and his ex-KGB colleagues coincided with a tenfold rise in world oil prices. Though its incompetent authoritarian rule is a tragic missed opportunity for the Russian people, Kremlin, Inc. has paid off the state's crippling debts and is restoring its clout at home and abroad. Inside Russia it has crushed every constraint, muzzling the media, brushing aside political opposition, castrating the courts and closing down critical pressure groups.[6]

So successful is Russia's return to the world stage that *Time* magazine chose Russian president Vladimir Putin as its 2007 Person of the Year for "taking Russia from chaos to a position of importance in the world today."[7] Although the Russian leader appears to have quelled chaos within his own country by use of autocratic power, he seems intent on fomenting chaos on the world stage by advancing a new cold war. He "accused the West of encroaching on Russia's borders and starting a new arms race,"[8] and "the United States of trying to impose its will on the world by military force."[9]

Attempting to justify his hostility toward the West, Putin said, "We [Russians] are striving to create a fairer world based on the principles

of equality . . . Time has shown our views find support in Arab and
other Muslim states."[10] In fact, "Russia is determined to further enhance
its relations with Muslim countries . . . We are all allies of the kingdom
in working to meet the world's need for energy."[11]

In October 2007, during Putin's first ever visit to Iran, an Iranian
newspaper reported that he "reassured Iran that the Bushehr nuclear
reactor, a billion-dollar energy project being built by Russia and
dogged by delays, would be completed." The report went on to suggest, "Maybe the most important result of Putin's trip is to show the
independence of Russia toward America and the West."[12] Putin
made other first-time-ever visits of a Russian leader to the Muslim
nations of Saudi Arabia, Qatar, Jordan, United Arab Emirates,
Indonesia, and most currently, Libya. By all reports, his visits were
successful financially, resulting in lucrative agreements and contracts
for further joint efforts in the production of oil and the exploration of
natural gas reserves.

Apparently the Russian president was successful politically as well.
In Libya, President Gadhafi and Putin agreed that the United Nations
"needs to be reformed in order to face an 'imbalance of forces' inter-
nationally," and especially "the Security Council with which we can
work together to resolve problems."[13]

Europe is not blind to what is going on in Russia. European leaders
have taken note of Russia's resurgence with growing alarm and dis-
may. According to a former German foreign minister, "Today, it is the
Kremlin that sets the agenda for EU–Russia relations, and it does so
in a manner that increasingly defies the rules of the game."[14] According
to one source, "Russia appears to be winning the energy dominance
game, signing individual deals with EU member states and moving
forward with . . . pipelines."[15] Among these EU member states are

several of Russia's former cubs. As the mother bear regains her strength, she is actively seeking to draw her brood back into her den.

Meshech and Tubal, the next names on Ezekiel's list, are usually mentioned together when they appear in the Bible. In the past, it has been widely assumed that these were ancient names for the modern cities of Moscow and Tobolsk. But very few scholars today identify Meshech and Tubal as Russian cities. One reason is Ezekiel's assertion that they were trading partners with ancient Tyre: "Javan, Tubal, and Meshech were your traders. They bartered human lives and vessels of bronze for your merchandise" (Ezekiel 27:13). It is highly unlikely that ancient Tyre (modern Lebanon) would be trading with Moscow and the Siberian city of Tobolsk. The more probable identification of Meshech and Tubal is as part of the present nation of Turkey.

The next country Ezekiel names is Persia, a name that appears thirty-five times in the Old Testament. Persia is easy for us to identify because it retained the name it had held since ancient times until March 1935, when it became the nation of Iran. Nearly four and a half decades later, Iran officially changed its name to the Islamic Republic of Iran. Today, with its population of 70 million people, Iran has become the hotbed of militant Islam and anti-Semitic hatred.

Iran's government is officially a theocratic republic whose ultimate political authority resides in the supreme leader, currently Ayatollah Ali Khamenei. This fact surprises many people who assume that the persistently vocal and visible president Mahmoud Ahmadinejad is the top man in Iran. But despite his virulent verbalizing, threats, and saber rattling, Ahmadinejad is only a figurehead under Khamenei. Iran's geographical location on the Persian Gulf and the vital Strait of Hormuz gives her great power. According to CIA reports in 2007, vast oil reserves and the upwardly spiraling price of crude oil gave Iran sixty billion dollars in foreign exchange reserves. Yet her people continue to live with high unemployment and inflation. Iran is identified as a prime player in the human trafficking trade. It is also a "key transshipment point" for heroin into Europe and has the "highest percentage of the populations in the world using opiates."[16] Additionally, the United States has identified Iran as a state sponsor of terrorism.

In a cat-and-mouse game that's been going on since August 2002, world governments have been in a continual on-again, off-again confrontation with Iran over its uranium enrichment capabilities. But world opinion seems to have no more effect on Iran than water on the back of a duck. As a US State Department spokesman recently commented, "the Iranian regime is continuing on a path of defiance of the international community."[17] Despite two rounds of sanctions and the possibility of a third, in February 2008 a defiant Ahmadinejad thumbed his nose at the UN Security Council's demand that Iran suspend uranium enrichment. He said, "With the help of Allah, the Iranian nation with its unity, faith, and determination stood and defeated the world powers and brought them to their knees."[18]

In a surprising reversal, the United States announced in early December 2007 that while Iran did have a secret nuclear weapons program at one time, the program had been abandoned, and Iran was no longer pursuing nuclear capabilities. Perhaps emboldened by the US announcement, in January 2008, five armed Iranian boats menaced three US Navy vessels in the Strait of Hormuz. The tense confrontation prompted a White House warning: "We urge the Iranians to refrain from such provocative actions that could lead to a dangerous incident in the future."[19]

The Iranian regime is well known for its hatred of Israel and its desire to eliminate her. In October 2005, the newly elected president Ahmadinejad declared to the World Without Zionism audience, "As the imam said, Israel must be wiped off the map . . . Anybody who recognizes Israel will burn in the fire of the Islamic nation's fury." He went on to say that any Islamic leader "who recognizes the Zionist regime means he is acknowledging the surrender and defeat of the Islamic world."[20]

Iran's militant influence extends beyond her own borders. In March 2008, Hezbollah chief Hassan Nasrallah railed, "The presence of Israel is but temporary and cannot go on in the region. We will see you killed in the fields, we will kill you in the cities, we will fight you like you have never seen before."[21] Hezbollah leaders do not have the authority to make such threats on their own. Hezbollah is an Islamic fundamentalist group, and though its base of operations is Lebanon, its authority comes from a source higher in the Islamic hierarchy. As Hezbollah's deputy chief, Sheikh Naim Qassem has said, "Even when it comes to firing rockets on Israeli civilians, that decision requires an in-principle permission from [the ruling jurisprudent]."[22] In this case the ruling jurisprudent would be the supreme leader of Iran— Ayatollah Ali Khamenei. "We ask, receive answers, and then apply. This is even true for acts of suicide for the sake of Allah—no one may kill himself without a jurisprudence permission [from Khamenei]."[23] Thus we can see that the aggressive and threatening influence of Iran infects and controls other Islamic terrorist organizations.

In reply to the Iranian-Hezbollah verbal bullying, UN secretary-general Ban Ki-Moon stated, "I am concerned by the threats of open war against Israel by the secretary general of Hezbollah."[24] Such deadly threats and utter disdain for world opinion is pretty convincing evidence that our national leaders are right on target in including Iran as a member of the Axis of Evil.

The next nation Ezekiel lists is Ethiopia. Some Bible translations render this nation as Cush, who is identified as a grandson of Noah, the first of Ham's four sons. "The sons of Ham were Cush, Mizraim, Put, and Canaan" (Genesis 10:6). In the verses that follow, we learn that the descendants of Cush settled in Arabia, Mesopotamia, and Assyria. The Cushites themselves, however, were established in Africa where they occupied a territory much larger than the modern Ethiopia, for the Ethiopia of ancient times included the present-day Sudan. This fact is significant to us, as Sudan is hardly a friend to the West. Sudan supported Iraq in the Gulf War and also harbored Osama bin Laden.

The next nation identified by Ezekiel is Libya. Some Bible translations render this nation as Put, which we find in Genesis 10 to be the name of another grandson of Noah. There is no ambiguity about the present identity of this nation, for ancient maps show that the territory occupied in Ezekiel's time by the nation of Put is now the modern nation of Libya. Since 1969, Libya has been under the dictatorial control of Colonel Mu'ammar al Gadhafi. It is an Islamic nation seething with a great hatred for Israel and, ominously, has recently formed a new alliance with Russia.

Gomer is next on Ezekiel's list. Gomer is mentioned in Genesis 10 as one of Japheth's sons. Genesis 10:3 helps us identify Gomer further by telling us that one of Gomer's relatives is Ashkenaz. Today, Israelis describe Jews from Germany, Austria, and Poland as *Ashkenazim*. This gives us a clue to Gomer's present-day identity, as this term associated with Gomer has likely been passed down through generations, retaining the identify of the people even as the name of the country has changed. Gibbon, in *The Decline and Fall of the Roman Empire,* said, "Gomer is modern Germany."[25] The modern nation identified as the ancient land of Gomer is usually thought to be either Germany or Turkey.

Ezekiel 38:6 refers to Gomer with "all its troops" (NKJV), or "all his bands" (KJV), or "all its hordes" (ASV), indicating that this nation will provide a powerful army in the assault on Israel. If ancient Gomer is part of the modern Turkey, as I believe it to be, it is a country with a growing allegiance to Russia. If we listen to the nightly news, we know that this nation has a strong military presence on the northern border of Iraq—quite possibly the "hordes" that Ezekiel refers to—and is already involved in the conflict over the control of the Middle East.

At the end of his list, Ezekiel added the house of Togarmah or, as it is rendered in some translations, Beth Togarmah (which is the same thing since the word *beth* is the Hebrew word for *house*). Secular historians usually place Beth Togarmah in the geographic location of Phrygia, a western kingdom in Asia Minor. Like Meshech, Tubal, and Gomer, Beth Togarmah was a part of the geographical area we currently call Turkey.

Thus Ezekiel completed his list of specifically identified nations that will come against Israel in the last days. And what a formidable list it is! Yet as if those nations were not enough, Ezekiel added that many more nations will also join the coalition to crush Israel: "many people are with you," he wrote. This is a reference to many smaller countries that have become allied with the more significant nations that Ezekiel specifically identifies. Nearly all of these nations are either Islamic or pro-Islamic. When this formidable mass of armies comes against Israel, there will be no possible human defense for the Israelis.

In a verse that follows this prophecy, Ezekiel spoke of some nations that will not be involved in the invasion of Israel: "Sheba, Dedan, the merchants of Tarshish, and all their young lions will say to you, 'Have you come to take plunder? Have you gathered your army to take booty, to carry away silver and gold, to take away livestock and goods, to take great plunder?'" (v. 13). Most Bible scholars believe that Sheba and Dedan refer to the peoples of the Arabian Peninsula, including modern-day Saudi Arabia, Yemen, Oman, and the Gulf countries of Kuwait and the United Arab Emirates.

Tarshish was a term that in ancient times described the western-most part of human civilization. Many scholars believe that "the merchants of Tarshish" and its "villages" and "young lions" refer to the market-based economies of Western Europe. Some scholars have even dared to be more specific. Dr. David L. Cooper wrote, "When all the historical statements are examined thoroughly, it seems that the evidence is in favor of identifying Tarshish as England."[26] Another scholar, Theodore Epp, agrees with this identification. He points out that the lion is a symbol for Britain and suggests that Britain's colonies, many of which have spun off to become nations of their own, are the cubs, or "young lions" in Ezekiel's prophecy. He said, "Great Britain's young lions, such as Canada, Australia, New Zealand, the African colonies, and the United States are strong enough to make an exhibit of disfavor in that day."[27]

If Theodore Epp and Dr. Cooper are right, it seems that the West in general will not participate in the invasion of Israel. What interests us in this study is that Ezekiel's prophecy of the alignment of nations, showing which ones will and which will not rise to crush Israel, squares very closely with the alignment of nations we see shaping up in the world right now. Thus we find that Ezekiel's ancient prophecy, written some twenty-six hundred years ago, informs us as to what is going on in the world today right before our very eyes.

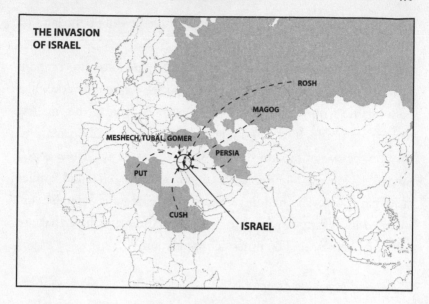

THE INVASION OF ISRAEL

# The Invasion of Israel

## *The Place of the Invasion*

Ezekiel clearly identifies Israel as the land that will be invaded by the nations named on the map above. He stresses this fact at least five times in chapter 38—sometimes obliquely, giving us some characteristic of the people to be invaded, and sometimes explicitly, identifying the land by name: "you will come into the land of those brought back from the sword and gathered from many people on the mountains of Israel, which had long been desolate; they were brought out of the nations, and now all of them dwell safely" (v. 8); "a land of unwalled villages; I will go to a peaceful people, who dwell safely, all of them dwelling without walls, and having neither bars nor gates" (v. 11); "a people gathered from the nations" (v. 12); "'On that day when My people Israel dwell safely'" (v. 14); "'You will come up against my people Israel'" (v. 16). There can be no question about

what nation these amassed armies will invade. It will be the land of
Israel.

When you look at Ezekiel's list of attacking nations and compare
them to the one nation to be invaded, you see a case of overkill like
nothing ever witnessed in world history. Israel is one of the smallest
nations on earth. It is one-nineteenth the size of California and
roughly the size of our third smallest state, New Jersey. Israel is 260
miles at its longest, 60 miles at its widest, and between 3 and 9 miles
at its narrowest. The nation of Israel is a democratic republic surrounded by twenty-two hostile Arab/Islamic dictatorships that are
640 times her size and 60 times her population.[28]

## The Period of the Invasion

Ezekiel does not give a specific date for the invasion, but he does give
us ways to identify the time when it will occur: "'After many days . . . in
the latter years . . .'" (Ezekiel 38: 8); "'On that day when My people Israel
dwell safely . . .'" (v. 14); "'It will be in the latter days that I will bring
you against My land'" (v.16).

The prophet tells us that the invasion of Israel will take place
sometime in the future (latter years). It will happen at a time when
Israel is dwelling in peace and safety and not involved in conflict with
other nations.

Has there ever been such a time in Israel's history? No, there has
not! Is today such a time? No! When will there be such a time? The
only period in Israel's life likely to meet this requirement comes
immediately following the Rapture of the church when the Antichrist
and the European Union make a treaty with Israel to guarantee her
peace and security. When this treaty is signed, the people of Israel will

relax the diligence they have been forced to maintain since the founding of their nation in 1948. They will rely on the treaty and turn their attention away from defense to concentrate on increasing their wealth. Israel will truly be a land of unwalled villages. Her defenses will be down, and she will be woefully unprepared for the invasion by the armies of Russia and the coalition.

## The Purpose of the Invasion

The nations in the battle of Gog and Magog will come down on the nation of Israel, pursuing three primary goals. The first goal will be to seize her land. As Ezekiel puts it, "to stretch out your hand against the waste places which are again inhabited" (Ezekiel 38:12). The second goal of the invaders will be to steal Israel's wealth: "To take plunder and to take booty, to stretch out your hand . . . against a people gathered from the nations, who have acquired livestock and goods, who dwell in the midst of the land . . . to carry away silver and gold, to take away livestock and goods, to take great plunder" (vv. 12–13).

And there is plenty of wealth to be plundered in modern Israel, as we can see by the following quote from a recent article in the *Jerusalem Post*: "Despite a population of only slightly more than 7 million people . . . Israel is now home to more than 7,200 millionaires . . . Of the 500 wealthiest people in the world, six are now Israeli, and all told, Israel's rich had assets in 2007 of more than 35 billion dollars . . . Israel's GDP is almost double that of any other Middle East country."[29]

Success and wealth in the high-tech industry has replaced earlier agricultural kibbutzim and started her on "the extraordinary road . . . from the socialist experiment of defiant European Jews to the high-tech revolution that has created a Silicon Valley in the Middle East, second only to the United States in start-ups.[30] In 2007, venture capitalists invested 1.76 billion dollars in start-up companies in developing "advanced telecom equipment" in Israel's "Silicon Wadi."[31]

According to one prosperity index, Israel exported goods and services of more than $70 billion last year, including $34.2 billion from the technology sector alone. "Israel is the highest-ranking Middle Eastern country in the index."[32] In 2007, she had a per capita gross domestic product index of $28,800, which compared favorably with the much larger European Union at $32,900.[33] Any way you measure it, Israel has become prosperous, and despite a recent recession and military conflict, her economy has continued to grow.

Finally, the invading nations have as their ultimate goal the wholesale slaughter of Israel's people: "I will go to a peaceful people, who dwell safely, all of them dwelling without walls, and having neither bars nor gates . . . to stretch out your hand . . . against a people gathered from the nations . . . You will come up against My people Israel like a cloud, to cover the land" (vv. 11–12, 16). The historical accumulated hatred for the Jews will drive these armies forward with the assurance that this time, the people of Israel will not escape death.

## The Particulars of the Invasion

"You will ascend, coming like a storm, covering the land like a cloud, you and all your troops and many peoples with you . . . Then you will come from your place out of the far north, you and many peoples with you, all of them riding on horses, a great company and a mighty army. You will come up against My people Israel like a cloud, to cover the land." (Ezekiel 38:9, 15–16)

In these passages Ezekiel tells us that the coalition of massive armies will gather from all the attacking nations and assemble on the mountains of Israel. One writer helps us understand the strategy of invading from these mountains:

> The mountains of Israel are mainly located on the country's northern borders with modern-day Syria, Lebanon, and northern Jordan (notably the strategically important Golan Heights). Since the Russian-Iranian coalition is described by the prophet as coming primarily from the north, it is reasonable to conclude that Syria and Lebanon are participants in the coalition. Jordan maybe as well, though this is not entirely clear.[34]

Now that we have set the stage for the invasion of the assembled armies against Israel by identifying the place, the timing, the purpose, and some of the particulars, let's look next at what will happen when this invasion actually begins.

## The Intervention of God

When the massive Russian-Islamic armies assemble on the northern mountains of Israel, ready to come against that tiny country, it will appear to be the most grossly mismatched contest in military history. The Israelis will be so outnumbered that there will be no human way they can win this war. Only intervention by God himself could possibly save them. And that is exactly what will happen. As Ezekiel tells us: "'And it will come to pass at the same time, when Gog comes against the land of Israel,' says the Lord GOD, 'that My fury will show in My face. For in My jealousy, and in the fire of My wrath I have spoken'" (Ezekiel 38:18–19a).

How will God accomplish this miraculous feat? What will be the results of His intervention? These are questions we can answer by continuing to explore Ezekiel's prophecy, and the answers will enable us to understand how today's events will play out to fulfill God's purposes in the near future.

## The Arsenal of Weapons

When God goes to war, He uses weapons unique to Him— weapons that render the arsenals of men as ineffective as a water pistol against a nuclear bomb. God will save His people Israel by employing four of these weapons simultaneously. First, he will rout the armies of Israel's attackers with massive convulsions in the earth. As Ezekiel explains:

> "For in My jealousy and in the fire of My wrath I have spoken: 'Surely in that day there shall be a great earthquake in the land of Israel, so that the fish of the sea, the birds of the heavens, the beasts of the field, all creeping things that creep on the earth, and all men who are on the face of the earth shall shake at My presence. The mountains shall be thrown down, the steep places shall fall, and every wall shall fall to the ground.'" (38:19–20)

God will follow these convulsions of the earth with His second weapon, which will be to create such confusion among the attacking troops that they will panic and begin killing one another: "'I will call for a sword against Gog throughout all My mountains,' says the Lord GOD. 'Every man's sword shall be against his brother'" (Ezekiel 38:21).

In the seventh and eighth chapters of Judges, we see a similar event reported. We are told that 135,000 Midianites had gathered against Israel. Gideon and his little band of three hundred men, under the direction of God and through the power of God, threw the enemy into total confusion, and the Lord set every man's sword against his brother. As a result, 120,000 Midianite soldiers died, largely by what today we would call "friendly fire."

In Ezekiel we can see how God's first two weapons work together in a one-two punch. A sudden earthquake in the mountains of Israel would certainly panic an army. With the ground moving like sea waves, the upheaval of the earth generating dense clouds of dust, it would be impossible for warriors to distinguish an enemy from an ally, and in their blind terror they would kill anything that moved.

The third divine weapon will be the contagion of disease: "And I will bring him to judgment with pestilence and bloodshed," asserts the Lord (38:22a). He will infect the invading troops with some debilitating disease that will render them incapable of carrying out an effective attack. God will follow this contagion with his fourth and final weapon: calamities from the sky. "I will rain down on him, on his troops, and on the many peoples who are with him, flooding rain, great hailstones, fire, and brimstone" (v. 22b).

We find the prototype for this strategy in God's judgment upon Sodom and Gomorrah, where the two decadent cities were forever buried under the briny waters of the Dead Sea by a storm of fire and brimstone. One man has written: "Every force of nature is a servant of the Living God, and in a moment can be made a soldier, armed to the teeth. Men are slowly discovering that God's forces stored in nature are mightier than the brawn of the human arm."[35] When God goes to war, no army on earth can stand against His formidable arsenal. The armies that come against Israel in the last days will learn that truth the hard way.

## The Aftermath of War

First, there will be a feast. There is strong irony in using the term *feast* for what will happen immediately following the destruction of Israel's enemies. It will not be a feast of victory for the rescued Israelis; it will be a feast for vultures and predators feeding on the incredible masses of bodies strewn across the battlefield. Here is how Ezekiel described the grisly banquet:

> "You shall fall upon the mountains of Israel, you and all of your troops and the peoples who are with you; I will give you to birds of prey of every sort and to the beasts of the field to be devoured. You shall fall on the open field; for I have spoken," says the Lord GOD . . . "And as for you, son of man, thus says the Lord GOD, 'Speak to every sort of bird and to every beast of the field:

> "Assemble yourselves and come;
> Gather together from all sides to My sacrificial meal
> Which I am sacrificing for you,
> A great sacrificial meal on the mountains of Israel,
> That you may eat flesh and drink blood.
> You shall eat the flesh of the mighty,
> Drink the blood of the princes of earth,
> Of rams and lambs,
> Of goats and bulls,
> All of them fatlings of Bashan.
> You shall eat fat till you are full,

And drink blood till you are drunk,

At My sacrificial meal

Which I am sacrificing for you.

You shall be filled at My table

With horses and riders,

With mighty men

And with all the men of war,'" says the Lord GOD. (Ezekiel 39:4–5,
   17–20)

This chilling prophecy uses the language of a feast—what God calls His "sacrificial feast"—to show how the intervention of God will result in a gruesome spectacle of uncountable bodies littering the landscape like debris from a tornado, creating a bountiful banquet for His guests, the birds of the air and the beasts of the field.

The second event that will occur after the destruction of Israel's enemies is a great funeral. Ezekiel described it:

It will come to pass in that day that I will give Gog a burial place there in Israel, the valley of those who pass by east of the sea; and it will obstruct travelers, because there they will bury Gog and all his multitude. Therefore they will call it the valley of Hamon Gog. For seven months the house of Israel will be burying them, in order to cleanse the land . . . They will set apart men regularly employed, with the help of a search party, to pass through the land and bury those bodies remaining on the ground, in order to cleanse it. At the end of seven months they will make a search. The search party will pass through the land; and when anyone sees a man's bone, he shall set up a marker by it, till the buriers have buried it in the Valley of Hamon Gog. (Ezekiel 39:11–12, 14–16)

Here Ezekiel painted another chilling and macabre picture of the horrendous death and destruction inflicted on Israel's invaders. This war will produce so many casualties that it will take seven months to bury all the bodies. In fact, the task will be so enormous that a special detachment of soldiers will be assigned to carry it out. According to the Old Testament, an unburied corpse is a reproach to God and causes a land to be defiled (Deuteronomy 21:23). Thus the Israelis will feel compelled to clean up the bloody battlefield and bury all the dead.

The third aftermath of the war against Israel will be a great and long-burning fire. Here's how Ezekiel explained the fire and its purpose:

> "Then those who dwell in the cities of Israel will go out and set on fire and burn the weapons, both the shields and bucklers, the bows and arrows, the javelins and spears; and they will make fires with them for seven years . . . They will not take wood from the field nor cut down any from the forests, because they will make fires with the weapons; and they will plunder those who plundered them, and pillage those who pillaged them," says the Lord God. (Ezekiel 39:9–10)

This passage indicates that the arsenal of weaponry and military equipment brought against Israel by the coalition of nations will be utterly staggering. While it will take seven months to bury the bodies, which is astonishing enough, it will take *seven years* to burn the weapons.

Some readers of Ezekiel are troubled that the prophet described these as weapons of ancient origin, whereas a battle that is yet to occur in the future will surely employ modern weaponry and highly sophisticated military equipment—guns, tanks, planes, bombs, missiles, and possibly even nuclear weapons. But we must allow common sense to prevail in our reading of Ezekiel. He did what all prophets have done: he spoke of the future using terms and descriptions that he and the people of his day would understand. If he had written of tanks and missiles and bombs, those living in his time would have been utterly mystified, and his message would have had no meaning to them.

The burial of the bodies and the burning of the weapons comprise what Ezekiel calls the "cleansing of the land" from the defilement of death and destruction wrought upon it by the enemies of God's people. These massive cleanup operations in the aftermath of the war give us an eye-opening picture of the enormity of the destruction predicted in Ezekiel's end-time prophecy. As we try to comprehend these cataclysmic events, we can only shake our heads in wonder and ask, "What in the world is going on?" I believe Ezekiel helps us to answer that question as we look further into his prophecy.

## The Sovereignty of God's Plan

### The Inevitable Accomplishment of God's Purpose

To understand what is going on in the war and destruction described in Ezekiel's prophecy, we must first consider the sovereignty of God's plan. Throughout this book we have observed that even in the most devastating of times, God is still in control. In fact, He often orchestrates events to bring about His purposes. He tells us what He will do to Israel's enemies in no uncertain terms: "I will turn you around, put hooks into your jaws, and lead you out, with all your army, horses, and horsemen" (Ezekiel 38:4); "It will be in the latter days that I will bring you against My land" (v. 16); "and I will turn you around and lead you on, bringing you up from the far north, and bring you against the mountains of Israel" (39:2).

Passages such as these confuse many people because of the seeming implication that God leads men to be evil or to do evil things. But the Bible never says that God instills evil in the hearts of men. Some would attempt to refute this claim by pointing out that during the Exodus, the Bible explicitly says that God hardened Pharaoh's heart. It does say that, of course, but the statement speaks about the nature of Pharaoh's heart, not about God overriding man's free will. Some hearts are like clay; the sun's heat will harden them. Others are like wax; the sun will cause them to melt. It's not the sun's fault that it hardens one substance and melts the other; it all depends on the nature of the material. Pharaoh's heart was the sort that would harden when exposed to God's light. It had nothing to do with God coercing him to do evil.

The Old Testament, especially, is intended to show that God is the sovereign ruler over all. Even though men try to thwart His plan and wreak great destruction, God's purpose will always win out. When Ezekiel wrote that God will bring the enemy against His land, he was simply saying that God will bring these nations to the doom that their wickedness inevitably demands. Everyone accomplishes God's will in the end. Those who conform to His will accomplish it willingly; those who do not conform accomplish it inadvertently as an unwitting tool in His hands.

## The Simplicity of God's Purpose

Secondly, let's look at the simplicity of God's purpose. As you read the following verses from Ezekiel's prophecy, you will have no difficulty picking out the defining purpose clauses:

I will bring you against My land, so that the nations may know Me, when I am hallowed in you, O Gog, before their eyes. (38:16)

Thus I will magnify Myself and sanctify Myself, and I will be known in the eyes of many nations. Then they shall know that I am the LORD. (38:23)

Then they shall know that I am the LORD. (39:6)

So I will make My holy name known in the midst of My people Israel, and I will not let them profane My holy name anymore. Then the nations shall know that I am the LORD. (39:7)

I will set My glory among the nations; all the nations shall see My judgment which I have executed, and My hand which I have laid on them. So the house of Israel shall know that I am the LORD their God from that day forward. (39:21–22)

It doesn't take a rocket scientist to figure out God's purpose in the cataclysmic battle of the last days. It is very clear and very simple. God intends for people to recognize Him as the Lord God of heaven, whose name is holy, whose glory fills the universe, and whom men must recognize as sovereign if they are to find the peace and joy He desires for His people.

## The Salvation of God's People

Finally, note the sovereignty of God's plan in rescuing His people. Ezekiel tells us that the ultimate outcome of the battle of Gog and Magog will be the salvation of the Jewish people:

Therefore thus says the Lord GOD: "Now I will bring back the cap-tives of Jacob, and have mercy on the whole house of Israel; and I will be jealous for My holy name—after they have borne their shame, and all their unfaithfulness in which they were unfaithful to Me, when they dwelt safely in their own land, and no one made them afraid. When I have brought them back from the peoples and gath-ered them out of their enemies' lands, and I am hallowed in them in the sight of many nations, then they shall know that I am the LORD their God, who sent them into captivity among the nations, but also brought them back to their land, and left none of them captive any longer. And I will not hide My face from them anymore; for I shall have poured out My Spirit on the house of Israel," says the Lord GOD. (39:25–29)

Thus Ezekiel ends his monumental prophecy on a high note, extol-ling God's tender love and compassion toward His people. No matter how great the evil in men's hearts, no matter how much destruction and death that evil brings about, God's ultimate purpose in confront-ing that evil, in revealing His glory among the nations, and in bringing His own from the lands of the enemy is always to accomplish the salvation of His people.

As Ezekiel shows us so vividly, God's destruction of the Axis of Evil in the last days will accomplish the salvation of his people, the nation of Israel. By identifying this Axis of Evil as modern nations who are unwittingly bent on fulfilling this devastating prophecy, we have answered another question about what is going on in the world today. We have shown how present events will lead to the ultimate accom-plishment of God's purposes.

As I close this chapter, I think it is important to point out that there is, in a sense, the potential for an axis of evil within the heart of every one of us. As the apostle Paul tells us, each of us has in our heart that "sinful nature" we inherited from Adam—a propensity for selfish evil that, if not controlled by the presence of God's Spirit, can run rampant and produce destruction in our own lives and in the lives of those about us.

But thanks be to God, His salvation is not for Israel only. All men and women today can choose to be among God's people. You don't have to be a Jew to receive salvation, nor does being a Russian or an Iranian force one to be a part of the Axis of Evil. God in His infinite love pours out His Spirit on all who believe and turn to Him. With that wonderful transaction, and as His Spirit is poured out on the redeemed, the axis of evil in our hearts is transformed by God's love.

I will conclude this chapter by passing on to you a fine and touching example of this principle, which I recently found in a true incident reported by Robert Morgan:

Daniel Christiansen tells about a relative, a Romanian soldier in World War II, named Ana Gheorghe. It was 1941, and troops had overrun the Romanian region of Bessarabia and entered Moldavia. Ana and his comrades were badly frightened. Bullets whizzed around them, and mortar shells shook the earth. By day, Ana sought relief reading his Bible, but at night he could only crouch close to the earth and recall verses memorized in childhood.

One day during a spray of enemy fire, Ana was separated from his company. In a panic, he bolted deeper and deeper into the woods until, huddling at the base of a large tree, he fell asleep from exhaustion. The next day, trying to find his comrades, he moved cautiously toward the front, staying in the shadows of the trees, nibbling a crust of bread, drinking from streams. Hearing the battle closing in, he unslung his rifle, pulled the bolt, and watched for the enemy, his nerves near the breaking point. Twenty yards away, a Russian soldier suddenly appeared.

*All my mental rehearsals of bravery served me nothing. I dropped my gun and fell to my knees, then buried my face in my sweating palms and began to pray. While praying, I waited for the cold touch of the Russian's rifle barrel against my head.*

*I felt a slight pressure on my shoulder close to my neck. I opened my eyes slowly. There was my enemy kneeling in front of me, his gun lying next to mine among the wildflowers. His eyes were closed in prayer. We did not understand a single word of the other's language, but we could pray. We ended our prayer with two words that need no translation: "Alleluia . . . Amen!"*

*Then, after a tearful embrace, we walked quickly to opposite sides of the clearing and disappeared beneath the trees.*[36]

# NINE

# Arming for Armageddon

GENERAL DOUGLAS MACARTHUR STOOD TALL ON THE DECK OF the USS *Missouri* in Tokyo harbor. It was September 2, 1945, and this man who had engineered America's hard-fought victory in the Pacific had just witnessed the signatures of Japan's leaders ending the bloody global struggle known as World War II. On that day, this authentic American hero uttered a profound warning, which he later repeated in his famous farewell address before the United States Congress: "We have had our last chance," he said. "If we do not now devise some greater and more equitable system, Armageddon will be at our door."[1]

Shortly after he was inaugurated as the fortieth president of the United States, Ronald Reagan was astounded by the complexities of the Middle East. Israel, on its thin strip of land, was surrounded by well-armed Arab enemies who were splintered like broken glass into countless factions and divisions impossible to reconcile. On Friday, May 15, 1981, scribbling in his diary, Reagan noted the intractable problems involving Lebanon, Syria, Saudi Arabia, the Soviet Union, and Israel. "Sometimes I wonder," he wrote, "if we are destined to witness Armageddon."

Only three weeks later, on Sunday, June 7, he received news that Israel had bombed the Iraqi nuclear reactor. That afternoon, Reagan wrote in his diary: "Got word of Israel bombing of Iraq—nuclear reactor. I swear I believe Armageddon is near."[2]

*Armageddon.* The very word chills the soul. Probably there are few adults who are not familiar with that word and what it implies. Why have our national leaders, in the twentieth and twenty-first centuries, begun to use that doomsday word in their speaking and writing? I believe it is because they can see how modern weaponry and international tensions are showing how quickly global equilibrium could get out of control, leading to a cataclysmic war such as the world has never seen before.

Our nation is no stranger to war. According to the US Army Military Institute, the United States has been involved in twenty-nine wars or military conflicts. This averages out to one war for every eight years of America's history. This number includes not only the major conflicts, but also lesser-known engagements, such as the Seminole wars, America's involvement in the Boxer rebellion, and the invasion of Panama. Approximately 1,314,971 troops have died for their country in these wars. This includes 25,000 who died in the War of Independence; 623,026 in the Civil War; more than 400,000 in World War II; more than 58,000 in Vietnam; and nearly 4,000 in the current conflicts in Iraq and Afghanistan. (That number has increased to more than 4,000 since the report was published.)[3]

The Bible tells us that there is yet another war to be fought on this earth. This war, called Armageddon, makes all the wars America has fought to date look like minor skirmishes. This war will draw the final curtain on modern civilization. In this chapter we will lift the biblical veil to show what is going on in the world that will lead to Armageddon. In fact, preparations for that war are underway right now throughout the world. The only thing holding back its rapid approach is the yet-to-occur disappearance of all true believers in Jesus Christ, the event we know as the Rapture of the church.

## The Preparation for the Battle of Armageddon

In the twelfth chapter of Revelation, the apostle John revealed how this conflagration will come about. "So the great dragon was cast out, that serpent of old, called the Devil and Satan, who deceives the whole world; he was cast to the earth, and his angels were cast out with him . . . Now when the dragon saw that he had been cast to the earth, he persecuted the woman who gave birth to the male Child" (vv. 9, 13).

These verses tell us that during the Tribulation, when Satan is cast out of heaven to the earth, he will begin immediately to persecute the woman who brought forth the male child. The "woman" is an obvious metaphor for Israel, through whom the child Jesus was born. Satan's first attempt at persecution will be the battle of Gog and Magog. As we learned in the previous chapter, this battle, which precedes the Battle of Armageddon, will be a massive, Russian-led coalition of nations coming against Israel like swarms of hornets against a defenseless child. As Revelation tells us, Satan will be the motivating force behind this invasion. But before he accomplishes his intended annihilation of Israel, she will be rescued by Almighty God.

The thwarting of the battle of Gog and Magog will be a setback to Satan, but he will not give up; he is relentless in his persecution of the

Jews. His purpose, beginning in the middle of the Tribulation period, is to destroy the Jewish people before Christ can set up His kingdom, thus wrecking God's prophesied rule over the earth. According to Revelation 16, Satan will employ two fearful personalities in these plans: "And I saw three unclean spirits like frogs coming out of the mouth of the dragon, out of the mouth of the *beast*, and out of the mouth of the *false prophet*" (v. 13, *emphasis added*).

Here John tells us that Satan will empower the beast, who is the head of the reestablished Roman Empire, and the false prophet, the head of the new world religious system. Thus Satan (the dragon), the Beast (the Antichrist), and the false prophet become the unholy trinity committed to the destruction of Israel. When the church of Jesus Christ is taken safely into heaven and the Tribulation period begins, the unrestrained satanic persecution of Israel will propel the entire world toward the Battle of Armageddon.

## The Place of the Battle of Armageddon

"And they gathered them together to the place called in Hebrew, Armageddon" (Revelation 16:16).

As we noted previously, the word *Armageddon* is much bandied about these days. It has become a synonym for every kind of dooms-day scenario. We hear talk of an impending *financial* Armageddon, an *ecological* Armageddon, an *environmental* Armageddon, and a *nuclear* Armageddon for which physicist Stephen Hawking tells us we should prepare by relocating ourselves "somewhere else in another solar system."[4] Obviously the popular imagination has captured the essence of the type of event that will occur at Armageddon, but people have missed the inherent meaning of the word by a country mile. Armageddon is not actually a battle; it is a place.

Given the enormous attention this word receives, it may surprise you that *Armageddon* is mentioned only once in the Bible—right here in the sixteenth chapter of Revelation. The Hebrew word *harmageddon* means "the mount of Megiddo." *Har* means mount, and *megiddo* means slaughter; so the meaning of *Armageddon* is "Mount of Slaughter." The mountain of Megiddo is an actual geographical feature located in northern Israel. It includes an extended plain that reaches from the Mediterranean Sea to the northern part of the land of Israel. Megiddo is about eighteen miles southeast of Haifa, fifty-five miles north of Jerusalem, and a little more than ten miles from Nazareth, the town where Jesus grew up.

While the word *Armageddon* is mentioned only once in the Bible, the mountain of Megiddo has a rich biblical history. It was at Megiddo that Deborah and Barak defeated the Canaanites (Judges 4–5). It was also there that: Gideon defeated the Midianites (Judges 7); Saul was slain during a war with the Philistines (1 Samuel 31); Ahaziah was slain by Jehu (2 Kings 9); and Josiah was slain by the invading Egyptians (2 Kings 23).

These are not by any means the only battles that have been fought on this bloody ground. Last year I stood at the top of Megiddo, overlooking the plain of Armageddon. If I could have watched past centuries fast-forward before my eyes, I would have seen a long succession of waged battles as great armies marched across the field one after the other—the Crusaders, the Egyptians, the Persians, the Druze, the Greeks, the Turks, and the Arabs. During World War I, British general Edmund Allenby led his army against the Turks in a fierce battle on the plain of Armageddon. According to scholar Alan Johnson, "More than 200 battles have been fought at or near there."[5] As you can see, Megiddo has earned its awful name: it is indeed a Mount of Slaughter.

Why Megiddo? Why will this be the location of the world's final conflict? One of the world's greatest military figures gives us the answer. In 1799, Napoleon stood at Megiddo before the battle that ended his quest to conquer the East and rebuild the Roman Empire. Considering the enormous plain of Armageddon, he declared: "All the armies of the world could maneuver their forces on this vast plain . . . There is no place in the whole world more suited for war than this . . . [It is] the most natural battleground on the whole earth."[6]

While it is no mystery why the earth's final battle will be fought at Armageddon, it is important to understand that the battle will be centralized on that field but not contained there. All the ancient prophets agree that this war will be fought throughout the entire land of Israel. In the book he edited on Armageddon, A. Sims wrote:

It appears from Scripture that this last great battle of that great day of God Almighty will reach far beyond Armageddon, or the Valley of Megiddo. Armageddon appears to be mainly the place where the troops will gather together from the four corners of the earth, and from Armageddon the Battle will spread out over the entire [country of Israel]. Joel speaks of the last battle being fought in the Valley of Jehoshaphat, which is close by Jerusalem and Isaiah shows Christ coming with blood-stained garments "from Edom," [present day Jordan]. So the battle of Armageddon, it seems, will stretch from the Valley of Megiddo in the north . . . through the Valley of Jehoshaphat, near Jerusalem, [and down to Jordan, south of Israel]. And to this agree the words of the prophet Ezekiel that the armies of this great battle will "cover the land" . . . But Jerusalem will no doubt be the center of interest during the battle of Armageddon, for God's Word says: "I will gather all nations against Jerusalem to battle."[7]

The words of the prophet Zechariah support Sims's view of Jerusalem as the center of conflict in the Armageddon war. "Behold, I will make Jerusalem a cup of drunkenness to all the surrounding peoples, when they lay siege against Judah and Jerusalem. And it shall happen in that day that I will make Jerusalem a very heavy stone for all peoples; all who would heave it away will surely be cut in pieces, though all nations of the earth are gathered against it" (Zechariah 12:2–3). So while we use the term *Armageddon* and localize the war to the plain of Megiddo, Scripture teaches that the battle will literally fill the whole land of Israel with war and bloodshed.

This war will be so horrific that the Bible says blood will flow in staggering torrents. "And the winepress was trampled outside the city, and blood came out of the winepress, up to the horses' bridles, for one thousand six hundred furlongs" (Revelation 14:20). If you translate these ancient measurements into the terminology of today, sixteen hundred furlongs is almost exactly two hundred miles—the distance from the northern to the southern tip of the land of Israel.

While that image may be hard for us to visualize, it is not unknown in human experience. Ancient historians Plutarch and Herodotus describe similar scenes during vicious battles of their days. Of the siege of Athens in 405–404 BC, Plutarch wrote:

About midnight Sylla entered the breach, with all terrors of trumpets and coronets sounding, with the triumphant shout and cry of an army let loose to spoil and slaughter, and scouring through the streets with sword drawn. There was no numbering the slain; the amount is to this day conjectured only from the space of ground overflowed with blood. For without mentioning the execution done in the other quarters of the city, the blood that was shed about the marketplace

spread over the whole [public square] . . . and passed through the gate
and overflowed the suburb.[8]

Similarly, writing of the fall of Jerusalem to the Roman hordes in
AD 70, Josephus wrote:

When they [Romans] went in numbers into the lanes of the city, with
their swords drawn, they slew those whom they overtook, without
mercy, and set fire to the houses wither the Jews fled . . . they ran every
one through whom they met with, and obstructed the very lanes with
their dead bodies, and made the whole city run down with blood, to
such a degree indeed that the fire of many of the houses was quenched
with these men's blood.[9]

We would actually be more accurate to refer to this conflict as the
"*Campaign* of Armageddon." The word translated as *battle* in Revelation
16:14 is the Greek word *polemos,* which signifies a war or campaign.
Armageddon will involve many battles fought throughout the entire
land of Israel over a three-and-one-half-year period of time.

## The Purpose of the Battle of Armageddon

Our sensibilities revolt when we read of the carnage the Bible pictures
when describing the Battle of Armageddon. And the horrible scene
raises all kinds of questions that many people find difficult to answer.
We wonder what is going on, not only in the world but also in the
mind of God. What is the purpose of this war in the plan of God?
Let's address these questions in order to show God's purpose, plan,
and intent in allowing the Battle of Armageddon to occur. Just what
are His purposes?

## To Finish His Judgment upon Israel

The Tribulation period is a time of divine indignation against the people of Israel, the people who rejected their Messiah and—time and time again after given the chance to return—failed to heed the corrective and punitive judgment of God. It is no accident that this future period of time is often referred to as "the time of Jacob's trouble" (Jeremiah 30:7).

## To Finalize His Judgment upon the Nations that Have Persecuted Israel

Those nations that have persecuted the Jewish people are finally gathered together in the Battle of Armageddon, in the Valley of Jehoshaphat, giving God the perfect opportunity to deal with them finally and decisively.

> I will also gather all nations,
> And bring them down to the Valley of Jehoshaphat;
> And I will enter into judgment with them there
> On account of My people, My heritage Israel,
> Whom they have scattered among the nations;
> They have also divided up My land. (Joel 3:2)

## To Formally Judge All the Nations that Have Rejected Him

"Now out of His mouth goes a sharp sword, that with it He should strike the nations. And He Himself will rule them with a rod of iron. He Himself treads the winepress of the fierceness and wrath of Almighty God" (Revelation 19:15).

This verse gives us another of God's purposes in bringing about Armageddon. Notice particularly that last phrase: "He Himself treads the winepress of the fierceness and wrath of Almighty God." To our time-bound senses, God's activity often seems so slow and ponderous that people pursuing ungodly goals tend to dismiss His judgment as a factor to be taken seriously. Thus the nations do not believe that a time is coming when God's judgment will inevitably descend. But be assured, He is storing up judgment against a day to come. The Bible is clear: one of these days God will have had enough, and His judgment will pour down like consuming fire against the world's wicked nations. "And men were scorched with great heat, and they blasphemed the name of God who has power over these plagues; and they did not repent and give Him glory" (Revelation 16:9).

This verse tells us just how incredibly wicked the nations will have become when God's judgment descends. Even when these men are writhing and screaming with the excruciating pain God inflicts upon them, they will continue to curse Him to His face. They will be so far gone, so given over to evil, that in their prideful defiance they will refuse to repent, even in the grip of fatal judgment.

## The Particularities of the Battle of Armageddon

Just to be sure there is no confusion about the wars in the Tribulation period, I want to make it clear that we have identified two separate battles. In the previous chapter we learned about the first battle, the one that will occur at the beginning of the Tribulation period when Gog (Russia) assembles a mass of nations against Israel that are thwarted by God's intervention. In this chapter we are learning about a second battle, one that will end the Tribulation period. It is easy to confuse the two, but the Bible presents them as two distinct events. The battle of Gog and the Battle of Armageddon are separated by several years and involve different participants. Here are some of the differences that will help us keep the two battles separate in our minds:

- In the battle of Gog, Russia and at least five other nations are involved (Ezekiel 38:2–6). In the Battle of Armageddon, all the nations of the world are involved (Joel 3:2; Zechariah 14:2).

- In the battle of Gog, the invaders will attack from the north (Ezekiel 38:6, 15; 39:2). In the Battle of Armageddon, the armies come from the north, south, east, and west (Daniel 11:40–45; Zechariah 14:2; Revelation 16:12–16).

- In the battle of Gog, the purpose of the armies is to "take a spoil, and to take a prey" (Ezekiel 38:12 KJV). In the Battle of Armageddon, the purpose is to annihilate the Jews and to fight Christ and His army (Zechariah 12:2–3, 9; 14:2; Revelation 19:19).

- In the battle of Gog, Russia will be the leader of the nations (Ezekiel 38:13). In the Battle of Armageddon, the Antichrist will be the leader (Revelation 19:19).

- In the battle of Gog, God defeats the northern invaders with the convulsions of the earth, the confusion of the troops, the contagion of diseases, and calamities from the sky. In the Battle of Armageddon, the armies are defeated by the word of Christ—"a sharp sword" (Revelation 19:15; see also verse 21 NKJV).

- In the battle of Gog, Israel's enemies will perish upon the mountains of Israel and in the open field (Ezekiel 39:4–5). In the Battle of Armageddon, those slain by the Lord will

lie where they fall, from one end of the earth to the other
(Jeremiah 25:33).

- In the battle of Gog, the dead will be buried (Ezekiel
  39:12–15). In the Battle of Armageddon, the dead will not
  be buried, but their carcasses will be totally consumed by
  the birds (Jeremiah 25:33; Revelation 19:17–18, 21).

- After the battle of Gog, war will continue among the
  nations involved (other than Israel) during the remainder
  of the Tribulation (Revelation 13:4–7). After the Battle of
  Armageddon, swords and spears will be beaten into
  plowshares and pruning hooks (Isaiah 2:4) and the nations
  will study war no more.[10]

## The Participants in the Battle of Armageddon

As we have noted, all the nations of the world will be involved in the
Battle of Armageddon, and they will be led by the Antichrist. But
the Bible gives us many more details about the motives and actions of
the participants in this battle. These are worth exploring, as they provide insights into the nature of the war and why it will be fought.

### The Deal Between Israel and Antichrist

Referring specifically to the Antichrist, Daniel tells us that "he shall
confirm a covenant with many for one week" (Daniel 9:27a). In prophetic language, this means a week of years, so the covenant will be
made for seven years. Until recently I thought Israel would simply be
duped into thinking this peace treaty would be a lasting agreement,
because I couldn't imagine any national leader taking seriously a peace

treaty that was openly proposed for a prescribed period of time. Until, that is, maverick peace broker and former president Jimmy Carter and the leadership of Hamas recently proposed a peace treaty, a *hudna*, to Israel with a ten-year time limit.[11] Apparently in the last days, Israel will be so wearied of continual threats of war that they will think any treaty, even one that gives them a short space of breathing room, will be better than no peace at all.

The Antichrist, who will at this time be the head of the European Union, will sign such a covenant with Israel, guaranteeing peace and security for seven years. Israel will view this man not as the evil Antichrist but as a beneficent and charismatic leader.

## The Worship of the Antichrist

On the heels of the covenant with Israel, this self-appointed world ruler will begin to strengthen his power by performing amazing signs and wonders, including even a supposed resurrection from the dead (Revelation 13:3). Then with his grip on the world greatly enhanced, he will boldly take the next step in his arrogant defiance of God: "Then the king shall do according to his own will: he shall exalt and magnify himself above every god, shall speak blasphemies against the God of gods" (Daniel 11:36).

Daniel goes on to give us a further description of the Antichrist's insidious methods:

> He shall regard neither the God of his fathers nor the desire of women, nor regard any god; for he shall exalt himself above them all. But in their place he shall honor a god of fortresses, and a god which his fathers did not know he shall honor with gold and silver, with precious stones and pleasant things. Thus he shall act against the

strongest fortresses with a foreign god, which he shall acknowledge, and advance its glory; and he shall cause them to rule over many, and divide the land for gain. (Daniel 11:37–39)

The Antichrist will be the epitome of the man with a compulsion to extend his dominion over everything and everyone. To achieve this end, the Antichrist will bow to no god but the "god of fortresses." That is, he will build enormous military might and engage in extensive warfare to extend his power throughout the world.

Daniel then describes how the swollen megalomania of the Antichrist will drive him to take his next step in Daniel 11:36, quoted earlier. John expanded on Daniel's description of the Antichrist's blasphemous acts by telling us that every living person will be required to worship this man. "He was granted power to give breath to the image of the beast, that the image of the beast should both speak and cause as many as would not worship the image of the beast to be killed" (Revelation 13:15). Step by step, the Antichrist will promote himself from a European leader, to a world leader, to a tyrannical global dictator, and finally to a god.

## The Decision to Fight Against the Antichrist

The Antichrist's grip on global power will not last long. The world will become increasingly discontented with the leadership of this global dictator, who has gone back on every promise he made. Major segments of the world will begin to assemble their own military forces and rebel against him.

The king of the south and his armies will be the first to come after the Antichrist, followed by the armies of the north. "At the time of the end the king of the South shall attack him; and the king of the North shall come against him like a whirlwind, with chariots, horseman, and with many ships" (Daniel 11:40). John Walvoord pinpoints the source of this army and describes the magnitude of the initial thrust against the Antichrist:

> Daniel's prophecy described a great army from Africa, including not only Egypt but other countries of that continent. This army, probably numbering in the millions, will attack the Middle East from the south. At the same time Russia and other armies to the north will mobilize another powerful military force to descend on the Holy Land and challenge the world dictator. Although Russia will have had a severe setback about four years earlier in the prophetic sequence of events, she apparently will have been able to recoup her losses enough to put another army in the field.[12]

The Antichrist will put down some of these first attempts at rebellion against him. But before he can celebrate and move on toward his goal of destroying Israel and Jerusalem, something will happen.

## The Disturbing News from the East

"But news from the east and the north shall trouble him; therefore he shall go out with great fury" (Daniel 11:44). The Bible leaves no doubt as to the source of the news that so disturbs and enrages the Antichrist: "Then the sixth angel poured out his bowl on the great river Euphrates, and its water was dried up, so that the way of the kings from the east might be prepared" (Revelation 16:12).

The Euphrates is one of the greatest rivers in the world. It flows from the mountains of western Turkey, through Syria, and continues on right through the heart of Iraq, not far from Baghdad. It eventually unites with the Tigris to become the *Shatt el Arab*, and finally empties into the Persian Gulf. The entirety of the Euphrates flows through Muslim territory. In Genesis 15 and Deuteronomy 11, the Lord specified that the Euphrates would be the easternmost border of the promised land. It serves both as a border and a barrier between Israel and her enemies.

Is it possible that a river the size of the Euphrates could be dried up? According to author Alon Liel, it is not only possible, it has recently happened. He wrote:

> On one occasion recently, the Euphrates was cut off. The headwaters of both the Euphrates and Tigris Rivers, on which both Syria and Iraq so heavily depend, are located in Turkish Territory, which makes Turkey's relations with those nations all the more sensitive. Tensions mounted in early 1990 when Turkey stopped the flow of the Euphrates River for an entire month during the construction of the Ataturk Dam . . . Having already showed it can completely cut off this flow, Turkey has strengthened its bargaining position in its complex relationships with its southern neighbors.[13]

What is the significance of the drying up of the Euphrates River, and why will that event have such a disturbing effect on the Antichrist? For an explanation, let's turn once more to John Walvoord:

> The drying-up of the Euphrates is a prelude to the final act of the drama, not the act itself. We must conclude then, that the most probable interpretation of the drying-up of the Euphrates is that by an act of God its flow will be interrupted even as were the waters of the Red Sea and of Jordan. This time the way will open not for Israel but for

those who are referred to as the Kings of the East . . . The evidence points, then, to a literal interpretation of Revelation 16:12 in relation to the Euphrates.[14]

It's no wonder the world dictator is disturbed and frustrated. He has just put down rebellions by defeating armies from the south and the north, and just when it appears that he is about to gain control of everything, he gets word that the Euphrates River has dried up and massive armies of the east are crossing it to come against him. He had thought himself safe, as no army could cross this barrier and come into the Israeli arena where he fought. But now that barrier is down, and an army of unprecedented numbers is marching toward him.

Just how large is that army? Listen to what John tells us: "Now the number of the army of the horsemen was two hundred million; I heard the number of them" (Revelation 9:16). Suddenly the Antichrist must divert the major portion of his attention to defending himself against an amassed force the size of which the world has never seen.

Is an army of two hundred million soldiers really believable? Dr. Larry Wortzel, a retired US Army colonel, is a leading authority on China and served as the director of the Strategic Studies Institute of the US Army War College. In October 1998, he filed the following report: "China's standing armed force of some 2.8 million active soldiers in uniform is the largest military force in the world. Approximately 1 million reservists and some 15 million militia back them up. With a population of over 1.2 billion people, China also has a potential manpower base of another 200 million males fit for military service available at any time."[15] So an army of that size is not only possible, the potential for it exists even at this moment.

When this unprecedented army crosses the bed of the Euphrates against the Antichrist, the greatest war of all history, involving hundreds of millions of people, will be set in motion. The major battleground for that war will be the land of Israel.

As if this news is not frightening enough, John tells us that all these events are inspired and directed by the demons of hell: "For they are spirits of demons, performing signs, which go out to the kings of the earth and of the whole world, to gather them to the battle of that great day of God Almighty" (Revelation 16:14).

> No doubt demonism in every shape and form will manifest itself more and more as the end draws near, until at last it all ends in Armageddon . . . But besides these hosts of human armies, there will also be present at Armageddon an innumerable host of supernatural beings . . . So Armageddon will truly be a battle of heaven and earth and hell.[16]

So just at the moment when the Antichrist is about to attack and destroy Israel and Jerusalem, a diversion occurs in the form of another massive army entering the field of conflict. Thus the stage is set for the last, stunning movement in the Battle of Armageddon.

## The Descending Lord from the Heavens

If you are a follower of Christ, what happens next may instill an urge to stand up and shout like a football fan watching the star quarterback come onto the field.

> Now I saw heaven opened, and behold, a white horse. And He who sat on him was called Faithful and True, and in righteousness He judges

and makes war. His eyes were like a flame of fire, and on His head were many crowns. He had a name written that no one knew except Himself. He was clothed with a robe dipped in blood, and His name is called The Word of God. And the armies in heaven, clothed in fine linen, white and clean, followed Him on white horses. Now out of His mouth goes a sharp sword, that with it He should strike the nations. And He Himself will rule them with a rod of iron. He Himself treads the winepress of the fierceness and wrath of Almighty God. And He has on His robe and on His thigh a name written: KING OF KINGS AND LORD OF LORDS. (Revelation 19:11–16)

The great Lord Jesus, the captain of the Lord's hosts, the King over all kings will descend to defend and protect His chosen people and put a once-and-for-all end to the evil of the Antichrist.

## Descending with His Saints

But the Lord Jesus, captain of the Lord's hosts, will not descend alone, as the following scriptures make abundantly clear:

Thus the LORD my God will come;
and all the saints with You. (Zechariah 14:5)

The coming of our Lord Jesus Christ with all His saints . . .
(1 Thessalonians 3:13)

When he comes, in that Day, to be glorified in His saints and to be admired among all those who believe. (2 Thessalonians 1:10)

Behold, the Lord comes with ten thousands of His saints. (Jude 14)

All those who have died in the Lord, along with those who were raptured before the years of the Tribulation, will join with the Lord and participate in the battle to reclaim the world for the rule of Christ.

## Descending with His Angels

The saints are not the only ones who will comprise the army of the Lord. Both Matthew and Paul tell us that the angels will also descend with Christ. "When the Son of Man comes in His glory, and all the holy angels with Him, then He will sit on the throne of His glory" (Matthew 25:31); "and to give you who are troubled rest with us when the Lord Jesus is revealed from heaven with His mighty angels" (2 Thessalonians 1:7).

How many angels are available for conscription into this army? The Bible shows their numbers to be staggering. In Matthew 26:52–53, Jesus told Peter in the Garden of Gethsemane, "Put your sword in its place . . . Do you think that I cannot call on My Father, and He will provide Me more than twelve legions of angels?" A Roman legion numbered about six thousand soldiers, so Jesus claimed instant access to the protection of seventy-two thousand angelic soldiers who would have rushed to His rescue had He but said the word. Revelation 5:11, at the very least, supports that number, saying, "I heard the voice of many angels around the throne, the living creatures, and the elders; and the number of them was ten thousand times ten thousand, and thousands of thousands." The Greek says literally, "numbering myriads of myriads and thousands of thousands." The *New Living Translation* renders the passage as "thousands and millions of angels."

Hebrews 12:22 sums it up by talking about innumerable angels in "joyful assembly" (NIV). Angels as far as the eye can see and the mind can imagine.[17]

This admixture of saints and angels calls to mind scenes from great fantasies such as *The Chronicles of Narnia* and *The Lord of the Rings*, where humans fight alongside other-worldly creatures to defeat the forces of evil. It's a thrilling picture to think of human saints side-by-side with God's angels doing battle.

The inception of the Battle of Armageddon has something of a historical precedent in miniature. Author Randall Price recounts the event:

The Yom Kippur War began at 2 P.M. on October 6, 1973. It was a surprise attack on Israel from the Arab nations of Egypt and Syria, which were intent on the destruction of the Jewish State. Overwhelming evidence of large-scale Arab military preparations on the morning of October 6 had compelled Chief of Staff David Elazar to ask the United States to help restrain the Arabs. U.S. Secretary of State Henry Kissinger urged Prime Minister Golda Meir to not issue a preemptive strike, but to trust international guarantees for Israel's security. To which Mrs. Meir, in her characteristic up-front manner, retorted, "By the time they come to save Israel, there won't be an Israel!"

When international intervention finally came in calling for cease-fire negotiations, Israel's casualties had mounted to 2,552 dead and over 3000 wounded. And it would have been much worse if Israel hadn't realized that if nobody was going to fight for them, they were going to have to fight for themselves. For that reason, Israel has come to rely upon their own defenses for their security. That attack is just a foretaste of what Israel can expect in the future, when the worst attack in its history will come and will be centered on Jerusalem. In that day there will be no allies, not even reluctant ones . . . But Scripture has prophesied otherwise. At the right time, Jerusalem's Savior will return.[18]

As Price tells us, Israel in this last war will be forced to rely on herself and not depend on assistance from allies. That is the similarity between the inception of the Battle of Armageddon and the Yom Kippur War, its miniature historical precedent. But what about the outcome? Will the end of the final war be anything like the end of Israel's Yom Kippur War? We will answer that question by telling the full story of the event in the next chapter.

We will close this chapter on a high note, (or perhaps on an acoustic guitar chord) by giving you the lyrics of an old country music song written by Roy Acuff and Odell McLeod and recorded by Hank Williams. The title is "The Battle of Armageddon":

There's a mighty battle coming and it's well now on its way.

It'll be fought at Armageddon, it shall be a sad, sad day.

In the book of Revelation, words in chapter sixteen say:

There'll be gathered there great armies for that battle on that day.


*Refrain:*

All the way from the gates of Eden to the battle of Armageddon

There's been troubles and tribulation, there'll be sorrow and despair.

He has said "ye not be troubled for these things shall come to pass."

Then your life will be eternal when you dwell with him at last.


Turn the pages of your Bible, in St. Matthew you will see,

Start with chapter twenty-four and read from one to thirty-three.

In our Savior's blessed words he said on earth, he prophesied,

For he spoke of this great battle that is coming by and by.

*Refrain*

There'll be nation against nation, there'll be war and rumor of war.

There'll be great signs in heaven, in the sun, the moon, the stars.

Oh, the hearts of men shall fail them, there'll be gnashing of the teeth.

Those who seek it will receive it, mercy at the Savior's feet.

Terrible and terrifying as the events we've discussed in this chapter may be, the last line of this old country song gives us the good news. We may be disturbed by the signs we see of coming catastrophic events. We may feel uneasy due to the continual reports of wars and wanton terrorism. We may quail at reports of nature turning against us. But the last line of this song is our bottom line: we who trust the Lord as our Savior need have no fear. He loves and protects His own, and whatever comes, if we seek Him and His will for our lives, we will be among those whom He saves from the wrath to come.

# TEN

# The Return of the King

IN A ROOM DECORATED FOR AN ALBANIAN FUNERAL, OUR missionary to Albania, Ian Loring, delivered a powerful Good Friday message about Christ's great sacrificial death. Afterward, he invited everyone to come back on Sunday to observe the "third day ritual." In Albanian culture, friends return three days after a funeral to sit with the family, drink bitter coffee, and remember the one who has died. More than three hundred people filled the room that Easter Sunday. Ian preached about the "not quite empty tomb," observing that Christ's empty grave clothes still bore His shape, but the napkin, which had been wrapped around His head, was placed away from the other grave clothes, folded. To Ian's congregation, that minor detail held great meaning and promise. In Albania, when a person has finished a meal and prepares to leave the table, he crumples up his napkin to indicate that he is finished. But if, instead, he leaves his napkin folded, it is a sign that he plans to come back. The application was obvious to the Albanians. Jesus is coming back!

The second coming of Christ is a central theme of much of the Bible, and it is one of the best-attested promises in all of Scripture. Christians can rest in the sure conviction that just as Jesus came to earth the first time, so He will return at the conclusion of the Great Tribulation.

As Christians, we are quite familiar with our Lord's first coming to earth because we accept the record of the four Gospels. It is history. The Bible clearly tells us that He is coming to earth again. Though the exact expression "the second coming of Christ" is not found in the Bible, it makes the assertion in many places. For example, the writer of Hebrews said: "And as it is appointed for men to die once, but after this the judgment, so Christ was offered once to bear the sins of many. To those who eagerly wait for Him *He will appear a second time,* apart from sin, for salvation" (9:27–28, *emphasis added*).

The Old Testament prophecies of Christ's first and second advents are so mingled that Jewish scholars did not clearly see them as separate events. Their perception of these prophecies was like viewing a mountain range from a distance. They saw what appeared to be one mountain, failing to see that there was another equally high mountain behind it, obscured from their sight through the perspective of distance. The prophets saw both comings of Christ either as one event or as very closely related in time. One Bible scholar has written: "Words spoken in one breath, and written in one sentence, may contain prophetic events millennia apart in their fulfillments."[1]

This mixing of two prophetic events into one may partially explain why the Jews as a whole rejected Christ. The prophecies speak of the Messiah both enduring great suffering and accomplishing a great conquest. They thought the suffering savior would become the conquering savior in one advent. They did not realize He would come a first time to suffer and then a second time to conquer.

It is evident that even Jesus' followers expected Him to fulfill the glorious promises relating to His second coming when He came the first time. Only after He ascended to heaven did they realize that they were living in the time period between His two appearances, as if on a plain between two mountains. Theologian John F. Walvoord explains:

> From the present day vantage point . . . since the first coming is history and Second Coming is prophecy, it is comparatively easy to go back into the Old Testament and separate the doctrine of Jesus' two comings. In His first coming He came as a man, lived among people, performed miracles, ministered as a prophet as the Old Testament predicted, and died on the cross and rose again. All these events clearly relate to His first coming. On the other hand, the passages that speak of His coming to reign, judging the earth, rescuing the righteous from the wicked, and installing His kingdom on earth relate to His second coming. They are prophecy, not history.[2]

Nothing could be more dramatic than the contrast between our Lord's first and second comings:

- In His first coming He was wrapped in swaddling clothes. In His second coming He will be clothed royally in a robe dipped in blood.

- In His first coming He was surrounded by cattle and common people. In His second coming He will be accompanied by the massive armies of heaven.

- In His first coming the door of the inn was closed to Him. In His second coming the door of the heavens will be opened to Him.

- In His first coming His voice was the tiny cry of a baby. In His second coming His voice will thunder as the sound of many waters.

- In His first coming, He was the Lamb of God who came bringing salvation. In His second coming, He will be the Lion of the tribe of Judah who comes bringing judgment.

| Rapture / Translation | Second Coming/ Established Kingdom |
|---|---|
| 1. Translation of all believers | 1. No translation at all |
| 2. Translated saints go to heaven | 2. Translated saints return to earth |
| 3. Earth not judged | 3. Earth judged and righteousness established |
| 4. Imminent, any moment, signless | 4. Follows definite predicted signs, including the Tribulation |
| 5. Not in Old Testament | 5. Predicted often in Old Testament |
| 6. Believers only | 6. Affects all humanity |
| 7. Before the day of wrath | 7. Concluding the day of wrath |
| 8. No references to Satan | 8. Satan bound |
| 9. Christ comes *for* His own | 9. Christ comes *with* His own |
| 10. He comes in the *air* | 10. He comes to the *earth* |
| 11. He claims His bride | 11. He comes with His bride |
| 12. Only His own see Him | 12. Every eye shall see Him |
| 13. Tribulation begins | |

Courtesy of Thomas Ice and Timothy Demy

# The Anticipation of Christ

Although Christians are most familiar with the first coming of Christ, it is the second coming that gets the most ink in the Bible. References to the Second Coming outnumber references to the first by a factor of eight to one. Scholars count 1,845 biblical references to the Second Coming, including 318 in the New Testament. His return is emphasized in no less than seventeen Old Testament books and seven out of every ten chapters in the New Testament. The Lord Himself referred to His return twenty-one times. The Second Coming is second only to faith as the most dominant subject in the New Testament. Let's look briefly at some of the most significant of these references.

## The Prophets Foretold the Second Coming of Christ

While many of the Old Testament prophets wrote concerning the second coming of Christ, it is Zechariah who has given us the clearest and most concise prediction of it:

> Then the LORD will go forth
> And fight against those nations,
> As He fights in the day of battle.
> And in that day His feet will stand on the Mount of Olives,
> Which faces Jerusalem on the east.
> And the Mount of Olives shall be split in two,
> From east to west,
> Making a very large valley;
> Half of the mountain shall move toward the north
> And half of it toward the south. (Zechariah 14:3–4)

Notice how Zechariah deals in specifics, even pinpointing the geographic location to which Christ will return: "In that day His feet will stand on the Mount of Olives" (14:4). Like Armageddon, the Mount of Olives is an explicitly identifiable place that retains its ancient name even today. Recently I visited a Jewish cemetery that has been on this site since biblical times. The prophet's specificity gives us confidence that his prophecy is true and accurate. Unlike vague fortune-tellers and prophetic charlatans, this prophet dared to be explicit and specific so that the truth of his prophecy cannot be missed when the event occurs.

## Jesus Himself Announced His Second Coming

Jesus, speaking from the Mount of Olives, affirmed His second coming to His disciples in dramatic and cataclysmic terms:

"For as the lightning comes from the east and flashes to the west, so also will the coming of the Son of Man be . . . Immediately after the tribulation of those days the sun will be darkened, and the moon will not give its light; the stars will fall from heaven, and the powers of the heavens will be shaken. Then the sign of the Son of Man will appear in heaven, and then all the tribes of the earth will mourn, and they will see the Son of Man coming on the clouds of heaven with power and great glory." (Matthew 24:27, 29–30)

## The Angels Announced that Jesus Would Return

Immediately following Christ's ascension into heaven, two angels appeared to the stunned disciples and spoke words of comfort to them. "Men of Galilee," they said, "why do you stand gazing up into heaven? This same Jesus, who was taken from you into heaven, will so come in like manner as you saw Him go into heaven" (Acts 1:11). The

next verse tells us "they returned to Jerusalem from the mount called Olivet" (v. 12). Did you catch that? Jesus ascended to heaven from the Mount of Olives. According to the angels, Christ will return to that very same spot—the Mount of Olives. The words of the angels conveyed both consolation for the disciples' present loss of Jesus and confirmation of His future return.

### John the Apostle Foretold Jesus' Second Coming

The prophecies of Christ's return are like bookends to John's Revelation. In the first chapter he wrote: "Behold, He is coming with clouds, and every eye will see Him, even they who pierced Him. And all the tribes of the earth will mourn because of Him" (v. 7). And in the last pages of the last chapter—indeed, almost the last words of the New Testament—our Lord emphatically affirms His second coming: "He who testifies to these things says, 'Surely I am coming quickly.' Amen. Even so, come, Lord Jesus!" (22:20).

Obviously we have excellent reason to anticipate the return of Christ. The Bible affirms it throughout as a certainty, describing it in specific terms and with ample corroboration.

## The Advent of Christ

Twice in the book of Revelation we are told that the door to heaven will be opened. It is first opened to receive the church into heaven at the time of the Rapture: "After these things I looked, and behold, a door standing open in heaven. And the first voice which I heard was like a trumpet speaking with me, saying, 'Come up here, and I will show you things which must take place after this'" (4:1). The door swings open a second time for Christ and His church to proceed from heaven on their

militant march back to earth (19:11,14). The first opening is for the Rapture of the saints; the second is for the return of Christ!

When Jesus arrives on earth the second time, His landing will dramatically herald the purpose of His coming. The moment His feet touch the Mount of Olives, the mountain will split apart, creating a broad passageway from Jerusalem to Jericho. As you can imagine, this will be an unprecedented geological cataclysm. In describing it, Dr. Tim LaHaye wrote: "There will be a Stellar Event. Celestial. Cosmic. Greater than earth. Greater than the heavens. And it will suck the air out of humanity's lungs and send men and women and kings and presidents and tyrants to their knees. It will have no need of spotlights, fog machines, amplified music, synthesizers, or special effects. It will be real."[3]

Thus Christ's return will be amplified by a devastating spectacle that will make Hollywood disaster movies look like Saturday morning child's fare. The world will see and recognize its rightful Lord and King. Whereas He came the first time in humility and simplicity, this time His glory and majesty will be spectacularly displayed for all to see.

Let's look briefly at the Bible's description of the glory and majesty Christ will display at His second coming.

## His Designation

In Revelation 19, the descending Lord is given three meaningful titles.

> Now I saw heaven opened, and behold, a white horse. And He who sat on him was called Faithful and True, and in righteousness He judges and makes war . . . He had a name written that no one knew except Himself . . . and His name is called The Word of God . . . And He has on His robe and on His thigh a name written: KING OF KINGS AND LORD OF LORDS. (vv. 11–13, 16)

These three names are not merely rhetorical embellishments or empty titles. Prophecy scholar Harry Ironside gives us insight into their significance:

> In these three names we have set forth first, our Lord's dignity as the Eternal Son; second, His incarnation—the Word became Flesh; and last, His second advent to reign as King of Kings and Lord of Lords.[4]

These three names encompass the entire ministry of the Lord Jesus Christ. The first name, the one known only to God, indicates His intimacy and oneness with the Father and thus His eternal existence, including His role in the Trinity as creator and sustainer of the world. The second name, the Word of God, harks back to the first chapter of John's gospel and indicates His incarnation when "the Word became flesh," walked as a man upon this earth, and revealed God to us. The third name, the majestic and towering syllables, King of kings and Lord of lords, is the title He will wear at His second coming, designating His role as the sovereign ruler over all the earth.

## His Description

*The eyes* of the returning Christ are described as burning like a flame of fire, signifying His ability as a judge to see deeply into the hearts of men and ferret out all injustice (Revelation 1:14; 2:18; 19:12). His eyes will pierce through the motives of nations and individuals and judge them for what they really are . . . not for how they hope their masks of hypocrisy will make them appear!

*The head* of the returning Christ is crowned with many crowns (Revelation 19:12), testifying to His status as the absolute sovereign King of kings and Lord of lords—the undisputed monarch of the entire earth. Famed nineteenth-century London preacher Charles

Haddon Spurgeon described the comfort and security that we derive from the sovereignty of Christ:

> I am sure there is no more delightful doctrine to a Christian, than that of Christ's absolute sovereignty. I am glad there is no such thing as chance, that nothing is left to itself, but that Christ everywhere hath sway. If I thought that there was a devil in hell that Christ did not govern, I should be afraid that devil would destroy me. If I thought there was a circumstance on earth, which Christ did not over-rule, I should fear that that circumstance would ruin me. Nay, if there were an angel in heaven that was not one of Jehovah's subjects, I should tremble even at him. But since Christ is King of kings, and I am his poor brother, one whom he loves, I give all my cares to him, for he careth for me; and leaning on his breast, my soul hath full repose, confidence, and security.[5]

*The robe* of the returning Christ is dipped in blood, reminding us that He is the sacrificial Lamb of God. Earlier in Revelation, John described Him as "the Lamb slain from the foundation of the world" (13:8). In fact, Jesus will be represented to us as the Lamb of God throughout eternity. In a sense, eternity will be an extended Communion service as we remember forever with love and gratitude the sacrifice of Jesus Christ that united us with God and gave us an eternity of joy with Him.

## The Armies of Christ

When Jesus returns to this earth to put down the world's ultimate rebellion, the armies of heaven will accompany him. John described these armies as "clothed in fine linen, white and clean, [following] Him on white horses" (Revelation 19:14).

In the short epistle that immediately precedes the book of Revelation, Jude described this epic event in verses 14 and 15:

Now Enoch, the seventh from Adam, prophesied about these men also, saying, "Behold, the Lord comes with ten thousands of His saints, to execute judgment on all, to convict all who are ungodly among them of all their ungodly deeds which they have committed in an ungodly way, and of all the harsh things which ungodly sinners have spoken against Him."

In one short verse, Jude used the word *ungodly* four times. This repetition is not accidental. Jude was emphasizing the fact that when Christ comes the second time, His long-suffering patience will have run its course. He will come to impose judgment upon those who have defied Him, and that judgment will be massive. At this point the people on the earth will have rejected the ministry of the 144,000 preachers and the two witnesses that God sent to them for their salvation, just as the prophet Jonah was sent to the Ninevites. In His loving mercy, God endeavored to turn them away from their fatal rebellion. But unlike the Ninevites, the people in the last days will have hardened their hearts beyond repentance.

In his second letter to the Thessalonians, Paul wrote in chilling terms of the judgment that will descend on these rebels:

The Lord Jesus is revealed from heaven with His mighty angels, in flaming fire taking vengeance on those who do not know God, and those who do not obey the gospel of our Lord Jesus Christ. These shall be punished with everlasting destruction from the presence of the Lord and from the glory of His power, when He comes, in that Day, to be glorified in His saints and to be admired among all those who believe, because our testimony among you was believed. (1:7–10)

As we learned in the previous chapter, the armies of heaven that accompany Christ in His second coming will be made up of saints and angels—people like you and me standing side-by-side with heavenly beings of immense power. These legions are dressed not in military fatigues but in dazzling white. Yet they need not worry about their pristine uniforms getting soiled because their role is largely ceremonial and honorary; they will not fight. Jesus Himself will slay the rebels with the deadly sword darting out of His mouth.

## The Authority of Christ

When the Lord returns to earth at the end of the Tribulation, the men and nations who have defied Him will no more be able to stand against Him than a spiderweb could stand against an eagle. His victory will be assured and His authority undisputed. Here is how John described the finality of His judgment and the firmness of His rule: "And he Himself will rule them with a rod of iron. He Himself treads the winepress of the fierceness and wrath of Almighty God. And He has on His robe and on His thigh a name written: KING OF KINGS AND LORD OF LORDS" (Revelation 19:15–16).

This grand title, King of kings and Lord of lords, identifies our Lord at His second coming. It speaks of His unassailable authority. At this name every king on earth will bow, and every lord will kneel. Don't be confused about the sword proceeding from Christ's mouth; it is not "the sword of the Spirit, which is the word of God" (Ephesians 6:17). This is an altogether different and fearful sword—the sword of judgment—a sharp instrument of war with which Christ will smite the nations into utter submission and establish His absolute rule.

When Christ returns the second time, He will finally fulfill the prophecy of Isaiah that we often quote and hear choirs sing to Handel's lofty music at Christmastime: "For unto us a Child is born, unto us a Son is given; and the government will be upon His shoulder. And His name will be called Wonderful, Counselor, Mighty God, Everlasting Father, Prince of Peace" (Isaiah 9:6). At His first coming, Jesus fulfilled the first part of Isaiah's prophecy, the heartwarming Christmas part. At His second coming, He will fulfill the second part—the part that reveals His iron-hard power and authority over all the nations. The government of the world will at last be upon His shoulder!

## The Avenging of Christ

The book of Revelation is divided into three sections. At the beginning of the book we are introduced to the world ruined by Man. As we move to the latter half of the Tribulation period, we witness the world ruled by Satan. But now as we come to Christ's return at the end of the Tribulation period, we see the world reclaimed by Christ.

Reclaiming the earth, however, is not merely a simple matter of Christ's stepping in and planting His flag. Before the earth can be reclaimed, it must be cleansed. You wouldn't move back into a house infested with rats without first exterminating and cleaning it up. That is what Christ must do before He reclaims the earth. All rebellion must be rooted out. He must avenge the damage done to His perfect creation by wiping the rebels from the face of the earth. The last verses of Revelation 19 give us an account of this purging and cleansing, and each step in the process is a dramatic story within itself. Let's briefly examine these avenging acts that will cleanse and reclaim the earth.

## The Fowls of Heaven

In the classic Alfred Hitchcock film *The Birds*, a coastal California town is terrorized by the escalating attacks of vicious birds. Throughout the film the terror increases to the point that birds merely sitting in rows on highline wires look ominous and foreboding. Instead of closing the film with his typical "The End," Hitchcock simply fades the screen to black, leaving the viewer with a lingering sense of terror as he drives from the theater and sees birds sitting on the high wires in his neighborhood. As horrifying as that story is, it pales in comparison to the grisly bird scene that John unveils.

> Then I saw an angel standing in the sun; and he cried with a loud voice, saying to all the birds that fly in the midst of heaven, "Come and gather together for the supper of the great God, that you may eat the flesh of kings, the flesh of captains, the flesh of mighty men, the flesh of horses and of those who sit on them, and the flesh of all people, free and slave, both small and great" . . . And all the birds were filled with their flesh. (Revelation 19:17–18, 21)

Words are hardly adequate to describe the horror of this appalling scene. The fowl of the earth's air all gather at Armageddon to feast upon the massive piles of human flesh that will litter the battlefield for miles upon miles. The word translated *fowl* or *birds* is found only three times in the Bible: twice here in Revelation 19 (verses 17 and 21), and once more in Revelation 18:2. It is the Greek word *arnin*, which designates a scavenger bird that is best translated into English as *vulture*.

In John's vision the angel is calling the vultures of the earth to Armageddon to "the supper of the Great God," where they will feast on the fallen carcasses of the enemies of the Lord. The text says that these corpses include both great and small, kings and generals, bond and free. As Harry Ironside wrote, "It is an awful picture—the climax of man's audacious resistance to God."[6]

The book of Revelation tells of another supper, one altogether different from that of the vultures on the field of Armageddon. In Revelation 19:7 we read, "Let us be glad and rejoice and give Him glory, for the marriage of the Lamb has come, and His wife has made herself ready." In verse 9, we read of the feast that will follow the wedding: "Then he said to me, 'Write: "Blessed are those who are called to the marriage supper of the Lamb!"'"

The marriage supper of the Lamb is a time of great joy, celebrating the wedding between the bridegroom Christ and His bride, the church. I am glad that I have a confirmed reservation for the marriage supper of the Lamb where I will feast at the table of heaven, for at the other supper—the supper of the Great God on the fields of Armageddon—the human participants will *be* the food.

I pause here to ask a few important questions: Which supper will you be attending? Have you made your reservation for the marriage supper of the Lamb? Have you accepted the saving work of the Lamb of God in your behalf? Have you confessed your sin and surrendered your will to the authority of the Lamb? I sincerely hope you have, for doing so secures your invitation to a celebration you don't want to miss.

Strangely, as W. A. Criswell pointed out, as glorious as this feast is, it is never described explicitly:

Concerning the marriage itself, is it not a strange narrative that God should omit to describe it? Nothing is said about it, no word is used to describe it. The Greek word here says, "*elthen* [aorist], the marriage is come . . ." and that is all. Just the fact of it. John just hears the Hallelujah chorus announcing it. He has a word to say about the wife, the bride of Christ, who has made herself ready. He describes the robe of our righteousness that shall be our reward at the Bema of Christ. But He never recounts the actual wedding itself. The event just happens and all heaven bursts into Hallelujahs concerning it.[7]

Yet in spite of the lack of description, John made it clear that this feast will be glorious through a writer's technique known as *indirection*. When an event is too wonderful for words, it is sometimes more effective to show the wonder through reactions to the event rather than through the event itself. Instead of describing the feast directly, John used the reactions of others to show its character indirectly. Thus, we are told of the glorious robe we'll wear, the loveliness of the bride, and finally of the hallelujahs that will spring from heaven expressing the pure joy of the occasion. Through these indirect impressions we can see that the marriage supper will be a celebration beyond anything we can imagine. I strongly urge you to RSVP immediately.

## The Foes of Heaven

"And I saw the beast, the kings of the earth, and their armies, gathered together to make war against Him who sat on the horse and against His army" (Revelation 19:19). Could there be anything more futile than creatures fighting against their Creator? Than little men stuck on one tiny planet, floating in the immeasurable cosmos, striking back at the Creator of the universe? Yet futility is not beyond hearts turned away from God. John warned that the beast and the false prophet will persuade the armies of the earth to go to war against Christ and the armies of heaven. It's like persuading mice to declare war against lions. This final war will be the culmination of all of the rebellion that men have leveled against Almighty God from the beginning of time! And there's not one iota of doubt about the outcome.

## The Fatality of the Beast and False Prophet

The Bible tells us that God simply snatches up the Antichrist beast and the false prophet and flings them into the fiery lake. "Then the beast was captured, and with him the false prophet who worked signs in his presence, by which he deceived those who received the mark of the beast and those who worshiped his image. These two were cast alive into the lake of fire burning with brimstone" (Revelation 19:20).

These two evil creatures have the unwanted honor of actually getting to that awful place before Satan, whose confinement occurs much later: "The devil, who deceived them, was cast into the lake of fire and brimstone where the beast and false prophet are. And they will be tormented day and night forever and ever" (Revelation 20:10). Satan does not join the beast and the false prophet there until the end of the Millennium, one thousand years later.

Once again I turn to Harry Ironside for an interesting sidelight concerning the nature of the punishment these two men experience: "'Note that two men, are taken alive' . . . These two men are 'cast alive into [the lake burning with fire and brimstone]' where a thousand years later, they are still said to be 'suffering the vengeance of eternal fire' (Jude 7)." He focuses our attention on two important truths from God's Word; the men are alive when they arrive, and they are still alive a thousand years later—and still experiencing suffering. He draws a profound conclusion: "the lake of fire is neither annihilation nor purgatorial because it neither annihilates nor purifies these two fallen foes of God and man after a thousand years under judgment."[8]

Hell has become an unpopular subject these days. As church historian Martin Marty noted, "Hell disappeared. And no one noticed."[9] There have been many attempts of late to soften the impact of this thoroughly biblical doctrine in favor of what C. S. Lewis called a grandfatherly God of indulgent kindness who would never consign anyone to hell, but says of anything we happen to like doing, "What does it matter so long as they are contended?"[10]

As God's judgment in Revelation clearly shows, God is not that soft. He intends to remake us in His own image, which is often a painful and self-denying process. If we refuse to be remade, we must endure the hellish consequence that choice brings. As John's vision shows us, hell is frightfully real. And it shows how deadly it is to be an enemy of the Almighty God. His power is infinite, and His justice is certain. No rebellion can stand against Him, and the consequences of such rebellion are terrible and eternal.

## The Finality of Christ's Victory over Rebellion

"And the rest were killed with the sword which proceeded from the mouth of Him who sat on the horse" (Revelation 19:21). Here is how John F. Walvoord describes the victory:

When Christ returns at the end of the tribulation period, the armies that have been fighting with each other for power will have invaded the city of Jerusalem and will have been engaged in house-to-house fighting. When the glory of the second coming of Christ appears in the heavens, however, these soldiers will forget their contest for power on earth and will turn to fight the army from heaven (16:16; 19:19). Yet their best efforts will be futile because Christ will smite them with the sword in His mouth (19:15, 21), and they will all be killed, along with their horses.[11]

Again we see the utter futility of fighting against God. Not only will the leaders of the rebellion be flung into hell, but also all the armies that joined them will be slaughtered by the mighty strokes of Christ's deadly sword.

## The Application of Christ's Second Coming

Throughout my years of ministry as a pastor and Bible teacher, I have talked to more than a few pastors and Christian leaders who expressed doubts concerning the relevance of Bible prophecy. They usually say something like this: "I don't preach on prophecy because it has nothing to do with the needs of my people today. I try to preach on more relevant topics. I leave prophecy to people like you, Dr. Jeremiah."

My response is that today there are few subjects more relevant than biblical prophecy. In fact, as we move into times that are so clearly depicted in the prophetic scriptures, some of my critics are beginning to get questions from their own congregants who are looking at today's headlines and asking, "What in the world is going on?" When I preached to my own church the messages that became the basis for this book, we recorded some of the highest attendance figures in the history of our congregation. I suspect that many had come to hear these messages because they were not getting meaningful answers from their own pastors. I cannot imagine being a pastor in today's cataclysmic world and not using the Word of God to give people God's perspective on world events.

In spite of the high value I place on understanding future events, I find that studying prophecy has an even higher and more practical value. It provides a compelling motivation for living the Christian life. The immediacy of prophetic events shows the need to live each moment in Christlike readiness. As revered Southern Baptist evangelist Vance Havner has put it, "The devil has chloroformed the atmosphere of this age." Therefore, in view of the sure promises of Christ's return, as believers, we are to do more than merely be ready; we are to be expectant. In our day of "anarchy, apostasy, and apathy," Havner suggests that expectant living means: "We need to take down our 'Do Not Disturb' signs . . . snap out of our stupor and come out of our coma and awake from our apathy."[12] Havner reminds us that God's Word calls to us to awake out of our sleep, and to walk in righteousness, in the light Christ gives us (Romans 13:11; 1 Corinthians 15:34; Ephesians 5:14).

Prophecy can provide the wake-up call that Dr. Havner calls for. When we have heard and understood the truth of Christ's promised return, we cannot just keep living our lives in the same old way. Future events have present implications that we cannot ignore. When we know that Christ is coming again to this earth, we cannot go on being the same people. From the New Testament epistles, I have gleaned ten ways in which we should be different as a result of our prophetic knowledge. For emphasis in each scripture quotation, I have italicized the words connecting the admonition with the promise of Christ's return.

1. *Refrain from judging others:* "Therefore judge nothing before the time, *until the Lord comes,* who will both bring

to light the hidden things of darkness and reveal the counsels of the hearts. Then each one's praise will come from God" (1 Corinthians 4:5).

2. *Remember the Lord's table:* "For as often as you eat this bread and drink this cup, you proclaim the Lord's death *till He comes*" (1 Corinthians 11:26).

3. *Respond to life spiritually:* "If then you were raised with Christ, seek those things which are above, where Christ is, sitting at the right hand of God. Set your mind on things above, not on things on the earth. For you died, and your life is hidden with Christ in God. *When Christ who is our life appears*, then you also will appear with Him in glory" (Colossians 3:1–4).

4. *Relate to one another in love:* "And may the Lord make you increase and abound in love to one another and to all, just as we do to you, so that He may establish your hearts blameless in holiness before our God and Father at *the coming of our Lord Jesus Christ* with all His saints" (1 Thessalonians 3:12–13).

5. *Restore the bereaved:* "But I do not want you to be ignorant, brethren, concerning those who have fallen asleep, lest you sorrow as others who have no hope. For if we believe that Jesus died and rose again, even so God will bring with Him those who sleep in Jesus. For this we say to you by the word of the Lord, that we who are alive and remain *until the coming of the Lord* will by no means precede those who are asleep. For the Lord Himself will descend from heaven with a shout, with the voice of an archangel, and with the trumpet of God. And the dead in Christ will rise first. Then we who are alive and remain shall be caught up together with them

in the clouds to meet the Lord in the air. And thus we shall always be with the Lord. Therefore comfort one another with these words" (1 Thessalonians 4:13–18).

6. *Recommit ourselves to the ministry:* "I charge you therefore before God and the Lord Jesus Christ, who will judge the living and the dead *at His appearing* and His kingdom: Preach the word! Be ready in season and out of season. Convince, rebuke, exhort, with all longsuffering and teaching" (2 Timothy 4:1–2).

7. *Refuse to neglect church:* "And let us consider one another in order to stir up love and good works, not forsaking the assembling of ourselves together, as is the manner of some, but exhorting one another, and so much the more *as you see the Day approaching*" (Hebrews 10:24–25).

8. *Remain steadfast:* "Therefore be patient, brethren, until the coming of the Lord. See how the farmer waits for the precious fruit of the earth, waiting patiently for it until it receives the early and latter rain. You also be patient. Establish your hearts, for *the coming of the Lord is at hand*" (James 5:7–8).

9. *Renounce sin in our lives:* "And now, little children, abide in Him, that *when He appears*, we may have confidence and not be ashamed before Him *at His coming*. If you know that He is righteous, you know that everyone who practices righteousness is born of Him" (1 John 2:28–29).

10. *Reach the lost:* "Keep yourselves in the love of God, *looking for the mercy of our Lord Jesus Christ* unto eternal life. And on some have compassion, making a distinction; but others save with fear, pulling them out of the fire, hating even the garment defiled by the flesh" (Jude 21–23).

## Hoping and Longing for Christ's Return

One of the finest stories I've heard about men longing for their leader's return is that of explorer/adventurer Sir Ernest Shackleton. On Saturday, August 8, 1914, one week after Germany declared war on Russia, twenty-nine men set sail in a three-masted wooden ship from Plymouth, England, to Antarctica on a quest to become the first adventurers to cross the Antarctic continent on foot. Sir Ernest Shackleton had recruited the men through an advertisement: "Men wanted for hazardous journey. Small wages. Bitter cold. Long months of complete darkness. Constant danger. Safe return doubtful. Honour and recognition in case of success."

Not only was Shackleton an honest man, for the men did experience all that his handbill promised, but he was also an able leader and a certified hero. His men came to refer to him as "the Boss," although he never thought of himself that way. He worked as hard as any crew member and built solid team unity aboard the ship, aptly named *Endurance*. In January 1915, the ship became entrapped in an ice pack and ultimately sank, leaving the men to set up camp on an ice floe—a flat, free-floating slice of sea ice. Shackleton kept the men busy by day and entertained by night. They played ice soccer, had nightly songfests, and held regular sled-dog competitions. It was in the ice floe camp that Shackleton proved his greatness as a leader. He willingly sacrificed his right to a warmer, fur-lined sleeping bag so that one of his men might have it, and he personally served hot milk to his men in their tents every morning.

In April 1916, their thinning ice floe threatened to break apart, forcing the men to seek refuge on nearby Elephant Island. Knowing that a rescue from such a desolate island was unlikely, Shackleton and five others left to cross eight hundred miles of open Antarctic sea in a 22.5-foot lifeboat with more of a hope than a promise of a return with rescuers. Finally, on August 30, after an arduous 105-day trip and three earlier attempts, Shackleton returned to rescue his stranded crew, becoming their hero.

But perhaps the real hero in this story is Frank Wild. Second in command, Wild was left in charge of the camp in Shackleton's absence. He maintained the routine the Boss had established. He assigned daily duties, served meals, held sing-alongs, planned athletic competitions, and generally kept up morale. Because "the camp was in constant danger of being buried in snow . . . and become completely invisible from the sea, so that a rescue party might look for it in vain," Wild kept the men busy shoveling away drifts.

The firing of a gun was to be the prearranged signal that the rescue ship was near the island, but as Wild reported, "Many times when the glaciers were 'calving' and chunks fell off with a report like a gun, we thought that it was the real thing, and after a time we got to distrust these signals." But he never lost hope in the return of the Boss. Confidently, Wild kept the last tin of kerosene and a supply of dry combustibles ready to ignite instantly for use as a locator signal when the "day of wonders" would arrive.

Barely four days' worth of rations remained in the camp when Shackleton finally arrived on a Chilean icebreaker. He personally made several trips through the icy waters in a small lifeboat in order to ferry his crew to safety. Miraculously, the leaden fog lifted long enough for all the men to make it to the icebreaker in one hour.

Shackleton later learned from the men how they were prepared to break camp so quickly and reported: "From a fortnight after I had left, Wild would roll up his sleeping bag each day with the remark,

'Get your things ready, boys, the Boss may come today.' And sure enough, one day the mist opened and revealed the ship for which they had been waiting and longing and hoping for over four months." Wild's "cheerful anticipation proved infectious," and all were prepared when the evacuation day came.[13]

Shackleton's stranded crew desperately hoped that their leader would come back to them, and they longed for his return. But as diligent and dedicated as Shackleton was, they could not be certain he would return. He was, after all, a mere man battling elements he could not control, so they knew he might not make it back. Unlike that desperate crew, we have a certain promise that the Lord will return. Ours is not a mere longing or a desperate hope, as theirs was, for our Lord is the Creator and Master of all, and His promise is as sure as His very existence.

The prophets, the angels, and the apostle John all echo the words of promise from Jesus Himself that He will return. God's Word further amplifies the promise by giving us clues in prophecy to help us identify the signs that His return is close at hand. The signs that tell us the second coming of the Lord is drawing near should motivate us as never before to live in readiness. As we noted in chapter 5, the Rapture, which is the next event on the prophetic calendar, will take place seven years before the events we have discussed in this final chapter. Future events cast their shadows before them. As we anticipate His return, we are not to foolishly set dates and leave our jobs and homes to wait for Him on some mountain. We are to remain busy doing the work set before us, living in love and serving in ministry, even when the days grow dark and the nights long. Be encouraged! Be anticipating! We are secure; we belong to Christ. And as the old gospel song says, "Soon and very soon, we are going to see the King!"

# APPENDIX A

## Jewish Population Statistics

| Country | 1970 | 2007 | Projected 2020 |
|---|---|---|---|
| World | 12,633,000 | 13,155,000 | 13,558,000* |
| Israel | 2,582,000 | 5,393,000 | 6,228,000* |
| United States | 5,400,000 | 5,275,000 | 5,200,000 |
| France | 530,000 | 490,000 | 482,000 |
| Canada | 286,000 | 374,000 | 381,000* |
| United Kingdom | 390,000 | 295,000 | 238,000 |
| Russia | 808,000 | 225,000 | 130,000 |
| Argentina | 282,000 | 184,000 | 162,000 |
| Germany | 30,000 | 120,000 | 108,000 |

* indicates anticipated Jewish population growth

Source: Jewish People Policy Planning Institute, *Annual Assessment 2007* (Jerusalem, Israel: Gefen Publishing House LTD, 2007)

# APPENDIX B

## Conventional Oil Reserves by Country
## June 2007

| Rank | Country | Proved reserves (billion barrels) June 2007 | Percentage world oil reserves |
|------|---------|----------------------|----------------|
| 1 | Saudi Arabia | 264.3 | 21.9% |
| 2 | Iran | 137.5 | 11.4% |
| 3 | Iraq | 115.0 | 9.5% |
| 4 | Kuwait | 101.5 | 8.4% |
| 5 | United Arab Emirates | 97.8 | 8.1% |
| 6 | Venezuela | 80.0 | 6.6% |
| 6 | Russia | 79.5 | 6.6% |

| Rank | Country | Proved reserves (billion barrels) June 2007 | Percentage world oil reserves |
|:---:|---|:---:|:---:|
| 8 | Libya | 41.5 | 3.4% |
| 9 | Kazakhstan | 39.8 | 3.3% |
| 10 | Nigeria | 36.2 | 3.0% |
| 11 | United States | 29.9 | 2.5% |
| 12 | Canada * | 17.1 | 1.4% |
| 13 | China | 16.3 | 1.3% |
| 13 | Qatar | 15.2 | 1.3% |
| | Total World Reserves | 1,208,200,000,000 | |

* When oil sands are included, Canada ranks second with 178.8 billion barrels of proved reserve. Currently oil sands are excluded from classification as reserves by the US Securities and Exchange Commission and are not included in BP statistics.

# NOTES

## Introduction: Knowing the Signs

1. "Speech by Dmitri A. Medvedev," *The New York Times* online, 11 December 2007, www.nytimes.com/2007/12/11/world/europe/medvedev-speech.html (accessed 2 June 2008).

2. "UN warns of more unrest over food shortages," EuroNews, 23 April 2008, www .euronews.net/index.php?page=info&article=482404&lng=1 (accessed 2 June 2008).

3. Pascale Bonnefoy, "Evacuation Ordered as Chilean Volcano Begins to Spew Ash," 7 May 2008, http://www.nytimes.com/2008/05/07/world/americas/07chile.html?ref=world (accessed 7 May 2008).

4. Adam Entous, "Gaza headmaster was Islamic 'rocket maker,'" Reuters wire service, 5 May 2008; available at www.thestar.com.my/news/story.asp?file=/2008/5/5 /worldupdates/2008-05-05T203555Z_01_NOOTR_RTRMDNC_0_-334136 -1&sec=Worldupdates (accessed 2 June 2008).

5. Skip Heitzig, *How to Study the Bible and Enjoy It* (Carol Stream, IL: Tyndale House Publishers, 2002), 96.

6. Tim LaHaye, *The Rapture* (Eugene, OR: Harvest House Publishers, 2002), 88.

7. William Zinsser, *Writing About Your Life* (New York: Marlowe & Company, 2004), 155–156.

## Chapter One: The Israel Connection

1. Romesg Ratnesae, "May 14, 1948," *Time*, http://www.time.com/time/magazine /article/0,9171,1004510,00.html (accessed 27 February 2008).

2. The Declaration of Independence (Israel), 14 May 1948, Israel Ministry of Foreign Affairs, "The Signatories of the Declaration of the Establishment of the State of Israel," http://www.mfa.gov.il/mfa/history/modern%20history/israel%20at%2050/the%20 signatories%20of%20the%20declaration%20of%20the%20establis (accessed 25 February 2008).

3. Rabbi Binyamin Elon, *God's Covenant with Israel* (Green Forest, AR: Balfour Books, 2005), 12.

4. Mark Twain, "Concerning the Jews," *Harper's*, September 1899, 535.

5. "Jewish Nobel Prize Winners," Jewish Virtual Library, http://www.jewishvirtuallibrary
.org/jsource/Judaism/nobels.html (accessed 26 February 2008); "Nobel Laureate Facts,"
Nobelprize.org, http://nobelprize.org/nobel_prizes/nobelprize_facts.html (accessed 27
February 2008); and "Jewish Nobel Prize Winners," The Jewish Contribution to World
Civilization (JINFO), www.jinfo.org/Nobel_Prizes.html (accessed 27 February 2008).

6. Jewish People Policy Planning Institute, *Annual Assessment 2007* (Jerusalem, Israel:
Gefen Publishing House LTD, 2007), 15.

7. David Jeremiah, *Before It's Too Late* (Nashville, TN: Thomas Nelson, Inc., 1982), 126.

8. Hal Lindsey, "I will bless them that bless thee," WorldNetDaily, 18 January 2008, www
.wnd.com/index.php?pageId=45604 (accessed 27 June 2008).

9. Elon, *God's Covenant with Israel,* 17.

10. Ibid.

11. Abraham Joshua Heschel, *Israel: An Echo of Eternity* (Woodstock, VT: Jewish Lights
Publishing, 1997), 57.

12. John Walvoord, "Will Israel Possess the Promised Land?" *Jesus the King Is Coming,*
Charles Lee Feinberg, ed. (Chicago: Moody Press, 1975), 128.

13. Quoted by Josephus, *Antiquities* xiv. 7.2, Leob edition, cited in A. F. Walls, "The
Dispersion," *The New Bible Dictionary* (Grand Rapids: Wm. B. Eerdmans Pub. Co.,
1962), 313–319.

14. Joseph Stein, *Fiddler on the Roof* screenplay, 1971.

15. Joel C. Rosenberg, from the audio track of the DVD *Epicenter* (Carol Stream, IL:
Tyndale House Publishers, Inc., 2007). Used with permission.

16. Rabbi Leo Baeck, "A Minority Religion," *The Dynamics of Emancipation: The Jew in the
Modern Age,* compiled by Nahum Norbert Glatzer (Boston: Beacon Press, 1965), 61.
Reprinted by permission of Beacon Press.

17. David McCullough, *Truman* (New York: Simon & Schuster, 1992), 619.

18. Gary Frazier, *Signs of the Coming of Christ* (Arlington, TX; Discovery Ministries, 1998),
67.

19. Chaim Weizmann, *Trial and Error* (New York: Harper & Brothers, 1949), 141–194.

20. Israel Ministry of Foreign Affairs, "The Balfour Declaration," http://www.mfa.gov.il
/MFA/Peace+Process/Guide+to+the+Peace+Process/The+Balfour+Declaration.htm
(accessed 27 February 2008); see also http://www.president.gov.il/chapters/chap_3
/file_3_3_1_en.asp.

21. Quoted in Gustav Niebuhr, "Religion Journal: Political Expressions of Personal Piety
Increase, as Bush and Gore Showed," *The New York Times,* 16 December 2000, http://
query.nytimes.com/gst/fullpage.html?res=990DEED61539F935A25751C1A9669C8B63
(accessed 27 February 2008).

22. Yossi Beilin, *His Brother's Keeper: Israel and Diaspora Jews in the Twenty-first Century*
(New York: Schocken Books, 2000), 99.

23. *The Jewish People Policy Planning Institute: Annual Assessment 2007* (Jerusalem, Israel:
Gefen Publishing House LTD, 2007), 15.

24. Milton B. Lindberg, *The Jew and Modern Israel* (Chicago: Moody Press, 1969), 7.

25. Clark Clifford, *Counsel to the President* (New York: Random House, 1991), 3.

26. Ibid., 4.

27. Ibid., 7–8.

28. Ibid., 13.

29. Ibid., 22.

30. McCullough, *Truman*, 620.

## Chapter Two: The Crude Awakening

1. "The Story of Oil in Pennsylvania," Paleontological Research Institution, www.priweb
.org/ed/pgws/history/pennsylvania/pennsylvania.html (accessed 1 October 2007).

2. Fareed Zakaria,"Why We Can't Quit," *Newsweek*, http://www.newsweek.com/id/123482
(accessed 25 February 2008).

3. Ibid.

4. Ronald Bailey, "Oil Price Bubble?" Reason Online, 26 March 2008, www.reason.com
/news/printer/125414.html (accessed 3 June 2008).

5. "This Week in Petroleum," Energy Information Administration, 19 March 2008, www
.tonto.eia.gov/oog/info/twip.html (accessed 26 March 2008); and International
Business Times: Commodities & Futures, "This Week in Petroleum", 19 March 2008,
http://www.ibtimes.com/articles/20080319/this-week-in-petroleum-mar-19.htm
(accessed 17 June 2008).

6. Dilip Hiro, "The Power of Oil," Yale Center for the Study of Globilization, 10 January
2006, http://yaleglobal.yale.edu/display.article?id=6761.

7. Oil-Proved Reserves, "BP Statistical Review of World Energy June 2007," BP Global,
http://www.bp.com/liveassets/bp_internet/globalbp/globalbp_uk_english/reports_and
_publications/statistical_energy_review_2007/STAGING/local_assets/downloads/pdf
/statistical_review_of_world_energy_full_report_2007.pdf (accessed 4 March 2008).
(Note: a complete chart with an explanation of Canadian reserves can be found in
appendix B.)

8. Daniel P. Erikson, "Ahmadinejad finds it warmer in Latin America" (editorial), *Los
Angeles Times*, 3 October 2007, www.latimes.com/news/opinion/sunday/commentary
/la-oe-erikson3oct03,0,5434188.story (accessed 3 October 2007).

9. Robert J. Morgan, *My All in All* (Nashville, TN: B&H Publishing, 2008), entry for April
22.

10. "Country Energy Profiles," Energy Information Administration, http://tonto.eia.doe
.gov/country/index.cfm (accessed 26 March 2008). (Note: this information is accessible
under the "Consumption" tab in the "Top World Oil Consumers, 2006" table.)

11. Zakaria, "Why We Can't Quit."

12. Sara Nunnally and Bryan Bottarelli, "Oil Consumption Statistics: the European
Union's Oil Consumption Growth," *Wavestrength Options Weekly*, 3 March 2007, www
.wavestrength.com/wavestrength/marketreport/20070307_Oil_Consumption
_Statistics_and_Global_Markets_Market_Report.html (accessed 3 June 2008).

13. Michael Grunwald, "The Clean Energy Scam," *Time*, 7 April 2008, 40–45.

14. "Jimmy Carter State of the Union Address 1980," 23 January 1980, Jimmy Carter Library & Museum, www.jimmycarterlibrary.org/documents/speeches/su80jec.phtml (accessed 3 June 2008).

15. "Confrontation in the Gulf: Excerpts from Bush's Statement on the U.S. Defense of Saudis," *The New York Times*, 9 August 1990, http://query.nytimes.com/gst/fullpage.htm l?res=9C0CE0DC1F3FF93AA3575BC0A966958260&sec=&spon=&pagewanted=all (accessed 26 March 2008).

16. Ann Davis, "Where Has All the Oil Gone?" *Wall Street Journal*, 6 October 2007, http://www.energyinvestmentstrategies.com/infoFiles/articlePDFs/100607SpeculatorsOilPri ces.pdf (accessed 17 June 2008).

17. Remarks by Abdallah S. Jum'ah, "The Impact of Upstream Technological Advances on Future Oil Supply," speech transcript, Third OPEC International Seminar, 12–13 September 2006, http://www.opec.org/opecna/Speeches/2006/OPEC_Seminar/PDF /Abdallah%20Jumah.pdf (accessed 21 August 2007).

18. "Oil War," Global Policy Forum, Security Council, 26 March 2003, http://www .globalpolicy.org/security/oil/2003/0326oilwar.htm (accessed 26 June 2008).

19. Paul Roberts, *The End of Oil: On the Edge of a Perilous New World* (Boston: Mariner Books, 2005), 337. Reprinted by permission of Houghton Mifflin Harcourt Publishing Company. All rights reserved.

20. Ibid.

21. "Mrs. Meir Says Moses Made Israel Oil-Poor," *The New York Times*, 11 June 1973.

22. Tim LaHaye, *The Coming Peace in the Middle East* (Grand Rapids, MI: Zondervan, 1984), 105.

23. Aaron Klein, "Is Israel sitting on enormous oil reserve?" WorldNetDaily, 21 September 2005, www.worldnetdaily.com/news/article.asp?ARTICLE_ID=46428 (accessed 27 August 2007).

24. Ibid.

25. Zion Facts, "What are the terms of the Joseph License?" and "What are the terms of the Asher-Menashe License?" http://www.zionoil.com/investor-center/zion-faqs.html (accessed 31 March 2008).

26. Dan Ephron, "Israel: A Vision of Oil in the Holy Land," *Newsweek*, 13 June 2007, http://www.newsweek.com/id/50060 (accessed 2 October 2007).

27. Paul Crespo, "Author: 'Something Is Going On Between Russia and Iran,'" Newsmax, 30 January 2007, http://archive.newsmax.com/archives/articles/2007/1/29/212432 .shtml?s=1h (accessed 26 March 2008).

28. Joel C. Rosenberg, *Epicenter* (Carol Stream, IL: Tyndale House Publishers, 2006), 113.

29. Amir Mizroch, "Israel launches new push to reduce its oil dependency," *Jerusalem Post*, 27 September 2007, posted at Forecast Highs, http://forecasthighs.wordpress.com/2007 /09/27/Israel-launches-new-push-to-reduce-its-oil-dependency (accessed 2 October 2007).

30. Steven R. Weisman, "Oil Producers See the World and Buy It Up," *The New York Times*, 28 November 2007.

31. Don Richardson, *The Secrets of the Koran* (Ventura, CA: Regal Books, 2003), 161.

32. Nazila Fathi, "Mideast Turmoil: Tehran; Iranian Urges Muslims to Use Oil as a Weapon," *The New York Times*, 6 April 2002, http://query.nytimes.com/gst/fullpage.htm l?res=9A05E5D6173DF935A35757C0A9649C8B63&scp=3&sq=Nazila+Fathi&st=nyt (accessed 25 June 2008).

33. Paraphrased by Timothy George, "Theology in an Age of Terror," *Christianity Today*, September 2006; from C. S. Lewis, "Learning in Wartime," *The Weight of Glory and Other Addresses* (New York: Macmillan, 1949), 41–52.

34. C. S. Lewis, "Learning in Wartime," *The Weight of Glory and Other Addresses* (New York: Macmillan, 1949), 26.

35. Vance Havner, *In Times Like These* (Old Tappan, NJ: Fleming H. Revell, 1969), 21.

## Chapter Three: Modern Europe . . . Ancient Rome

1. Adapted from David Jeremiah, *The Handwriting on the Wall* (Nashville, TN: Thomas Nelson, Inc., 1992), 15–16.

2. "The Mists of Time," Amazing Discoveries, http://amazingdiscoveries.org/the-mists-of -time.html (accessed 21 March 2008).

3. Tim LaHaye, Ed Hindson, eds., *The Bible Prophecy Commentary* (Eugene, OR: Harvest House Publishers, 2006), 226.

4. "The European Union," *Time*, 26 May 1930, http://www.time.com/time/magazine /article/0,9171,739314,00.html (accessed 8 October 2007).

5. William R. Clark, *Petrodollar Warfare: Oil, Iraq and the Future of the Dollar* (New Society Publishers, 2005), 198; see also W. S. Churchill, *Collected Essays of Winston Churchill, Vol. II* ( London: Library of Imperial History, 1976), 176–186.

6. "The History of the European Union," Europa, http://europa.eu./abc/history (accessed 8 October 2007).

7. Compiled from "The EU at a glance—Ten historic steps," Europa, http://europa.eu (accessed 8 October 2007).

8. Michael Shtender-Auberbach, "Israel and the EU: A Path to Peace," The Century Foundation, 3 November 2005, http://www.tcf.org/list.asp?type=NC&pubid=1129 (accessed 10 October 2007).

9. Council of the European Union Presidency Conclusions, http://www.consilium.europa .eu/ueDocs/cms_Data/docs/pressData/en/ec/94932.pdf (accessed 17 June 2008).

10. "How are we organized?" Europa, http://europa.eu/abc/panorama/howorganised /index_en.htm (accessed 5 March 2008).

11. Alex Duval Smith, "Blair kicks off campaign to become EU President," *The Guardian*, 13 January 2008, http://www.guardian.co.uk/uk/2008/jan/13/politics.world (accessed 5 March 2008); see also Dan Bilefsky, "2 Leaders Back Blair as European Union President," *The New York Times,* 20 October 2007, http://www.nytimes.com/2007 /10/20/world/europe/20europe.html?_r=1&oref=slogin (accessed 5 March 2007).

12. Arno Froese, *How Democracy Will Elect the Antichrist* (Columbia, SC: Olive Press, 1997), 165.

13. Quoted in David L. Larsen, *Telling the Old, Old Story: The Art of Narrative Preaching* (Grand Rapids, MI: Kregel, 1995), 214.

14. Jim Madaffer, "The Firestorm—Two Weeks Later," City of San Diego, www.sandiego .gov/citycouncil/cd7/pdf/enews/2003/the_firestorm.pdf (accessed 5 March 2008).

15. "Burned Firefighter Describes Cheating Death," NBC San Diego, 14 November 2007, www.nbcsandiego.com/news/14598732/detail.html (accessed 15 November 2007); Tony Manolatos, "Cal fire report recounts tragic incident, rescue," *Union Tribune* (San Diego), 9 November 2007, http://www.signonsandiego.com/news/metro/20071109 -9999-1n9report.htm (accessed 5 March 2008); Tony Manolatos, "Pilot who rescued fire crew didn't feel like a hero," *Union Tribune* (San Diego), 30 October 2007, http:// www.signonsandiego.com/news/metro/20071030-1400-bn30pilot.html (accessed 31 October 2007); and Tony Manolatos, "During rescue effort that turned tragic, an act of heroism," *Union Tribune* (San Diego), 23 October 2007, http://www.signonsandiego .com/news/metro/20071023-9999-bn23firedead.html (accessed 26 October 2007).

## Chapter Four: Islamic Terrorism

1. Georges Sada, *Saddam's Secrets: How an Iraqi General Defied and Survived Saddam Hussein* (Brentwood, TN: Integrity Publishers, 2006), 285–286.

2. Ibid., 289.

3. "Public Expresses Mixed Views of Islam, Mormonism," Pew Research Center Publications, 25 September 2007, http://pewresearch.org/pubs/602/public-expresses -mixed-views-of-islam-mormonism (accessed 1 October 2007).

4. Sada, *Saddam's Secrets,* 289–290.

5. Adapted from "New Poll Shows Worry over Islamic Terror Threat, to Be Detailed in Special Fox News Network Report," Fox News, 3 February 2007, www.foxnews.com /story/0,2933,249521,00.html (accessed 16 October 2007).

6. "Hamas TV puppet 'kills' Bush for helping Israel," Reuters wire service, 1 April 2008, http://www.reuters.com/article/worldNews/idUSL0146737420080401 (accessed 1 April 2008).

7. Reza F. Safa, Foreword to Don Richardson, *The Secrets of the Koran* (Ventura, CA: Regal Books, 2003), 10.

8. Will Durant, *The Age of Faith* (New York: Simon & Schuster, 1950), 155.

9. Statistics compiled from "Major Religions of the World Ranked by Adherents," Adherents.com, http://pewresearch.org/pubs/483/muslim-americans (accessed 17 October 2007); and "Muslim Americans: Middle Class and Mostly Mainstream," Pew Research Center, www.adherents.com/Religions_By_Adherents.html (accessed 17 October 2007).

10. Durant, *Age of Faith*, 163.

11. Robert A. Morey, *Islam Unveiled: The True Desert Storm* (Sherman's Dale, PA: The Scholar's Press, 1991), 49.

12. Abd El Schafi, *Behind the Veil* (Caney, KS: Pioneer Book Company, 1996), 32.

13. Winfried Corduan, *Pocket Guide to World Religions* (Downers Grove, IL: InterVarsity Press, 2006), 80–85.

14. Information on the five pillars adapted from Norman L. Geisler and Abdul Saleeb, *Answering Islam*, 2nd ed. (Grand Rapids, MI: Baker Books, 2006), 301.

15. Benazir Bhutto, *Reconciliation: Islam, Democracy, and the West* (New York: HarperCollins, 2008), 2–3, 20.

16. "Text of Ibrahim Mdaires's Sermon," *The Jerusalem Post*, 19 May 2005.

17. Richardson, *Secrets of the Koran*, 69–71.

18. Oren Dorell, "Some say schools giving Muslim special treatment," *USA Today*, 25 July 2007, http://www.usatoday.com/news/nation/2007-07-25-muslim-special-treatment -from-schools_N.htm (accessed 16 October 2007); see also Helen Gao, "Arabic program offered at school," (San Diego) *Union Tribune*, 12 April 2007, http://www .signonsandiego.com/news/education/20070412-9999-1m12carver.html (accessed 16 October 2007).

19. Tony Blankley, *The West's Last Chance* (Washington, DC: Regnery Publishing, Inc., 2005), 21–23, 39.

20. Sada, *Saddam's Secrets*, 287.

21. Philip Johnston, "Reid meets the furious face of Islam," (London) *Telegraph*, 21 September 2006, http://www.telegraph.co.uk/news/uknews/1529415/Reid-meets-the -furious-face-of-Islam.html (accessed 13 March 2008).

22. Nick Britten, "Religions collide under the dreaming spires," (London) *Telegraph*, 4 February 2008, http://www.telegraph.co.uk/news/uknews/1577340/Religions-collide -under-the-dreaming-spires.html (accessed 13 March 2008).

23. "Sharia law in UK is 'unavoidable'," BBC News, 7 February 2008, http://news.bbc .co.uk/2/hi/uk_news/7232661.stm (accessed 13 March 2008).

24. Jonathan Wynne-Jones, "Bishop warns of no-go zones for non-Muslims," (London) *Telegraph*, 5 January 2008, http://www.telegraph.co.uk/news/uknews/1574694 /Bishop-warns-of-no-go-zones-for-non-Muslims.html (accessed 13 March 2008).

25. "Vatican: Muslims now outnumber Catholics," *USA Today*, 30 March 2008, http:// www.usatoday.com/news/religion/2008-03-30-muslims-catholics_N.htm (accessed 2 April 2008).

26. "Ahmadinejad's 2005 address to the United Nations," Wikisource: United Nations, http://en.wikisource.org/wiki/Ahmadinejad's_2005_address_to_the_United-Nations.

27. "Ahmadinejad: Wipe Israel off map," Aljazeera News, 28 October 2005, http://english .aljazeera.net/English/archive/archive?ArchiveId=15816 (accessed 4 June 2008).

28. Stan Goodenough, "Ahmadinejad: Israel has reached its 'final' stage,'" *Jerusalem Newswire*, 30 January 2008, www.jnewswire.com/article/2314 (accessed 4 June 2008).

29. Mark Bentley and Ladane Nasseri, "Ahmadinejad's Nuclear Mandate Strengthened After Iran Election," Bloomberg News, 16 March 2008, www.bloomberg.com/apps /news?pid=20601087&sid=aGUPH1VLn.7c&refer=home (accessed 4 June 2008).

30. John F. Walvoord and Mark Hitchcock, *Armageddon, Oil and Terror* (Carol Stream, IL: Tyndale House Publishers, 2007), 44.

31. "Roman Catholic Bishop Wants Everyone to Call God 'Allah,'" Fox News, 16 August 2007, http://www.foxnews.com/story/0,2933,293394,00.html (accessed 14 March 2008).

32. Stan Goodenough, "Let's Call Him Allah," *Jerusalem Newswire*, 21 August 2007, http:// www.foxnews.com/story/0,2933,293394,00.html (accessed 14 March 2008).

33. "Roman Catholic Bishop," Fox News.

34. Ibid.

35. Hal Lindsey, "Does God care what He's called?" WorldNetDaily, 17 August 2007, www
    .wnd.com/index.php?pageId=43089 (accessed 27 June 2008).

36. Adapted from Dr. Robert A. Morey, *Islam Unveiled,* (Shermandale, PA: The Scholar's
    Press, 1991), 60.

37. Edward Gibbon, *The Decline and Fall of the Roman Empire* (London: Milman Co.,
    n.d.), 1:365.

38. "A Testimony from a Saudi Believer," Answering Islam: A Christian-Muslim Dialog and
    Apologetic, http://answering-islam.org./Testimonies/saudi.html (accessed 20 April
    2006).

## Chapter Five: Vanished Without a Trace

1. "Firefighters Gain Ground as Santa Ana Winds Decrease," KNBC Los Angeles, 24
   October 2007, http://www.knbc.com/news/14401132/detail.html (accessed 26 October
   2007).

2. Bruce Bickel and Stan Jantz, *Bible Prophecy 101* (Eugene, OR: Harvest House
   Publishers, 1999), 124.

3. *Merriam-Webster Online*, s. v. "rapture," www.merriam-webster.com/dictionary/rapture
   (accessed 5 June 2008).

4. Alfred Tennyson, "Break, Break, Break," *Poems, Vol. II* (Boston: Ticknor, Reed and
   Fields, 1851), 144.

5. Tim LaHaye, *The Rapture* (Eugene, OR: Harvest House Publishers, 2002), 69.

6. "100 Nations' Leaders Attend Churchill Funeral," Churchill Centre, www
   .winstonchurchill.org/i4a/pages/index.cfm?pageid=801 (accessed 4 March 2008).

7. Bickel and Jantz, *Bible Prophecy*, 123.

8. Arthur T. Pierson, *The Gospel, Vol. 3* (Grand Rapids, MI: Baker Book House, 1978),
   136.

9. Wayne Grudem, *Systematic Theology* (Grand Rapids, MI: Zondervan, 1994), 1093.

10. Gig Conaughton, "County Buys Reverse 911 System," *North County Times*, 11 August
    2005, http://www.nctimes.com/articles/2005/08/12/news/top_stories/21_13_388_11_05
    .txt (accessed 4 March 2008); see also "Mayor Sanders Unveils New Reverse 911
    System," KGTV, 6 September 2007, http://www.10news.com/news/14061100/detail.html
    (accessed 4 March 2008); Gig Conaughton, "Officials Laud High-Speed Alert System,"
    North County Times, 27 October 2007, http://www.nctimes.com/articles/2007/10/26
    /news/top_stories/21_36_2110_25_07.txt (accessed 18 March 2008); Scott Glover, Jack
    Leonard, and Matt Lait, "Two Homes, Two Couples, Two Fates," Los Angeles Times, 26
    October 2007, http://www.latimes.com/news/local/la-me-pool26oct26,0,3755059.story
    (accessed 26 October 2007).

## Chapter Six: Does America Have a Role in Prophecy?

1. Adapted from Newt Gingrich, *Rediscovering God in America* (Nashville, TN: Integrity, 2006), 130.

2. Peter Marshall and David Manuel, *The Light and the Glory* (Old Tappan, NJ: Revell, 1977), 17, 18.

3. "President's Proclamation," *The New York Times*, 21 November 1982, http://select .nytimes.com/search/restricted/article?res=F30611FB395DOC728EDDA80994 (accessed 15 April 2008).

4. "The Journal of Christopher Columbus (1492)," The History Guide: Lectures on Early Modern European History, www.historyguide.org/earlymod/columbus.html (accessed 2 November 2007).

5. "Washington's First Inauguration Address, April 30, 1789," Library of Congress, www .loc.gov/exhibits/treasures/trt051.html (accessed 5 June 2008).

6. John F. Walvoord, "America and the Cause of World Missions," *America in History and Bible Prophecy*, Thomas McCall, ed. (Chicago: Moody Press, 1976), 21.

7. Gordon Robertson, "Into All the World," Christian Broadcasting Network, http://www .cbn.com/spirituallife/churchandministry/churchhistory/Gordon_Into_World.aspx (accessed 1 November 2007).

8. Luis Bush, "Where Are We Now?" Mission Frontiers, 2003, http://www .missionfrontiers.org/2000/03/bts20003.htm (accessed 1 November 2007).

9. Abba Eban, *An Autobiography* (New York: Random House, 1977), 126.

10. Ibid., 134.

11. "The Worst of the Worst: The World's Most Repressive Societies," Freedom House, April 2007, http://www.freedomhouse.org/template.cfm?page=383&report=58 (accessed 1 November 2007).

12. Ronald Reagan, "Inaugural Address, January 20, 1981," Ronald Reagan Presidential Library Archives, National Archives and Records Administration, www.reagan.utexas .edu/archives/speeches/1981/12081a.htm (accessed 5 June 2008).

13. Quoted in Newt Gingrich, *Winning the Future: A 21ˢᵗ Century Contract with America* (Washington, DC: Regnery Publishing, Inc., 2005), 200.

14. John Gilmary Shea, *The Lincoln Memorial: A Record of the Life, Assassination, and Obsequies of Abraham Lincoln* (New York: Bunce and Huntington Publishers, 1865), 237.

15. Benjamin Franklin, "Speech to the Constitutional Convention, June 28, 1787," Library of Congress, http://www.loc.gov/exhibits/religion/rel06.html (accessed 18 June 2008).

16. William J. Federer, ed., *America's God and Country—Encyclopedia of Quotations*, (St. Louis: Amerisearch, Inc., 2000), 696.

17. Ibid., 697–698.

18. Jared Sparks, ed., *The Writings of George Washington*, 12 vols. (Boston: Little, Brown and Company, 1837), vol. III, 449.

19. "The Gettysburg Address," http://www.loc.gov/exhibits/gadd/gadrft.html (accessed 18 June 2008).

20. Charles Fadiman, ed., *The American Treasury* (New York: Harper & Brothers, 1955), 127.

21. Jay Gormley, "LISD to Repaint 'In God We Trust' on Gym Wall," CBS11TV.com, 1 April 2008, http://cbs11tv.com/business/education/LISD.Repaints.motto.2.689875.html (accessed 7 April 2008).

22. "Laus Deo," Snopes Urban Legends Reference Pages, www.snopes.com/politics /religion/lausdeo.asp (accessed 7 April 2008); see also "Washington Monument," www .snopes.com/politics/religion/monument.asp (accessed 7 April 2008).

23. Tim LaHaye, as cited by Dr. Thomas Ice, "Is America in Bible Prophecy?" Pre-Trib Research Center, http://www.pre-trib.org/article-view.php?id=14 (accessed 18 June 2008).

24. Tim LaHaye, "The Role of the U.S.A. in End Times Prophecy," *Tim LaHaye's Perspective*, August 1999, http://209.85.173.104/search?q=cache:ZEQ46V4CQRYJ:www .yodelingfrog.com/Misc%2520Items/(doc)%2520-%2520Tim%2520LaHaye%2520 -%2520The%2520Role%2520of%2520the%2520USA%2520in%2520End%2520Times %2520Prophecy.pdf+%22Does+the+United+States+have+a+place+in+end+time+pro phecy%3F%22&hl=en&ct=clnk&cd=1&gl=us&lr=lang_en (accessed 18 June 2008).

25. John Walvoord and Mark Hitchcock, *Armageddon, Oil and Terror*, (Carol Stream, IL: Tyndale House Publishers, 2007), 67.

26. "President Bush Meets with EU Leaders, Chancellor Merkel of the Federal Republic of Germany and President Barroso of the European Council and President of the European Commission," press release dated 30 April 2007, The White House, http:// www.whitehouse.gov/news/releases/2007/04/20070430-2.html (accessed 28 March 2008).

27. "Transatlantic Economic Council," European Commission, http://ec.europa.eu /enterprise/enterprise_policy/inter_rel/tec/index_en.htm (accessed 28 March 2008).

28. Jerome R. Cossi, "Premeditated Merger: Inside the hush-hush North American Union confab," WorldNetDaily, 13 March 2008, http://www.worldnetdaily.com/index .php?fa=PAGE.view&pageId=58788 (accessed 28 March 2008).

29. Ibid.

30. Walvoord and Hitchcock, *Armageddon*, 68.

31. Ed Timperlake, "Explosive missing debate item," *The Washington Times*, 5 March 2008, http://www.washingtontimes.com/news/2008/mar/05/explosive-missing-debate-item (accessed 28 March 2008).

32. Ed Timperlake, "Explosive missing debate item," *The Washington Times*, 5 March 2008, http://www.washingtontimes.com/news/2008/mar/05/explosive-missing-debate-item (accessed 28 March 2008).

33. Ed Timperlake, "Explosive missing debate item," *The Washington Times*, 5 March 2008, http://www.washingtontimes.com/news/2008/mar/05/explosive-missing-debate-item (accessed 28 March 2008).

34. "U.S. says N. Korea missile tests 'not constructive,'" Reuters, 28 March 2008, http:// www.reuters.com/article/idUSWAT00920520080328 (accessed 28 March 2008).

35. Walvoord and Hitchcock, *Armageddon*, 65.

36. La Shawn Barber, "America on the Decline," La Shawn Barber's Corner, 25 February 2004, http://lashawnbarber.com/archives/2004/02/25/brstronglatest-column-america-on-the-declinestrong/ (accessed 28 March 2008).

37. Adapted from Carle C. Zimmerman, *Family and Civilization* (Wilmington, DE: ISI Books, 2008), 255.

38. Mike Evans, *The Final Move Beyond Iraq* (Lake Mary, FL: Front Line, 2007), 168.

39. Herbert C. Hoover, *Addresses upon the American Road 1950–1955* (Palo Alto, CA: Stanford University Press, 1955), 111–113,117.

40. Mark Hitchcock, *America in the End Times*, newsletter, The Left Behind Prophecy Club.

41. Herman A. Hoyt, *Is the United States in Prophecy?* (Winona Lake, ID: BMH Books, 1977), 16.

## Chapter Seven: When One Man Rules the World

1. Erwin Lutzer, *Hitler's Cross* (Chicago: Moody Press, 1995), 62–63.

2. Tim LaHaye and Ed Hinson, *Global Warning* (Eugene, OR: Harvest House, 2007), 195.

3. Charles Colson, *Kingdoms in Conflict* (Grand Rapids, MI: Zondervan, 1987), 129–130.

4. Lutzer, *Hitler's Cross*, 73.

5. Arthur W. Pink, *The Antichrist* (Minneapolis: Klich & Klich, 1979), 77.

6. Marvin Kalb and Bernard Kalb, *Kissinger* (New York: Little, Brown and Company, 1974), 201–202.

7. Colson, *Kingdoms in Conflict*, 68.

8. Ibid.

9. Thomas Ice, "The Ethnicity of the Antichrist," Pre-Trib Research Center, www.pre-trib.org/article-view.php?id=230 (accessed 5 June 2008).

10. *Conservapedia*, French Revolution, http://www.conservapedia.com/French_Revolution (accessed 18 June 2008).

11. W. A. Criswell, *Expository Sermons on Revelation*, vol. IV (Dallas: Criswell Publishing, 1995), 109.

12. David E. Gumpert, "Animal Tags for People?" *Business Week*, 11 January 2007, www.businessweek.com/smallbiz/content/jan2007/sb20070111_186325.htm?chan=smallbiz_smallbiz+index+page_today's+top+stories (accessed 11 April 2008).

13. Gary Frazier, *Signs of the Coming of Christ* (Arlington, TX: Discovery Ministries, 1998), 149.

## Chapter Eight: The New Axis of Evil

1. "President Delivers State of the Union Address," press release dated 29 January 2002, The White House, http://www.whitehouse.gov/news/releases/2002/01/20020129-11.html (accessed 10 March 2008).

2. John F. Walvoord, *The Nations in Prophecy* (Grand Rapids, MI: Zondervan, 1978), 107.

3. Erik Hildinger, *Warriors of the Steppe: A Military History of Central Asia, 500 B.C. to 1700* (New York: DaCapo Press, 2001), 33.

4. Walvoord, *Nations in Prophecy*, 106.

5. Ibid.,101.

6. Edward Lucas, "The New Cold War," www.edwardlucas.com (accessed 6 June 2008).

7. Mike Celizic, "*Time*'s Person of the Year Is Vladimir Putin," *Today*: People-msnbc.com, 19 December 2007, http://www.msnbc.msn.com/id/22323855 (accessed 17 April 2008).

8. Nabi Abdullaev, "Speech Suggest Best Is Yet to Come," *Moscow Times*, 11 February 2008, http://www.moscowtimes.ru/article/1010/42/302320.htm (accessed 11 February 2008).

9. Oleg Shchedrov, "Putin in Jordan to demonstrate regional ambitions," Reuters AlertNet, 12 February 2007, www.alertnet.org/thenews/newsdesk/L12935084.htm (accessed 6 June 2008).

10. Ibid.

11. Hassan M. Fattah, "Putin Visits Qatar for Talks on Natural Gas and Trade," *The New York Times*, 13 February 2007, www.nytimes.com/2007/02/13/world /middleeast/13putin.html (accessed 17 April 2008).

12. Scott Peterson, "Russia, Iran Harden Against West," *Christian Science Monitor*, 18 October 2007, http://www.csmonitor.com/2007/1018/p06s02-woeu.html (accessed 18 June 2008).

13. "Russia scraps Libya's debts as Putin visits Tripoli," AFP (Agence France-Presse), April 2008, BNET Business Network, http://findarticles.com/p/articles/mi_kmafp/is_200804 /ai_n25344293 (accessed 17 April 2008).

14. "EU should unite behind new Russia strategy: study," ViewNews.net, 7 November 2007, http://viewnews.net/news/world/eu-should-unite-behind-new-russia-strategy-study .html (accessed 18 June 2008).

15. Andris Piebalgs, "Gas warms EU-Russian ties," repost of *New Europe*, 7 April 2008, http://www.mgimo.ru/alleurope/2006/21/bez-perevoda1.html (accessed 21 July 2008).

16. "Iran," CIA-The World Factbook, https://www.cia.gov/library/publications/the-world -factbook/geos/ir.html (accessed 26 June 2008).

17. Borzou Daragahi, "Tehran sharing more nuclear data, agency says," *Los Angeles Times*, 31 August 2007, http://articles.latimes.com/2007/aug/31/world/fg-irannukes31 (accessed 31 August 2007).

18. "Ahmadinejad in new attack on 'savage animal,'" AFP news wire, 20 February 2008, http://afp.google.com/article/ALeqM5g_nrxYSrTbp_LIZcVU4VGCBpQ0hQ (accessed 6 June 2008).

19. Thom Shanker and Brandan Knowlton, "U.S. Describes Confrontation with Iranian Boats," *The New York Times*, 8 January 2008, http://www.nytimes.com/2008/01/08 /washington/08military.html?scp=2&sq=U.S.+Describes+Confrontation+With +Iranian+Boats&st=nyt (accessed 26 June 2008).

20. Nazila Fathi, "Iran's President Says 'Israel Must Be Wiped Off the Map,'" *The New York Times*, 26 October 2007, http://www.nytimes.com/2005/10/26/international /middleeast/26cnd-iran.html (accessed 18 April 2008).

21. "UN boss alarmed by Hezbollah's threat against Israel,"Agence France-Presse, 3 March 2008, http://findarticles.com/p/articles/mi_kmafp/is_200803/ai_n24365391 (accessed 3 March 2008).

22. Aaron Klein, "Hezbollah: Rockets fired into Israel directed by Iran," WorldNetDaily, 7 May 2007, http://www.worldnetdaily.com/news/article.asp?ARTICLE_ID=55572 (accessed 5 September 2007).

23. Ibid.

24. "UN boss alarmed by Hezbollah's threat against Israel," Agence France-Presse, 3 March 2008.

25. Edward Gibbon, *The Decline and Fall of the Roman Empire* (London: Milman Co., London, n.d.), 1:204.

26. David L. Cooper, *When Gog's Armies Meet the Almighty* (Los Angeles: The Biblical Research Society, 1958), 17.

27. Theodore Epp, *Russia's Doom Prophesied* (Lincoln, NE: Good News Broadcasting, 1954), 40–42.

28. Barry L. Brumfield, "Israel; Politically and Geographically," Israel's Messiah.com, www.israelsmessiah.com/palestinian_refugees/israel_vs_arabs.htm (accessed 6 June 2008).

29. Matthew Kreiger, "7,200 Israeli millionaires today, up 13%," *Jerusalem Post*, 28 June 2007, http://www.jpost.com/servlet/Satellite?pagename=JPost%2FJPArticle%2FShowFull&cid=1182951032508 (accessed 17 April 2008).

30. Serge Schmemann, "Israel Redefines Its Dream, Finding Wealth in High Tech," *The New York Times*, 18 April 1998, http://query.nytimes.com/gst/fullpage.html?res=9502EED7123CF93BA25757C0A96E958260&sec=travel (accessed 6 June 2008).

31. "Land of milk and start-ups," *Economist*, 19 March 2008, www.economist.com/business/displaystory.cfm?story_id=10881264 (accessed 29 April 2008).

32. "Israel," Legatum Prosperity Index 2007, Legatum Institute, http://www.prosperity.org/profile.aspx?id=IS (accessed 29 April 2008).

33. "Israel," CIA-The World Factbook, https://www.cia.gov/library/publications/the-world-factbook/geos/is.html (accessed 26 June 2008).

34. Joel C. Rosenberg, *Epicenter* (Carol Stream, IL: Tyndale House Publishers, 2006), 131.

35. H. D. M. Spence and Joseph Excell, eds., *The Pulpit Commentary*, vol. 28 (New York: Funk & Wagnalls, 1880–93), 298.

36. Robert J. Morgan, *From This Verse* (Nashville, TN: Thomas Nelson, Inc., 1998), entry for December 29.

## Chapter Nine: Arming for Armageddon

1. Douglas MacArthur, "Farewell Address to Congress," delivered 19 April 1951, American Rhetoric, www.americanrhetoric.com/speeches/douglasmacarthurfarewelladdress.htm (accessed 6 June 2008).

2. Douglas Brinkley, ed., *The Reagan Diaries*, (New York: HarperCollins, 2007), 19, 24.

3. "American War Deaths Through History," Military Factory.com, www.militaryfactory.com/american_war_deaths.asp (accessed 6 June 2008).

4. Sylvie Barak, "Stephen Hawking says NASA should budget for interstellar travel: rising for the moon," The Inquirer (blog), 22 April 2008, www.theinquirer.net/gb/inquirer /news/2008/04/22/stephen-hawking-argues-nasa (accessed 6 June 2008).

5. Alan Johnson, *The Expositor's Bible Commentary* (Grand Rapids: Zondervan, 1981), 12:551.

6. Vernon J. McGee, *Through the Bible,* vol. 3 (Nashville, TN: Thomas Nelson, Inc., 1982), 513.

7. A. Sims, ed., *The Coming Great War,* (Toronto: A. Sims, Publisher, 1932), 7–8.

8. John Dryden, trans., *Plutarch's Life of Sylla*. Public domain.

9. Josephus, *The Wars of the Jews, Book 6* from *The Works of Josephus*, translated by William Whiston (Peabody, MA: Hendrickson Publishers, 1987); available online: "Josephus Describes the Roman's Sack of Jerusalem," Frontline, http://www.pbs.org /wgbh/pages/frontline/shows/religion/maps/primary/josephussack.html (accessed 26 June 2008).

10. J. Dwight Pentecost, *Things to Come—A Study in Biblical Eschatology* (Findlay, OH: Dunham Publishing Company, 1958), 347–48.

11. "Hamas offers truce in return for 1967 borders," Associated Press, 21 April 2008, www .msnbc.msn.com/id/24235665/ (accessed 6 June 2008).

12. John Walvoord and Mark Hitchcock, *Armageddon, Oil and Terror* (Carol Stream, IL: Tyndale House Publishers, 2007), 174.

13. Alon Liel, *Turkey in the Middle East: Oil, Islam, and Politics* (Boulder, CO: Lynne Rienner Publishers, 2001), 20–21.

14. John F. Walvoord, "The Way of the Kings of the East," *Light for the World's Darkness,* John W. Bradbury, ed. (New York: Loizeaux Brothers, 1944), 164.

15. Larry M. Wortzel, "China's Military Potential," US Army Strategic Studies Institute, 2 October 1998, www.fas.org/nuke/guide/china/doctrine/chinamil.htm (accessed 6 June 2008).

16. Sims, *The Coming Great War,* 12–13.

17. Robert J. Morgan, *My All in All* (Nashville: B&H Publishers, 2008), entry for July 16.

18. Randall Price, *Jerusalem in Prophecy* (Eugene, OR: Harvest House Publishers, 1998), 1179–1180.

## Chapter Ten: The Return of the King

1. Lehman Strauss, "Bible Prophecy" Bible.org, http://www.bible.org/page.php?page _id=412 (accessed 27 November 2007).

2. John F. Walvoord, *End Times* (Nashville, TN: Word Publishing, 1998), 143.

3. Tim LaHaye, *The Rapture* (Eugene, OR: Harvest House Publishers, 2002), 89.

4. Harry A. Ironside, *Revelation* (Grand Rapids, MI: Kregel, 2004), 187–188.

5. Charles Spurgeon, "The Saviour's Many Crowns," a sermon (no. 281) delivered 30 October 1859, The Spurgeon Archive, www.spurgeon.org/sermons/0281.htm (accessed 7 June 2008).

6. Ironside, *Revelation*, 189.

7. W. A. Criswell, *Expository Sermons on Revelation*, vol. 5 (Grand Rapids, MI: Zondervan, 1966), 31.

8. Ironside, *Revelation*; 189–190.

9. Kenneth Woodward, "Heaven," *Newsweek*, 27 March 1989, 54.

10. C. S. Lewis, *The Problem of Pain* (New York: Macmillan, 1940, 1973), 28.

11. Walvoord, *End Times*, 171.

12. Vance Havner, *In Times Like These* (Old Tappan, NJ: Fleming H. Revell Company, 1969), 29.

13. Based on Sir Ernest Henry Shackleton, *South! The Story of Shackleton's 1914–1917 Expedition*, public domain, available at Project Gutenberg, www.gutenberg.org /files/5199/5199-h/5199-h.htm (accessed 7 June 2008).

## Appendix B: Conventional Oil Reserves by Country, June 2007

1. Oil-Proved Reserves, "BP Statistical Review of World Energy June 2007," BP Global, http://www.bp.com/liveassets/bp_internet/globalbp/globalbp_uk_english/reports_and _publications/statistical_energy_review_2007/STAGING/local_assets/downloads/pdf /statistical_review_of_world_energy_full_report_2007.pdf (accessed 4 March 2008).

# Living with Confidence in a Chaotic World

To Marvin L. "Buzz" Oates

whose love for God and His Word has touched all of us at *Turning Point*
and will, from this day forward, help us touch the rest of the world
with the unchanging message of God's Word

# Acknowledgments

EVERY DAY OF MY LIFE I HAVE THE PRIVILEGE OF DEVOTING MY time and energy to the only two things in the whole world that are eternal: the Word of God and people. I am so blessed to be surrounded by a team that is deeply committed to these two priorities.

At the center of that team is my wife, Donna, whose office is right next to mine and whose heart has been next to mine for forty-six years. Together we have dreamed and planned and worked toward the goal of influencing our world for Christ. More than ever before, we have been seeing our dreams come true. Like every book I have written, this one has Donna's fingerprints all over it.

Our son, David Michael, is our managing partner at *Turning Point Ministries*. His role continues to expand each year, and it is because he has taken so much off of my administrative plate that I am able to produce books such as the one you are about to read.

Diane Sutherland is my administrative assistant at our media center, and she coordinates my schedule, my travel, my partnerships . . . basically my life! All of us at *Turning Point* wonder how we ever got along without Diane.

Cathy Lord is the coordinator of research and editing. She not only provides considerable research herself, but she works with our team to assure that our information is timely and accurate. Cathy is a stickler for details and a sleuth when it comes to locating original sources.

Rob Morgan and William Kruidenier have worked with me at *Turning Point* to enrich my work. These have to be two of the most well-read men in America. I am constantly amazed at the helpful insights they bring to our writing projects. Rob Suggs is the gifted wordsmith who adds his artistry to the final product.

For the last three years, *Turning Point* has been aggressively involved in the marketing of our books. Our creative department, led by Paul Joiner, has developed some of the finest marketing strategies I have ever seen. Everyone who has seen Paul's work agrees with my assessment. Paul Joiner is one of God's best gifts to *Turning Point*.

The people of the Shadow Mountain Community Church hear what you are reading long before it is written, and they often send me notes which say, "This is going to be a book, isn't it?" Their notes are passed to me through the office of Barbara Boucher, who has been my administrative helper at Shadow Mountain for seven years. Thank you, Barbara, for your faithfulness.

Once again, as with all my other writing projects, I am represented by Sealy Yates of Yates and Yates. I am convinced that no one understands the publishing world like Sealy. He is my agent, my attorney, the chairman of our board, and, most of all, my friend.

None of us deserve to have our name on the same page with the name of our Lord and Savior, Jesus Christ. Together we all want to say,

*This is really all about Him. This is His Message! We are His people!*
*Whatever glory comes from this endeavor belongs to Him and Him alone.*
*He is the only One who is worthy!*

# Knowing the Signs

**HOW ON EARTH DID WE GET INTO THIS MESS?**

Sure, we realized the good times couldn't last forever. Everybody knows that economies move through seasons and cycles, just like everything else. What goes up must come down—just basic common sense, right?

Still, those realizations didn't quite prepare us for the reality. It was as if the United States of America went to the doctor's office for its annual checkup. The nurse said, "This will hurt just a little bit," then picked up a mallet and smashed us a good one on the head! There was a bad financial story in the headlines, then another, and the hits just kept coming. As the late Senator Everett Dirksen is credited with saying, "A billion here, a billion there, and sooner or later it adds up to some real money."[1]

For months, the pundits had been tossing around what they called "the R word"—*Recession*. Then, almost overnight, they were talking about "the D word"—*Depression*. And sure enough, we were all a little depressed.

The numbers tell the story in their cold, hard fashion. By the end of the year 2008, American investors had lost $6.9 trillion in the stock market. (One sign of the times in this grave new world, by the way, is that we find ourselves talking in numbers usually reserved for those astronomers who watch distant galaxies. *Trillions!* Can you wrap your mind around such sums of money?)

Here is a number that fits my level of comprehension: *one half.* That's the portion of the total wealth of the United States and, in fact, of the entire world that did a vanishing act in just months—fifty cents of every dollar; half of every yen, pound, mark, shekel, or whatever is used for money in your corner of the world. We've seen the illusionist make the rabbit disappear, but we always know it's merely sleight of hand; the rabbit always makes a return appearance.[2]

If only that could happen today. If only one of these brainy economists could walk onto the world stage and pull half the world's wealth out of his top hat. So many of our friends would have their jobs back. Young couples wouldn't lose their homes. We can only dream.

Wealth is a fluid thing. If all this capital vanished in a cloud of collapse and selling off, it can reappear in a cloud of demand and buying. But the experts tell us that is unlikely, at least in the near future. The buyers are presently nursing their wounds. This economic tsunami has been a sign before them, written in glaring red letters that read, "Let the buyer beware!" Economies boom in an atmosphere of confidence, when people go to market with the assurance that buying and selling are safe options. Toxic credit has poisoned the well on Wall Street; bad mortgages have left a trail of disaster; and banks have collapsed like a series of dominoes.

*Forbes* magazine compiles an annual list of the world's billionaires. These lists tend to resemble exclusive clubs, with the membership carrying over from one year to the next. At least they did so in the past. In the 2009 list, 30 percent of the 2008 membership dropped off the list, billionaires no more. Those members had lost an accumulated two trillion dollars—in one year! The best of times had become the worst of times.[3]

The cynic will say, "How sad about those poor, suffering billionaires! Now that they're only *millionaires,* how will they pay their water and power bills?" But you see, we're all interconnected. No man is a financial island in this world economy. The truth is that the net worth of US households fell by $11.2 trillion in 2008. We've seen the steepest decline in the housing market since 1951, and in stocks since 1946. The total nonfinancial household debt in the US is now $13.8 trillion.[4]

Throwing the word *trillions* around makes me dizzy. So let's talk about unemployment. At this writing, the national figure stands at 14.5 million or 9.4 percent of the workforce, the highest in more than two decades.[5] People who don't hold jobs don't make mortgage payments; therefore, it's not surprising that foreclosures climbed 30 percent in a single, horrible month.[6] What could be sadder than all those empty houses being sold by the banks? Our beautiful Southern California avenues are cluttered with them. I drive by them on my way to our church and shake my head; but when I look across the congregation and see the sad faces of those without jobs and homes, the truth of it really touches home. *How did we get here, Lord? How could we have not foreseen that this storm was coming?*

World leaders are meeting, working desperately to put aside political and cultural differences to find ways to stop the bleeding. Everyone looks to the United States for leadership, (also for blame—it goes with the territory). The US Congress passed a stimulus package and a $787 billion recovery plan to inject some life into a very sick economy. The new US Treasury Secretary has indicated that "as much as $2 trillion could be plowed into the financial system to jump-start lending."[7] Is it too much, too soon? Too little, too late? We hear every kind of answer, every variety of opinion. The truth is that no one really knows. We hope and pray that our economic experts are applying the right remedies, but none of them saw the crash coming—so what qualifies them as experts?

Meanwhile, across the sea, the European Central Bank has cut interest rates to a new ten-year low. There, too, the effort is to infuse more money to stimulate the economy of the European continent. Germany expects the global economy to shrink "at the worst rate since the Great Depression." Switzerland's National Bank has been negatively impacted despite its safe haven status. Obviously there is no such thing as a safe haven.[8]

In Australia, unemployment is rampant even as the government injects billions of dollars into the country's financial system. China tries its own hand at a stimulus package to fill the gap left by the loss of its export markets. As many as twenty million Chinese are out of work.

Forty heads of state met at the World Economic Forum in Switzerland. Chinese Premier Wen Jiabao urged "greater cooperation . . . in tackling the global crisis and building a new world economic order." Russian Prime Minister Vladimir Putin declared the world economic crisis to be a "perfect storm." He voiced his nation's willingness to join with other nations to address the crisis. And not surprisingly, the tensions began to rise. Mr. Putin exploited the opportunity to disparage American delegates who, the previous year, had declared "the US economy's fundamental stability."[9] Economic crises may come and go, but political bitterness is forever.

Nor was Russia the only nation to complicate an already horrendous problem by taking jabs at the United States. In a series of provocative and dangerous maneuvers, Chinese ships harassed two US naval vessels in open seas, coming within twenty-five feet of the USNS *Impeccable*.

More ominously, North Korea has again expelled UN nuclear inspectors from its Yongbyon nuclear plant,[10] conducted an underground nuclear test and launched six short-range rockets (all in the space of one week), and appears poised to launch a long range ICBM, all in direct violation of UN Security Council Resolutions.[11]

In the Middle East, tension is the status quo. Iran's Ahmadinejad continues to blame the West for the global economic situation and declared that "the capitalist system is on the brink of disintegration."[12] Meanwhile, his government continues to push forward with its nuclear program, threatening others with disintegration. The launch of a multistage rocket early this year now enables the Iranians to place satellites in the Earth's orbit, adding to concerns over a nuclear-armed Iran's ability to wreak havoc in the world.

Had enough? Me too. Say what you want about this past year, but you have to say it hasn't been dull. I actually made a point to compile a list of global crises that have occurred during the last twelve months, and I came up with one or more for every letter of our alphabet. How that will come in handy, I have no clue.

Think about this. You and I have lived through some tumultuous times. The twentieth century is surely the most remarkable hundred years in the history of our planet. There will be some readers who remember Pearl Harbor, D-Day, the atomic bomb, the advent of television, the revolutions of the 1960s, Neil Armstrong's walk on the moon, the end of the Berlin Wall, the arrival of personal computers and the Internet. Some of us have parents who can tell us about the

Great Depression of the 1930s. But I would suggest that there's never been a time like this one in our collective memory. Even that earlier depression, though it had an international scope, came before the age of the "global village." Today we are more interconnected than ever as passengers on the voyage of Spaceship Earth.

Some of you may have read my previous book, entitled *What in the World Is Going On?* In that book I summarized ten world events and related them to the prophetic Word of God. Among other things, we talked about the rebirth of Israel as a nation, the redistribution of wealth through oil, the realignment of Europe, the rise of radical Islam, and the resurgence of Russia. You know how rapidly the world landscape can change these days. Just as the book was finished and ready to hit the bookstores, along came the reversal of the financial markets. Any one of these events by itself might not cause us a concern, but all of them, taken together, present a frightening picture.

Now I wish to paint for you a separate picture. It couldn't create a starker contrast with the one we've just described, the landscape of current events. Yet this other picture is every bit as real, every bit as true. It simply lies in the future rather than the present.

We serve a loving heavenly Father who wants us to know that this world and its troubles will not last forever. In His inspired Word, He offers us a preview of a time that is so wonderful, so blessed, that the tribulations of any historic era—whether this present hour, the Hebrew captivity in Babylon, Rome's persecution of the young church, or any other you might name—would seem like a swiftly fading headache. Just before Jesus Christ returns to earth, keeping the promise He made to His disciples, this troubling time will finally arrive. And, my friends, it's quite possible that we have entered the early stages of those events.

In Paul's first letter to the Thessalonians, we are told: "But concerning the times and the seasons, brethren, you have no need that I should write to you. For you yourselves know perfectly that the day of the Lord so comes as a thief in the night. For when they say, 'Peace and safety!' then sudden destruction comes upon them, as labor pains upon a pregnant woman. And they shall not escape" (1 Thessalonians 5:1–3).

As I think about that passage, I find myself observing how that metaphor, about labor pains, perfectly fits the headlines I'm reading. An expectant mother endures quite a trial as she prepares for the birth of her child. She has morning sickness, she goes through all kinds of other drastic bodily changes, and then the labor pains arrive. As that child is preparing to enter the world, the mother's discomfort is amplified—it's a message that God doesn't want her to miss. *Rejoice! Your child is on the way!*

Similarly, our world is in pain even now. When the time comes for the blessed event that awaits all of creation, we will feel it as the nations quake. *Rejoice! Your Redemption draweth nigh!* This pain, this confusion, this anxiety is only for a little while longer.

What about these *catastrophes*? That's a word that seems to be recurring more frequently in the news media. Financial, societal, even natural catastrophes are rending this globe and all of its occupants. It's an odd four-syllable word, isn't it? The word *catastrophe* represents the union of two Greek words, *cata*, meaning "over," and *strophe*, meaning "to turn." The full picture is one of overthrow, of everything turning over in sudden and violent change.

Ask any Californian about sudden and violent changes. Living on or near various fault lines, we take these things in stride. During the most recent week, for example, we had more than seven hundred earthquakes in our region, or so I'm informed from the latest Southern California Earthquake Data Center Web site.[13] Nonchalant as we may appear, we all have that identical thought in the back of our minds: *the big one*. The ground could open up any second now. "It's California," someone will tell you. "Deal with it! You don't like it, move!" Then, just as he finishes those words, that familiar tremble of the foundations may begin. Even quakeproof buildings are suddenly doing that frightening dance. And the fellow who told you to "deal with it" is doing so himself, with a frantic dash toward the exit.

All of us are brave while we're under the impression that the coast is clear. However, here's one more statistic: Did you know that there has been a 42.8-percent spike in earthquakes measured worldwide between 2000 and 2008?[14]

Labor pains or simple geology? You make the call.

We could just as well talk about the terrible tsunami that hit Asia, or the unprecedented storms that hit the Gulf Coast, or any number of increasingly violent storms that are now becoming a fixture in the daily news. Tornadoes, hurricanes, ice storms, blizzards, floods, extremes of heat and cold. The Weather Channel has a growing audience and a show entitled *Storm Stories*.

We could also discuss eruptions in the spiritual world. We are seeing an outpouring of pure, unrestrained evil such as we would never have thought possible even a few years ago. It's the clear symptom of a culture in disintegration. I don't need to say much here; you need only turn on your television set to agree that too much freedom of a certain kind can lead to the worst enslavement. Our society has lost its moorings, so that reports of mass shootings, many involving someone's own family, are no longer particularly shocking to us. We read of fathers imprisoning their own children for immoral purposes and mothers selling their young children to representatives of the sickest underbelly of a lost culture.

Clergy misconduct, I'm sad to say, is never far from the headlines. And we've read of the monumental fraud of Bernard Madoff, which represented friendships exploited into the loss of billions of dollars. Our newspapers, ironically in their own death throes at a time when there is more news than ever before, look more and more like super-market tabloids. Current events are just that appalling.

If even churches, families, and friendships no longer provide a safe haven, what does that suggest about the future of humanity? Could we really be approaching the terminal point of the human experience? In plain terms, something's got to give.

A year ago my question was, "What in the world is going on?" Today there can be but one question: "Is there any way for us to live with confidence in a chaotic world?" You see, we no longer have the luxury of sitting back in our recliners, stroking our chins, and examining this spectacle from some distance. Now we are all players in world events. If you have not lost a job or a home, you undoubtedly know someone who has. By this time, virtually every American has been affected by the cultural fallout that has been highlighted by our economic system. If you and I are up to our ears in this, then, what on earth can we do? We need a plan, and we need one as quickly as possible.

In our last book we examined the passages that describe the future return of Jesus Christ to this earth. But what if I told you that those same texts contain clues for how we are to live in the meantime? In scouring the books of the New Testament, I discovered ten practical strategies to help us live with confidence in a chaotic world. We *can* know what on earth to be doing when our challenges exceed our courage.

As we face the uncertainty of our troubled generation, we cannot afford to turn away from the priceless counsel of the Word of God. We need it more than ever because it provides a firm foundation even when the world seems in the grip of quicksand's undertow.

As I feel the anxiety of these times, I draw profound peace from the promise that Jesus gave to His disciples—that includes you and me—in the Upper Room. He told them that He would never leave them without comfort: "The Helper, the Holy Spirit whom the Father will send in my name, will teach you all things, and bring to your remembrance all things that I said to you. Peace I leave with you, My peace I give to you; not as the world gives do I give to you. Let not your heart be troubled, neither let it be afraid" (John 14:25–27).

In those words I can hear Jesus speaking to our generation. He assures us that we need never live in fear, no matter what the newspaper says. Jobs can be lost, homes can be lost, but the love of Christ is forever. Understanding that calms our spirits and allows us to begin thinking—really thinking—about the new world around us. As we work through the ten chapters of this book together, I pray that you will see your own circumstances with new eyes; and that you will look within, finding new courage not in your own strength or skills, but in the unlimited resources of Christ, in whom we can do all things. Then, as we finish these pages, we will smile in the midst of it all and agree: in the power and love of Almighty God, we *can* live with confidence in an age of chaos.

—David Jeremiah
San Diego, CA
June 2009

# ONE

# Stay Calm

FUNNY HOW IT NEVER RAINS IN BEIJING WHEN AMERICAN PRESI-dents arrive for high-profile visits. It's no coincidence. Military meteorologists in China seed the clouds and empty them of their moisture in advance.[1] The weather is tailor-made for the occasion. That's why the skies were picture-perfect for the opening ceremonies of Beijing summer Olympics in 2008. Using an arsenal of rockets, artillery, and aircraft, Chinese scientists blasted the clouds right out of the sky. "We can turn a cloudy day into a dry and sunny one," boasted Miam Donglian of the Beijing weather bureau.[2]

That's nothing to what's coming. Weather modification is a rapidly developing technology, spurred on by billion-dollar investments in climate change and global warming. It's the new science, and its rami-fications aren't lost on military planners. Secret laboratories in military installations around the globe are developing what may be the most underreported arms race on earth: weather warfare.

Many military and environmental scientists believe we can learn to use powerful chemicals and electromagnetic scalar waves to manipulate and control short-term weather patterns in ways that can alter the world's balance of power. According to some reports, the US Air Force is determined to "own the weather" by 2025; but other nations and terrorist states have timetables of their own.[3]

Former Secretary of Defense William Cohen warned that military manipulation of the biosphere is a frightening threat, saying that some countries are engaging "in an eco-type terrorism whereby they can alter the climate, set off earthquakes and volcanoes remotely through the use of electromagnetic waves." He said, "There are plenty of ingenious minds out there that are at work finding ways in which they can wreak terror upon other nations. It's real . . ."[4]

I don't know if it's real or not; but if some doomsdayers are right, technology is being developed that could trigger earthquakes by well-placed underground nuclear explosions, or by earth-penetrating electromagnetic waves, or by injecting superfluids into major fault zones. Blizzards could be pulled down. Volcanoes could be cooked up. Typhoons and tsunamis could be triggered and aimed against unfriendly coasts. Communications could be disrupted by heated plumes of supercharged particles altering the atmosphere.

Writing in *The Ecologist*, Michel Chossudovsky of the University of Ottawa warned that "the world's weather can now be modified as part of a new generation of sophisticated electromagnet weapons. Both the US and Russia have developed capabilities to manipulate the climate for military use . . . Weather manipulation is the pre-emptive weapon par excellence. It can be directed against enemy countries or 'friendly nations' without their knowledge, used to destabilize economies, ecosystems and agriculture. It can also trigger havoc in financial and commodity markets."[5]

When we read what's coming, we feel like we're either hurtling into the age of science fiction or stepping into the pages of the book of Revelation. The last book of the Bible indicates that catastrophic disruptions in earth's meteorological patterns will wreak havoc on the world during the Great Tribulation.

But here's what I want to know: as we await the Lord's return, the atmospherics of your heart and mine should be calm. The Bible says we have a God who calms the storm and a Savior who rebukes the wind and waves so they are calm (Psalm 107:29; Luke 8:24). The writer of Psalm 131 said, "Surely I have calmed and quieted my soul." Proverbs 17:27 tells us that a person of understanding has a calm spirit; and in Isaiah 7:4 (NIV), the Lord tells us, "Be careful, keep calm, and don't be afraid. Do not lose heart."

*Calm* is an interesting word that is known more for what it is not: agitation, fear, or turbulence. But "calm" does require some kind of storm or we would never notice it. The weather world gave us the word in the first place. It means wind that is moving one mile per hour or less. The Beaufort Scale has "Calm" at one end and "Hurricane" at the other—extreme opposites.

Take a moment and evaluate your own life. As you attempt to move through these chaotic days, where would the Beaufort Scale register the winds of your soul?

A September 2008 American Psychological Association poll indicated that 80 percent of us were under significant stress because of the economic mess. That figure represented a rise of fourteen percentage points in only five months. And we don't even have the numbers for early 2009, when the unemployment epidemic really cut a swathe through the American workplace. If you haven't lost your job, your home, or your savings, you're probably worried that it could happen, and you're concerned for those of your friends who have been so devastated.

One industry is actually doing very well: pharmaceutical medicines for anxiety. I've read claims that fifteen million Americans suffer from enough anxiety to need medication.[6] While this may represent a wise option in cases of clinical stress, there are deeper causes for panic attacks and anxiety that medication will never penetrate.

Perhaps this is a good time to remember why I wrote this book and why you have chosen to read it. We are trying to determine what on earth we should be doing in these stressful times. And we have discovered that God has given us solid answers to our questions in the very passages that tell us of His Son's return to earth.

In this chapter, and in every chapter that follows it, I have identified instruction for living life while we are looking for the Savior. I can find no better resource for our troubled days. Jesus, for example, spoke to His disciples about His purposes after leaving earth. Here is how He began: "Let not your heart be troubled" (John 14:1). He would not have said these calming words unless His followers needed them. Their hearts were troubled; He knows that ours are too. Each one of us has a different "anxiety quotient."

Some people believe that when they accept Christ, they will receive a *Get Out of Stress Free* card and live a life of uninterrupted bliss. To be honest, when I became a believer, I picked up a few new problems I hadn't had before. Jesus never offered a false promise. At every point, He warned us that troubles would follow our path and that obedience to Him would actually increase our persecution. But He is also the one who said, "These things I have spoken to you, that in Me *you may have peace.* In the world you will have tribulation; but be of good cheer, I have overcome the world" (John 16:33, emphasis added).

Jesus Himself felt pressure. He was distressed as He watched Mary weep over the death of her brother Lazarus. He "groaned in the spirit and was troubled" (John 11:33). As He contemplated the cross, He felt genuine anxiety (John 12:27). As He waited for Judas to betray Him, He was troubled (John 13:21). He is a high priest who can "sympathize with our weaknesses" (Hebrews 4:15).

As the death of our Lord Jesus nears, His disciples begin to be anxious about their life situations, and Jesus comforts them with these words:

> "Let not your heart be troubled; you believe in God, believe also in Me. In My Father's house are many mansions; if it were not so, I would have told you. I go to prepare a place for you. And if I go and prepare a place for you, I will come again and receive you to Myself; that where I am, there you may be also. And where I go you know, and the way you know." Thomas said to Him, "Lord, we do not know where You are going, and how can we know the way?" Jesus said to him, "I am the way, the truth, and the life. No one comes to the Father except through Me." (John 14:1–6)

## The Ultimate in Comfort

We need to return to this passage whenever we are besieged by worry. Remember, Jesus didn't say these words as He stood beside a Galilean stream on a sunny day, without a care in the world. He said them as He stood near the jaws of hell itself. He didn't speak from the all-protective shelter of His Father's arms. He sat with His frightened disciples in the Upper Room, preparing for the worst of humanity and the silence of heaven. His words were, "Let not your heart be troubled."

It encourages me to realize that He faced what He did, felt the worst of what we would feel, and still drew enough strength to comfort others. He looked at His friends and felt compassion for them. These were men He had asked to follow Him. For three years He had been their life. Then He had begun to speak of leaving them. In John 13, He had told them that the time was drawing near for Him to leave, and that this time they would not be able to follow Him. Peter asked Him exactly where He was going. Jesus told him again that it was a place to which he could not come until sometime in the future (John 13:36).

This conversation would have been terribly upsetting for the disciples who had depended upon Jesus for everything. Our Lord's words of encouragement to His close friends were preserved by the apostle John, so that they are available to give comfort to us as well. Jesus gave His disciples some things to believe, things to hold onto. He asked them to put their trust in four things that He promised would provide courage and renewed strength for their troubled hearts. I think you will discover as you read the following pages that these timeless truths are just what you and I need in these chaotic days.

## Jesus Asks Us to Believe in a Person

When a child is afraid during the night, who but a parent can provide comfort? The child will cling to Mommy or Daddy and begin to feel calm. That's how it is with Jesus. His comfort begins with His very identity. "Let not your heart be troubled," He tells us. "You believe in God, believe also in Me" (John 14:1).

The people of Judea believed in one God. The center of their faith was expressed in the *Shema*: "Hear, O Israel: The LORD our God, the

LORD is one! You shall love the LORD your God with all your heart, with all your soul, and with all your strength" (Deuteronomy 6:4–5). These Jewish followers of Jesus had been trained since infancy to love God exclusively. Now Jesus was telling them something shocking; He wanted them to believe in Him in the exact same way—because He was God's Son. If the divine nature of Jesus is difficult for us to understand, you can imagine how the disciples would have struggled to wrap their minds around such an idea. In fact, it wasn't until after His resurrection that they began to process what He was telling them.

Jesus was asking men who had been schooled in the Hebrew Scripture to expand their faith in their heavenly Father to include His Son, their earthly teacher. Calling upon His full authority as the Lord of heaven and earth, He said, "I and the Father are one" (John 10:30 NIV). To believe in what I say, you must believe in who I am.

## Jesus Asks Us to Believe in a Place

Now Jesus tells His disciples, "In My Father's house are many mansions; if it were not so, I would have told you. I go to prepare a place for you" (John 14:2).

A man takes a new job in another city. He is in the process of moving his family to a brand new home there, but he must travel ahead of them and start his work earlier. His child cries because he will be gone for a week, but the father stoops, pulls him into an embrace, and says, "I'll be there getting your new room ready. You're going to have a place to ride your bicycle, and I'll be starting on that tree house we're going to build." The tears dry as the child sees all this in his mind. That's a picture of what Jesus is doing here. He encourages His disciples to think of the wonderful future He is planning for them.

The Scriptures include many synonyms for heaven. We know it is vast, we know it is beautiful and wonderful beyond all imagining. We know it is a country, one about which our most gorgeous earthly landscapes are only rough drafts. It is, in another way, a magnificent city, built and perfected by the architect of this universe. Then we can think of it is as a kingdom, the realm of the powerful king. Heaven is also called *paradise*, a word suggesting its supreme beauty.

Those metaphors are beautiful pictures of our future home, but Jesus' description of heaven is my favorite: "My Father's house." We know what that means. Many of us had favorite grandparents we visited. We think, "This is where Dad was a little boy. This is my father's house!" It holds a special charm and wonder for us, associated with Christmas, joy, and laughter. I like to think of heaven that way.

There was a special house where I grew up. My parents, as they grew older, finally moved away from it, and that was hard for me to take. I hadn't lived there for some time, but the house symbolized my whole past, my first memories, my childlike innocence and security. It was part of me. Praise God, He never decides to move to a smaller home. There is ultimate security in the eternal nature of heaven. Author Thomas Wolfe wrote a book called *You Can't Go Home Again,* but there is one home we can never lose or leave. Christ has gone there to prepare it for us, and that gives us comfort.

Heaven is real. Cloud-and-golden-gate–laden cartoons, movies, and jokes have reduced heaven to a stereotype. We need to realize just what is being stolen from the sanctified imagination when this precious image is made trivial to us. We are not yet in heaven, but it has power for us right now. It extends its hope to us. It guides our aspirations. It soothes our hearts when we lose a loved one. And when we think of its eventuality, we realize there is nothing mundane or insignificant about any of us—we are children of the kingdom; we are bound for heaven! It is real, and it is home.

## About Those Mansions

Many of us are familiar with the phrase "many mansions," as we learned it in our King James Bibles. Newer translations substitute something like "many rooms" or "many dwelling places." The explanation is that this word, now associated with the homes of millionaires, originally meant a simple dwelling place. Jesus is actually saying, "In my Father's house are many rooms." But please don't think we'll all be tenants of a large boarding house, with cramped quarters and a shared bathroom down the hall. Heaven is the infinite expanse of God's glory; it is perfection, and the idea of a mansion is more than appropriate.

This language of an ultimate home is a powerful balm to the heart. Home means something different to every person, but it's a longing we all share. Home, no matter how humble, is the place where we begin life. It is the place we must inevitably leave to build an adult life. And the yearning to recapture that basic security and sense of belonging remains in us. Ecclesiastes 3:11 says that God has set eternity in our hearts, and that's heaven, our ultimate home.

On one occasion, Dr. Paul Tournier, the brilliant Swiss Christian medical doctor, counseled a young man from a troubled home situation. "Basically, I'm always looking for a place—for somewhere to be," said the man. Tournier explained that each of us long for a true home.[7]

You can see this longing through history. The first thing men do upon becoming substantially wealthy is to build the "dream home." In some cases they've become consumed by this quest. In the nineteenth century, King Ludwig II of Bavaria nearly bankrupted his German nation by building palace after palace. He had to be removed from power, and his greatest castle remained incomplete.[8]

In the United States, two palatial houses qualify as "castles." North Carolina has the Biltmore House while California has its Hearst Mansion. The Biltmore House has over 250 rooms, including 35 bedrooms and 43 bathrooms. George Washington Vanderbilt nearly depleted his incredible fortune in completing the estate, then died after only a few years of enjoying it. The home of William Randolph Hearst has a mere 165 rooms, with 127 acres of gardens, terraces, pools, and walkways. Again, a heart attack took the founder before he could enjoy the fruit of his labor. In both cases, tourists have come out as the true winners.

Today we have every kind of television show about homes and making them perfect. The yearning never dies. But no matter how luxurious a palace we build, no matter how much we spend, we can't take it with us, nor will any moat or drawbridge keep death from the front door. These architectural obsessions simply prove our longing for the one and only home that will be enjoyed throughout eternity. Can you imagine living in the Biltmore House or Hearst Mansion? Beside the home Jesus is preparing, either would seem like a run-down tool shed.

## What Makes a Home?

There will be some readers who have lost their homes, or come close to it, in the recent mortgage crisis. I realize this subject is a sensitive one for you, and I don't wish to cheapen the loss you've experienced with trite assurances. Even so, I truly believe that God can help you experience the reality of your eternal home, and in that way give you comfort and reassurance. We must remember that a house is not a home, any more than the church is a building. A true home is an intangible thing, composed of love, relationships, and peace. Heaven may be like a mansion or a billion mansions—but no ornamentation or architecture will make it precious to us. Only the presence of our Lord will do that.

As we continue to explore what on earth we should be doing now, let us not forget about our Lord's words concerning heaven.

None of us know what the future holds for our own crisis. My prayer for you is that you come through your crisis strong. This can be a time of maturity for all of us, helping us to understand that we are not citizens of this world, and that we cannot place our faith in any of its establishments or institutions. As we await His return, we trust Him to care for our every need, and we remember that Jesus himself said, "Foxes have holes and birds of the air have nests, but the Son of Man has nowhere to lay His head" (Matthew 8:20).

Do we really long for that ultimate and eternal home, rather than simply a place to lay our heads? C. S. Lewis writes that sometimes it seems as if we have no desire for heaven at all; other times, it seems to him we've never desired anything else. In truth, he says, our yearning for heaven is "the secret signature of each soul." It is the thing we have desired all along and will continue to desire, even when we don't realize it's the thing we most want.[9]

## Jesus Asks Us to Believe in a Promise

A particularly wonderful aspect of the Bible is its many promises. When God makes a promise, it is our rock. Jesus comforts us with this promise: "And if I go and prepare a place for you, I will come again

and receive you to Myself; that where I am, there you may be also"
(John 14:3).

Some interpret this as a description of what happens when we die.
The problem is that we have no specific scriptural support for the
idea of Christ returning for each believer at death. Luke 16:22 suggests that the angels handle that task. No, this verse is certainly a
description of the triumphant return of Christ. Our comfort is in
looking forward to His return, when He will take us away from all the
problems and heartbreaks of this life.

What I have just said is certainly nothing that hasn't been said
countless times before. I doubt it's the first time it's been expressed to
you in similar wording. And yet it is the most profound statement in
all of history. Here is the very heart of Jesus' message to His troubled
disciples. The deepest, most far-reaching truth in the entire universe
is not expressed in any of Einstein's laws but in a children's song that
goes, "Jesus loves me, this I know, for the Bible tells me so." It's nothing new, but it's the best news you'll ever hear. How much different
would our lives be if we could only begin to embrace the truth that
the God of heaven desires to spend eternity with us? Listen to our
Lord as He puts this desire into prayer: "Father, I desire that they also
whom You gave Me may be with Me where I am, that they may behold
My glory which You have given Me; for You loved Me before the foundation of the world" (John 17:24).

We need our Lord's promise as we continue to walk the uncharted
roads of our current crisis. We might lose our jobs or our homes; the
devil may win the battle—but Christ has already won the war.

In the darkest days of the Second World War, as defeated US
troops in Bataan awaited promised reinforcements, President Roosevelt
ordered the ignominious General Douglas MacArthur to leave the

Philippines for Australia—virtually deserting his men. Upon his arrival in Australia, he made a speech promising those troops and the Filipinos, "I shall return." US government officials asked him to change the line to, "*We* shall return," but he stood firm.[10] His promise, therefore, became a personal one that he fulfilled four years later when he triumphantly reappeared in that part of the world to retake the lost ground and free the captives. By the way, MacArthur understood the concepts we're discussing. On April 9, 1942, in a tribute to the troops of Bataan, he stated, "To the weeping mothers of its dead, I can only say that the sacrifice and halo of Jesus of Nazareth has descended upon their sons, and that God will take them unto Himself."[11]

If a general can keep his promise to return, how much more certain is the covenant of that same Jesus of Nazareth? He will come back to take *all* of us unto Himself. And even now, He has ascended into heaven, and is preparing our place. That's how much He loves us! Can we begin living like it?

## Winning the Battle

There is hope in trusting a future that Jesus has guaranteed, but there is still the daily battle. I don't want you to feel that I would attempt to minimize the anxiety or hardship you may be experiencing. This world's problems are real. But we need to fully grasp that God's solutions are too. When Jesus says, "Let not your heart be troubled," He means it. And not just for the men who were in that room with Him two thousand years ago; He means it for every troubled time and every troubled person.

We can master anxiety. But we can't do it with a fatalistic attitude about problems—that loses the battle before the first shot is fired.

When we believe in the victorious Christ, and trust Him to guide us forward toward positive solutions, we will begin to live with supreme confidence.

Jesus says, "Believe in me. Believe in the reality of my home. Then believe my promise. *Believe.*" For some, believing can be difficult to accept because the problems of this world are visible and tangible, but the hope and power come from an invisible reality. Our only bond to that world is our faith—our decision to *believe.* When we do that, we are declaring victory over this world's problems before they occur, in the name of Jesus, who is the object of our faith. We will still have sorrow and setbacks, but we stubbornly view them only in the much larger context of eternity—today's tears making tomorrow's joy sweeter.

Our growth over the years helps us with this perspective. After forty years as a pastor, I can testify that I see problems in a different light than I once did. There are disappointments that would have knocked me down years ago. Today I have more readiness to chalk them up to the challenges of my profession, and to simply move on. By now I've had enough opportunities to see what the Lord does with the worst of circumstances. He has more than won my trust, so it will take a far greater blow than it took yesterday to knock me down today.

## Jesus Asks Us to Believe in a Plan

Finally, Jesus has a plan for us to trust. It is revealed in John 14:5–6. Thomas, always uncertain, asks Jesus, "Lord, we do not know where You are going, and how can we know the way?"

Jesus answers him: "I am the way, the truth, and the life. No one comes to the Father except through Me."

If Jesus was leaving, Thomas wanted a map. Global Positioning

System (GPS) receivers were not available. Thomas was asking, "Can't you even leave a forwarding address?"

Jesus' answer is surely not what Thomas is expecting to hear. Jesus says that He *is* the map. He is the Global Positioning Savior. He shows the way to heaven, takes us there, and ultimately is the journey Himself.

Now imagine you're on a business trip and stop at a convenience store to ask directions. The cashier gets that all the time, so he fires the turns at you in rapid succession: first right, third traffic light, dog-leg left, straight at the Methodist church, then go through four or five intersections, if you see the Jiffy Burger you've gone too far, what you want is the second left past the old gas station . . .

All of this was spewed out before you could get the cap off your pen, and there's a look of abject despair on your face. So the cashier glances at his watch and says, "Know what? I get off in three minutes, and it's on my way home. I'll lead you right there myself."

Now you're smiling. That cashier has become the way. He not only has the directions but is the means for getting there. He is your new best friend. William Barclay says that this is what Jesus does for us. "He does not tell us about the way; He is the Way."[12]

I'm told that in many of the "big box" stores today, employees are trained to become the way when someone asks where something is—to walk the customer there. That level of service is sacrificial and well appreciated. And it's the way of Jesus.

But Jesus says something else that many people would rather skip over or explain away. Jesus says not only that He will take us to heaven, but that He is the only one who can: "No one comes to the Father except through Me."

Those who remember their grammar lessons know the difference between a definite and indefinite article. The former signifies "the one and only"; not just *a* restaurant but *the* restaurant. A restaurant is indefinite; we could be talking about any eating establishment. When Jesus says He is "the way," He uses the definite article, and He is definitely clear about it. He never said He was *a* way, but *the* way. Then, to clinch the issue, He added that no one could come to the Father "except through Me."

Today we have decided that this ancient, inspired, and specific article of Christian doctrine is no longer politically correct. It is, we are told, bigoted and intolerant. According to some recent polls, a majority of Americans—70 percent—think some non-Christian religions also provide paths to salvation. Pollsters at Pew Research Center were amazed to find how many respondents accredited more than one way to heaven. Fifty-seven percent of evangelicals said they believed *many* religions can lead to eternal life. In other words, nearly half of American evangelicals were left in the category of believing Jesus is not the exclusive way to heaven.[13]

Respondents to an online poll by the evangelical periodical *Christianity Today* indicated a similar belief pattern. Forty-one percent believe there is more than one way to heaven.[14]

What part of John 14:6 do we not understand?

## Overwhelming Evidence

This last year I had the privilege of meeting Billy Graham's grandson, Will, and to hear him preach. He gave me an idea of what it was like to be the grandson of Billy Graham. "Everybody wants to meet you," he said. "Then, as soon as they meet you, you discover they don't really want to meet you, but they want you to help them to meet your grandfather." He shared his humorous response for dealing with that inevitable question: "The Bible says the way to the father is through the son, not through the grandson."

Jesus' words in John 14:6 clearly teach the exclusive, one-way nature of salvation. But this truth is not isolated to one text, as the following references demonstrate.

- "Enter by the narrow gate; for wide is the gate and broad is the way that leads to destruction, and there are many who go in by it." (Matthew 7:13) Narrow gate or narrow mind? You be the judge.
- "Therefore I said to you that you will die in your sins; for if you do not believe that I am He, you will die in your sins." (John 8:24)
- "Nor is there salvation in any other, for there is no other name under heaven given among men by which we must be saved." (Acts 4:12)
- "For there is one God and one Mediator between God and men, the Man Christ Jesus." (1 Timothy 2:5)

The Scriptures are remarkably clear on this issue. Jesus is the one and only way, the one and only truth, and the one and only life. If that is narrow-minded, so be it. I'm happy to be narrow-minded if that's what God is because this is His truth, not mine.

What about the other religions? Again the Bible says, "There is a way that seems right to a man, but its end is the way of death" (Proverbs 14:12). It's not about what seems right that counts; it's about what *is* right. The various world religions are neither different versions of the same story nor parallel steps leading skyward on some pyramid of truth where all the differences melt away. Other religions teach starkly different versions of reality. Life is either a circle, as Eastern religions have it, or time is linear with a beginning and end, as the Word of God has it. There is either endless reincarnation as those religions insist, or it is given to man but once to live, once to die, as the Bible teaches in Hebrews 9:27.

Most scientists would agree with me that there is only one law of gravity, and that we don't get a vote on it. Science, mathematics—neither of these disciplines is democratic. Neither has a "choose your own truth" policy. Why should the spiritual realm be any different?

Let's not build up false charges of narrow-mindedness when the obvious character of Jesus is one of love, forgiveness, and total sacrifice. He wants to take us to heaven—all of us. But He is the only way. He invites us to come to Him—to be saved by grace, received through our faith as it responds to Him. He demands no sacrifice, no achievement, nothing other than a sincere *yes* from the human will.

Then He wants to enter our hearts and give us joy and wisdom for the rest of this life, and His glorious presence in the next. He has written that invitation in the blood of His own hands. And when we accept His invitation, He has promised to write our name in the Lamb's Book of Life.

Dr. Ruthanna Metzgar is not your general run-of-the-mill church wedding singer. She is a professional. Her résumé is impressive. She has sung in the United States, Canada, Europe, and Japan. She is world-renowned as an instructor, lecturer, and conductor of both choirs and orchestras.

She also has an impressive repertoire. Her versatile soprano voice has performed everything from classical, sacred, musical theater to contemporary gospel. She is also a gifted communicator about her personal faith in Christ. It is in that context that I first came across her story.

Anyone who has taken voice lessons, sung in a top-notch college choir, or played in an adult orchestra knows the penchant directors and conductors have for detail. They leave nothing to chance. They almost obsess over every difficult passage, making sure it is practiced and polished and performance ready. They don't like surprises at an important presentation.

Well, Ruthanna must have been very preoccupied because she missed a very important detail. It isn't often that even a professional singer is asked to sing at the wedding of a millionaire. Ruthanna was. The wedding took place in the tallest skyscraper in Seattle—on the top two floors! She described the "atmosphere as one of grace and sophistication." From that vantage point the view of Puget Sound and both the Cascade and the Olympic Mountains was spectacular.

After the ceremony, "the bride and groom approached a beautiful glass and brass staircase that led to the top floor." They ceremoniously cut the satin ribbon that had subtly acted as a lustrous boundary and invited their guests to follow them up to the reception. Just one more detail and Ruthanna and her husband, Roy, would be among the honored guests at the gala dinner.

At the top of the stairs stood a tuxedoed gentleman with an ornately bound book, who asked, "May I have your name please?" Ruthanna gave him their names and expected to be ushered directly into the party. But, as hard as he looked, as carefully as she spelled her last name, he firmly announced, "I'm sorry, but your name is not here. Without your name in this book, you cannot attend this banquet."[15]

Ruthanna explained to him there must be a mistake; she had just sung at the wedding. With a hundred or so guests waiting on the steps below her, he simply replied: "It doesn't matter who you are or what you did, without your name in the book, you cannot attend this banquet." He promptly signaled for them to be escorted to the service elevator and taken to the parking garage.

Roy Metzgar wisely waited until they were well on their way home before he asked what had happened. In tears, Ruthanna replied, "When the invitation arrived for the reception I was very busy and I never bothered to return the RSVP . . . Besides, I was the singer, surely I could go to the reception without returning the RSVP!"

There was no shrimp, smoked salmon, no luscious hors d'oeuvres, no exotic beverages for her that night. Rather there was only the sad realization of the overwhelming evidence against her. She had failed to follow the only plan that would get her into that banquet. She didn't mean to refuse the invitation; she merely let the opportunity slip away. It was really a decision to take no action.

Fortunately, Ruthanna's inaction held only a temporary consequence. You have a similar opportunity to make a decision. You have been issued an invitation with eternal consequences. There is just one plan. I urge you to make take the action that leads to eternal life in heaven. A confirmed reservation for a joyous eternity is the evidence that provides the settled calm that can carry us through any storm.

Mark Twain once quipped, "Everybody talks about the weather, but nobody does anything about it."[16] Well, no longer. As we step into the era of designer skies and weather weaponry, let's keep our eyes on the master of earth and skies, knowing He controls all the elements of our future.

Because of Christ, we have a better forecast and a cloudless future.

# TWO

# Stay Compassionate

ARIEL, THE MODERN CITY, IS LOCATED LESS THAN FORTY MILES due north of Jerusalem in the "occupied territories." Its ancient olive trees belie the establishment of the city just thirty years ago. The gospels relate Jesus' journeys and ministry in this area known then, as now, as Samaria. I love the way the King James puts it: "and [Jesus] must needs go through Samaria" (John 4:4). Samaria was definitely on Jesus' radar screen! He loved the people of Samaria.

Today, David Ortiz is the pastor of a small congregation of mostly Palestinian Christ-followers. However, there are some in the town of Ariel who loathe Christians. Ironically, the Ortiz family learned the depths of this hatred on the joyous holiday of Purim in 2008. Gifts of food and drink are sent to friends, and gifts are made to charity to celebrate the preservation of the Jews from the total extinction that had been planned for them by Haman (Esther 9:18–32).

As if in celebration of the holiday, a gift basket was delivered to the Ortiz home. Fifteen-year-old Ami was home alone, and he tore into the package with the anticipation of some candy or some other sweet treat. He certainly did not anticipate the explosion that ripped into his young body. Hundreds of shards, including pieces of metal, safety pins, and screws, pierced him and left him in critical condition. He was blinded by the shrapnel imbedded in his eyes, and both eardrums were punctured, leaving him with a significant loss of hearing.

Ami spent five months in the hospital, lost some toes through amputation, and endured nearly a year in a pressure suit to assist in his healing from his severe burns. More than a year later, he still faces several more surgeries. In a recent television interview in Israel, he told a reporter, "It was a shock. I didn't know what to do. Just to find out you're missing parts of your body. It's kind of hard."

Israeli television anchorwoman Ilana Dayan described Ami as "probably the Israeli who has been injured the worst by Jewish terror."[1] You read that correctly. After viewing the real-time video of the attacker dressed in an Israeli Defense Forces (IDF) uniform placing the basket at the door, police believe that the bomb was the work of radical Jews. The man has not yet been arrested.

No one would blame Ami for hating these neighbors and for desiring to seek revenge. But when Ami was questioned by the reporter about his attitude toward those who did this evil to him, he replied: "I don't feel hate. I don't see a reason for it. I could say they're blinded by their hate. They think it's the right thing. You can't blame a blind person for running over you, so I don't see [how I could blame them]. It's just not there. It wasn't there from the beginning. I don't even know how to explain it, but it's just not there. No hate at all."

Ami knows what it is like to be blinded. Thankfully, several successful surgeries have restored his sight. Perhaps his physical blindness explains his compassion on the spiritual blindness of those who do not know Christ.

The antithesis of hate is compassionate love. Ami and his family seek to demonstrate Christ's compassion to their neighbors, knowing that at any time, any place, they might again become targets. Instead of retreating into their fear, every Thursday Ami and his family help out at a soup kitchen that also provides a small medical clinic and clothes to those in need. Recently, his mother Leah wrote, "It is an important and vital work being done in the name of *Yeshua*. I never have realized before how much the Lord wants us to be His eyes, hands, and feet in these last days."[2]

Thankfully, most of us will never have our capacity for compassion tested at such a heinous level. But in these chaotic days, we are being tested to decide if we will be self-centered takers or compassionate givers. One such decisive moment happened in Sacramento a few months ago.

The drink was a Grande Gingersnap Latte. Nothing too special, except that it created a small, public statement about the power of kindness.

It was the Monday of Thanksgiving week, and a woman was at the Starbucks drive-through window, picking up her morning beverage. As she reached for her pocketbook, some inspirational quirk inspired her to do something extravagant: she paid for the customer behind her—someone she didn't know.

That driver, needless to say, was startled—and sufficiently moved to follow suit. He paid for the driver behind him. In the end, one hundred nine people had gotten in on the fun and paid for the next customer's coffee. An employee told the local TV station that those working the windows caught the fever too. "We're all in this economy thing together," she said.[3]

A popular movie from a few years ago helped spread the "pay it forward" principle, but the idea can be traced back as far as 1784, when Benjamin Franklin advocated progressive kindness. He received what used to be called a "begging letter" from a man in financial need. Franklin responded, "I do not pretend to give such a sum; I only lend it to you . . . When you meet with another honest man in similar distress, you must pay me by lending this sum to him . . . I hope it may thus go thro' many hands before it meets with a knave that will stop its progress."[4]

Being part of a good works chain is rewarding.

When the bottom falls out of our economy, as it has recently done, we see two equal and opposite reactions. One is the hardening of the heart, fueled by cynicism and despair. "Time to take care of my own," says this type of person. "The rest of you are on your own. Me, I'm locking the door and hunkering down. Wake me when the recession is over; I'll be sleeping with my wallet under my pillow."

Of course, there's an alternative response. It's the behavior we would expect from children of God's kingdom, who try to live in a way that will please him and minister to a hurting world. During that nightmarish week, when global stock markets declined by seven trillion dollars, *Time* magazine asked Christian author Philip Yancey for his take on how Christians should pray at such times. Yancey said the first part is simple: Cry, "Help!" He said that he had stopped editing his prayers for sophistication and the ring of maturity because God wants us to be ourselves.

Then, he explained, the second stage was that of listening to God in meditation and reflection. The question here would be, "What can we learn from this catastrophe?" One possible lesson would be that we're foolish when we place our ultimate trust in governments and economies.

The third stage, Yancey told the magazine, was to ask God for help in taking our eyes off our own problems "in order to look with compassion on the truly desperate." He concluded, "What a testimony it would be if, in 2009, Christians resolved to increase their giving to build houses for the poor, combat AIDS in Africa, and announce kingdom values to a decadent, celebrity-driven culture. Such a response defies all logic and common sense—unless, of course, we take seriously the moral of Jesus' simple tale about building houses on a sure foundation."[5]

Yes, it's clear that our next step forward in tough times is to protect and even extend our spirit of compassion. The apostle Paul wanted the church at Thessalonica to understand that during its own rough period. As Paul wrote them a letter, he broke into prayer: "Now may our God and Father Himself, and our Lord Jesus Christ, direct our way to you. And may the Lord make you increase and abound in love to one another and to all, just as we do to you, so that He may establish your hearts blameless in holiness before our God and Father at the coming of our Lord Jesus Christ with all of His saints" (1 Thessalonians 3:11–13).

Concerning that last phrase, the New Testament teaches us that Jesus will return. That is a 100 percent biblical certainty, and it could happen any day. It's Paul's context for the instruction he gives here. So does he advise the Thessalonians to shut everything down, put on their Sunday best, and sit patiently in their pews until the wonderful day? Not in the least. He consistently commands believers to be busy in the interim period, doing kingdom business—our hands busy with the earth, our hearts occupied with heaven.

This particular letter to the Thessalonians, perhaps the second of all his letters (the first being Galatians), is one of the essential documents pertaining to our Lord's return. Paul wanted to visit Thessalonica and help the believers work through some problems. But it was evidently not God's will for him to do so. Make no mistake; this was not a rejection slip from Paul to one more congregation competing for his time ("We regret that present scheduling will not allow for a visit from the apostle"). His language in this letter betrays his intense personal desire to be with his friends.

The problem was that "Satan hindered us" (1 Thessalonians 2:17–18). That's a common occurrence. The devil will present obstacles to God's work whenever he can—though God, who uses all things for His glory and our good, turns the worst crises to His own advantage. Here is how God did it in this situation: if Paul had gone to the city as he wanted, you could erase the amazing letters to the Thessalonians from your Bible. We wouldn't have the invaluable teachings we've enjoyed for twenty centuries. The devil, you see, has a way of winning the battle but losing the war. Now we have two incredible letters to the Thessalonians that tell us what we need to know about the return of Christ and what on earth we should be doing as we wait.

Paul couldn't see how God would use his letter; seldom do we live long enough to see the ultimate fruit of our service to God. That's something to remember when we feel discouraged. Paul couldn't have dreamed that his private correspondence would bless untold billions of people in the future. From his perspective, the church at Thessalonica was a group of his friends who were suffering—persecuted for loving Christ—struggling just to get by. They were experiencing hard times not too different from the ones that inspired this book. So how did they handle it? Did they pull in their heads, give in to self-pity, and harden their hearts, as some might do? How are you responding? Always remember that what life does to us depends upon what life finds within us. In school, you perform on a test based on how you studied for that test. If you fail, don't blame life or the school—you had every opportunity for preparation. You perform in life's testing, too, based on how you've readied yourself. Paul knew these people of Thessalonica. He realized they could be strong under trial, but he sensed they were overmatched.

Paul understands their discouragement, but he wants to bolster his friends, keep them from giving in to self-pity, and motivate them to serve God with deeper resolve. He wants to offer them a prayer, but what do you pray for people under intense pressure? Would you ask God for protection? Courage? Perhaps removal of the problem? Paul doesn't take any of those roads. He asks God to teach the Thessalonians to be more loving and compassionate toward one another. It seems counterintuitive, doesn't it?

Have you stopped and considered that the real purpose of your struggles, at a given moment, might be the heart of compassion that God is building within you? Smooth sailing doesn't develop such a thing, you know. Trials develop our humility, and humility opens our eyes to the needs of others. If we look to do His service during tough times, we will come out better rather than bitter. That's Paul's prayer for the struggling church at Thessalonica.

## The Essence of Compassion

The world is cold and cruel in the best of times; on tough days, things only get worse. In this present crisis, we expect a new age of cynicism and the hardening of hearts. While cutting our own budgets back, or even worrying about the loss of a career, the temptation is to shut out the problems of those who have it worse than we do. Yet this is the very time when the world needs us most of all. What's the use of a sunny-day Christian? We need devoted followers of Christ who are at their best when the clouds come out.

Someone will say, "That's all fine and good, but I'm just not feeling it. At this moment, my heart is not 'abounding and overflowing with love.'" That's to be expected. Don't worry, the heart of God overflows so magnificently that we need only stand under it and catch the spray. And a little of that is enough for a miracle. It's His love the world really needs, after all. "The LORD is gracious and righteous; our God is full of compassion" (Psalm 116:5 NIV). We also read that "His compassions fail not" (Lamentations 3:22). Notice, by the way, that the latter verse comes from a book of lamentations, of all things. Sad times are good times for realizing God's goodness.

No matter what we face, the abounding love and compassion of God are more than sufficient for us to enjoy ourselves and to share with someone else—and when I say "no matter what," I mean it. In *Campus Life* magazine, author Shannon Ethridge remembers a terrible day from her eleventh grade year. Attempting to apply lipstick while driving on a bumpy country road, she struck and killed a bicyclist. That was the beginning of her nightmare. What stunned her most was what the victim's husband said, upon being told he had lost his wife. His first question was, "How is the girl? Was she hurt?"

It was inconceivable to Ethridge that anyone could take such a devastating blow and have immediate concern for the author of the tragedy. The night before the funeral, she forced herself to visit the bereaved husband. "As I entered the house," she writes, "I looked down the entry corridor to see a big, burly middle-aged man coming toward me, not with animosity in his eyes, but with his arms opened wide."

The man was a Wycliffe Bible Translator named Gary Jarstfer. He gave her a large, compassionate embrace, and she dissolved into tears.

Over and over she wept the words, "I'm sorry, I'm sorry!" Jarstfer gently spoke to Ethridge about the life and legacy of his beloved wife. He added, "God wants to strengthen you through this. He wants to use you. As a matter of fact, I am passing Marjorie's legacy of being a godly woman on to you. I want you to love Jesus without limits, just like Marjorie did."

Gary Jarstfer insisted that all charges against the distraught eleventh grader be dropped. Then he began to look out for her and encourage her in the development of her life. Ethridge writes, "Gary's merciful actions—along with his challenging words to me that night before Marjorie's funeral—would be my source of strength and comfort for years to come."[6]

The logic of such behavior is never found in the world but only in the Word. The love capable of such abounding compassion is never found within ourselves but only as we are in Christ. Human nature dictates that we act very differently when things go wrong. The flesh (in Paul's terminology) encourages us to go inward and look to self. The Spirit encourages us to go outward and become all the more loving and forgiving—including forgiving oneself.

Therefore, when the men and women of Thessalonica are being treated terribly simply for loving and worshiping the one true God, Paul doesn't pray that they will be stronger in fighting evil. He doesn't ask God to strike down the oppressors. His prayer is that the people will be abounding in love and compassion. As Jesus said, "Love your enemies, bless those who curse you, do good to those who hate you, and pray for those who spitefully use you and persecute you, that you may be sons of your Father in heaven" (Matthew 5:44–45a).

The essence of identifying with someone else is the Incarnation —God wrapping Himself in flesh and becoming a man, then taking on our sins at the cross. All that we do in this world should be an echo of what Christ has done on the cross. We love. We are compassionate. We identify with others and their problems, and we take up their crosses for them. Gary Jarstfer is a perfect example. He had his own grief to handle, but he identified with the very person who would have been the object of anyone else's bitterness. He empathized with Shannon Ethridge, felt her pain even as he had plenty of his own, and took up her cross, making sure that her tragedy could be turned to triumph.

Don't you think the world needs more of that kind of love? What would happen if we replaced the here-today-gone-tomorrow love of contemporary marriage with the ironclad, unconditional love of 1 Corinthians 13? What would happen if every Christian in America went to work tomorrow after making a granite-solid personal covenant to love everyone at the office in the way God loves them? Can you imagine what would happen to our society?

God and only God can give us this love. Left to ourselves, we would make a hopeless mess of any difficult relationship. This is why we can't be too upset at our nonbelieving friends who don't love us unconditionally. Just as we wouldn't be angry with a blind man for stepping on our toes, we should be nothing but compassionate to people who don't know Christ.

Sometimes I listen to the news, hear the griping, the complaining, and the whining, and have to stop and remember that these people don't know the Jesus we know. There is so much anger, so little forgiveness; so many demands, so little service. I think Longfellow had it right when he wrote, "If we could only read the secret history of our enemies, we should find in each man's life sorrow and suffering enough to disarm all hostility."[7] It takes godly compassion to live with that outlook.

What God wants from us in the midst of this crisis is compassion—broken-hearted compassion that sees the hurts of those around us as an invitation to express God's love in meaningful acts of kindness.

## The Expression of Compassion

Let's think about the focus of all this compassion. It is expressed "to one another and to all" (1 Thessalonians 3:12). That pretty much covers everyone you can think of, doesn't it?

There is a basic standard for love, as John describes it: "If someone says, 'I love God,' and hates his brother, he is a liar; for he who does not love his brother whom he has seen, how can he love God whom he has not seen? And this commandment we have from Him: that he who loves God must love his brother also" (1 John 4:20–21).

Jesus set forth this standard to His disciples in the Upper Room, only hours before He was arrested: "By this all will know that you are My disciples, if you have love for one another" (John 13:35).

An e-mail circulated recently, telling the story of one of those angry drivers who was tailgating everyone, sitting on his horn, honking when people stopped for a yellow light, and so on. Then, in his rearview mirror, he saw the blue, revolving light. Soon the police officer was asking the man to exit the car with his hands up.

He took the driver to the station and had him searched, fingerprinted, photographed, and placed in a holding cell. Finally the staffers came for him, brought him back to the booking desk, and returned his personal effects. The arresting officer was very apologetic. "I made a mistake," he explained. "I was behind you in traffic while you were blowing your horn, making hand gestures, and cursing at the guy in front of you. When I saw the *What Would Jesus Do?* bumper sticker and the chrome-plated Christian fish emblem on the trunk, I assumed you had stolen the car."

People are watching, and they watch more closely when they know we are people of faith. It has been said that we are the only Bible some people will ever study. They have the right to expect our walk to reasonably match our talk even though consistent love and compassion don't come easy. Henri J. M. Nouwen expresses it this way: "Compassion is hard because it requires the inner disposition to go with others to the place where they are weak, vulnerable, lonely, and broken. But this is not our spontaneous response to suffering. What we desire most is to do away with suffering by fleeing from it or finding a quick cure for it."[8]

Dionysius, a second-century bishop in the city of Corinth, wrote letters describing how Christians behaved in the grip of a rampant plague:

> Most of our brethren showed love and loyalty in not sparing themselves while helping one another, tending to the sick with no thought of danger and gladly departing this life with them after becoming infected with their disease. Many who nursed others to health died themselves, thus transferring their death to themselves . . . The heathen were the exact opposite. They pushed away those with the first signs of the disease and fled from their dearest. They even threw them half dead into the roads and treated unburied corpses like refuse in hopes of avoiding the plague of death, which, for all their efforts, was difficult to escape.[9]

The world is watching how we treat each other. Will they see a difference?

The biblical standard is simply to love one another. But now we come to the difficult part. If we stayed with the basic standard to love each other, our faith would be little different than any belief system in this world. But there is a higher standard of love, and Jesus came to give it the definitive expression through His life and teachings. In the words of Eugene Peterson's paraphrase, he said, "If all you do is love the lovable, do you expect a bonus? Anybody, can do that" (Matthew 5:46 MSG). Paul is referring to the basic standard when he uses the phrase "one another" and the higher standard when he adds, "and to all."

Loving our loved ones is a good start. If we can't do that, we definitely have a problem. The higher standard, on the other hand, sends a strong, clear message that we, the people of Christ, are not your average, everyday human beings. Those who are watching us don't weigh the size of the Bibles we carry. They don't keep a calendar for totaling the number of Bible study meetings we attend, nor do they give us a test on mastery of biblical trivia. But they watch with intense interest to see how we treat others: first, those close to us and then—the championship round—everyone else. Paul writes, "May the Lord make you increase and abound in love to one another *and to all*" (1 Thessalonians 3:12). Those final three words are the tricky part.

For the Thessalonians, *all* was a difficult word. *All* constituted certain people who were abusing and persecuting them. "As you abound and increase in love," Paul is saying, "Don't forget these!" We don't like that at first because we know we can't individually get it done. Just as Jesus said, we can love our families, our buddies, and our friendlier neighbors all by ourselves. So can those who don't know God. But if we're going to love beyond those comfortable boundaries, if we're going to advance this love into hostile territory—well, we're going to need to rely on a greater source. We're going to need the power of the Holy Spirit. And of course, once we realize that, He has us right where He wants us.

C. S. Lewis helps us with this in one of his writings. He says that an unbeliever makes his choice as to whom he will show kindness, but a Christian has a different secret. He writes that we shouldn't waste our time worrying about whether we love our neighbors—just act as if we did. The difference between worldly people and Christians is that the worldly treat people kindly when they like them; Christians try treating everyone kindly and thus find themselves liking more people—including some they'd never have expected to like![10]

Christians, in other words, let their actions lead and their feelings follow. Human nature feels its way into acting (which can be a long wait). Christ-centered faith acts its way into feeling (which is quick, powerful, and liberating). To put it simply, we followers of Christ are realists. We understand that, naturally speaking, we're never going to like certain people. We know we're not prone to doing the right thing when left to our own devices. But for the sake of Christ, we're going to walk in the Spirit and treat others well because it's the very nature of who Jesus is. Therefore (if we're living as we ought to), we treat our enemies as benevolently as our friends and soon enough discover we have no enemies anymore.

Think about that person you simply don't like. You keep your distance and harbor ill feelings. What do ill feelings do when we give them free reign? They grow more ill; they are never self-healing. But what happens if you ignore the ill feelings and put your best foot (the "Christ" foot, if you will) forward? You find that friendliness with that person isn't as bad as you thought. Much of the time, that person (sensing or outright knowing your dislike) is surprised, shamed, or hopefully inspired into returning the friendliness. This is what Paul, quoting Proverbs, calls "heaping hot coals on someone's head" (Romans 12:20). And in the next verse of Romans, Paul adds, "Do not be overcome by evil, but overcome evil with good." That's leading with actions and letting the feelings follow, and when we do it, we begin to look an awful lot like Jesus.

Some call it the "As If" principle. If you act as if you feel a certain way, you'll find you really do soon enough. You're becoming your own self-fulfilling prophecy. Call it what you will, but it's really walking by faith, being obedient and trusting God to make you the person you haven't yet become. Sometimes the growth in us is what God's agenda has been all along. He wants to see how we'll respond to difficult personalities and whether we'll be obedient when it demands sacrifice on our part. It's the only way we can grow and become transformed to the image of Christ. Living and loving by faith is one of the great adventures of life.

## The Example of Compassion

The essence of compassion is that we increase and abound in love for one another. The expression of it is acting out our love for others, including those difficult to love. What about the example of compassion? Paul completes the thought: "May the Lord make you increase and abound in love to one another and to all, just as we do to you" (1 Thessalonians 3:12).

Paul is saying, "I'll lead. You follow." He has established a consistent model, and that gives him the luxury of saying not only "Do as I say," but also "Do as I do." The New Testament implies that when Paul first visited Thessalonica, he wasn't initially accepted. But he persisted, kept putting his "Christ" foot forward, and let his love for them increase and abound. The evidence is in plain view, all throughout this letter. Here are a few of the ways he demonstrated his love for the people of this city:

- *He thanked God for them.* "We give thanks to God always for you" (1 Thessalonians 1:2*a*). He offered his gratitude to God, a perfect strategy for building love in our hearts for someone.

- *He prayed for them.* "Making mention of you in our prayers" (1:2*b*). How else do we grow a sturdy love for another person? We pray for their needs. The end result of that is always compassion as we are given God's heart for the person.

- *He preached the Gospel to them.* He writes: "But even after we had suffered before and were spitefully treated at Philippi, as you know, we were bold in our God to speak to you the gospel of God in much conflict" (2:2). People don't always appreciate having the gospel preached to them, but that's our work, and it is the greatest evidence of our love.

- *He was gentle, kind, and considerate toward them.* "But we were gentle among you, just as a nursing mother cherishes her own children. So, affectionately longing for you, we were well pleased to impart to you not only the gospel of God, but also our own lives, because you had become dear to us" (vv. 7–8). This is precisely what compassion looks like.

- *He sacrificed for them.* "For you remember, brethren, our labor and toil; for laboring night and day, that we might not be a burden to any of you, we preached to you the Gospel of God (v. 9). This is the ultimate proof of compassion.

What is Paul talking about in that ninth verse? As he was building his relationship with the church at Thessalonica, he refused to let these friends pay for his preaching service. Instead, he worked an extra job as a tentmaker. You may remember that was his "practical" craft. In order to preach for his brothers and sisters in Christ at no cost, he supported himself with his hands. Now you can see how Paul is able to say, "Follow my example."

Read that list of five proofs of compassion again, but this time substitute the name of Jesus for Paul. Did Christ not do each of those things for us? Does He not call us to imitate Him? I challenge you to think of one person you know who is in need. Then, systematically follow the procedure Paul has laid out: Thank God for him. Pray for him. Talk to him about Christ and what He has done for you. Suffer for him in helping him. Be gentle, kind, and considerate. Then, however necessary, sacrifice yourself in some way in behalf of that person.

A woman once asked me, "How do I minister to somebody who won't even let me talk about Jesus? I want her to go to heaven, but she simply isn't open to hearing about the Lord. How do I witness to someone like that?"

My reply was, "You have to be Jesus to her."

She wanted me to explain my comment. I said, "You have to love her well. If she rejects your love, be resolute and keep on loving. Don't worry about what to say because words aren't necessary in cases like this. She's not listening to anything but your actions. Words can be refuted, but actions overwhelm every defense. That's how Jesus did it for us; that's what the cross is all about. So love her as Jesus loves you."

Paul, the author of this Thessalonian letter, was not born loving. He was a hater and hunter of Christians. He approvingly watched the death of Stephen, the first Christian martyr. He knew all the words that made up the law, but when he met Jesus on the road to Damascus, he experienced something far more powerful than words.

A more recent persecutor of Christians in the Middle East is named Tass Saada. They called him "Butcher." He was a PLO sniper, and one of Yasser Arafat's bodyguards. Like Paul, he had an encounter with the living Christ. By the power of the Holy Spirit, he was transformed into a brand-new person. The Butcher became a man of love and compassion. But that made him very unpopular with his family, and some wanted to kill him because of his conversion.

Today Tass and his American wife, Karen, have a compassion ministry to those living in miserable poverty and daily danger in Gaza and the West Bank. It was there that Joel Rosenberg and his wife traveled to meet the Saadas not long ago. They were there to visit a hospital that treated victims of the border clashes, both Jew and Arab. The Israeli doctors couldn't believe Saada's stories about the man he had once been—a PLO killer capable of murdering all the Jews to whom he was presently speaking. Now he was a man helping to finance a hospital, rather than putting people in one.

How on earth, he was asked, had such a change come about? It wasn't a matter of earth but heaven. Taas gave the credit to Christ and the glory to God. His heart, he said, was completely transformed so that he had a deep love for the Jewish people. As a matter of fact, Taas said, he now had something to ask. He wanted each member of the hospital staff to forgive him. The moment was transcendent. A man of hatred had become an ambassador of God's love for all humanity.[11]

If God could do this for killers such as Paul and Taas, do you have any doubt that He can fill your heart with abounding love?

## The Effect of Compassion

What is the effect of compassion? "That He may establish your hearts blameless in holiness . . ."

This is a purpose clause. It shows exactly why we are to be loving others. The purpose of all those years of school is to have an education and be knowledgeable. The purpose of going to work forty hours a week is to earn a living. What is the purpose of loving others? It is to develop holy, blameless hearts.

*Christian* means "little Christ." We want to be just like Him, to imitate Him in every way possible so that we could be mistaken for Him. How do we do it? By following His lead; by doing what He did.

Some people believe they can become Christ-like by reciting numerous Scripture verses. Some believe they can do it by mastering the spiritual lingo and delivering the most impressive spoken prayers. Some of those things are good, some are worthless; none make us like Jesus.

And how did Jesus live? He loved people everywhere He went. He touched lepers, befriended social pariahs, cured sick people, cherished children, and had compassion for everyone in His path. His last acts were to pray for the forgiveness of His murderers, and then to look beside Him and feel compassion for a dying thief, whom He encouraged and assured of salvation. In His deepest hours of agony, never for a moment did He take a break from loving others. In the Upper Room, He told His disciples that their main work would be to love one another. The more difficult His life became, the more crowded He was by the demands of people, and the closer to a torturous death—the more loving, compassionate, and forgiving He became.

"Who could follow that act?" you ask with reasonable incredulity. "Who could have such a heart?"

That's irrelevant when you're at the starting line of loving someone. Just do it and worry about motives later. Love, as Paul describes it in this chapter, is a living thing. It starts from the tiny seed of obedience and blooms as we water it with our actions. Go love and serve, and you will find a miracle happening within yourself: a holy and blameless heart.

## The Exercise of Compassion

There are so many fringe benefits to living the way God wants us to live. Here is another one: showing compassion has measurable therapeutic value for our lives.

Allan Luks was the executive director of the Big Brothers and Big Sisters charity for eighteen years leading up to his retirement. In his book *The Healing Power of Doing Good,* he describes a study of three thousand volunteers of all ages throughout the country. The results of a computerized questionnaire demonstrated a clear cause-and-effect relationship between helping others and good health. He concluded that helping contributes to the maintenance of good health, even diminishing the effect of diseases and disorders: serious and minor, psychological and physical.

Doing good for others does good for us. It reverses the destructive process of self-absorption, moves us into the healthy arena of seeing the needs of others, and ultimately opens us up to the reality of God and His destiny for us.

William Booth, the founder of the Salvation Army, was passionate about showing compassion, especially for the downtrodden of the London slums. One day his son Bramwell entered the room early and found his father furiously brushing his hair, brushes in both hands, as he frantically finished dressing for the day. No time for "Good morning"; Booth looked at his son and cried, "Bramwell! Did you know there are men sleeping outdoors all night under the bridges?" He'd been in London late the preceding night, and this had been a shocking sight on his way home.

"Well, yes," said Bramwell. "A lot of poor fellows, I suppose."

"Then you ought to be ashamed of yourself for having known it and done nothing for them," answered William Booth.

Bramwell began constructing elaborate excuses. He could never add such a complex project to all the things he had going on in his life, which he now began to name. His plate was full.

His father simply barked, "Go and do something!"

That moment of resolve was the beginning of the Salvation Army Shelters, a special ministry that changed the lives of hundreds of homeless men during the early days of the Salvation Army work in London.[12]

Have you ever had a Booth moment, when suddenly you saw some person or situation through God's eyes and developed a fiery determination to see it change?

Roy Anthony Borges had a moment like that in prison. Having become a Christian, he had to begin unlearning everything life had taught him—particularly everything prison had taught him. Hate, they taught, was the thing that made you survive. And every inmate had far more enemies than friends.

A typical enemy for Borges was Rodney, who stole his radio and headphones one day while Borges was playing volleyball in the prison yard. It was an expensive radio, a gift from his mother. The earphones had been a Christmas present from his sister. In a prison cell, such a thing is a treasure to cherish. Borges was angry and his heart went directly to the possibility of revenge. But he was wise enough to pray, and he began to feel in doing so that God was testing him.

The anger was not so easily removed. Every day he had the impulse to jump Rodney, to wipe the arrogant grin off his face. But there was a Bible verse that wouldn't get out of his mind. It was Romans 12:20–21, Paul's instruction to forget about vengeance, to leave all that to God. Finally Borges actually began to see his enemy from a perspective he'd never had: God's view. He began praying for the man, and expecting something miraculous to happen in the life of the man who had stolen his radio.

It got even stranger. Before he knew it, Borges was helping his enemy, talking to him about Jesus, entirely forgetting to hate Rodney. One day he saw the miracle. Rodney was kneeling next to his bunk, reading the Bible on his own. He said, "I knew [then] that good had overcome evil."[13]

In these difficult days, there will be stress and tension. You will be more prone than usual to give in to bitterness. It will be an easy time to nurture a potent grudge against someone else. Maybe you'll give in to those impulses. You can rationalize it by saying you've had a hard time, that you'll get back to being Christ-like when times are better, and that God will understand. But that vaults you onto the sad, downhill slope toward living in the hopelessness of this world, where people's happiness is based solely upon circumstances. In this world, it will never be convenient to be godly on those terms.

There is another way, and that's the way of responding to crisis by doubling down on patience, kindness, longsuffering, and compassion. Let your love increase and then abound. The result will be a joy that transcends these circumstances. And if enough of us get in on that, then even the circumstances cannot hold out. The love of God is the one thing that can and will turn this world upside down. Let's get to work.

# THREE

# Stay Constructive

ATHEISM HAS TAKEN OVER THE BUSES. IN NEW YORK, THEY'RE chugging past the Empire State Building bearing twelve-foot long signs announcing: *You Don't Have to Believe in God*. Thousands of people in Chicago are getting on and off buses emblazoned with a similar message: *In the Beginning Man Created God*. In Indiana, the bus banners say: *You Can Be Good Without God*.

In other American cities, the buses are wrapped in this message: *Why believe in a god? Just be good for goodness' sake!* Another slogan gives this bit of atheistic reassurance: *Don't Believe in God? You're Not Alone*.

Riders in Genoa, Italy, are bouncing around in vehicles that declare: *The Bad News Is that God Does Not Exist. The Good News Is that You Do Not Need Him*.

(Let me get that straight. The atheists are admitting their core teaching is *Bad News*?)

And then there's the slogan of the original atheistic bus campaign in London. It said: *There's Probably No God. Now Stop Worrying and Enjoy Your Life*.

Let me rephrase that.

- There's Probably No God. So Your Life Has No Ultimate Meaning.
- There's Probably No God. So You Came From Sludge and Are Returning to Dust.
- There's Probably No God. So You Can Never Be Forgiven of Your Sins.
- There's Probably No God. So Good Luck Dealing with Your Problems.
- There's Probably No God. So You'll Never See Your Loved Ones in Heaven.
- There's Probably No God. So Live for Fun and Die in Despair.
- There's Probably No God. So There's No Hope, No Life, No Grace, No Heaven.

I don't know who'd want to believe that message, let alone advertise it. For that matter, I've never met anyone who could actually prove that God doesn't exist. There are no true atheists. Nevertheless, a new, aggressive, in-your-face brand of atheism is gaining millions of adherents in these last days.

Atheists are ready to come out of the closet, and they're itching for a fight. They've gotten a boost from President Barack Obama, who included a reference to "nonbelievers" in his inaugural address. *USA Today* said that Obama's inaugural address represents the first time in inaugural history that an American president has explicitly acknowledged atheists and atheism.[1]

Atheism is finding its voice because our culture has become

totally secularized, and secularization is not neutral; it's inherently anti-Christian.

But there's nothing constructive about secularization or atheism. Look at what the twentieth century's most famous atheists did to the world: Lenin, Stalin, Hitler, and Mao Zedong. Without God, we can only tear down. With Christ, we're in the business of building up.

As Christians face these perilous times, our message is fresh, positive, exciting, energetic, and eminently constructive.

In the Old Testament there is a beautiful passage about the shifting seasons of life. One of its statements is, "There is a time to tear down, and a time to build up" (Ecclesiastes 3:3b NASB). Within living memory, we've seen generations dedicated to both.

Half a century ago, there was a time to build up. The late author Stephen Ambrose wrote extensively about the Second World War and the generation of young men who returned from it. Ambrose's father came home from the war, put up a backboard, and a whole squad of ex-GIs from the neighborhood came over regularly to play basketball. Ambrose never remembered their last names, but he remembered the scars on their arms and chests. As he reflected on their accomplishments he wrote:

> But in fact these were the men who built modern America. They had learned to work together in the armed services in World War II. They had seen enough destruction; they wanted to construct. They built the interstate highway system, the St. Lawrence Seaway, the suburbs (so scorned by the sociologists, so successful with the people), and more. They had seen enough killing; they wanted to save lives. They licked polio and made other revolutionary advances in medicine. They had learned in the armed forces the virtues of solid organization and

teamwork, and the value of individual initiative, inventiveness, and responsibility. They developed the modern corporation while inaugurating revolutionary advances in science and technology, education and public policy.[2]

They labored, they filled their station wagons and ranch-style homes with children, and they retired. Perhaps they really are the "Greatest Generation."

Then came the time to tear down. You've lived through that time, and so have I—decades of national division. Future generations will look back and see this as a season of wanton destruction. From top leadership on down to the man on the street, we've been about the business of demolition rather than construction. We've become adept at poisoning the wells of culture, politics, business, spirituality, the family, and every other sphere. For reasons unknown, we've begun tearing down everything between ourselves and the horizon:

We've torn down integrity.
We've torn down purity.
We've torn down honesty.
We've torn down respect.
We've torn down national pride.
We've torn down ideals.
We've torn down dreams.
We've torn down our sense of shame.
We've torn down political aspiration.
We've torn down everything we began building at the birth of our nation.

We began the new millennium with terrorism on our own soil, with high school shootings, and with dramatic rollbacks of traditional moral boundaries. The Cleavers, the Brady Bunch, and the Huxtables no longer mirror our complex families. Diversity is the new state religion, with tolerance demanded in all things except for traditional Judeo-Christian values.

Paul tells us not to be surprised:

> Don't be naive. There are difficult times ahead. As the end approaches, people are going to be self-absorbed, money-hungry, self-promoting, stuck-up, profane, contemptuous of parents, crude, coarse, dog-eat-dog, unbending, slanderers, impulsively wild, savage, cynical, treacherous, ruthless, bloated windbags, addicted to lust, and allergic to God. They'll make a show of religion, but behind the scenes they're animals. Stay clear of these people. (2 Timothy 3:1–5 MSG)[3]

Does that sound to you like a picture of today's world? I realize it's easy to be discouraged. We could throw up our hands and simply quit. Such is not a godly attitude, according to the Scriptures. In a time of tearing down, we are to be about His work of building up. In a destructive world, we are to maintain constructive attitudes.

## The Final Follow

It will not surprise you to learn that a lot of tearing down and building up have occurred in every generation, including in Bible days. There had been a time for tearing down in the apostle Peter's life. He had watched his Lord arrested and taken for execution—that alone almost tore down the life of Peter. But to make things worse, he himself had failed the most basic test of love and loyalty. Even with a prediction from Jesus that should have served as a warning, Peter had denied his affiliation with his wonderful master—not once but three times.

In spite of our Lord's patient preparation of His impetuous disciple, Peter was constantly demonstrating the frayed fabric of his life. Time and time again Peter proved that without Jesus he was nothing. Now it looked like he would once again be a fisherman—no more teachers, no more dreams.

In the comforting simplicity of the net and sea spray, Peter surely thought back to the last time he had been a serious fisherman. The Master had come along then and said, "Follow me." He had seen a miraculous catch, knelt before the teacher, and said, "Depart from me, for I am a sinful man, O Lord!" That experience, too, had been a tearing down, a humbling, a confrontation with his own unworthiness. Even so, Jesus had wanted him, and he had followed. Jesus had said, "Do not be afraid. From now on you will catch men" (Luke 5:8, 10).

"Follow me." That's what Jesus had said and that's what Peter had done. Now, having failed his Lord, he was just a fisher of fish again. He must have wondered if his following days were finished. The final chapter of John's gospel, however, brings Peter full circle. Again, Jesus will say to him, "Follow me." This will be the final "follow." And again Peter will drop his nets and go—this time to the Ascension; to Pentecost; to the building of the Jerusalem church; and all the way to Rome, where he will die (according to tradition) as a martyr, a coward no more, but the courageous man Jesus had said he would be.

We all love Peter. And why not? There is so much reality, so much familiar humanity that comes through the ancient pages of Scripture to make him real for us. There is Peter who was the first to recognize Jesus as the Christ; Peter who denied he was even a friend. There was

Peter who stepped out of the boat, and Peter who almost drowned when his faith short-circuited. Jesus called him "the Rock" one time, "Satan" another. Peter was so much like us—one step forward, two steps back, animated by wild faith and paralyzing doubt. He was a man of highs and lows, mountains and valleys, and that's why he makes a perfect study for times like these. As a preacher I tend to operate on the "what comes next" principle. I keep things simple and chronological, starting at the first verse and moving along. This chapter is an exception. The novelist Kurt Vonnegut Jr. once advised writers to start as close to the end as possible.[4] That's what I'm going to do here. I find it intriguing to start at the end of the story in John 21, then go back to pick up the details.

John 21 is the final chapter of the final gospel. It's considered a kind of epilogue and contains the last recorded words of the Savior before He ascended to heaven. There are more recorded conversations between Jesus and Peter than with any other disciple, so it's fitting that this last one is also with Peter. It's also fitting that it's a tale of restoration because that's what Jesus does. He is always reconciling, always reconstructing, always bringing people home.

Jesus is completing a conversation with Peter, once again foretelling what lies ahead for the fisherman. "When you were younger you dressed yourself and went where you wanted," He says. "But when you are old you will stretch out your hands, and someone else will dress you and lead you where you do not want to go" (John 21:18 NIV).

On the night of His arrest, Jesus had correctly predicted an act of denial. Now He predicts an act of devotion. According to tradition, Jesus is saying that Peter will reach his latter years, but that he will die with his hands outstretched—a euphemism for what He Himself has been through. Tertullian and Eusebius, early historians of the

Christian movement, each report that Peter followed his Lord to the cross.

Jesus saw it through the mist of the future and foretold Peter's three denials—just as He sees our future with its failures and successes. Now that Peter is a fallen disciple, Jesus repeats once more the words that defined His disciple's life mission: "Follow Me." It is as if none of the heartbreak in between has ever happened. Jesus looks beyond it and says, "Follow Me."

## "What About Him?"

As this exchange occurs, Peter notices that someone else is already following. According to John 21:20, Peter turns and sees "the disciple whom Jesus loved" keeping pace with them. This, of course, is John, the only disciple who rivaled the closeness that Peter enjoyed with Jesus. So much is happening right now between Jesus and Peter, but the impetuous disciple momentarily loses sight of all that. He wags a thumb at the trailing John and says, "But Lord, what about this man?" (v. 21).

The preceding conversation has been gentle and compassionate, soothing the bruising of Peter's soul. Now Jesus is blunt. He says to Peter concerning John, "If I want him to remain alive until I return, what is that to you?" And one more time, He says these words with an added urgency: *"You must follow me"* (v. 22 NIV; emphasis added). In His answer to Peter, Jesus mentions His own "return," reminding us again that instructions for practical living are often found in the context of future predictions.

Jesus' final words to Peter were—*You must follow Me!* His last command to Peter should be the first concern of each of us today. Whatever things distract you—what is that to you? You must follow Him!

I wanted to begin right there, framing the story for this chapter with that crucial command. Now let's go back and examine the fascinating conversation that led up to it—the story of the recommissioning of a fallen disciple, a failure who became a follower again.

Moving back to John 18 we find the disciples in crisis. Jesus has been arrested, and two disciples have followed at a distance. One, loving and loyal John, will follow all the way to the cross; the other, Peter, will experience another relapse of doubt. Just as he has sunk into the waves after a glorious moment of water-walking, now he sinks back into an alley. Hours previously, he has promised to follow Jesus to death itself—to occupy the next cross (Matthew 26:35). Peter is always so near, and yet so far. He has followed Jesus to the point at which his courage fails. And beside a fire, where peasants warm their hands, a stranger voices the very question which Peter is silently asking of himself: "You are one of His disciples, are you not?" (John 18:25).

Peter hears himself say, "I am not!" Worst of all is the growing suspicion that he is telling the truth. Peter is given two more chances to redeem himself, but each time the answer is the same. Three is a number of completion, and Peter understands himself to be a complete failure in following Jesus.

We've all been there, doing or saying something wrong, feeling the sting of conviction, and hearing the voice inside us asking, "You are one of His disciples—are you not?" We also know that our first act of disobedience can be a slippery slope that becomes an avalanche.

## Love or Like?

Now there is another fire, this one on an early-morning beach at the Sea of Tiberias. A few of the disciples had gone with Peter when he said, "I am going fishing" (John 21:3). Their fishing trip ends just as on that memorable occasion when they fished all night and caught nothing. One of the disciples notices a man watching them by the shore. It's Jesus, though He is initially unrecognized. And soon He's duplicating the wonderful miracle of the net-bursting catch—one hundred fifty-three fish are suddenly spilling over the nets. John counted them. And soon, there is a campfire, a breakfast, a reunion, laughter, and probably many, many questions. Ignoring all the chatter around the fire, however, John wants us to know only what Jesus said to Peter.

Three times Jesus asks him, "Do you love Me?" and Peter answers in the affirmative—but there are certain significant variations on the theme. We see the word *love* in our Bibles all three times. But in the Greek it's not so. For the first two questions, Jesus uses the word most associated with godly love—*agape*. This is supreme, sacrificial love. "Peter, do you love Me with the love of God, committed and costly?" Each time Peter answers with a different word—the one that means "brotherly affection." *Do you love Me? Yes, I'm fond of You.*

The first time Jesus asks, "Do you [*agape*] Me more than these?" Peter replies that he is fond of Him.

The second time it is, "Do you [*agape*] Me?" He has dropped the phrase of comparison. Peter offers the same reply.

The third time, Jesus makes another change. He abandons the elevated *agape* and asks if Peter is fond of Him. It may be one of Jesus' saddest remarks, and it has the effect of, "Well, Peter, are you even *fond* of Me? Really?"

Peter, wounded from his great failure, no longer wants to boast of his unmatched love or how he will follow Jesus to the cross. Humbled, he is saying, "I can give you only this much from my heart," and Jesus is asking, "Are you sure you even have that much to give?"

As we read this passage, understanding the Greek language and all its implications to their subtle discourse, we can almost make out the sound of Peter's heart breaking. It is a time for tearing down. Jesus had called him the Rock. What kind of rock can be shattered into so many pieces?

## Feed and Follow

What we've just discussed is the content of a sermon countless pastors have preached. The intricacies of the conversation between Jesus and Peter make for such a terrific lesson that we often miss elements in the story that are equally important. We focus on the love, but we miss out on the lambs. Let me tell you what I mean.

Jesus is asking Peter about the depth of his love and commitment. But He is also giving Peter a commission with every response. The first time, when Peter says, "Lord, You know that I'm fond of You," Jesus immediately says, "Feed My lambs." The second time, Jesus says, "Tend My sheep." And the third time Jesus combines the two and says, "Feed My sheep."

What Jesus is saying to Peter is this: "Peter, it's not about some abstract love that you have, and how that love might be measured on some emotional scale. It is about your willingness to do what I do—to care for My children." Jesus instructs Peter to feed the lambs; tend them; feed the sheep. These words *feed* and *tend* refer to providing spiritual nurture to the soul, or building someone up by promoti the spiritual welfare, in the way a shepherd would care for his fl "This is what I do," Jesus is saying. "You do it too."

And Jesus adds the final commandment, which sums up thing: "Follow Me." In that conversation, Peter may be feelin than he ever has, having the very measure of his love for Jesus sized up. And yet Jesus is saying, *"Follow Me!"*

I read that chapter one more time, in the light of all that is going on in our nation and world, and I'm struck by the way Jesus takes something broken and rebuilds it into something strong and fruitful. He does that with twelve confused, slow-learning disciples. In our broken world we are witnessing just the opposite. I'm a Christian and a patriot, someone who loves his country and believes God has blessed it. But as I write these words our nation is being deconstructed, torn down piece by piece.

I could write another chapter, or perhaps another book, about the things that are being destroyed before our very eyes. And the temptation for each of us is to either throw up our hands in surrender, or climb onto a soapbox and start condemning the ones doing the damage. But I believe that if Jesus were to counsel us on how to respond, He would say just what He has said to Peter. He would say, "Tend My lambs. Feed My sheep. And keep following Me."

## The Art of Body Building

One of the beautiful words in our language, in both sound and sense, is *edification*. The Greek version has a nice ring to it too: *oikodomeo*. It is two words combined, *oikos* ("house") and *domeo* ("to build"). So when we speak of edifying—building up—one another, the Greek understanding is building one anothers' house. The word *edifice*, or building, comes from this root.

Here's an example of how it's used in the literal sense, in the New Testament: "Therefore whoever hears these sayings of Mine, and does them, I will liken him to a wise man who builds his house [*oikodomeo*] on the rock" (Matthew 7:24). In Matthew 24:1, we find the word used in reference to building the temple—the *oikodomeo*, or the edifice. That's a house, but it's God's house.

Through the years, the meaning of this word has shifted. We use this expression to talk about building people rather than buildings. In other words, we've taken the word exactly where I believe God would want us to take it. If you'll remember, Jesus had a history of making things. His early occupation was carpentry, making things with His hands. But even before that, He is the One who made the universe by the power of His Word (John 1:1–3, 10; Colossians 1:16, 17; Hebrews 1:1, 2, 10). His earthly ministry involved shaping people into living stones.

When He ascended to heaven, we, the living church, became His body, and one of the great themes of the New Testament is the building up of the body of Christ. Peter writes, "You also, as living stones, are being built up a spiritual house, a holy priesthood, to offer up spiritual sacrifices acceptable to God through Jesus Christ" (1 Peter 2:5). This is a divine metaphor telling us that we are one great building under construction, so that God can come to take residence in that building. At the same time, we are *individual* buildings—Paul said that your personal body is God's temple as well (1 Corinthians 3:16). We build each other up individually and corporately.

This should be the most beautiful process visible on this earth: people constantly edifying one another, building each other up to be holy dwelling places for God. Yet sometimes it goes awry. I've read books about the "toxic church," describing church leaders who have broken people down instead of building them up. And nothing could be more tragic. The Bible exhorts us to edify one another, to build up one another. As a pastor, my passion is to be in the building business, raising up men and women to be beautiful structures of God.

When Jesus said, "I will build My church, and the gates of Hades shall not prevail against it" (Matthew 16:18), He was referring to the eternal body of believers that was christened on the day of Pentecost. Many empires have raged against that church and failed. It continues to rise taller and taller with each generation. The exterior is built through evangelism, and the interior through edification.

Today, the world is doing everything in its power to tear down the church, and often within the church, we are tearing each other apart. We seem to have forgotten that *we are God's building*. We are eternal; we are the living body of Christ. When we feel beaten down by this world, we should be strengthened by our knowledge of God's plan for His church. And then we should love one another as the eternal living stones of that church, and continue to build each other up instead of tearing down. Here are some things to keep in mind as we strive to become better builders.

## Edification Is Not About You: It's About Others

I only know of one passage that speaks of self-edification. The New Testament is a collection of "we" writings. It's always speaking in the second person plural. The major emphasis is upon the building up of one another.

Sadly, we have more than our share of demolition experts. I'll never forget being a young preacher and traveling to various churches to preach. One day I was the guest preacher at a church in northern Ohio. As I often did back then, I sang a solo and then delivered my sermon.

A woman walked up to me afterward and said, "Son, I've heard you preach a lot. You need to sing more."

The interesting thing is that she was trying to do exactly what we're talking about—she wanted to build me up as a vocalist. But I was devastated because my passionate calling was to preach. We need to be thinking, lovingly and sensitively, about the best way to uplift others. Paul gives us a solid tip: "All things are lawful for me, but not all things are helpful; all things are lawful for me, but not all things edify. Let no one seek his own, but each one the other's well-being" (1 Corinthians 10:23–24).

These are challenging words for the "Me Generation." In Erwin McManus's book, *An Unstoppable Force*, he bemoans the fact that we seem to have lost sight of this core value of the church. He writes: "Unfortunately, for too many people, when the conversation is no longer about them, there's not much left to be said."[5] To that assessment he adds that since we are each the center of the universe (is that even possible?), everything is evaluated on whether or not it meets our own specific and "special" needs.

The logical phenomenon derived from that mind-set is what I would call "church shopping myopia." This malaise has become as common in Christians as seasonal allergies. Physical myopia is a condition that causes vision to become defective—it sees things only within a very narrow range. The myopic church shopper's spiritual vision is distorted by a focus on convenience—"What does the church have to offer me?"—instead of focusing on relevance—"How will this church help me to 'serve the lost and broken world?'"

Rather than obediently following Jesus' command to feed His sheep, church shopping is too much about being fed and too little about exercising our faith.

While there is only one visible body of Christ on earth today, no one person is that body. All of us together as followers of Jesus, each doing the part ordained for us by God, make up His body.

For the church of Jesus Christ, it's always "*We* over *Me*." As the athletes say it, "There's no 'I' in *team*." Paul uses this principle when he writes, "He who speaks in a tongue edifies himself, but he who prophesies [that is, *preaches*] edifies the church" (1 Corinthians 14:4). The implication is that what serves the body takes precedence over what serves the individual.

In the New Testament there are many references to "one another" and "each other." Here's one of them: "Therefore comfort each other and edify one another, just as you also are doing" (1 Thessalonians 5:11). I've met many self-educated men and women, but no self-edified ones.

I read about a group of women who were having dinner together shortly after one of them returned from Europe. One of the women, a stay-at-home mom, was particularly low in spirit that day. She hadn't been to Europe or anywhere else exciting. Her life felt so drab she felt like she was invisible. She was surprised when her returning friend presented her with a gift. It was a book about the great cathedrals of Europe. Inside the cover, her friend had inscribed, "With admiration for the greatness of what you are building when only God sees."

Inside the book she read the account of how one of the cathedrals was built. A visitor saw a workman carving a tiny bird on the inside of a beam. He watched the craftsman's concentrated movements for a few minutes then looked up at the entire massive edifice, under constant construction for a century. He asked the carver, "Why are you spending so much time chiseling a tiny bird into a beam that will be covered by the stone roof? It will be hidden from everyone's view?"

Without looking away from his work, the craftsman replied, "Because God sees."

As the woman read this story, she thought of the things in her life that were hidden from view: baking for church receptions, sewing patches on children's jeans, bandaging scrapes, cleaning the house, then cleaning it again when it was left messy—she remembered now that God saw, and she felt better. Most of all, she realized that her friend had done a little carving on the weary beams of her soul. It was uplifting, edifying encouragement from a friend just at the right time—which is the way God uses us within the body, even when we don't realize it.[6]

We must try to be ready for those moments, watching closely for the moods of our friends, ready to apply the salve of a good word in season. That's the work of edification. On the other hand, there is a corresponding warning to heed: "Let no corrupt word proceed out of your mouth, but what is good for necessary edification, that it may impart grace to the hearers" (Ephesians 4:29). Even our most casual words are to be spoken with regard to the ripple effect that ensues. It's not about us, but about others.

## Edification Is Not What You Profess: It's What You Pursue

Building is long and deliberate work, but destruction is the work of a thoughtless moment.

Some of us build up while others tear down. It seems as if cynicism and sarcasm are a kind of cultural lingo these days. It takes a conscious effort to be a positive, uplifting person when we have so few role models doing it. I catch myself slipping into a sarcastic mode as I talk to staffers at our church. Someone kids me, I zing him back, and pretty soon it escalates into sarcasm that leaves a bruise somewhere behind the smile.

Have you ever realized that aggressive humor can be hurtful? Humor has a double edge. It can be used to strengthen a bond or to strike a blow.

"Therefore," Paul tells us, "let us pursue the things which make for peace and the things by which one may edify another" (Romans 14:19). Pursuit is intentional—it's not something that happens on its own. As far as humor goes, the joke that comes naturally will often be at someone's expense. The joke you'll need to be intentional about is the one that sets others at ease, perhaps by making it at your own expense. I do this, for example, when I tell you I'm directionally challenged. We laugh together, no one is hurt, and the laughter bonds us.

Pursuing edification means staying on task. Paul writes to Timothy to avoid those time-wasters "which cause disputes rather than godly edification which is in faith" (I Timothy 1:4). So many silly distractions keep us from building each other up. By the way, what do we call those time-wasters? That's one of those ideas that needs a word of its own. I've invented one: *posteriorities*. I'm hoping that all the new dictionaries will pick up on my brilliant new word!

Here's what it means. If priorities are all those things you intend to do, in the order you intend to do them, then posteriorities are all the things you're *not* going to do, in the order you don't intend to do them. If our priorities are to edify one another, then what are our posteriorities? Silly arguments about inconsequential religious questions; squabbles over church politics, carpet colors, and who gets to be on what committee; and all that kind of thing. Let's establish our posteriorities and start avoiding them immediately.

If it is true that Christ is coming back soon, shouldn't we feel a sense of urgency over the things at the top of His list for us to accomplish? Building up one another is a priority, not a posteriority. Wouldn't you love for churches to chart all their activities and all their budget expenses, and find out which ones edify people and which don't?

On a personal level, how are you measuring up with your priorities? Use this little poem to chart your own profile:

> I saw them tearing a building down,
> A group of men in a busy town,
> With hefty blow and lusty yell,
> They swung with zest,
> And a side wall fell.
> Asked of the foreman,
> "Are these men skilled?
> The kind you would hire if you had to build?"
> He looked at me, and laughed, "No, indeed!
> Unskilled labor is all I need.
> Why, they can wreck in a day or two,
> What it has taken builders years to do."
> I asked myself, as I went my way,
> Which of these roles have I tried to play?
> Am I a builder with rule and square,
> Measuring and constructing with skill and care?
> Or am I the wrecker who walks the town,
> Content with the business of tearing down?
> —Author Unknown

## Edification Is Not About How Much You Know: It's About How Much You Care

"Knowledge puffs up, but love builds up" (1 Corinthians 8:1 NIV). Another translation reads: "While knowledge may make us feel important, it is love that really builds up the church" (NLT).

Have you ever been hurting over something when someone wanted to give you a detailed advice list—when all you wanted was a listening ear and a soft shoulder? It's amazing how few of us learn that those in pain need comforting more than they need information. We men in particular can live our whole lives without figuring that out. We want to tell our wives how to fix things; what they want is to know that we care, we empathize, and we hurt with them.

We need to realize that with everything we do at church. Doctrine and instruction will never cease to matter, but people wander into church because they are lonely, hurt, and disconnected. Why did people seek Jesus out? He loved them and cared for their needs. Then, through tears of gratitude, they heard His teachings. Jonathan Edwards, America's great preacher and theologian, said, "Our people do not so much need to have their heads turned as to have their hearts touched, and they stand in the greatest need of that sort of preaching which has the greatest tendency to do this."[7]

## It's Not About Your Gifts: It's About Your Goals

What about the question of spiritual gifts? Paul says, "Now concerning spiritual gifts, brethren, I do not want you to be ignorant" (1 Corinthians 12:1). The Barna research organization has identified the fact that Paul is not getting his wish; many people are ignorant on this subject.

As you may know, we all have at least one spiritual gift that we use within the body of Christ. These aren't the same as natural abilities, but are specially adapted to strengthen and unify the church. More than 20 percent of those surveyed by Barna claimed "gifts," such as: sense of humor, creativity, and clairvoyance.

The problem is that these are not spiritual gifts by any New Testament definition. As for the genuine gifts, 28 percent of American Christians failed to claim a single one of them. If they are indeed followers of Jesus Christ, they can be certain that they possess at least one of the gifts specified in Romans 12:6–8, 1 Corinthians 12, Ephesians 4:7–13, or 1 Peter 4:10–11.[8]

Spiritual gifts aren't like Christmas or birthday gifts, intended for private enjoyment. They are for the express purpose of building up fellow believers. Whether your gift is teaching, service, faith, helps, or any of the others, it is "for the edification of the church that you seek to excel" (1 Corinthians 14:12). Therefore the question is not which gift did you receive, but how you intend to use it.

When we bring these gifts to church, Paul says, "let everything be done for edification" (1 Corinthians 14:26). Paul saw people boasting about tongues or prophecy, and he pointed out that the only thing we should boast about is how strong and unified the fellowship is becoming. Self-centeredness slips into the church, reflecting the world we live in, while the work of building one another must be humble and unselfish. Our gifts are nothing to brag about—they are on loan from God for the wonderful work of body building.

## It's Not About Your Wisdom: It's About His Word

There is a final principle that will help us be the encouragers and edifiers that God wants us to be. When Paul visited Ephesus, he delivered a beautiful address to the elders there, including these words: "So now, brethren, I commend you to God and to the word of his grace, which is able to build you up and give you an inheritance among all those who are sanctified" (Acts 20:32).

The Word of God is a Book that builds. When you feel torn down by all that is happening in this world, you'll find so much strength and encouragement in the Bible. When you think you're in no condition to help others when you need so much encouragement yourself, it is all here for you in the ageless Scriptures. God speaks through this Book. He takes its inspired words and applies them to your life so that you feel a ray of hope in the darkening gloom.

It's a difference maker. But don't make the mistake of believing a weekly sermon, a book like this one, or even a fellowship group will make this happen for you. It's important that you delve deeply into the Word yourself. You need to be studying it and reflecting on it every day of your life. The word of His grace, according to Paul, is able to build you up. And do you remember earlier in the chapter when I mentioned finding only one passage that speaks of building ourselves up? Jude 20–21 is that very passage: "But you, beloved, building yourselves up on your most holy faith, praying in the Holy Spirit, keep yourselves in the love of God, looking for the mercy of our Lord Jesus Christ unto eternal life."

So yes, the real work is done in fellowship. But we must never neglect the deep, private work of building that only the Holy Spirit can do within us, through the Scriptures, through prayer in the Holy Spirit, and through privately entering into his presence.

My question to you is, who said you need to choose between the two? You can excel at both, keeping the discipline of a daily appointment with God, to build the inner person, and also ministering among the body at your church. What a wonderful balance it makes when we do both well. What a great joy to be found doing them both when Christ appears in the sky.

Many people stop during the autumn to take in the spectacle of geese migrating in flocks, high in the sky. They fly in a distinctive V formation. We enjoy the natural beauty of that, but have you ever wondered about its functionality? The V is more efficient than flying in a line or randomly. The flapping of the wings creates an uplift of air, an effect that is increased at the rear of the formation. There is one goose at the point of the V, and after a certain time, he'll drop off and fly to the end of the formation. The weaker birds also remain close to the rear and on the inside where their work is decreased. In this way, the geese take care of one another. The stronger birds lead until others rotate to the front and take their places. By cooperating and uplifting one another, the geese achieve long migrations that would be otherwise impossible. In numbers, they're better protected. I think those geese have something to teach us.[9] We are so much stronger together than we are on our own.

I cannot predict what the condition of the world will be as you read these words. Nor do I know anything of the circumstances of your life. But of certain truths I can be extremely sure. One is that Christ's return is closer than it was when we began this book together. Another is that His church will endure because it is eternal. And finally, I know that you have a place in that church—a place where you can heal and be healed; a place where you can take the lead and fall back for rest; a place where you can build up others, and be built up yourself.

The world outside can grow only to a finite level of darkness, but inside the church, we've yet to see the ultimate brightness of pure light. We've yet to see the perfection of genuine love. We've yet to become those people that we're destined to become, through the strengthening of the body of believers, and through the work of Christ Himself.

When He returns, we'll see the brightest, most intense, most beautiful light in all creation. Jesus said, "I am the light of the world" (John 8:12; 9:5). I hope you are drawn to that light like a moth to flame. What on earth should we do now? Gather together. Serve Him. Await His return.

*There Is a God. Christ Is Returning. The Best Is Yet to Come.*

You can put that on your bus, and drive it!

# FOUR

# Stay Challenged

FOR ALL OF HIS SEVENTY-SIX YEARS, ROMANIAN-BORN LIVIU Librescu met life's challenges head-on. As a child in Romania during World War II, he was confined to a Jewish ghetto while his father was sentenced to a forced labor camp. But he survived the Holocaust, determined to fulfill his dream of becoming an engineer. And he did, in spite of the Communist Party ruling Romania during his young adult years. He completed an undergraduate engineering degree at the Polytechnic University of Bucharest and then a PhD at the Institute of Fluid Mechanics at Romania's Academy of Science. As a brilliant professor he was widely esteemed—within Romania. Communist rule prohibited him from publishing his research outside of Romania. So, at great risk, he smuggled his papers out of Romania to publishers in other countries.

After three years of overcoming obstacles, Dr. Librescu and his wife were granted permission to emigrate to Israel in 1978. After teaching at Tel-Aviv University for seven years, he accepted a one-year position as a visiting professor in the Virginia Tech (Virginia) Department of

Engineering Science and Mechanics. In 1985 his family joined him in Blacksburg, Virginia, and they became part of the university family. He became one of Virginia Tech's most popular and respected professors and researchers in the field of aeronautical engineering. Throughout his career, Dr. Librescu compiled a list of awards and recognitions too long to detail here, but they were evidence of how the man lived his life—with strenuous and lavish commitment and generosity to his opportunities, his vocation, his family, and his university.

Dr. Librescu was Jewish. For all of his seventy-six years, he exemplified in his life the kind of diligence that reflects the image of God in human beings. Dr. Ishwar Puri, head of Dr. Librescu's department at Virginia Tech, said of his colleague, "He loved his position as a professor. A prolific researcher and wonderful teacher, he devoted himself to the profession, solely for the love of it."

When the professor himself was asked, in 2005, why he continued to work so hard, he said, "It is not a question of organizations or calculations. If I had the pleasure to do this, then I will put time aside to do this. It is personal freedom. If you are limited, then you miss the freedom. And I—I would like to be fluid. I would like to be free as a bird and fly everywhere."

The way Dr. Librescu lived his life—overcoming obstacles for more than seven decades to give his all to what he loved—would be a lesson by itself in diligence. He continued to teach at Virginia Tech well past retirement age because life itself was a challenge for him. He never gave himself permission to stop as long as his students needed him. In fact, it was his diligence that cost Dr. Librescu his life, and served as the ultimate illustration of what it means to live with no reservations.

On April 16, 2007, when a heavily armed, deranged student entered the classroom buildings on the Virginia Tech campus and began randomly killing and wounding students and staff, Dr. Librescu was teaching a class of around twenty students. As soon as it became obvious that the shooter might target his classroom, the seventy-six-year-old professor immediately threw himself against the inside of the classroom door while instructing the students to flee out the windows to safety. One of the last students to exit the classroom remembers seeing the professor leaning against the door and then falling, fatally wounded by bullets that came through the door. All twenty students, some with broken legs from the two-story fall, survived.

What would make someone sacrifice himself for the sake of others? For Liviu Librescu, it was the culmination of a life of overcoming challenges and remaining diligent to the end. After the attack, a student summarized the professor's actions: "It's one of those things where every little thing you do can save somebody's life."

I tell Liviu Librescu's story for a reason expressed by Dr. Puri, his department head: "[Professor Librescu] was an extremely tolerant man who mentored scholars from all over our troubled world." The professor was no stranger to trouble, but he wasn't intimidated by it. From childhood his commitment to living for others created peace in "our troubled world." Christians live in the same world. And we are called by God to take up our cross and march into the trouble for the sake of Christ—not knowing but that one little thing we do might save someone's life in time or for eternity.

Learning to live an exceptional life—a life of sacrifice, diligence, and generous commitment—is a process that never ends.[1]

The apostle Peter clues us in on the importance of living this kind of life: "Therefore, beloved, looking forward to these things, be diligent to be found by him in peace, without spot and blameless" (2 Peter 3:14). As always, the theme is that Christ is returning, so how shall we then live in this chaotic world? As you can see, the idea this time is to be diligent.

It isn't the first time Peter has used this word. Note what he has already written in an earlier chapter: "But also for this very reason, giving all diligence, add to your faith virtue, to virtue knowledge" (1:5). His message to us is to be motivated because our Lord is coming back. Don't stop the good things you're doing, but work even harder. If you do that, the world will never trip you up.

## The Purpose of Diligence

At the beginning of this epistle, we catch a glimpse of how the idea of diligence fits into Peter's overall theme: "As his divine power has given to us all things that pertain to life and godliness, through the knowledge of him who called us by glory and virtue, by which have been given to us exceedingly great and precious promises, that through these you may be partakers of the divine nature, having escaped the corruption that is in the world through lust" (2 Peter 1:3–4).

You may need to read that rich paragraph more than once. As you do so, note that Peter offers two focal points. First there is the astonishing idea that every follower of Christ has been given everything pertaining to life and godliness—not some things, not most things, but *everything*. Have you ever realized that? All that you need is already yours.

But wait! Where can we find these things? Peter says they have been given to us through the "exceedingly great and precious promises" of God's Word. That means your Bible is a full utility kit for everything you need to live with confidence in this chaotic world.

There's nothing else tangible in life that is as wonderful and complete as the written Word of God.

My wife, Donna, was recovering from surgery recently, and it fell to me to buy groceries. That is one of those things in life that just wasn't meant to be. She gave me a nice, neat list, and I wandered in confusion from aisle to aisle, occasionally finding some product but clueless as to why it was in the place where I found it. Yet I can find my way through the Bible like an old scout.

The Word is so beautifully organized and presented for us. We have history, poetry, and prophecy neatly grouped and giving us the story of God's people. Then we have the Gospels and our narrative of the early church, then the letters of those apostles that offer so much clear guidance for life. Everything we need for life and godliness is found in a neat package you can hold in a hand and bury in a heart. You can carry a New Testament in your shirt pocket or even, in software form, inside a cell phone these days.

Those who know me know how I feel about God's Word. But there's a disclaimer. It's possible to become so enamored of the Bible that we forget we need to interact with it. It's not enough to say, "What a beautiful leather Bible," and promptly stick it away on the shelf or under the car seat. Some Christians hear that "it is God who works in [us] both to will and to do for His good pleasure" (Philippians 2:13), and they think they can sit back and relax. They tend to miss the verse that came right before it, telling them to work out their own salvation "with fear and trembling" (2:12). That doesn't sound relaxing to me.

We do need to be careful how we speak of "working out" our salvation. This doesn't mean we can earn salvation—only the blood of Jesus Christ can give us that. In terms of the true reconciling work of forgiveness, we have no part. But we are to work *out* what God has worked *in*. I call that the "divine cooperative." The gift is delivered to us through the work of God, and we take it and practice due diligence in working to perfect ourselves as followers of Christ.

Isn't this how we look upon all gifts? If someone gives you a nice shirt for your birthday, it's up to you to wear it. If you receive a book, you're the one to read it. We are the recipients, but we must act on what we have been given or the gift is wasted upon us. Donna and I have two athletically gifted sons. I often told them while growing up that their ability was God's gift to them, and what they did with it was their gift to God. We receive gifts from the Holy Spirit too. I hope you have a firm grasp on what your spiritual gift is and that you are intentionally using it rather than tucking it away to admire.

We have the gift in hand. We've been provided with everything we need for life and godliness, and the Bible is the set of instructions that will get us up and running. More than that, it can make the very difference in our survival during the toughest of times. Consider the example of Geoffrey Bull, a British missionary who was taken prisoner when the communists took over China in 1949.

Geoffrey was kept in solitary confinement, but that wasn't the worst of it. His cell wasn't much larger than a phone booth. For twelve years his captors made him the subject of constant brainwashing attempts. "Not only did they want my confession," he said, "they wanted my soul." Convinced he was a British spy, the Chinese were after him every day, using diabolical mental tortures. But one thing made a difference for Geoffrey Bull. As a boy, his parents had encouraged him to memorize impressive portions of the Scriptures. Those verses lived in his heart, in the one stronghold the wardens could not penetrate, and they gave Geoffrey strength and power.

One night, with the cell doors bolted and padlocked, Bull knelt to pray. The guard began shouting through the keyhole, "You are not to pray!" He entered the cell and forced him from his knees. Even so, Geoffrey clung to every word of Scripture he possessed, turning it over in his mind, feeling its warmth. God gave him a patience and peace that few of us can imagine. When he would finish with the verses, he would name the names of his captors, praying for every one of them. The seeds of bitterness found no place in his heart.

After he was finally released, Geoffrey Bull faced many months of recuperation. After that, you might have expected him to retire. Not him. He married and resumed his missionary career, this time in Borneo. There was still much work to be done—to be done *diligently*.[2]

## The Prerequisite for Diligence

Faith is the prerequisite for diligence. Peter begins right there, telling us in verse 5 what to add to our faith. A list of "add-ons" follows, but the steam engine that pulls the train is faith. Without it, we're going nowhere.

Faith is the lowest common denominator in the mathematics of this passage. Have you noticed? Grace and peace are "multiplied" in verse 2, then a number of sums are "added" in verses 5–7. If you pay close attention, you will notice that God does the multiplying, and we do the adding. That's the divine cooperative at work.

So faith is the beginning of the process. We accept Christ by faith and are saved completely by God's grace. We want to move forward as believers by adding on to this faith. How do we do it? By taking responsibility for our growth. And this is what Peter wants to help us understand.

# The Principles of Diligence

Now it's time to understand the meaning of the word that I believe is the key to the Christian life. What is the word *diligence* all about?

- *To strenuously give of yourself. Strenuous* is an athletic word. It is demanding and sweat-producing. It means "to give all strenuous activity toward." Indeed it comes from the athletic world of intense concentration on the goal of becoming a champion. Diligence is the picture of the sprinter coming around the bend toward the finish tape, exerting every muscle in his body, even when it seems like he has nothing left to give. He has practiced for months or years, working on every tiny characteristic of his motion. He has run countless miles, pushing his body toward faster finish times. And now, as he runs the big race, he is even more focused. Just saying *strenuous* seems to make us huff and puff.

- *To lavishly give of yourself.* Understanding what it means to strive strenuously can include the idea of *lavish* extravagance. In New Testament times, wealthy patrons loved sponsoring Greek plays. Fierce competition ensued, as each patron tried to top his rivals in financing the latest and the greatest props, scenery, and performers. When his friends viewed his lavish production, they'd have a new benchmark, and they'd be determined to set yet another. These wealthy donors were "out-lavishing" one another. Peter uses the Greek word *choregeo,* which means to supply things extravagantly, without limit or cost considerations. It is the word from which we get our word *choreography*, and it is what we mean when we say, "Money is no object."

The great age of the Greeks has passed, but the idea lives on. The college bowl games, televised around New Year's, strenuously try to out-lavish one another in their glitzy halftime shows. But they all pale in comparison to the Super Bowl, when tens of millions of dollars are spent on world-class performers, fireworks, light shows, and whatever else will make the viewers say, "Wow!" The official sponsors of the game spend budget-busting sums to produce the TV commercial that will be most discussed around tomorrow's water cooler. As for those who actually play the game, they hold nothing back, either. They are strenuous in their ferocity. No one gives half of his effort during the biggest game of the season.

We see the same phenomenon every four years in the Olympic Games. Each host city wants to be proclaimed the best ever at putting on a show for the entire world. More than one hundred million dollars was spent in Beijing, more than doubling what was spent four years earlier in Athens.[3]

Many of the athletes compete with one another all through the year at other venues, and they know each other well. But they save something extra for the world stage of the Olympics, and we love seeing strenuous competition at its very best.

With all of that modern imagery in mind, think about what the Word of God, through Peter, asks us to do. We are to be characterized by a strenuous diligence, lavishing all that we are, and all that we have, upon growing in Christ. He tells us that we have all the tools when it comes to life and godliness. Now it's up to us to pour it on as we make our lives the most exciting, adrenaline-pumped, God-glorifying testimonies of service that we can produce through the power of the Holy Spirit.

In his book *Knowing Scripture,* R. C. Sproul writes about the "Sensuous Christian." Sproul doesn't mean that in the usual physical use of that word. He defines that term as the domination of the Christian life by the intangibles of feelings. "Many of us" he writes, "have become sensuous Christians, living by our feelings, rather than through our understanding of the Word of God. Sensuous Christians cannot be moved to service, prayer, or study unless they 'feel like it.'"[4] This hapless believer does good things when he is feeling close to God. But when he is depressed, he does nothing of service to Christ. He therefore looks for stimuli to ignite his emotions because he wants to *experience* God rather than genuinely know Him. The sensuous Christian evaluates the Word by his feelings rather than the other way around, and he stays immature because he believes this is childlike faith, when it's actually childish. The Word constantly admonishes us to grow in our faith, but the sensuous Christian simply wants an experience of some kind. What eventually happens? He encounters tough times but he lacks the wisdom to meet the challenge.

Sproul makes me realize I need to ask this question of myself, just as I ask you to ask yourself: *Is my walk with God all about emotions and feelings? Or is it driven by faith and the Word?* When I have one of those days when I don't feel the victory of my faith, do I continue to serve Him in obedience? Or do I let my feelings hurt my faith? Strong faith is based upon the facts of God's Word—the truth of our salvation, the historic fact of Christ's resurrection, the understanding that He will come again. Those things are true even if I'm not as excited about them as I should be on a gloomy day. Peter is talking about laying a foundation of faith based on the solid and substantial Word, so that no bad day, no bad event, no national recession can shake it. These are the times when God smiles upon our response—when the world is treating us poorly, when our spirits are low, yet we pray anyway; we serve anyway; we open the Word anyway and say, "God, I'm not my best today, but all that I have is still yours." Any child that tells Him that is going to be taken up in His embrace and comforted.

His promises don't fluctuate with our whims. We can cling to those promises and find a powerful emotional equilibrium. Living based on feelings is like riding a roller coaster without a seat belt. Living rooted to His Word is more like building a house with a foundation of pure, tempered steel. You're going to be ready for anything that comes along. What Peter is saying to us is, "Start digging! You have your shovel, you have your earth-moving equipment, now lay down that sure foundation." You do so by applying all that is in the Word.

I'm the first to admit that I process through a series of emotions as I prepare to preach. Like most communicators, I'm always putting myself into the shoes of my listeners. How will this sound to them? What if they hear this sermon and it drives them away from striving for Christian maturity? There's always the temptation to give the people what they want, which may not be the same as what they need.

Every preacher of the Word struggles with this urge, but in the end, he knows that God has called him to be true to the Word. He knows the terrible implications of conforming his message to the world, rather than letting his message be transforming through the true Word of Christ. I get a sense of Peter having these same thoughts as he wrote the first chapter of his letter:

> For this reason I will not be negligent to remind you always of these
> things, though you know and are established in the present truth. Yes,

I think it is right, as long as I am in this tent, to stir you up by remind-ing you, knowing that shortly I must put off my tent, just as our Lord Jesus Christ showed me. Moreover I will be careful to ensure that you always have a reminder of these things after my decease (2 Peter 1:12–15).

His "tent" is the old, tattered human body that he knows will soon perish. He can't make small talk. He can't spend time telling people the feel-good messages that massage the ear. The situation is urgent, and he is already making arrangements to see that his words outlive him—as they have certainly done, in that we're discussing them right now. Peter is nothing if not strenuous and lavish in training his brothers and sisters in the faith.

## The Priorities of Diligence

Peter offers us seven priorities of diligence, all built upon that founda-tion called faith. Like many biblical lists, this one isn't exhaustive—other positive traits could be listed. But I believe these seven are special. They form the basic girders that make up the architecture of the Christian life that we build. These are the seven elements you should look for periodically when checking up on the vital signs of your walk with Christ.

- *Faith + Virtue.* "Add to your faith virtue" (2 Peter 1:5). Do you know what virtue is? *Courage.* This is the New Testament word for moral goodness: having the courage to do the right thing no matter what the circumstances might dictate. People with strong integrity are consistent from one situation to another.

They act from their moral base rather than from consensus or popular opinion. This kind of virtue develops as we become steeped in God's Word and begin to show the mind of Christ in our actions. The Spirit of God, rather than the spirit of the age, guides our decisions.

- *Virtue + Knowledge.* "To virtue knowledge" (1:5). This one means exactly what it says. We are to continue growing in the knowledge of God's Word. In fact, the word *knowledge* is found five times in the first chapter of 2 Peter. What we need is knowledge anchored in truth, and we have it in the Scriptures. It only remains for us to extract that knowledge and make it part of us. You'll never find a devout believer who doesn't have a deep familiarity with the Word of God. This is simply essential.

- *Knowledge + Self-control.* "To knowledge self-control" (v. 6). Most of us are very comfortable hearing that we're going to be gaining knowledge, but our smiles fade a bit when we hear about self-control. This concept implies that we have choices. We can choose what we do, what we say, and what we think. This is about (here comes another unpleasant word) *discipline.* Anything worth achieving in life is going to come because of personal discipline and self-control. You might have shown a little of it by picking up this book rather than turning on the television. You exercise it by rising from bed to attend church when you're a little sleepy. We could all use more self-control.

I spoke to a San Diego Charger about his routine for personally motivated discipline. Every morning his alarm clock would sound at a very early hour, and he would take off running toward the hills. He did this day after day, and how could he keep it up? He told me that with every footfall he would say to himself, "My competitors are still in bed. My competitors are still in bed." He wanted to attain that slight edge that would set him apart, win him a starting job, earn him a place on the All-Pro team, and help him contribute to team goals. In the end, he realized every one of his goals.

- *Self-Control + Perseverance.* "To self-control perseverance" (v. 6). Perseverance is a glorified synonym for patience. It is to "voluntarily and continually endure difficulties and hardships for the sake of honor."[5] Self-control gets the football player out of bed in the morning, but perseverance finishes the routine today, tomorrow, and the next day. Many of us have the self-control to start diets or exercise programs, but lack perseverance, and therefore never cross the finish line.

  Perseverance is silencing your body when it begins to complain. It's forcing yourself awake to study the Bible in the morning when you know you could use another fifteen minutes of sleep. Perseverance is the trademark of champions.

- *Perseverance + Godliness.* "To perseverance godliness" (v. 6). What exactly is godliness, and how does it grow from perseverance? The word means reverence and deep respect toward God, and it begins to take form in us only when we continue with Him—serving Him as Lord, growing through His Word, accepting the Spirit's correction and guidance, all across time. It's not about being a Sunday Christian or a mountain-top experience believer, but an everyday, long-haul follower of Jesus Christ.

  We need real godliness all the time, but it is especially

necessary in chaotic days like the ones we are currently experiencing—and I don't mean the everyday run-of-the-mill pattern that passes for "godliness." Today we seem to be presenting our concept of God in a more casual, user-friendly way, and I see certain dangers there. We want unbelievers to see a positive faith, and that is good. We want them to see a God of love instead of one who is relentlessly angry, and that, too, is good. But I worry that bit by bit, we're losing the concept of His holiness, His majestic and infinite magnitude, and yes, His judgment of sin. Our God is an awesome God, a glorious King, and so much more than a kindly grandfather in heaven.

I bring this up because the godly Christian is the one who is truly humble before Almighty God. It is impossible to pursue our Lord over the years and still maintain a childish, superficial, lame and tame conception of him. To be godly is to reflect, more and more clearly, His image in us. Our minds can't take in His greatness, but we need to at least be humbled by the thought of it.

- *Godliness + Brotherly Kindness + Love.* I have combined the last two priorities of diligence because they are so closely related. To godliness we are to add brotherly kindness, and to brotherly kindness, we add that supreme mark of the Christian called love (v. 7).

Does it seem strange that we first add self-control, which is tough, then perseverance, which is a little harder, then we begin to become godly, which is an ultimate goal of life—and then we add, of all things, brotherly kindness? It almost seems a step backward, something rather mundane compared to godliness. But brotherly kindness and love are what truly set us apart as believers, when we practice them consistently. You can have knowledge without love and kindness. You can have faith without it, perseverance, and all the rest. But godliness makes love overflow from within us!

It's a tribute to the goodness of God that if we are truly like Him, the first thing people will see in us is the warmth of brotherly kindness. All of the Ten Commandments are summarized in the word *love*. Jesus spoke constantly of love, and showed this trait more than any other in His life. And it's the one and only virtue that God is described as *being*: "God is love" (1 John 4:8, 16). That's how significant love is in our faith.

This list is a kind of godliness obstacle course for the believer. Make a checklist of the seven traits, put it where you'll see it every day, and evaluate how you're running the course. It's a slow process, but trust me—be a diligent disciple and one day you're going to look at the list, notice you're beginning to match up with it, and you'll realize that you have become a different creature.

## The Possibilities of Diligence

Peter now offers us two three-part pictures—one for the diligent life, one for the nondiligent.

Three things that will happen if you are diligent:

- *You will have stability in your Christian life.* Peter wants us to know that if we pursue God and focus on these qualities, we'll see them begin to come together for us. Character is the result of persistent action, and a pattern of diligence will lead to stability. One by one, old and unhelpful habits will fall by the wayside in your life. You'll simply find that you don't want to do those things anymore because walking in the Spirit is so much more satisfying.

You'll be more resistant to the ups and downs of the world that trouble most people, and therefore you'll have stability. What about sin? You'll never be totally free of its everyday challenge—not in this life. We're not talking about a plan for perfection, but a life of constant growth. None of it comes easily. If it did, we would see stable and fruitful lives all around us. The church would be filled with supersaints! No, it's not easy, but those who are diligent, those who continue to pursue the consistent Christian life, will enjoy a maturity that causes them to live with confidence in chaotic times.

- *You will have vitality in your Christian life.* Vitality is defined as abundant mental and physical energy. It's what people tend to lose when they leave their youth behind—that ability to spring out of bed and greet the new day; the propensity to embrace change rather than fear it; and so many other signs of a lively heart. Make a close study of the mature saints you know, and you'll see that vitality, even deep into their golden years. There's some quality about them that remains forever young. Wouldn't you love to grow with grace like that? These qualities, lived out diligently, make it happen.

Christ came into this world to give us life and to give it *abundantly*, as Jesus tells us in John 10:10. He's not interested in helping us survive. He wants us to thrive. Peter is telling us in verse 8 that we'll come to the place where all these qualities of diligence will create a joy and vitality that overflows from us, as if we were fountains of God's goodness. The godlier qualities of our lives will become infectious, so that other people begin to seek Him because they want what they see in us.

- *You will have reality in your Christian life.* Third, Peter tells us that we'll have true reality in our lives. Peter says we will be neither barren nor unfruitful in the knowledge of Jesus Christ. That means we'll know His truth deeply, and it will bear real fruit all around us. We will be involved in the real world, connecting the truth of the gospel to the needs that we see. Some people believe faith is some kind of fantasy world in which we escape the problems of the day and become "so heavenly minded that we're no earthly good." That's not the profile of the truly devout follower. Real Christians keep it real.

Now, what about the other side of the coin? What does life look like for the believer who chooses not to pursue this course?

Three things that will happen if you are not diligent:

- *You will lack spiritual power.* Peter speaks of life "for he who lacks these things" (2 Peter 1:9), referring to the list he has just given. There are millions of people who profess to be Christians, yet manage to avoid going after virtue, knowledge, self-control, patience, godliness, brotherly kindness, and love. You can have a reunion with them after thirty years and find they're at the same level of spiritual maturity now as then—a real tragedy. Once, a little boy fell out of his bed during the night and told his mother, "I went to sleep too close to where I got in." That's what happens to too many of the children of God. They remain children by dozing off at the very entry point of their faith. They don't learn to pray through a trial. They can't minister to a friend who needs loving care. They have no idea how to grow in grace, and the voice of the Holy Spirit is so still, so small, that they can't hear it above the culture's clamor. They lack spiritual power.

- *You will lack spiritual perception.* "Shortsighted, even to blindness," is the way Peter speaks of the immature Christian (1:9). We live in an era in which keen eyes are essential spiritual equipment—and you realize what kind of sight I'm talking about. We need to see truth, as if looking through the eyes of God. Growing believers enjoy increasing communication with the Holy Spirit, their counselor and advisor in all things. Nongrowing ones are like armies without reconnaissance reports, fighting away in the fog. They are shortsighted to the point of blindness.

  As we read the headlines, consider our own business and housing decisions, and wonder what's just around the corner in our culture, we need to pray daily that we be granted the ability to see with the eyes of God, think with the mind of Christ, and walk in the power of the Holy Spirit. Do those things, and you have an outrageous advantage on those who don't! We have a direct line to the One who knows what happens on the next page because He has written the whole story.

- *You will lose spiritual privilege.* Thirdly, the nondiligent believer will eventually come to the place where he "has forgotten that he was cleansed from his old sins" (1:9). These sins, of course, were those committed before salvation. Can you imagine experiencing the miracle of salvation, the cleansing of Christ's blood, the arrival of the Holy Spirit, and the joy of Christian fellowship, only to forget that miracle that started it all in motion? It seems impossible, but when we look at the world, we see how often it happens. Christians live in such a way that there is no discernible difference between their lives and those outside the kingdom. In other words, they have lost all the spiritual privileges and graces that make life worth living. These are the people who ask, "Am I really saved? How can I be certain?" If the question even needs to be asked, there is something terribly wrong.

This is why we want to live with passion, focus, and diligence, growing in the traits that Peter mentions. Everything we could possibly need to be difference-makers in this world has already been given to us. There's really no limit to what we can achieve in this life for the glory of God, and our own abundant life.

The goal of my life is to reach that place where diligence to God's will is my total passion.

## The Promise of Diligence

Now God offers us this promise: "If you do these things you will never stumble" (2 Peter 1:10). What is a stumbling block to anyone else becomes a stepping-stone for us. This doesn't mean we'll have no problems. To the extent that we diligently pursue the Christian life, however, we will walk victoriously and upright, and we'll avoid the classic mistakes.

There is another intriguing promise. "For so an entrance will be supplied to you abundantly into the everlasting kingdom of our Lord and Savior Jesus Christ" (1:11). What kind of entrance? This is actually a nautical image. Heaven, in Peter's imagery, has a harbor. We sail Godward toward that harbor, moving through the storms and rocks that lurk in the waves. Some ships barely make it into port—the crew is exhausted and near mutiny, the rigging is torn, supplies are low, and the ship has sprung many leaks. It's not exactly a hail-the-conquering-hero kind of arrival. But we don't have to float into the harbor with our sails down and our spirits defeated. Peter is telling us that diligent believers are like diligent captains and sailors: they sail with discipline, manning the watchtower, maintaining the ship, keeping morale high among the crew. That's a picture of the well-lived Christian life. The storms will come, but God has given us what we need to come through them all the stronger.

In other words, this isn't about going to heaven. If you have trusted Jesus Christ, your name is on that crew list by order of the Captain. What's at issue here is the quality of your voyage. Think about the sailors of old—the life they led on the sea, the confinement of a small ship, the dangers of storm, snare, and shipwreck. The hard life of the open sea required absolute discipline, unquestioned diligence, and particularly an unquestioning obedience to the admiral—no matter how desperate the voyage became.

How strong is your faith? Are you disciplined and diligent enough to weather the storm? Think about that as you hear the story of Sabina

Wurmbrand. She was a Jewish convert to Christianity in the Romania of the 1930s and '40s. She and her husband, Richard, accepted Christ and together founded an underground church. Sabina was arrested for covert Christian activities, including smuggling Jewish children out of the ghettos.

The Romanian Communist Party sponsored a "religious conference." Ministers were required not only to attend but to profess loyalty to Communism. Sabina insisted that her husband stand up for Christ, even if that would make her a widow because, she told him, "I don't wish to have a coward for a husband." Four thousand were on hand to watch, and the whole nation listened on radio, as Richard Wurmbrand professed allegiance only to Christ. He was imprisoned and placed in solitary confinement, much like Geoffrey Bull in China. His book, *Tortured for Christ*, describes fourteen excruciating years of suffering for his Lord.

Sabina's story is less famous, though she spent much time in prison and under house arrest as well. When the family was finally ransomed and allowed to leave Romania in 1966, Sabina begin a speaking ministry, telling the world what it meant to live behind the Iron Curtain as a disciple of Jesus Christ, particularly from a woman's point of view. The women worked for hour upon hour at slave labor, scooping out a canal by hand. Empty stomachs kept them awake at night, though they were bone-tired. Sabina wondered about her nine-year-old son, Mihai, now a homeless orphan. Her captors would gather children and beat them, just to torment the parents in the camp.

The wardens kept them alive and working with promises that they might see their children if only they would keep laboring. This hope energized them when all heart and strength should have been gone. Finally the day came for Sabina to meet with Mihai. There were only a few moments, and her heart was too full for speech. Little Mihai was pale and thin. As they led him away, she managed the words, "Mihai, love Jesus with all your heart!"

Those words and the intensity of her love were more powerful than all the cruelty of the Eastern Communist Bloc. Her husband and son both came through those dark days as strong Christians, pushing on boldly for the kingdom of God.[6]

Don't you hear the voice of the Spirit saying the same words to you? "Christian! Love Jesus with all your heart!" I don't know what dangers, toils, or snares life has thrown in your path in these recent months. I can't say exactly what the coming months will hold. But I know that on this wondrous gospel ship, daily diligence to the chores of kingdom life will bring us through—no matter what we face.

# FIVE

# Stay Connected

"I HAVE YOUR CHILD!" IS THERE ANY MORE TERRIFYING NEWS? Add to that the words, "You will never see this child again," and you have a serious situation. Authorities on the East Coast had one of these on their hands early this year. A nine-year-old Athol, Massachusetts, girl had been taken by her grandmother. The little city of Athol has some big-league, technically savvy police officers. The police first connected with the grandmother through the girl's cell phone number. She promised to return the girl. When she failed to do so, Officer Todd Neale went into action.

He was aware of a fact that many people do not know. He knew that since 2005 there has been a US law that requires mobile phone providers to be able to locate 67 percent of callers within 100 meters (0.18 miles).[1] The technology can only be used in cases of lost or missing people or when a life is clearly in danger.

Officer Neale contacted the girl's cell phone service provider to request that they provide him with GPS coordinates every time the phone was used. While he knew enough to take those steps, he needed the services of a more experienced cell phone tracker. He called on Athol's Deputy Fire Chief, Thomas Lozier, who had that experience. The two successfully tracked the kidnapped girl through GPS and Google maps to a hotel six states away from her home. The local state police took over from there, arrested the grandmother, and reconnected the girl with her frantic family. The cell phone posse rejoiced.

Cell phones are wonderful tools for making connections. Besides their obvious use for making voice contact with friends or loved ones, they can also be used to text silent messages when a verbal conversation would be rude—like in a restaurant. Newer phones even have full keyboards for doubled-handed input.

But simple texting has become "so last year." Today there is Twitter. With one action you can send a 140-character message with all of the minutiae of your life to two hundred of your closest friends simultaneously and in real time. "The social warmth of all those stray details shouldn't be taken lightly," says *Time* in a recent cover story.[2] In this increasingly impersonal world, people really want to connect with one another. Twitter became the primary real-time connection within Iran and to the rest of the world during the demonstrations following the disputed presidential election of June 12.

So many people seek to make connections with someone who will care about them that it is apparently very common for a Twitterer (if that is a word) to receive an error message: "Twitter is over capacity. Too many Tweets! Please wait a moment and try again."[3]

May I suggest a better place to make meaningful connections—without busy signals? The church.

Oh, I know. There are those like *Newsweek* who are proclaiming the "Decline and Fall of Christian America." Others like the *Boston Globe* have also carried stories about how that state's mainline churches are dying slow deaths; in the Roman Catholic Church, the Archdiocese of Boston has closed nearly one quarter of its churches during the last decade.[4] A report from March 2009 shows significant declines in both of the two largest faith communities, Roman Catholic and Southern Baptist. Until recently, both of them had steady growth.[5]

The American Religion Survey, also released in March 2009, indicates a sharp uptick in the number of people who profess no religion at all. In fact, "no religion" is the only area of growth—and that's across the board, in every state in the union. True, a few faith groups are reporting growth: evangelicals, Mormons, and Muslims. According to the report, Muslims in America have doubled since 1990.

In his book, *Bowling Alone: The Collapse and Revival of American Community,* Robert D. Putnam observes that since the 1960s, Americans have become 10 percent less likely to be church members and 25 to 50 percent less likely to be involved in religious activities. In other words, there are now fewer church members, and a great many are less active ones. During the 1950s, there was a boom in church attendance. Putnam believes those strides have been reversed—and perhaps even overcompensated for in the other direction.[6]

People are not only staying away from churches, they are staying away from community groups such as clubs, service organizations, and adult sports leagues. Charles Colson notes that the age of personal computers has pushed individualism to a new level. Rather than connecting with people face to face, they do it electronically through Internet social networking, e-mail, and instant messaging—much of the time with "handles" rather than names, and faceless anonymity replacing deep, knowing friendship.[7]

Cyber-community seems nice until something bad happens, and then we want face time rather than Facebook. In the aftermath of

September 11, 2001, people came looking for genuine community. The same thing happened with the subsequent series of crises that followed. On the Sunday after 9/11, our large sanctuary couldn't contain all the members and guests who wanted to be part of a worship service. When we feel insecure, a computer screen seems cold and irrelevant. Television is impersonal. We need to be with fellow members of the human race, created, like ourselves, in the image of God.

When the economic bottom fell out late in 2008, the *New York Times* had this headline: "Bad Times Draw Bigger Crowds to Churches." The article studied the spikes in attendance of evangelical churches during every recession cycle of the last forty years. Each time, growth jumped 50 percent in the wake of the bad news—before settling back into its routine as people became more comfortable.[8]

How does this affect society? How does it influence individuals? Theologian Leonard Sweet writes that "each of us lives on many levels, and we need multileveled relationships with different kinds of people to be healthy and whole. With the decline of extended families in Western cultures, this becomes all the more important."[9]

We could be seeing the results of that already. Two studies found that over the last nineteen years, the number of people reporting that they had no one with whom they could really share important issues had tripled. Nearly half of all Americans, claimed the studies, had either one intimate friend or none at all. Meanwhile, virtual social networks have become all the rage. We suspect that people long for authentic community, and perhaps they're looking for love in all the wrong places. Online friendship isn't ultimately satisfying. It's possible to have three hundred "connections" on Facebook, two hundred "following" you on Twitter, and still feel as if no one really knows you at all.

During tough times, we're seeing a widespread craving for genuine soul-to-soul connection.[10] How many online friends will come to visit us if we check into the hospital? How many will hold us accountable for living with godly integrity?

## A Church that Looks Like God

It was our Creator who said, "It is not good that man should be alone." He brought Eve into the world to provide rewarding human interaction for Adam (Genesis 2:18).

Relationships are part of our basic design. We require a relationship with God's only Son, Jesus Christ, in order to be saved. After that, a great deal of our growth as believers comes through the accountability that fellow Christians provide within spiritual community. Together, we become something much larger than the sum of our parts. According to the New Testament, we are the one body of Christ—an assembly of parts that only function in unison. This we call the church.

Have you ever noticed the great "3:16" verses in the Bible? The greatest, of course, is John 3:16, which tells us God loved the world so much that He sent His only Son. "The world" is all of us together. 1 John 3:16 tells us "we know love because He laid down his life for us. And we also ought to lay down our lives for the brethren." In other words, God set the pattern that we follow with each other. Philippians 3:16 encourages us to "walk by the same rule [and] be of the same mind"—a definition of community. And in Malachi 3:16, in the last book of the Old Testament, we read: "Then those who feared the LORD spoke to one another, And the LORD listened and heard them; So a book of remembrance was written before Him for those who fear the LORD and who meditate on His name."

That last verse tells us that when God-fearing people begin to speak to one another, He listens to them and their conversation becomes part of eternity through His "book of remembrance." Remember, Jesus said, "For where two or three are gathered together in My name, I am there in the midst of them" (Matthew 18:20). We can always experience the presence of God alone, and we should do so every day. But special things happen when believers gather together to share in Him.

Dr. Russell Moore of Southern Seminary believes there is a reason for that. He says that our need for connection, communion, and community is rooted in the triune nature of God himself. Genesis 1:26 and 11:7 quote the Lord as saying, "Let *Us* . . ." He is multipersonal, and as individuals created in His image, we need the multiple personalities available to us through community. Moore also points out that the members of the Trinity glorify one another. God is glorified on the divine level by the Father glorifying the Son, the Son glorifying the Father, and the Spirit glorifying the Son.[11]

A close study of the gospel of John shows these triune relationships as a clear theme. For example, Jesus answers our prayers to bring glory to the Father. He said, "And I will do whatever you ask in My name, so that the Son may bring glory to the Father" (John 14:13 NIV). John 17:1 in particular shows the power of this mutual glorification: "Father, the hour has come. Glorify Your Son, that Your Son also may glorify You."

## As We See the Day Approaching

There is a powerful and positive relationship among the three Persons of the Godhead as each glorifies the other. Any strong church or fellowship reflects this principle. When we love and perfect each other, we are reflecting the work of the Holy Trinity and participating in His ancient and everlasting love. As we mentioned earlier, the New Testament has a pattern of "one another" and "each other" tasks (encourage one another, love one another, bear with one another, to name three). As we carry these out, we experience a unique form of godliness that can't be attained as separate human entities. We reflect the roles and relationships of the Triune God, and we really do become the people of God, the body of Christ, and the fellowship of the Holy Spirit.

If we are going to be able to live courageous lives in these chaotic days, we will need to be calm in our hearts, compassionate toward others, constructive in our relationships, challenged to grow, and connected to the church. We were created to live in community, not in isolation.

Mary Saunders, a Southern Baptist missionary in Africa, described a regular meeting she had with a new Christian in Somalia. The regular appointment was secret because the area was predominantly Islamic and often intolerant. On this particular evening, Mary reviewed the memory verse the young Somali had been learning: "This is the day which the LORD hath made; we will rejoice and be glad in it" (Psalm 118:24 KJV). After discussing the verse, Mary sang the familiar chorus based on that verse. The young man was delighted. The idea of singing raised a question for him: "When there is more than one Christian, what other things do you do?"

Mary realized that the ideas of corporate worship, music, praying together, Bible study—all these things she took for granted—were unimaginable to someone whose experience was limited to private Bible study and prayer.[12]

This book is about what on earth we should be doing in times like these, based on passages about the return of Christ. The Bible teaches that we should be living every day with an attitude of expectancy, and the New Testament writers had to preach that same message: "And let us consider one another in order to stir up love and good works, not forsaking the assembling of ourselves together, as is the manner of some, but exhorting one another, and so much the more as you see the Day approaching" (Hebrews 10:24–25).

We follow daily events and realize that this present age could end very soon, and that Christ's return could be approaching. The realization of that motivates us, more than ever, to be busy with our Father's business. And it's very clear that part of that business is to stay connected to one another through the fellowship of the church. We are to devote ourselves to one another and to begin preparing the body of Christ, as we prepare ourselves, for that day when He arrives to reclaim us. As we "see the Day approaching," in the words of Hebrews, we should be gathering together more frequently instead of less.

Hebrews 10:24–25 constitute the New Testament's central statement on the connectivity of God's people. By the way, in the course of this chapter, you're likely to notice that this is one of my favorite words: *connectivity*. In the current climate, people hear that term and think of networks, the Internet, and the world of business. Our world of spiritual business is the ultimate connectivity, the kind Jesus described to His disciples when He said, "I am the vine, you are the branches. He who abides in Me, and I in him, bears much fruit; for without Me you can do nothing" (John 15:5). In that marvelous analogy, we are all interconnected through our attachment to the true vine, Jesus Christ. We cannot afford to be cut off from each other or from the vine that sustains us, that feeds us, and that helps us to grow.

As we have that connectivity with Him and with one another, we begin to bear much fruit (15:8).

## The Imperative of Connectivity

Let's take a closer look at this passage to discover the imperative of connectivity. Notice the wording: "Not forsaking the assembling of ourselves together, as is the manner of some."

There are three exhortations given to us by the Lord through the writer of this passage in Hebrews which are set apart by the key words, "let us."

- "*Let us draw near* with a true heart in full assurance of faith" (v. 22). This is our responsibility to God—coming to him wholeheartedly.
- "*Let us hold fast* the confession of our hope" (v. 23). This is our responsibility to ourselves—to live hopefully.
- "And *let us consider one another* in order to stir up love and good works" (v. 24). That's our responsibility to one another, and we fulfill it by "not forsaking the assembling of ourselves together" (v. 25).

For the writer of Hebrews, worship attendance isn't an option for Christians. Take a close look at the first generation of believers, and you'll see how strongly they felt about it. According to Acts, the narrative of that era, those first Christians assembled in two ways: publicly and privately. One was the more formal expression of the church in the temple and in synagogues; the other more informal and intimate, in homes.

## Connectivity in Public Meetings

Those first Christians were "continuing daily and with one accord in the temple" (Acts 2:46). Did you notice that I said "in the temple and in synagogues"? Isn't that the last place you would expect Christians to gather, in the wake of the hostility against Jesus? You'd think that the followers of Christ were looking for trouble by gathering there.

The truth is that most of the first Christians were also Jewish. The temple was the greatest symbol of worship and spiritual community that they could imagine. And a closer examination of the language in Acts 2:46 shows that it was actually the temple *courts* where the believers met. The crowds were tremendous in the wake of the Resurrection, which was followed, a few weeks later, by the coming of the Holy Spirit.

As impressive a city as Jerusalem was, there weren't any modern civic or convention centers available for the huge crowds coming together to worship Christ. So the temple, with its expansive courts, made sense.

This matter of gathering together is highly significant. The phrase is actually a single word in the language of the New Testament. It occurs only a couple of times—once here in Hebrews 10 and again in 2 Thessalonians. In his second letter to the Thessalonian church, Paul writes these words: "Now, brethren, concerning the coming of our Lord Jesus Christ and our *gathering together* to Him, we ask you . . ." (2 Thessalonians 2:1).

From these uses of this word, we learn that there are two "gathering together" seasons in the church: a present day gathering together on earth, and a future reunion with Christ in the air. That ultimate event is thrilling to the soul, but the current fellowship is just as exciting, just as supernatural, and Christ is just as present. As we come together, we are slowly causing each other to conform to His image. We also experience His presence on an entirely different level as He comes to be enthroned upon our praises. As a matter of fact, gathering together in His power in the midst of a world in turmoil is very much like those first believers who boldly ventured every day to the temple, where they could not help being seen by the Pharisees and the priests. That Judean world was in turmoil, too, and it's no wonder that people were flocking to the joy and hope they witnessed among the believers.

The devil would love for us to hang on to our mundane ideas and images of fellowship: doughnuts and coffee, a handshake, a little football talk—little more than what happens at the water cooler from Monday to Friday; the fellowship of the saints reduced to a friendly chat at the country club. Yet New Testament fellowship—*koinonia*—includes the idea of a holy partnership, of genuine communion of souls, best illustrated when we share the bread and the cup together in the Lord's Supper. It connects us as children of the same Father, blessed by salvation from the same Savior, and filled with the same Spirit. We experience a supernatural oneness with each other when we meet in the name of Christ. And if you've ever been a part of that, you know that Monday morning at the water cooler can't ever compare to Sunday morning at the throne of grace. Country clubs and lodges all pass away, but Christ's church is eternal.

Regardless of the stern warning in Hebrews, many believers don't take church attendance seriously. As a pastor, I hear words such as, "Oh, I'm spiritual, but I don't particularly need the church or 'institutional religion.'" When someone tells me, "I've learned to worship God on the golf course," I'm tempted to reply, "That's a good trick, and just about as easy as playing golf in the sanctuary." Indeed, I would love to see ordinary people approach sporting events with the same attitudes they bring to Christian fellowship. An anonymous wit posted a tongue-in-cheek sampling of what that would be like. Here is his list of reasons for no longer attending professional sports games:

1. Every time I go, they ask me for money.
2. The people I sit by aren't very friendly.
3. The seats are too hard and uncomfortable.
4. The coach never comes to call on me.
5. The referees make decisions I don't agree with.
6. Some games go into overtime, and I'm late getting home.
7. My parents took me to too many games when I was growing up.
8. My kids need to make their own decisions about which sports to follow.

It's true that some have legitimate reasons for not attending church, and those people are one of the reasons we have a radio and television ministry. But our faithful listeners are familiar with the point I regularly make on Friday broadcasts: our programs can never take the place of participation in the local church. The church is an up-close-and per-sonal thing; accept no substitutes. We must not forsake our assembling together. We need public connectivity.

## Connectivity in Private Meetings

There is also a need to connect with other believers in smaller gather-ings. This requirement may be less well known, but it's just as important. We crave the sense of belonging that comes through a more intimate group of like-minded believers who can hold one another truly accountable. The last part of Acts 2:46 captures this necessity: "Breaking bread from house to house, they ate their food with gladness and simplicity of heart." Isn't that a wonderful description of what goes on in many home Bible study and fellowship groups today?

The early church had a wonderful balance between corporate worship in the temple court and dinner meetings in individual homes. Every day there were brand-new believers in Jerusalem, coming to the large gathering and funneling into the small one for growth and socialization in God's kingdom. At my own church, we first called our home groups 20:20 groups because of Acts 20:20: "I kept back nothing that was helpful, but proclaimed it to you, and taught you publicly and from house to house." Spiritually speaking, it's a good way to gain 20/20 vision.

Small group ministry is commonplace in churches today, but the very first network was in Jerusalem, and the groups were led by apostles and the growing leadership of the new church. What a wonderful, balanced way for us to mature in Christ together—through "big" church and small group. Wherever this pattern is imitated, we see the same thing happen as what transpired in the birthplace of our faith. Rapid growth occurs.

When we think about all the good things that come out of church fellowship and small group ministry working together, we can't help wondering why or how anyone could ever live without it. Yes, we come together out of obedience to God. But we also do it because nothing else gives us such joy and sustenance.

## The Importance of Connectivity

What are some of the good things that happen because we are connected? A single chapter in a book would never be sufficient for naming them all, but we can touch on a few.

One is simply that it's a priceless privilege. Can you imagine how you would feel about freedom of worship if it were ever denied you? Joel Rosenberg tells about a rapidly growing church in Iran. It's made up of converts from Islam, and the pastor broadcasts his weekly worship service and teaching via satellite. People are eager to hear these sermons and lessons because they worry about what would happen if the secret police were to catch them attending a Christian church. They don't dare play Christian music in their homes or sing praise songs aloud because neighbors could turn them in. So they depend completely upon the pastor's broadcasts for their worship and fellowship in the Word.[13]

Consider what happens when we become a part of each other's lives.

*We promote love.* "And let us consider one another in order to stir up love" (Hebrews 10:24). Here's the phrase again. "One another" is one of Paul's favorite phrases: he uses it thirty-eight times in his epistles, and we find it occurring sixty-eight times from Acts through Revelation. The New Testament is a "one another" book, not something written for the hermit in the wilderness. The writer of Hebrews wants to remind us that coming together keeps us connected by *agape* love.

Simple togetherness is one of the main ingredients of love—so simple we almost miss it. If we neglect to gather together, we drift apart from one another and become disconnected. Being together reminds us of the needs we each have. We share the concerns of our hearts, we laugh and eat together, we worship at the throne of grace side by side, and God knits our hearts in love. Then human love increases our love for that same God who binds us.

Faith, hope, and love grow within us as we come to church and interact together: faith in Christ, hope in the future, and love for each other as our hearts intertwine into a true spiritual family. That's something we all long for in this crisis-driven world. Deep in our souls, we don't want to sit anonymously in the pews. We are unsatisfied by coming, hearing a sermon, and going home. We want to know and be known, not only by God but by His children. We have to put ourselves forward, and we have to risk the bumpy stretches that come with any kind of relationship. But this is a deep need, to stir up the love that God has given us to share.

The phrase *stir up* is translated, "to provoke, to incite." In the Greek, it suggests an "exasperated fit." The choice of words would seem strange in association with love and good works, but it's very intentional. Fellowship should have an energy that provokes everyone toward God's work. We should get stirred up!

The baseball player Reggie Jackson referred to himself as "the straw that stirs the drink."[14] Cocky and outspoken, he had a knack for keeping the adrenaline flowing among his teammates. Hebrews is telling each of us to be the straw that stirs the drink in fellowship together as we stir up love among God's people. I envision a church that is, if you'll pardon the expression, "stir crazy"—a place in which people rise from their beds each week with a relentless purpose and think, *By the grace of God, I will find a way to show love to a new friend today. Lord, please give me a word of encouragement and guide me to just the soul who needs to hear it! My life is filled with blessings, and I'm going to be a blessing to at least one person today.*

A friend told me about an example of that recently. At church, Barbara sat next to Sherry, a younger woman she vaguely knew. Then, at a certain time in the service, Barbara touched Sherry's arm and whispered, "I bought this little angel ornament yesterday. It's just a tiny thing that I thought was pretty—and I felt God leading me to give it to you, Sherry. I've also sensed He has been guiding me to get to know you better." That afternoon, Barbara called the young woman on the phone. She was just a little nervous, being unaccustomed to such assertiveness. But she said, "Please don't think I'm a crazy woman! I really did feel my heart moved to make friends, and I thought I would call you and break the ice."

From there, the two had a wonderful conversation. Barbara's friendly gesture had moved the younger woman to tears. Sherry had been desperately seeking the personal and genuine touch of God. She had wanted to know if He really acted in this world, or if it was all just talk. This unexpected encounter, just as she was wondering, eventually led her to Christ. That's the kind of event that Hebrews is telling us about when it says, "Please! Don't drift out of fellowship. Stir each other up!"

*We provoke good works.* We are better together. Together we can do more for Christ that we could do by ourselves. Together we can attempt great things for God and expect great things from God. Together we can reach out to the whole world in providing financial and intercessory support for multitudes of missionaries. Together we can link up with radio, television, Internet, and print media . . . literally touching every person on planet Earth.

Being among the people of God should be provocative—not a retreat from the world but an order to advance! The sermon should bring on an "exasperated fit" to go tell people about the Lord. The music should inspire the soul and provoke us to bring our friends to hear it. Hearing what God is doing overseas—or on the other side of town—should stir us up to go and help. The question for believers is this: Is your church fanning your gifts into flame? The question for pastors is this: Are your church's ministries stirring up people for service?

Let's be certain we're clear. We are not saved *by* good works, but we are saved *for* them (Ephesians 2:10). Throughout its history, the church, at its best, has blessed the surrounding world. In the first centuries there was persecution. But as soon as churches became free to gather throughout the empire, Christians began helping the sick. St. Basil built the first hospital in Caesarea of Cappadocia, and soon institutions like that began appearing in many cities.

In his book, *How Christianity Changed the World*, Alvin J. Schmidt tells how Christians had been erecting hospitals for nearly four centuries before Arabs took their example and began building them in their own countries. So the Christian influence led to the healing of the sick not only in Western but in many Middle Eastern countries. Then through the missions movement, believers were helping the sick and needy across the globe. Schmidt concludes, "Christ's parable of the Good Samaritan had become more than merely an interesting story."[15] Our faith was designed by God to be a productive one.

Philip Yancey is one writer whose books I read from cover to cover. In his book *Reaching for The Invisible God*, he tells about a time when a man came up to him after a speaking engagement and said blusteringly, "You wrote a book titled *Where Is God When It Hurts*, didn't you?" When he nodded yes, the man continued, "Well, I don't have time to read your book. Can you tell me what it says in just a sentence or two?"

After some thought, Yancey replied, "Well, I suppose I'd have to answer with another question, "Where is the church when it hurts?"

You see, he explained, the church is God's presence on earth, his body. And if the church does its job—if the church shows up at the scene of disasters, visits the sick, staffs the AIDS clinics, counsels the rape victims, feeds the hungry, houses the homeless—I don't think the world will ask that question you asked with the same urgency. They will know where God is when it hurts: in the bodies of His people, ministering to a fallen world. Indeed, our consciousness of God's presence often comes as a byproduct of other people's presence."[16]

*We provide encouragement.* "Not forsaking the assembling of ourselves together, as is the manner of some, but exhorting one another" (Hebrews 10:25). Another translation of the word *exhorting* is the word *encouraging.* In other words, we should be constantly encouraging each other as we gather in fellowship. If you're discouraged with life—out of a job, worried about health concerns, or simply stressed out by the modern pace—church activity should encourage you rather than give you even more stress.

Ted Engstrom tells about a literary group that once gathered at the University of Wisconsin. The members wanted to be poets, novelists, essayists, and authors—and they had the talent to be successful. These young men met regularly to read and critique each other's work. After a while, they began calling themselves the Stranglers because they were very tough in their evaluations. Members competed with each other to see who could parse each word and phrase most critically. After a while, it was like having one's precious creativity dissected with a sharp scalpel.

That group was all male, which may explain the competitive spirit. But a group of women formed a sister group and called themselves not the Stranglers but the Wranglers. When they read their works aloud, something much different occurred. They offered constructive suggestions tinged with positive encouragement. They erred on the side of motivation rather than mutilation.

Twenty years later, an alumnus studied the careers of his classmates and made a surprising discovery. Not one of the gifted male Stranglers had made a significant literary accomplishment. But at least six successful authors were former Wranglers. One of them was Marjorie Kinnan Rawlings, author of the classic *The Yearling*.[17]

To encourage is to "pour courage" into someone who needs it. Christians are blessing dispensers and hope ambassadors. Wherever they go, accomplishment and fruitfulness should bloom all around them because of the relationships left in their wake.

When the church goes about its business and becomes a greenhouse for inspiration and evangelism, you cannot stop it from growing or from turning the world upside down. Who wouldn't want to be a part of a place that makes everyone stronger and more confident? In our time, the world has all the Stranglers it needs. It specializes in finding fault, knocking people down a peg. The workplace is making people angry. Marriage and parenting seem harder than ever. We are brewing a culture of despair, and that's fertile soil for the church to step in and provide real encouragement, real relationships, and real love through the authentic power of Jesus Christ. Nothing else can come close to competing with the hope and the peace we can offer.

Living outside the fellowship of the church carries its own penalty. It's like a world with no sky, or one with no music but plenty of noise. Why would anyone want to deprive himself of the good gifts of God? Fellowship in a local church is the most beautiful of all.

Yes, the church—as we experience it—has its faults, but remember: the church as God sees it is perfect and spotless because of the cleansing blood of Christ.

# The Power in Your Hands

I've always been fascinated by the life and ministry of Charles Spurgeon, the "Prince of Preachers," whose preaching took England by storm during the 1800s. I recently read a new biography of him and learned a brand new tidbit about his conversion—a subject I thought I knew well.

As a teenager, Spurgeon was a nonbeliever. He was planning to become a farmer when he decided to study Latin and Greek instead. He really didn't know where his career was heading. At the school in Newmarket, his life was impacted by one particular individual. No, it wasn't a professor or instructor; neither was it a classmate or friend. Charles Spurgeon had his life changed by the school's cook, an elderly woman named Mary King. She invited him to attend her church one day, and that led to many conversations with her about her faith, eventually setting him on the path to salvation. Years later, he learned of Mary King's retirement, and supplemented her income from his own pocket.[18]

Here's what that story says to me. If a cook from the kitchen can prepare the path for the greatest preacher of the century, what does that imply God might do through you? We rarely recognize the full extent to which God has used ordinary, available human beings for His greatest purposes. Many millions of people owe Mary King a debt of gratitude because of Spurgeon's contribution to their faith.

If such power was in Mary King's hands, it's in yours as well. It's not difficult to encourage, inspire, and edify another human being. You could do it today, using the telephone, a written card, an e-mail, an automobile, your spoken voice—or a strategic pew. What if you made a covenant with every other believer you know concerning this goal? You and your coconspirators would be determined to give a powerful word of encouragement to at least one soul every time you came to church. And someone just might walk up and encourage you. If you were to do this, God would make a determination of His own. He would begin sending people across your path from every direction—hearts in need of hope, ears in need of edifying words. You can't imagine the joy you would experience simply by being a willing vessel for holy encouragement.

I realize there are times when you need a lift too. Don't forget the very best source of all: God's Word. "For whatever things were written before were written for our learning, that we through the patience and comfort of the Scriptures might have hope" (Romans 15:4). Open the Bible and God will begin speaking to you through it. I have my own set of Scriptures that always lift my spirits. I hope you have yours as well.

## The Incentive of Connectivity

The writer of Hebrews tells us that our faithfulness in church attendance should increase as we see our Lord's return on the horizon. We don't know when the day of His return will be, though many signs seem to be coming into alignment. It is a sure thing that each day that passes draws us closer to its eventuality. Each day it doesn't happen, it's that much more likely that tomorrow it will.

If there were no promised Second Coming, the condition of the world itself would be all the incentive we needed to cling to the wonderful fellowship of God's people. But we know that Jesus will return. I want to be found faithful to everything that matters to Him, and nothing matters more than His church.

Even in the midst of national crisis, when worship attendance temporarily surges, the habit of most is to find other things to do; Sunday is the new Saturday. In what is being called a "post-Christian America," church attenders are now in the minority compared to the Sunday golfers, joggers, and late-sleepers who see no particular reason to worship their Creator.

As we see the day approaching, we should be motivated to build the body of Christ into something that justly glorifies God. We should take fewer Sundays off and be more faithful to our church classes and small groups. And when we are in attendance, not only should we be there, but we should be there body, mind, and spirit, devoting all of ourselves to the work of Christ through the church, giving generously of our resources as the first Christians did. When your pastor announces a need, whether it's workers for the nursery, people to cut the church lawn, or funding for missions, he should be overwhelmed by volunteers. And when the new members are introduced, he should have to read so many names that he becomes hoarse.

The church is not a building. No, it is not even the people. It is actually the living presence of a holy God in a fallen world. It is the tangible evidence of an invisible hope, dressed in the skin of all the people who have found that hope. And when society comes unglued, as we've seen it do lately, the church becomes God's lighthouse, shining the way for our ships to avoid the rocks, survive the tempest, and come into safe harbor. If there was ever a day when we needed the church, this is it. If there was ever a greater opportunity to invite our faithless friends, we have it now.

There's a legend about a church in southern Europe called the "House of Many Lamps." It was built in the sixteenth century and had no provision for artificial light except for a receptacle at every seat for the placement of a lamp. In the evenings, as the people came to church, they would carry their own light with them. When they entered the church building, they would place their lamp in the receptacle as they began to worship. If someone stayed away, his place remained dark. If more than a few stayed away, the darkness seemed to spread. It took the regular presence of every member to illuminate that sanctuary.[19]

When you forsake assembling—when that little light of yours is not allowed to shine—you leave a spot of darkness. If enough people heed your example and take Sundays off, a great darkness begins to fall across the house of many lamps. It's discouraging to walk into a half-empty house of God, and there are a great many today that have more empty seats than full ones. In Europe, the darkness has nearly engulfed a continent that once dominated Christendom—a continent that gave us Luther, Calvin, Wycliffe, Wesley, Spurgeon, and so many others. The absence of your light also produces a sense of cold emptiness.

On a cold and blustery winter evening, a husband and wife made themselves as comfortable as they could before the crackling fireplace as they awaited the arrival of their pastor. He had made the appointment earlier in the day. The husband steeled himself against the anticipated rebuke. They had previously been in the habit of attending every service, every week. But over the past year, they rarely made it once a month. "We're just as good as some people who go to church twice every Sunday, and I am going to make it clear to our pastor too!" the husband blustered.

The doorbell rang, and the pastor entered. Remaining in his overcoat, he silently walked directly to the fireplace, took up the tongs, lifted a brightly glowing coal from out of the fire, placed it on the hearth, and, still silent, stepped back to watch.

The husband eventually joined him in an oddly silent observation. After a very long time, the once red-hot glow turned into a cold, dark mass. Finally, the pastor wordlessly turned to the man and gave him a look that spoke volumes. The man got the message. Like that coal, we burn brightly when we are together, but we burn out when we stand alone.[20]

As for me, here I stand—squarely on the side of God's church. As a young man, I gave my heart to Christ and my hands to the church. I have had wonderful days there, as well as a few painful ones. If Christ comes tomorrow (a wonderful thought), I want Him to find me faithfully serving in the fellowship of the saints, the gathering of the holy priesthood.

# SIX

# Stay Centered

LAURA LING AND EUNA LEE KNEW THEY WERE TAKING A GREAT risk when they went to the border region between China and North Korea earlier this year to film an investigative report on human trafficking. Ling had previously produced a television documentary on the underground church in China and was working in conjunction with a Christian agency from South Korea. The women were captured, tried, and convicted of a "grave crime" against the regime of Kim Jong Il.[1]

On the same day that the journalists were sentenced to twelve years at hard labor, the government threatened the world with a "merciless offensive means to deal a just retaliatory strike to those who touch the country's dignity and sovereignty even a bit."[2] This rhetoric is couched in the context of UN Security Council discussions about stronger new sanctions against North Korea for their recent nuclear test and barrage of rocket tests.

Two days before the women were sentenced, the Voice of the Martyrs organization received a threat via fax from North Korea.

"Something very bad will happen to you," the communiqué read, if the ministry continued its weekly outreach into the Communist nation with faxed messages of Christ's love.[3]

To be a follower of Christ in North Korea is considered equal to being a traitor to the government, where only worship of the ailing President Kim Jong Il and his late father is permitted. North Korea has the dubious distinction of holding the number one spot on Open Doors World Watch List not just for 2009 but for the seventh straight year. The list contains the names of the fifty countries of the world where Christians are most severely persecuted for their faith in Christ.[4]

Despite the extreme poverty and intense persecution of Christians in North Korea, it has been estimated that there are as many as four hundred thousand Christians who risk their lives to gather in secret worship services![5] As many as 10 percent of those believers are currently incarcerated in North Korea's notoriously atrocious political prison camps.[6]

North Korea is a hostile environment in which to be a follower of Jesus Christ, but so are forty-nine other countries. Even right here in America Christians are reporting greater persecution. When we hear such things, many of us are caught off guard. But if we believe the Word of God, we know that persecution has always been part of the believers calling (2 Timothy 3:12).

Most of us will never experience the persecution that Laura Ling and Euna Lee are facing. But neither can we escape the new hostility and intolerance that is being directed toward followers of Christ in our post-Christian nation. As never before, we must build our lives around the core values of our faith. We must stay centered on Christ, or we will become discouraged and defeated warriors.

When the apostle Paul wrote to a group of Christians who were living in a time similar to ours, he helped them to find their spiritual center: "If then you were raised with Christ, seek those things which are above, where Christ is, sitting at the right hand of God. Set your mind on things above, not on things on the earth. For you died, and your life is hidden with Christ in God. When Christ who is our life appears, then you also will appear with Him in glory" (Colossians 3:1–4).

In Paul's last statement, in verse four, there is a reference to the return of Christ, so we know that we're on the right track. Practical instructions follow prophetic insights. What Paul wrote to the Colossian believers, he wrote for us.

## Set Your Hearts on Christ

Think back to a time when you set your heart on something. Can you remember how that idea loomed before you, galvanizing your spirit every single day?

I need only talk to people for a few minutes before their "heart-set" comes tumbling out. They want to find their life's partner and marry. They long to start families, or they have compelling visions to build their own businesses. They dream of becoming famous musicians or faithful missionaries.

When we set our heart on something, it motivates us, changes us, and energizes us: it makes our eyes shine, puts a spring in our step, and focuses all our divided attentions into a single, laser-intense direction.

Kevin Everett lay facedown on the Buffalo Bills' home turf, trying desperately to get up. The crowd silenced as the Bills and Broncos gathered in prayer. Kevin realized that he was paralyzed from his fierce tackle in the season opener. He tried to give a thumbs-up as he was finally lifted off the field. "I tried my hardest, you know, put all my heart into it. Just to let them know that I was all right. But it wasn't all right."

Early reports indicated it was a potentially life-threatening injury, and should he live, the chances of his walking were almost nonexistent. Through a series of miracles, some of which were medical, and a lot of intense work on his part, Everett not only lived but also walked unaided onto that same playing field one year later. His heart had become set on doing whatever it took to make a recovery. One reporter asked Everett if he had ever thought about giving up. "That's not me," he responded. "I don't give up. I don't settle for less. I kept plugging away, working hard."

Although he will never play the game again, he has a new heart-set. Gratitude to the Lord has become his transforming strength and has given him a new focus in life. "You put your faith in God and let him show you the way."[7]

I'm sure you've been through trying times, perhaps the loss of a job or a loved one. While surrounded by sorrow, you might have found that it helped to fix your mind on one thing, something positive and productive. For instance, work can be a true blessing. We call it "staying busy." But Paul counsels us to set our hearts on Christ in such a way that every facet of this life is transformed by its relationship to Him.

We know we are destined for heaven. We realize we are citizens of another world. Therefore we are to set our hearts on the things of God, which are perfect and beautiful, rather than the things of this world, which are in disarray even at the best of times. When Paul wrote this statement, he used a verb tense that means "keep on doing this," as opposed to a one-time action. In other words, it's not "think about heaven at this moment." It's "*Keep on* keeping your mind immersed in God and His Word, all the time." This is a discipline too few of us have mastered: the art of heaven-based thinking. Some call it the practice of the presence of God.

We need to understand what it means to "set our hearts." According to Paul it means that our "desires and thoughts, wishing and thinking, the whole of our emotional and intellectual energy is to be directed toward [heaven], where Christ reigns at God's right side."[8] I imagine every one of us has centered our desires and thoughts, all our emotional and intellectual energy, on various earthly goals in the seasons of life. Can we think and feel with the same intensity about Christ?

In times such as these we have to look somewhere for answers. The psychologist tells us we should look within. The opportunist tells us we should look around. The optimist says we should look ahead, and the pessimist says we should look out. But God says we should look up—even when we feel down.[9]

Think for a moment about a compass that you might carry on a hike. You can turn your feet in any direction, but the arrow of the compass will faithfully point to magnetic north. That way, should you ever become lost, the compass will align your position for you. In life, our true north is Christ. Whatever direction our world's path may twist, however off-path it may wander, our lives should point faithfully to the one and only Lord of every place, every time, every situation. When He is our determining point, everything will find its proper orientation.

"Our citizenship is in heaven, from which we also eagerly wait for the Savior, the Lord Jesus Christ" (Philippians 3:20). The wise old preacher Vance Havner put it this way:

"Christians are not citizens of earth trying to get to heaven, but citizens of heaven making their way through this world."[10]

If we reach deep into Christian history, back to about AD 149, we find a letter called "The Epistle of Mathetes of Diognetus." The unknown writer described Christians this way:

> They dwell in their own countries, but simply as sojourners. As citizens, they share in all things with others, and yet endure all things as if foreigners . . . They pass their days on earth, but they are citizens of heaven. They obey the prescribed laws, and at the same time surpass the laws by their lives. They love all men and are persecuted by all. They are unknown and condemned; they are put to death, and restored to life. They are poor, yet make many rich; they are in lack in all things, and yet abound in all; they are dishonored, and yet in their very dishonor are glorified.[11]

Or consider the oath of allegiance that is required of newly nationalized US citizens, in which they "declare on oath" that they "freely and without any mental reservation" relinquish ties of loyalty to their former homelands and that they will defend the United States against all enemies.[12]

As Americans, we expect new citizens to be loyal and trustworthy, never betraying their new home. How much more important is our role as citizens of heaven. This is the most basic statement of our true identity, and it's more critical than any other fact about us.

## Set Your Minds on Christ

We've discussed matters of the heart; now let's talk about the mind. Having our hearts set on Christ means that our wills, our emotions, our hopes and dreams are centered on Him.

The phrase *set your mind* means "to have understanding; to be wise; to feel, to think, to have an opinion, to judge; to direct one's mind to a thing; to seek or to strive for, to seek one's interests or advantage." In other words, it is the mental discipline of directed thinking.

That's the positive command, but it is accompanied by a warning against the negative: "Seek those things which are above . . . not those things which are on the earth" (Colossians 3:1–2). Immediately we find ourselves questioning that way of life. Paul isn't telling us to forego the physical challenges and chores of everyday life, while sitting and ruminating on heaven and angels. He *is* saying that our ultimate concern should be with heavenly realities and values, governed by the presence and power of Christ, who sits at the right hand of the Father.[13] Therefore the physical impulse may be to roll over in bed on that Saturday morning and catch an extra hour of sleep, but the Holy Spirit may be whispering in your ear that He wants you to go and minister to someone's needs. The Christian trains his mind to see those two alternatives, and to give precedence to the things of God.

Sometimes, God wants you to take care of earthly business. We do live in this physical world, and we should do everything, including everyday responsibilities, as unto the Lord. In the ancient world, it was the Gnostics who wanted to twist Christianity into bearing contempt for this physical realm. But that's not the teaching of Scripture. Christ is Lord of body, mind, and spirit.

In his letter to his friends in Corinth, Paul gives us a heavenly perspective on earthly things: "Because of the present crisis . . . the time is short. From now on, those who . . . buy something [should live] as if it were not theirs to keep; those who use the things of this world, as if not engrossed in them. For the world in its present form is passing away" (1 Corinthians 7:26 31 NIV).

So is it okay to buy a car, to invest in a home? Of course. But we don't set our hearts and minds on perishable things because they will pass away. The eternal things have our allegiance. Allow me to share with you an analogy that helps me think of what it means to have an earthly life with a heavenly mind.

Travel is a necessary portion of my ministry, and that means I must often move between time zones. If I fly across the United States, that three-hour time change can really make a difference in such matters as eating and sleeping. In the airports I'll see people stepping from the jetway as they reset their watches to the local time. Me, I'm too stubborn. My watch shows Pacific Time, all the time. I glance at my wrist and do the math, based on how many times zones I'm separated from the home I love. I also think about what's happening back home according to the time. If it's Sunday, I'll visualize people getting ready for worship in our sanctuary, and a little pang of regret will pass through me because I'm absent. It may be nighttime where I am, but in San Diego, "God's Country" to me, the skies are sunny and the aisles are filled with people chatting, finding their seats, and preparing to worship God.

For some reason, the consistency of the watch connects me to home. I don't mind adding or subtracting the necessary hours, and calculating my local time in relation to Pacific Time. I believe Paul is making a similar point here in this passage. Keep your mental clock set on heavenly time. Look to Christ first, and then do the math to know how to function in this world. You have to live in this world for a time, just as I have to leave California from time to time. Learn to say with the psalmist, "Whom have I in heaven but You? And there is none upon the earth that I desire besides You" (Psalm 73:25).

The discipline of centering our hearts and minds on Christ will require us to focus. Here, from Paul's written words to the Colossians, are four truths that will help us to stay centered on Christ:

## Focus on His Connection to You

Colossians 3:1–4 reads, "If then you were raised *with* Christ . . . your life is hidden *with* Christ . . . you also will appear *with* Him in glory" (emphasis added).

I've highlighted the word *with* to show just how critical it is in this frame of thinking. *With* is a word of connection, our lifeline to Christ. When He died, we died with him. When He was buried, so were we. And we shared in His glorious resurrection, so that now we can be seated in the heavenlies with Him.

When the Bible says that Jesus died for us, it doesn't mean simply that He died in our behalf; it means He died in our place. He died where we should have died. Just as Adam was the personal embodiment of our fall into sin, Christ is the personal embodiment of our salvation and glory. "For as in Adam all die, even so in Christ all shall be made alive" (1 Corinthians 15:22). We fell with Adam, but we were resurrected with Christ.

Do you see the importance of that little word *with* in our spiritual destiny? The great Chinese Christian preacher and writer, Watchman Nee, grasped it. In 1927, he had been struggling with issues of temptation and his sinful nature. One morning he was sitting upstairs reading the book of Romans, and he came to the words, "Knowing this, that our old man was crucified with Him . . ." (6:6). For Nee, it was as if the words had come to life on the page. He leapt from his chair, ran downstairs, and grabbed a kitchen worker by the hands. "Brother," he shouted. "Do you know that I have died?"

The worker only stared in puzzlement. Nee blurted out, "Do you not know that Christ has died? Do you not know that I died with Him? Do you not know that my death is no less truly a fact than His?"

It was all Watchman Nee could do to keep himself from running through the streets of Shanghai, shouting about his death and new life. From that day on, his faith was confident and strong. His biographer wrote that it was impossible to say anything that might offend Nee. Why should he be offended? That Watchman Nee was long since dead![14]

Charles Spurgeon had his own way of explaining this amazing phenomenon of dying with Christ:

> I suppose that, if you were to meet your old self, he would hardly know you, for you are so greatly altered. I dare say he would say to you, "Come, old fellow, let us go to the theater, or turn into this beer-shop, or let us go home, and find out some way of amusing ourselves."
>
> You would reply, "No, sir; I cut your acquaintance a long time ago, and I do not mean to have anything further to do with you, so you may go about your business as soon as you like. I am not what I was, for I have been crucified with Christ, and I am dead, and my life is hid with Christ in God."[15]

One day Martin Luther was answering a knock at his door. "Does Dr. Martin Luther live here?" asked the visitor. "No," Luther answered, "he died. Christ lives here now."[16] Can we understand that this truth is just that radical? The old you is dead and in the grave; the new you is raised to walk in newness of life, and to live victoriously for Christ. Why not take a few moments today and mull this truth over in your mind!

# Focus on His Control over Everything that Concerns You

What image comes to your mind when you think of Jesus? Do you think of the uninspiring media stereotype of "gentle Jesus," a rather weak teacher? Or do you imagine the risen and ascended Lord, the glorious one in whose name "every knee should bow, of those in heaven, and of those on earth, and of those under the earth, and that every tongue should confess that Jesus Christ is Lord, to the glory of God the Father" (Philippians 2:10–11)?

Mental images make a difference. The reality is that Jesus is risen, that He sits at the right hand of the Father, and that when we see Him again, He will be revealed in all His magnificence. When we focus our attentions on *that* Lord, on His power and authority, our faith surges. I love the way Eugene Peterson captures it in his creative paraphrase of Ephesians 1:20–23:

> All this energy issues from Christ: God raised him from death and set him on a throne in deep heaven, in charge of running the universe, everything from galaxies to governments, no name and no power exempt from his rule. And not just for the time being, but forever. He is in charge of it all, has the final word on everything. At the center of all this, Christ rules the church. The church, you see, is not peripheral to the world; the world is peripheral to the church. The church is Christ's body, in which he speaks and acts, by which he fills everything with his presence (MSG).

Let those words soak through your mind for a few minutes. Afterward, I challenge you—no, I *dare* you—to feel the same anxiety over the state of current affairs. Our Lord sits enthroned at the center of this universe, ruling all things. Do you think He can handle a stock market in turmoil? He defeated death itself. Do you feel confident He could defeat a tough housing market? All nations, all creatures will bow before Him. Under His protection, do we have anything to fear?

Even when the world seems to spin out of control, be calm: this is only how it seems. In reality, Almighty God is still on His throne, and in the words of that old spiritual, "He's got the whole world in His hands."

## Focus on His Care for You

Colossians 3:3 reads, "For you died, and your life is hidden with Christ in God."

*Hidden.* Just as your hand might gently enfold a rose petal, God's hand gently enfolds you—again, *with* Christ. The phrase is "*with* Christ, *in* God." I certainly can't think of a more secure place to be.

I don't feel secure about my own abilities. I have no ultimate faith in our economy, our military prowess, or anything else in this poor, fallen world. But in Christ, I do feel utterly safe and secure. He is my rock, my shelter in a time of storm.

Note that we are not commanded to hide ourselves in God. Your life "is hidden." In other words—done! This is an accomplished fact, a here-and-now thing, not something for which to anxiously hope. If you are a Christ-follower, then you are with Christ, in God, and you are ultimately free and safe. Next time you feel worried, go somewhere alone and simply reflect on that.

The Bible is actually filled with imagery and language about this security. We imagine ourselves with Shadrach, Meshach, and Abednego, thrown into a roaring furnace yet receiving not even a deep tan. A fourth man is beside them—that would be Christ (Daniel 3:25). We ride the whirlwind with Elijah, and ordinarily it might be frightening. But Elijah finds peace there, and so do we. With the mighty arms of the tempests buffeting him, whirling and thundering all about him, he smiles, as comfortable as if he were home in bed (1 Kings 19:10–12). Instead of sitting around worrying about the stock market, housing, or unemployment, is there any reason, after all these thousands of years, for God to no longer protect us? Our security is not found in the things of the earth, but in our position with Christ, in God—where we are *hidden*.

## Focus on His Commitment to You

Colossians 3:4 reads, "When Christ who is our life appears, then you also will appear with Him in glory."

Part of being with Christ is becoming more like Him. Today, we are being transformed to something just a bit closer to His image every day, but when He returns in glory, the change will be sudden and dramatic. He will come in His glorious resurrection body, and we will then have perfect resurrection bodies too.

Paul reiterates this point that Christ will "transform our lowly body that it may be conformed to His glorious body" (Philippians 3:21). Does that sound good to you?

As we grow older, we have a deepening appreciation for bodily wellness. I don't know about you, but my "tent" is growing a bit more tattered all the time. One day I get to trade it in on a new and deluxe model. This is Christ's commitment to me, and to you as well. Place your faith in Him, and you will be fully and wonderfully renewed—spirit, mind, and even body—upon His return.

In John Ortberg's book, *Faith and Doubt,* he reminds us that to stay centered in Christ, we will need to learn the difference between hoping *for* something and hoping *in* Someone. Hoping for something, he writes, means wanting a particular outcome—a job, a house, a cure. But all these earthly hopes ultimately disappoint us. They wear out, fall apart, melt away, or perhaps they never materialize. All of us learn to live with the inevitability of dashed hopes.

At those sobering moments, the question becomes, "Is there some deeper hope?" Is there anything, anyone in this life that will never once disappoint us? The Bible, Ortberg writes, points to one Man, one hope, one God who is worth trusting, not because of any particular thing He can give us. We trust Him because of who He is. He is the one *in whom* and *by whom* we can hope. "Hope," he concludes, "is faith waiting for tomorrow."[17]

## Three Ways to Stay Centered in Christ

Hopefully, I have convinced you of the importance of staying centered in Christ. If so, then your question may be, *Just how do I go from being earth-centered to being heaven-centered?* Here are three suggestions to help you in your quest for Christ-centeredness.

*Seek God's Will.* "But seek first the kingdom of God and His righteousness, and all these things shall be added to you" (Matthew 6:33).

What is it about this verse? People insist on reading it backwards, as though from some spiritual strain of dyslexia: "Add all these things unto you, then seek the kingdom of God and His righteousness in whatever time is left." Blessed are those who read it as written, as intended, as the truth happens to be. One missionary rephrased it well: "Take care of the things that are important to God, and He will take care of the things that are important to you."

As a college student Richard Greene learned this lesson. He was fretting over bills and he grew agitated and afraid. "Where will the extra money come from?" he asked aloud. "Please, Lord, help me pay these bills."

A short while later he received an unexpected scholarship. Then a friend handed him a check for the month's rent. All these things were added unto him. God cared for Greene's educational needs, and he went on to serve the Lord at Trans World Radio, beaming the message of Scripture around the world.[18]

*Search God's Word.* Jesus was a guest in the home of Mary and Martha one day, as Luke's gospel tells us. He found Himself caught in the crossfire of warring priorities. Martha was playing hostess and housekeeper, while Mary sat at Jesus feet and listened intently to His teaching. It didn't seem fair to Martha, and she told Jesus so—Mary, she said, should do her part. As always, Jesus gave the least expected response: "Martha, Martha, you are worried and troubled about many things, but one thing is needed, and Mary has chosen that good part, which will not be taken away from her" (Luke 10:38–42).

We face this choice every single day. Staying centered on Christ requires us to stay focused on God's Word. Geoffrey Thomas has written, "The love of Christ is the strongest constraint to knowing the Scriptures, and if we have little desire for the Bible, we should ask if we indeed know the Savior." In other words, our relationship with the Bible mirrors our relationship with Christ.[19]

At the age of fourteen Jerry Bridges was the lone witness to his mother's very sudden and frightening death. His dad became lost in his own sorrow and neglected to minister to his son. Years later, Bridges was an ROTC engineering student at the University of Oklahoma. One night while studying, he happened to reach toward the shelf for a textbook. His eye caught a Bible his parents had given him when he was a boy. A thought flashed through his mind that now that he was really a Christian, he ought to read the Bible. And he followed up on that impulse over many years.

As it turned out, hearing deficiencies kept Bridges from the naval career he had wanted. He settled in California and worked as a writer of technical manuals for an airplane manufacturer. Though his career wasn't following the intended script, Bridges turned even more attention to what his Bible said about life in this world. He found a passion for the Scripture that led him to fifty years not with the Navy but the Navigators, the international ministry dedicated to Bible study and memorization.[20]

Along the way, Bridges found himself writing booklets, which led to major Christian books that have fed millions of hungry souls. All his literary endeavors sprang from his own intimate walk with God and his daily navigation of the Word—his lifeline when he was seeking to cope with his deflated career dreams. His book for troubled times, *Trusting God,* has this to say: "The moral will of God given to us in the Bible is rational and reasonable. The circumstances in which we must trust God often appear irrational and inexplicable . . . It is only from the Scriptures, applied to our hearts by the Holy Spirit, that we receive grace to trust God in adversity . . . The faith to trust God in adversity comes through the Word of God alone."[21]

This is what it means to set our minds on God through His Word. As Bridges affirms, the Scriptures often turn worldly logic on its head. People may think we are unreasonable. The truth is that only those with their minds set on God know what reason really is; only God's course is the course that will ultimately prevail.

*Support God's Work.* Our final secret to staying centered in Christ is so simple, so powerful, and so often forgotten. Simply go where His action is—and if you can't go there, find other ways to get involved.

In the Sermon on the Mount, again through the rewording of Eugene Peterson, Jesus tells us, "Don't hoard treasure down here where it gets eaten by moths and corroded by rust or—worse!—stolen by burglars. Stockpile treasure in heaven, where it's safe from moth and rust and burglars. It's obvious, isn't it? The place where your treasure is, is the place you will most want to be, and end up being" (Matthew 6:19–21 MSG). We might call that an investment manifesto for children of the kingdom. Pour yourself into eternal things, things that affect the invisible world; things that change the population of heaven.

Jesus says that our hearts naturally follow our treasures. What we value most is a magnet for our thoughts and emotions. Therefore we must learn to value God's things the most. The more we give ourselves to His purposes, the more centered on Christ we will become. Here's a quick way to test that: Talk to someone who has just returned from short-term mission work. Maybe you've had that experience yourself. How did you feel upon returning? What was your experience of giving a few days or weeks completely to the advancement of the gospel? Most of us feel like entirely different people. As the old song reminds us, "the things of earth will grow strangely dim, in the light of His glory and grace"[22]—and in the sanctified sweat of His service.

Our earthly treasures begin to look shabby indeed when we place them next to the treasures of God's kingdom. And all we need to do to prove that is to support the work of God. In his book *The Treasure Principle*, Randy Alcorn writes, "By telling us that our hearts follow our treasure, Jesus is saying, 'Show me your checkbook, your VISA statement, and your receipts, and I'll show you where your heart is.'"[23]

Alcorn offers the illustration of buying a stock for investment purposes. (His principle is especially valid given the current market volatility.) When we buy a particular stock, we have a vested interest in that firm. Its forecasts, its dividends, and its earning statements can directly affect our personal financial fortunes. They can rise or fall, depending on how that company performs in the marketplace. So we watch the financial pages and read our Google alerts for any hint of change. When we see articles about "our company" or even any industry related development, we read every word. A month earlier we would not have given that same news a passing glance.

This is simply the logical behavior of the wise investor, and when we invest ourselves in God's kingdom, our minds and hearts follow in that same way. If we begin sending money to help African children with AIDS, Alcorn continues, we begin to read more on that subject than we used to. If we're supporting a new church in India and we hear of an earthquake, we are glued to the news, praying all the while. The compass point always goes north, and our hearts go where our money leads.[24]

It may be simple, but it's also a matter of obedience. Are you willing to reallocate your resources to help center your heart and mind on Christ? It will work every time. The more you give to His purposes, the more centered on Him you become.

There are many other means of staying centered on Christ in chaotic times. But if we start with seeking Him first and searching for Him in the Scriptures, if we remember that our heart follows our treasure and we invest that treasure in things above, we will be well on our way toward staying centered in Christ.

When tough times come, as they've done lately, it serves us well to look to the examples of those who have suffered much more deeply. We often have a great deal to learn from them. A perfect example is Viktor Frankl, who survived a Nazi concentration camp. Cruelty, torture, hard labor, starvation, and an environment of death were his daily life for several years. He was married for only nine months when he and his young wife were separated. She was deported to Bergen-Belsen, and he was sent to Auschwitz.

In his book *Man's Search for Meaning*, Frankl describes an early morning prison march with a regiment of hungry, listless men, stumbling through the darkness, tripping on stones, and splashing through the mud as the guards shouted viciously and clubbed them with rifle butts. No one added a word to the icy wind. But finally the man next to Frankl muttered through the cover of his coat collar, "If our wives could only see us now! I hope they are better off in their camps and don't know what is happening to us."

When he said that, Frankl's thoughts immediately turned to his own young wife. He thought about her face, examining every feature in the sanctuary of his memories where even the Nazis could not invade. He thought of her encouraging smile and serious mind. The sun was beginning to rise, but the thought inside him was brighter, and it somehow strengthened his legs and insulated his body.

Over the coming months, stronger men gave up hope and died all around him. Why did Frankl trudge onward through the miserable landscape of his days? He credited this to the power of the human concentration. He simply kept his mind fixed on the powerful image of his wife, and he derived strength and comfort there, purpose and meaning for a life starving for it. "I understood how a man who has nothing left in this world may still know bliss," he wrote. "Be it only for a brief moment in the contemplation of his beloved."

Love, he discovered, is the most profound of all motivators. He could finally comprehend the words of an old proverb: "The angels are lost in perpetual contemplation of an infinite glory."[25] Those angels know, better than we, where the real joy is to be found. That abundant source is a well with no bottom, and when we are weak and thirsting from the trials of this life, we would be well advised to find that well and drink deeply.

Several years ago, my wife and I were invited to Oxford, England, to attend the expository preaching conference sponsored by *Preaching Magazine*. The meeting was held at St. Andrew's Church, and I was invited to give one of the sermons from the historic pulpit where Dr. G. Campbell Morgan had once taught the Word of God. When I returned to the United States after the conference, I was the surprised recipient of several books about G. Campbell Morgan, including the book *In The Shadow Of Grace: The Life and Meditations of G. Campbell Morgan*.

I discovered in the reading of this book that G. Campbell Morgan had ministered the Word of God during a period that included the sinking of the *Titanic*, the First World War, and the Second World War. All these events personally impacted the lives of members of his congregation.

*In The Shadow of Grace* presents portions of the sermons that Morgan preached during times of tragedy and war. According to his own words, Morgan was a pacifist. Yet with the advance of the German armies toward England, he found it necessary to speak in favor of the war and the protection of his nation.

On March 3, 1916, G. Campbell Morgan preached a sermon he

called "The Fixed Heart in the Day of Frightfulness." In his own words, he simply encouraged his listeners to stay centered on Christ.

> Men who are strong are always men who are fixed somewhere, who have a conviction from which they cannot be separated by argument, which cannot be changed, whatever the circumstances in which they live. Sometimes these men are very narrow, but they are wonderfully strong; they are singularly obstinate, but they are splendidly dependable. Consequently, we always know where to find these men. The fixed heart is the secret of courage. Courage is an affair of the heart; courage is the consciousness of the heart that is fixed . . . What, then, shall we do in the day of frightfulness? We shall do our duty; the thing that is nearest; the thing we have to do tomorrow morning. We will do that, and do it well; and do it cheerfully . . . What this nation needs, now just as much, and perhaps more, than anything else, is the multiplication of strong, quiet souls who are not afraid of evil tidings, even though the zeppelins may be coming, and will not add to the panic that demoralizes, but will do their work.[26]

That's called being centered. No level of persecution, no newspaper headline, no stock collapse, no housing bubble can taint the tiniest drop of that peace, joy, and love. Give Christ your mind and your heart. Invest yourself in the things that matter to Him. You'll find there a whole new world, one ruled perfectly and lovingly by our Lord—and pretty soon, you'll understand that the events of this earthly life are just as firmly in His wonderful hands.

# SEVEN

# Stay Confident

BILL MAHER IS BEST KNOWN AS THE HOST OF TWO NIGHTTIME television talk shows. The name of the second show—*Politically Incorrect*—pretty well sums up Maher's tone, personality, and subject matter. As a stand-up comedian, he is known for his acid-tongued commentaries on everything traditional—especially faith.

But in 2008 Maher added to his comedic résumé by writing and starring in a documentary film called *Religulous* that opened in theaters on October 3. His goal was to attack organized religion, especially Christianity and its belief in the Bible. Being an equal-opportunity agnostic, Maher also tried to split open the foundations of Judaism and Islam as well.

And because each of the three major religions is based on the teachings of a holy book—Islam, the Koran; Judaism, the Old Testament; Christianity, the Old and New Testaments—these books became the targets of Maher's focused scorn. In an interview on *The CBS Early Show* with host Harry Smith, Maher said, "My motivation [with *Religulous*] is to make people laugh. I mean, religion, to me, is a giant elephant in the room of comic gold because, you know, we're talking about a garden with a talking snake. If you can't find humor there—people are just used to [these stories]. That's why they don't laugh at [them]."[1]

Some people are surprised when they hear Maher say he's not an atheist—but less surprised when they read his answer to the question, "Is there a God?" Since he rejects the divine origin of the Bible, he rejects what it says:

> I believe there's some force. If you want to call it God—I don't believe God is a single parent who writes books. I think that the people who think God wrote a book called The Bible are just childish. Religion is so childish. What they're fighting about in the Middle East, it's so childish. These myths, these silly little stories that they believe in fundamentally, that they take over this little space in Jerusalem where one guy flew up to heaven—no, no, this guy performed a sacrifice here a thousand million years ago. It's like, Who cares? What does that have to do with spirituality, where you're really trying to get, as a human being and as a soul moving in the universe? But I do believe in a God, yes.[2]

Bill Maher is not the first skeptic in history to doubt the veracity of the Bible, and he won't be the last. But he is certainly emblematic of something the apostle Peter wrote nearly two thousand years ago: "Scoffers will come in the last days, walking according to their own lusts" (2 Peter 3:3). Having been raised in the church as a young person, Maher also fits the description of some the apostle Paul predicted would come: "Now the Spirit expressly says that in latter times some will depart from the faith, giving heed to deceiving spirits and doctrines of demons" (1 Timothy 4:1).

My prediction, though not divinely inspired, is that we haven't seen anything yet. There will be more arrogant skeptics to join Maher's critical and comedic chorus against the Bible and the faith. The warning for true Christians is not, "The skeptics are coming!" but that they have such a well-publicized, public platform. Their voices enter the ears of believers through the media. Christians, therefore, must be prepared to "always be ready to give a defense to everyone who asks you a reason for the hope that is in you, with meekness and fear" (1 Peter 3:15).

One man who has learned to do just that—defend his faith with meekness and fear—started down a road not unlike Bill Maher: the road of scathing skepticism of the Bible's authority. Piyush Jindal, better known as Bobby Jindal, is the governor of Louisiana. He's the first Indian-American elected to statewide office in US history. Governor Jindal's story has captured national imagination over recent months for a variety of reasons. Helping to rebuild a state devastated by storm and flood, he understands the idea of public crisis.

Jindal, born and raised a Hindu, converted to Christianity after a careful reading of the Bible. It began a spiritual journey to Christ he describes as "gradual and painful." Young Jindal first picked up the Word with ulterior motives: He wanted to disprove a faith—one he both "admired and despised." This is a familiar old story in Christianity: the skeptic who is converted by following an investigative trail, undermining his own skepticism in the end. Our Bible does a powerful job of defending itself when confronted.

Jindal was expecting to find a pack of myths inside those covers. But something happened as he opened his New Testament. Its pages worked like a mirror. "I saw myself in many of the parables," he says. Jesus seemed to be speaking across the centuries, telling stories written just for him.

His curiosity now in overdrive, Bobby Jindal began to seek out works about the historical accuracy of the Bible. To his own surprise, he found himself convinced that here were sacred words that had traveled with integrity through two thousand years—firsthand accounts of the ultimate miracle, God in human form. It was intellectually impossible to deny that Jesus Christ had risen from the dead, then ascended to heaven.

"However," he says, "my perspective remained intellectual and not spiritual." Jindal was shaken by what he found, but he was unwilling to give in to what his mind told him was the real thing. After many hours of counseling with a patient pastor, he finally embraced his new Lord and Savior.[3]

Bobby Jindal is an emblem of his era. Last year the *New York Times* reported on a change in the interests of college students. After decades of obsession with the more "practical" curriculum, many young scholars are gravitating toward courses in philosophy. They're feeling a deep need to make sense of the world, and they're finding that contemporary thinkers and leaders give them no ultimate answers. Therefore, they are digging into the wisdom of writers from distant centuries.[4]

We Christians believe there is only one of those ancient texts that is eternally relevant. The pressing questions of our past, present, and future are all answered by this Book because the Scriptures, like Christ, are eternal—authoritative yesterday, today, and forever. They explain life, but they also give us strength and comfort for the rigors of life's journey. Perhaps greater than anything we have discussed so far, the Bible is the key to living with confidence in a chaotic world.

If the history of human experience teaches us anything, it is this, the Bible is no ordinary book. Composed of sixty-six shorter books, written by some forty different authors over many centuries, it is a kind of multicentury anthology with no earthly reason to be so perfectly unified. It is incredible that it should speak with one authoritative voice, or that all its various sections, chapters, and verses should hold such power over human lives after several millennia. There is no explanation for any of this unless it is the eternal Word of God. I am convinced that this miraculous Book provides an accurate account of history and the *only* account of the future. We need the life-changing message of the Bible right now.

Beth Moore writes that we should desire a steady diet of Scripture because of what it says about itself: it is "living and active" (Hebrews 4:12 NIV). This is no dusty, ancient document with a lingering passage or two of vague interest. The Greek word for *living* suggests that the Word is teeming with life. Moore concludes that if we believe this, and if we accept that it is "God-breathed" (2 Timothy 3:16 NIV), "we might say that every breath comes to us still warm from the mouth of God. As if He just said it."[5] I wish I had written that!

When you open this Book, you are not just opening a book. When you read the Word, you are doing more than reading words. You are not simply taking in information; you are taking in *life*, warm from the breath of God. Nor are you studying the works of dead writers—rather you are hearing the voice of the living Lord. And when this world is in crisis, and up seems down, and right has gone wrong, this Book holds the answers you need. You and I should inhabit its pages more fully than we reside in our physical houses. We should consume its truth as surely as we eat the food upon our tables. When there's no other visible source of confidence, we can stay confident in the Word of God.

# A Cure for Itching Ears

Timothy was a young man with an uphill struggle before him. His mentor, the apostle Paul, had left him in Ephesus to guide its church. That was going to be no easy task.

Paul understood the encouragement his young protégée needed. Sitting in prison shortly before his execution by the Romans, Paul could have used a little encouragement himself. But the tentmaker from Tarsus was wise and godly by this late season of his life, and he wasn't given to self-pity. Always abounding in the joy of God's work, he wrote a letter counseling Timothy to stay focused on a task with eternal implications. The letter carries an urgency that stands out among his New Testament epistles. Perhaps he felt what Jesus felt in the Upper Room: time was short, and the stakes were high for the kingdom of Christ.

Ephesus was a cultural melting pot in which people, even believers, were becoming more worldly every day. God's inspired Word was being trivialized, so Paul wrote to Timothy, "I charge you therefore before God and the Lord Jesus Christ, who will judge the living and the dead at His appearing and His kingdom: Preach the word! Be ready in season and out of season. Convince, rebuke, exhort, with all long-suffering and teaching" (2 Timothy 4:1–2).

Notice the phrase "I charge you." It's used on six other occasions in Scripture. It always precedes a clear and urgent command. Even without the charge, these words would have carried the same weight as any other scriptural command. But the extra notice is a way of underlining the words that follow. It tells us, "Listen very carefully—this next part is life-and-death stuff." Then comes the phrase, "before God and the Lord Jesus Christ, who will judge the living and the dead at

His appearing and His kingdom." Can you feel the solemnity with which Paul fashions this word of counsel? Once again, here is an end-time reference in a present time call-to-action context.

The twenty-first century is not dissimilar from the first. Our culture, like the city of Ephesus, subjects the Word of God to scorn and ridicule. Paul wrote of a time when people will "not endure sound doctrine, but according to their own desires, because they have itching ears, they will heap up for themselves teachers; and they will turn their ears away from the truth, and be turned aside to fables" (2 Timothy 4:3–4).

We live in an age of ten thousand competing voices, all of them tantalizing, all designed to scratch the itching ears of a directionless society. People are inventing new religions by the day. If Paul were writing in our era, he might call them "ear candy." They sound sweet but have no nutritional value whatsoever. Consider the books that ride the best-seller list at the moment of this writing, each of them offering a "new," suspiciously convenient way to find truth, meaning, and purpose without breaking a sweat. Listen to the gurus who populate the talk shows. You'll notice that the trendy new "religions" play to the ego while making almost no demand on obedience or sacrifice.

Pluralism and tolerance are the watchwords of the day, but they result in more turmoil, not more peace. All the answers people seek are in the Word of God, where they've awaited us for two thousand years. But the masses would rather have their ears tickled than their souls renewed.

## A Famine of Hearing

Long before Paul, the prophet Amos warned: "Behold, the days are coming . . . that I will send a famine on the land, not a famine of bread, nor a thirst for water, but of the hearing of the words of the LORD" (Amos 8:11). It's a strange kind of famine, isn't it? The problem is not with the corn but the ears.

We may well be in the early stages of the hearing famine. For generations, God's Word has been at the center of church preaching. Today, even in the major faith communities, questioning scriptural authority is in vogue. Popular speakers advocate processing God's Word through the cultural filters of the day, rather than the other way around. We once understood that we don't stand in judgment of the Bible; it stands in judgment of us. But many today are air-brushing the Word of God to make it palatable to those who go in for spirituality that costs nothing but the cover price of a best seller. Instead of our being conformed to the image of Christ, we want to conform His image, and everything else in Scripture, to our sad conditions. Thirty years ago, people were saying, "If it feels good, do it." Today, it's more subtle. We say, "If it sounds good, believe it."

When we are trying to figure out how on earth we can live with confidence in this crazy, chaotic world, we ought to be running to the Bible and not away from it, as so many are doing. We are like survivors of the *Titanic*, the great luxury ship, floating helplessly on the tides. At that boat's launch an employee of the White Star Line boasted, "Not even God himself could sink this ship."[6] No matter how modern and luxurious the ship was, however, it went down— and its passengers were left scrambling for scraps of wood to keep them afloat.

That's a picture of you and me right now. Our culture of prosperity seemed to be an unsinkable vessel, but it's in pieces right now. Though everything else may fail us, God's Word never will. Jesus, who calmed the storm and walked across the waves, is still in control. Double-digit unemployment, trillion-dollar debts and bailouts—what are these to One who created every star in the sky? He still reigns, He still speaks, and His Word still offers the provision for every need we have in such a time.

So what exactly are these needs? Paul is going to give us a clue. In so many ways, the great apostle is telling Timothy what the church in Ephesus, and the church in our own cities, need to hear when the preacher stands up to speak.

## We Need a Sure Word from God

Paul gives Timothy five commands in this text. The mentor's directives nearly jump off the page in their urgency and forcefulness:

> Preach!
> Be ready!
> Convince!
> Rebuke!
> Exhort!

Remember, Paul has been working in a state of urgency for three decades, planting churches across as much of the globe as he can possibly reach. He knows that his ministry is almost complete, even though the fire still burns within him for new lands and new souls. Now he must place the future of all his labor in the hands of the next generation of evangelists, preachers, and teachers—including Timothy, his prize pupil. Paul yearns to see the Holy Spirit take hold of Timothy's young life.

He writes, "For I am already being poured out as a drink offering, and the time of my departure is at hand. I have fought the good fight, I have finished the race, I have kept the faith" (2 Timothy 4:6–7). Can't you hear the passion in his words?

In the previous chapter of this letter, Paul has spoken to Timothy about truth and the importance of upholding it. He has foreseen a time when religious leaders will be addicted to pleasure rather than fellowship with the Father, and will clothe themselves in the appearance of godliness—without the power of it. "From such people stay away!" he has concluded (2 Timothy 3:4–5). Now, in the fourth chapter, Paul tells Timothy that it's not enough to just *acknowledge* what is right, he must *announce* what is right. He must preach this truth!

The word he uses for *preach* means "to proclaim with formality, gravity, and an authority that must be listened to and obeyed." We know that from the beginning, preaching has been God's vehicle for inviting people into His kingdom. Paul speaks of "the foolishness of preaching" (1 Corinthians 1:21) because the very words that are divine revelation to the believer seem like nonsense to the rest of the world. The Holy Spirit, of course, makes the difference. Puritan Thomas Watson explained, "Ministers knock at the door of men's hearts; the Spirit comes with a key and opens the door."[7]

*Turning Point* is our international ministry for doing exactly what we're discussing: preaching the Word to the world. We use television, we use radio, we use the Internet, we use prerecorded media, print media, and sometimes we do it the good old-fashioned way: we go to the various corners of the world and preach the gospel in person.

On one such trip to Wake Forest, North Carolina, I was preparing to speak at a dinner meeting. Someone told me that a US Army chaplain wanted to share a word. This is not something that occurs at our meetings with much frequency, but God had big things in mind that evening. Let me share his incredible story with you.

His name is Brad Borders. He was a young man whose life had been characterized by poor decisions. From his mid-teens he had been confused and aimless, and the future seemed to hold no promise for him. But one day in 1994, while driving through the Smoky Mountains of North Carolina, he concentrated on keeping his car on the road through the precipitous turns as he turned up the radio. Of all things, it was some Bible preacher—and of all subjects, he was preaching from the book of Revelation, one of the most difficult books in the Bible.

Brad described for our audience the strangeness of listening to biblical teaching as an atheist. As Paul said, it can seem like nothing more than sheer folly to an unbeliever. Brad had always rejected this kind of thing quite easily. But on this day, the message finally came in loud and clear. It must have been like listening to someone speaking a foreign language, then, in one moment, receiving the ability to understand every word being spoken. It just *clicked*.

*There is a God,* he thought abruptly.

The next thought was, *And Jesus Christ is His Son. And I don't know Him. And if that doesn't change, my life will remain in shambles.*

Strange how you can be driving along a road, he said, and suddenly you believe your entire destiny hinges on the words from a two thousand-year-old book! What would make someone believe that? What mysterious power could bring an adult mind to that conclusion in the space of one instant?

Suddenly the pastor (that was me) was speaking directly to Brad. He was calling on every listener to stop for a moment and consider one question. *What's going to happen on the day you die?*

Brad had absolutely no answer for that question. He had no defense, no diversion. He needed Jesus. He needed forgiveness. He was certain that God, the maker of everything, was alive, and suddenly Brad wanted more than anything in the world to know him. Sitting behind the wheel of a '92 Saturn, Brad prayed his heart out. He asked for forgiveness, for salvation, and for the privilege to know Christ personally. God granted his every request.

Fourteen years passed, bringing this same man to a microphone at our dinner, where he held the audience spellbound. During the intervening years, he had been mentored and discipled, just as Paul had done with Timothy. He had gone through seminary, been ordained as a pastor, enlisted as a chaplain, and commissioned as a servant of the gospel, traveling to places he never dreamed he would see. I was amazed as I listened to his story. I had never met Brad or heard a word of his story. I only learned it because I happened to visit North Carolina. I had to wonder what else God was doing out there through our ministry that he hadn't let me know about. Praise God, this is the tip of the iceberg; His Word never returns void. He has promised us:

> For as the rain comes down, and the snow from heaven,
> And do not return there,
> But water the earth,
> And make it bring forth and bud,
> That it may give seed to the sower
> And bread to the eater,
> So shall My word be that goes forth from My mouth;
> It shall not return to Me void,
> But it shall accomplish what I please,

And it shall prosper in the thing for which I sent it.
(Isaiah 55:10–11)

In case there's any doubt about the return on God's Word, consider this. Since Brad Borders became a chaplain, he has led more than seven hundred soldiers to Jesus Christ.

That's the ultimate power of the Word of God through preaching. It has nothing to do with me. Believe me, I couldn't convince you or anyone else to believe in the reality of Christ and to commit your life totally to Him—not unless the Holy Spirit empowered the words of my mouth. In ordinary circumstances, Brad, an atheist without direction, could never have suddenly turned his life on a dime, becoming someone capable of leading more than seven hundred soldiers to Christ. Even then, it would be even less likely to happen based upon a sermon from the book of Revelation. Although Brad didn't believe a word of it, the preacher obviously did. In other words, it was a sure word from God.

You'd be amazed how many times something as unlikely as that has happened, always beginning with the Word being preached. There is an account of a woman on her deathbed. She described how she was saved by reading a crumpled, ragged piece of wrapping paper in a package shipped from Australia. Someone had used the printed text of a sermon by Charles H. Spurgeon to wrap a package for shipment. The sermon was preached in England, printed in America, shipped to Australia, then sent back to England as wrapping paper, where the woman read it and encountered Jesus Christ. The Word traveled thousands of miles on the cheapest, most crumpled and smeared newsprint. But the truth shone brilliantly through the simplest of media, and God's Word did not return void.[8]

## We Need a Serious Word from God

We need a sure word but also a serious one. Paul writes, "Be ready in season and out of season."

The words *be ready* mean "to stand by; to be on hand." This phrase conveys more than the idea of just being alert. There is urgency and vigilance in being ready the way Paul describes. It's the idea of a soldier standing on the wall at midnight, knowing the enemy is within firing distance. "In season and out of season" basically means this: the right time *and* the rest of the time. We proclaim the Word of God when it is readily accepted, and we proclaim it when it is not. People always need a serious word from God.

Those of us who are charged with the responsibility of teaching God's Word must understand that it is serious business! Nothing could be sadder than the feast of God's Word served up at lukewarm heat, with little flavor. We're approaching issues that concern our hearts, our souls, and our heavenly destiny. The element of solid reasoning is important, as we'll see, but the heart of preaching is . . . the heart. We preach the Word to change lives.

It is possible to be intellectually stimulated without being changed from within. This is why we are to proclaim the Word, to the hearts of our people, with authority and certainty.

A cartoon by my friend Rob Suggs in *Leadership Journal* showed a sad pastor studying a chart that showed his plunging church attendance. Apparently most of his congregation had drifted away. A friend was gently suggesting to the pastor, "I'm no expert, Bob, but maybe it would help if you didn't close each sermon with, 'But then again, what do I know?'"[9]

Paul commands Timothy to boldly proclaim the message of the

Gospel. People need a serious word from God, so we need to deliver our message as if tomorrow depends upon it; the truth is, it does.

## We Need a Systematic Word from God

We also need a systematic word from God. We must be bold with our message. We share it with most certainty and urgency. But we must also share it intelligently.

Paul uses three important words here: *convince, rebuke,* and *exhort.* Those are known to writers as "strong verbs"—action words in which the action is aggressive. What can we learn from these words that will help us during times of national and world crisis?

*Our Minds Need to Be Convinced by the Word.* To convince is "to present an argument or a strong appeal"—something like an attorney presenting a brief. We're trying to change the mind of the hearer.

J. Sidlow Baxter wrote: "To my own mind, the most satisfying proofs that the Bible is divinely inspired are not those which one 'reads up' in volumes of religious evidences or Christian apologetics, but those which we discover for ourselves in our own study of the Book. To the prayerful explorer the Bible has its own way of revealing its internal credentials."[10]

The nineteenth-century scholar, A. T. Pierson, agreed: "Every study of the Bible is a study of the evidences of Christianity. The Bible is itself the greatest miracle of all."[11]

That miracle once did its work upon a young G. Campbell Morgan. He had grown up in a Christian home, never questioning that the Bible was the Word of God. But in college, his faith was severely challenged and he began to entertain doubts. "The whole intellectual world was under the mastery of the physical scientists, and of a materialistic and rationalistic philosophy," he later said. "There came a moment when I was sure of nothing."

That was an era when it was fashionable to launch attacks on the veracity of Scripture. The new crowd hired out great lecture and concert halls across England for the purpose of attacking the authority of the Bible. Armed with all their intellectual artillery, the army of skeptics troubled the young Morgan. He studied every book he could find—for and against the Bible, for and against Christianity—until his mind was reeling with arguments and counter-arguments.

He finally heaved a sigh, gathered up all the volumes, and locked them in a cupboard. He then walked to a bookshop and purchased a brand-new Bible. He had decided it was time to let the venerable old Book speak for itself. The young Morgan believed that if the Bible truly was divinely inspired, and if he would simply read it with an open mind, then the Book would do its own convincing. So he opened its covers and began to read.

The Bible spoke to him with eloquence and authority. The unity of the sixty-six inspired books, the many literary forms gathered across time, and the depth of the message itself—all these elements of the Bible experience overwhelmed him. The clear power and presence of God could be encountered here! "That Bible found me," he later said. After that year, 1883, he was a devoted student of the Scriptures for the balance of his life.[12]

Our cynical culture would like you to believe that the Christian life is a mindless thing, built around an ordinary book that is a dusty grab bag of mythology. It's all so much emotion, they claim, so much self-deception. According to the stereotype, you check your mind at the door when you take up Christianity, and smart folks should stay away.

Now for the truth of the matter: the Word of God is the most rational, accurate, well-documented body of literature in the history of the world. It requires our God-given intellect to even begin the life-long process of embracing its many dimensions of profound teaching. Great thinkers throughout the ages have discovered just that: Sir Isaac Newton, who gave us our basic laws of physics; Blaise Pascal, world-class mathematician and scientist; Sir Francis Bacon, who introduced the scientific method; Michael Faraday, foundational pioneer of chemistry and electromagnetism. And today, to give one example of many, there is Professor Henry F. Schaefer, one of the most distin-guished physical scientists in the world, a five-time nominee for the Nobel Prize, and a devout follower of Jesus Christ.[13] Here is what many of these men would tell you: if it requires faith to be a Christian, how much more faith does it require to dismiss this amazing, timeless book called the Bible? People today say the age of miracles is over, and that they've never seen one. But if you own a Bible, you hold a living mir-acle in your hand.

*Our Wills Need to Be Convicted by the Word.* Paul's second word is *rebuke.* It's not my favorite word or yours, but it's a necessary part of life and faith. It means "to reprimand." It is synonymous with the word *convict.* In a spiritual context, it means to speak out against sin where we find it.

In today's church, that can be an adventure. But to some extent, human nature has always been tough on truth-tellers. We understand why pastors often shy away from "telling it like it is," but truthfully, they often find they've underestimated their listeners. People are starv-ing to hear an unvarnished gospel. They need a sure word from God!

Too many modern pastors attempt to be user-friendly and give no offense. I don't set out to preach or not preach about sin. I want to reach seekers too. But my goal is to be faithful to the Word of God. I preach through its pages and disregard the politics of addressing this or that topic. It just so happens that occasionally the Bible has something to say about sin! If the Bible says it, we need to say it too. And more often than not, it's the message people are longing to hear.

John Steinbeck, the author of *The Grapes of Wrath*, was not known for writing from an evangelical perspective. But in another of his books, *Travels with Charlie*, he gives an interesting account of his reaction to a sermon he once heard in a New England church:

*It is our practice now, at least in the large cities, to find from our psychiatric priesthood that our sins aren't really sins at all but accidents that are set in motion by forces beyond our control. There was no nonsense in this church. The minister, a man of iron with tool-steel eyes and a delivery like a pneumatic drill, opened up with prayer and reassured us that we were a pretty sorry lot. And he was right. We didn't amount to much to start with, and due to our own tawdry efforts we had been slipping ever since. Then, having softened us up he went into a glorious sermon, a fire-and-brimstone sermon . . . He spoke of hell as an expert, not the mush-mush hell of these soft days, but a well-stoked, white-hot hell served by technicians of the first order. This reverend brought it to a point where we could understand it, a good hard coal fire . . . For some years now God has been a pal to us, practicing togetherness . . . But this Vermont God cared enough about me to go to a lot of trouble kicking the hell out of me. He put my sins in a new perspective. Whereas they had been small and mean and nasty and best forgotten, this minister gave then some size and bloom and dignity . . . I wasn't a naughty child but a first rate sinner . . .*[14]

Missionary poet Amy Carmichael wrote: "If you've never been hurt by a word from God, it's probable that you've never heard God speak."[15] The Bible does many things. It will uplift your spirit, it will make you cry tears of sheer joy, and it will drive you to worship. But there are also times when it seizes you by the collar, pulls you up close, and shows you the sin in your life in such a way that there's nowhere to hide. When you listen to the Word—through preaching, through small groups, or through personal study—do you ask God to shine His light on the dark places of your character, convict you of sin, and give you victory over it?

In his letter to Titus, Paul describes what a true teacher must do! "Have a good grip on the Message, knowing how to use the truth to either spur people on in knowledge or stop them in their tracks if they oppose it." (Titus 1:9 MSG).

Paul also touches upon the ultimate goal of preaching: "Warning every man and teaching every man in all wisdom, that we may present every man perfect in Christ Jesus" (Colossians 1: 28). We can't present every man and woman perfect in Christ Jesus without confronting imperfections where we find them. That's just how it works; our wills need to be convicted by the Word.

*Our Hearts Need to Be Comforted by the Word.* In her book *Edges of His Ways*, Amy Carmichael is right on target when she points out that no matter what our need may be, what dark cloud may hang over us, we will find just the right word in the Bible somewhere; just the remedy we need. It may not be the first passage we see when we open the Book, but if we search the Scriptures diligently, the Bible will answer every issue that arises.[16]

The Bible speaks to every part of who we are. It convinces the mind, convicts the will, and comforts the heart. In Paul's advice to Timothy, the relevant word is *exhort—encourage* in some translations—"to encourage with the goal of bringing someone along a path toward a positive end result." There is no comfort, no encouragement, like the kind that can be experienced through God's Word. Paul writes to the Thessalonians, "Therefore comfort one another with these words" (1 Thessalonians 4:18). And in 1 Corinthians 14:3, we learn that prophecy is for the purpose of comfort: "But he who prophesies speaks edification and exhortation and comfort to men."

Yes, God gives us His Word for guidance, but He also gives it for comfort because He loves us. We look around us and wonder what the future holds. We have questions about the direction of our nation and our world. We have worries about our finances. But when we open God's Word, we receive profound comfort. We are reminded on every page that kings, countries, and economies don't hold the fate of the world; only God does, and He is a God of comfort and love. He has a future and a hope for us.

Once our hearts are lifted, we can lift the hearts of others. The Bible tells us in so many passages to encourage and comfort one another, and it's one of the most important things we do as we gather together for fellowship. One stumbles, another lifts him up. One has an anxious heart, her brothers and sisters pray for her and surround her with love and support. The church shines in these moments as we allow the Holy Spirit to minister encouragement through God's Word.

I assure you that the most remarkable and powerful words of comfort and encouragement you'll ever encounter are all in the Bible. But do you know where to find them? The Psalms, in particular, speak to every condition of the human heart, but do you know your way around in that section of your Bible? If you will simply take the time to learn how to find what you need in the Scriptures, you will have an incredible remedy for fear and anxiety. Better yet, if you will memorize key passages, the Holy Spirit will call up those words from your mind again and again. Burying His Word in your heart is the wisest way you can spend your time.

## We Need a Sensitive Word from God

We want to notice a final word from Paul in this amazing passage. He has outlined for Timothy both the message and the method for ministry in chaotic times. The leader should convince, rebuke, and exhort. But he must make sure he does so "with all long-suffering and teaching." What exactly does Paul mean here?

As I read the words, I realize that Paul is speaking particularly to me as a pastor. As I teach God's Word, I need to be very patient. We leaders can be discouraged; there are times when we feel that no one is listening. We look out across the sanctuary and ask ourselves, "Is anyone really interested in learning about God's Word today? Is there any chance that someone out there will actually apply this to their lives?" God's instruction for me is to be longsuffering; to wait however long it takes; to do the work of ministry and remember the harvest is His. If I begin to play God, insisting that things work on my schedule, I will drive people away.

And this patience is not just for preachers. For example, there are wives who have grown deeper spiritually than their husbands. They've been able to attend the Bible studies or spend time in personal study while their husbands were devoted to their careers. Wives, too, need to be longsuffering and patient; be gentle and loving while letting God do the work of admonishment and conviction.

All of us, as followers of Christ, need to be sensitive. We forget that the Spirit of God is always on the move, always seeing the big picture that we don't see. We can't know what is in the minds of others or what the future holds. What we can do is be obedient to Christ and to His Word, and that means being loving, patient, gentle, and longsuffering.

## Where to Bury the Treasure

It was February of 1944 when the little Dutch clock shop was raided. An agent of the Nazi Gestapo stood in the living room of Corrie ten Boom's family, his eyes studying the books on a shelf. "You! The old man there," he barked. "I see you believe in the Bible."

It was true. Each morning, before he opened his watch shop, Corrie ten Boom's father, Casper, held devotions with his family. The focal point was a large, brass-hinged Bible. Casper would read a chapter, lead a prayer, and begin the business day. Then, as the sun set, the family would gather again and take up where they had left off in the morning's reading.

His youngest child, a daughter, remembered him reading, "Thy word is a lamp unto my feet, and a light unto my path . . . Thou art my hiding place and my shield: I hope in thy word" (Psalm 119:105, 114). The child had wondered what it all meant. A hiding place? What kind? How could a word be a hiding place, and what was there to hide from?

This was the dark day when she would discover her answer. Old Casper, his four adult children, and one grandchild were ordered out of their home and marched to police headquarters. There they awaited an uncertain fate, having been charged with secretly sheltering Jews who were under persecution by the Germans. In the holding cell, the ten Booms ate the meager meal they were given, huddling together in the encroaching darkness. Only one thing gave them a taste of home: time together in the Word. Casper led devotions as if it were any other day, any other place. The great Bible was out of reach, and there was no light for reading anyway. But it didn't matter because he had buried the Word in his heart—the hiding place no enemy could invade. He knew the passages of comfort, chapter and verse.

His daughter Corrie wrote, "His blue eyes seemed to be seeing beyond the locked and crowded room, beyond Haarlem, beyond earth itself, as he quoted from memory, 'Thou art my hiding place and my shield: I hope in thy word . . . Hold thou me up, and I shall be safe'" (Psalm 119:114, 117).[17]

Later, in the concentration camp, she managed to get a Bible and to read it to fellow prisoners. "The blacker the night around us grew," she recalled, "the brighter and truer and more beautiful burned the Word of God."[18] And indeed the nighttime of her life grew black. She endured the deaths of her father and her beloved sister, Betsie. She survived humiliation, cruelty, and neglect. But the Word of God, and the peace of God flowing from it, brought her through the long nightmare so that she might emerge to bless the world with her message of hope.

## Hidden in Plain Sight

Does that story or, perhaps, something else in this chapter help you to feel differently about that Book collecting dust on your shelf or on the back seat of your car where you left it on Sunday? It's not my intention to deal in guilt but to motivate and encourage you to experience the great blessing that comes to those who read and love the Bible as people over the ages have done.

Some of the stories in this chapter have shown you how the Word of God has worked miracles in people's lives. It traveled on newsprint across the world to lead a woman to salvation in England. It strengthened a small knot of suffering humanity in a concentration camp. It captured the intellect of a future Indian-American governor of an American state. A rebellious young man had his life changed on a North Carolina road. Do you notice the pattern? These lives reflect many times and cultures; and each dealt with intense crisis in some way or another. Time after time, the Word of God was their lamp, and the light of their way.

That light seems to shine brightest of all when darkness falls upon our surroundings. Our world is now in crisis, and many people I know are living with a sense of loss and a fear of the future. The Word of God is available to convince your mind, to convict your will, and to comfort your heart. If you will read it, cherish it, and let it dwell within you richly, you'll see the darkness retreat as the light of God's truth shines brightly in your life.

If you remember the Bible's warnings—that the Bible and the faith will come under increasing attacks as we get closer to the return of Jesus Christ—you will not cower in fear when skeptics raise their voices. Whether they are comedians who try to soften your defenses with humor, scholars who try to overwhelm your beliefs with intellectual arguments, or religious leaders who try to convince you that the Bible is just a book, you will be ready. You will remember that "the grass withers, the flower fades, but the word of our God stands forever" (Isaiah 40:8).

# EIGHT

# Stay Consistent

"DO YOU HAVE A REGULAR MEETING IN YOUR HOME?" THE CITY official asked.

"Yes," the pastor's wife replied—she was the one who answered the door.

"Do you say, 'Amen'?" was the next question.

"Yes."

"Do you pray?"

"Yes."

"Do you say, 'Praise the Lord'?"

"Yes."

The city official went on to tell the pastor's wife that the Bible study they held in their home was in violation of local ordinances. A few days later the couple received a written warning that listed "unlawful use of land" and warned them to "stop religious assembly or apply for a major use permit"—a process that could cost tens of thousands of dollars in legal and other fees.

If you think this took place in Albania, you'd be wrong. China?

Nope. Cuba? Not even close. A former Soviet Eastern Bloc nation? Good guess, but no.

Believe it or not, this took place in May 2009 in San Diego, California, in a neighborhood quite near to where I live. The church I pastor has more than two hundred small group Bible studies that meet in our members' homes weekly, throughout our vast county. The saddest part about it is this: when I heard this report in our local news I wasn't really surprised. Not that this is typical of the local governments in our area. Rather, it is indicative of a growing trend in our nation and our world—a trend that requires Christians to be tolerant of everyone and requires no one to be tolerant of Christians.

And this trend—which is going to increase as the world's tolerance for Christianity decreases in the years ahead—is going to present a new dilemma for Christians in America and other nations: do I live a consistent Christian life, or do I compromise when the pressure gets intense?

As it turns out, some neighbors had complained to local authorities about the number of cars that were parked at the pastor's home during the weekly Bible study. And that's all it took for authorities to begin an investigation as to whether a religious meeting was being held without an appropriate permit. As I write these words, the matter is still under deliberation.[1]

I say "Three cheers!" for the pastor's wife, who boldly and truthfully answered the questions the local official asked. She was consistent. Instead of answering yes each time, what if she had said, "Uh, we have met here occasionally"; "No, we don't say 'Praise the Lord' or 'Amen'"; or "Yes, we pray—sometimes we say grace before we eat, but not every time"? Let's face it; she didn't know if she was about to be arrested or something worse. As far as she knew, her fate lay in her answers.

Consistency. It's the act of living true to what you believe regardless of the cost. Christians need to consider how consistent they are going to be before, not after, they hear a knock on their door.

The truth is, the world itself is inconsistent enough. I doubt its condition has grown any less chaotic since you began reading this book. Our stock market is the very study of inconstancy with its roller-coaster gains and losses. Nothing is stable about international politics, and on a social level, we see marriages struggling and careers going bust. The only consistent thing about our world is that it's inconsistent.

What about you? Are you the same person on Mondays that you are on Sundays? Do solid biblical principles guide each section of your life? How about marriage and parenting, if those apply—do you have consistent principles there, and do you live by them? These are hard questions, and issues that aren't always pleasant to consider. But one of the biblical essentials for getting through times like these is to live a life of solid consistency—to be one person through and through, to be an example of tough-minded integrity that does not throw out the game plan just because things have gotten tougher.

Sports fans will understand what I'm talking about. In 2001, rookie head coach Mark Richt led his Georgia Bulldogs up to Knoxville, Tennessee, to play national title contender Tennessee. Georgia was a serious underdog and hadn't won in Tennessee's raucous, one hundred thousand–seat stadium in twenty years. Before leading his team onto the field, Richt told his players, "Men, if they blow the doors off us early, keep your composure. Believe in the plan." As the game began, Tennessee indeed jumped out to a big lead and pushed Georgia's smaller linemen around. The rout-hungry fans were deafening. But

Georgia's players remembered the coach's advice, each man holding to his part in the game plan, and the Bulldogs pulled off an upset still remembered as one of the greatest college games ever broadcast by CBS.[2]

We can all agree that "the doors have been blown off" in our own game lately. Our temptation is to do what undisciplined athletes might do—throw caution to the wind, forget our training, and declare that it's every man for himself. Yet calm assurance and the right plan are the keys to pulling through. We have God's Word in these times. David the psalmist said that those who don't know God are like chaff (dust) that the wind blows away, but the one who loves the Word of God "is like a tree planted by the rivers of water, that brings forth its fruit in its season, whose leaf also shall not wither; and who shall prosper in whatever he does" (Psalm 1:3).

## Confidence + Consistency

Not only do we want to lead lives of consistency, but we depend upon it in others. When I climb onto an airplane, I insist upon a consistent pilot—let him be dull and predictable in his routine, as long as he delivers me to my destination in one piece. If a surgeon is operating on me, I don't want him to be the kind of doctor who has good days and bad days; I want to know that his results have been consistent in past operations. Coaches such as Mark Richt want quarterbacks who are reliable, who will make the right reads and throw the ball to players wearing the right color jersey—*consistently*.

As a matter of fact, we want these people to be confident as well as consistent. Their self-assurance becomes our self-assurance. Confident and consistent: Both of these words begin with the prefix of *con*, which means "with." *Confidence* means "with faith" while *consistency* translates to "with a place"—that is, the idea of standing firm like the tree planted by the river. It has a place, its roots are deep, and it's not budging an inch. When we are centered in Christ and confident in His Word, we can be consistent. We can stand firm because our faith is built on nothing less than Jesus and His righteousness. And when the sky is falling and everyone else is running around frantically, we can walk calmly in the Spirit.

Sometimes we read God's Word and think: *What do you want from me, Lord? I'm doing the best I can!* It's a tough world, and we often feel that we have to be many kinds of people to survive—the rough-and-tumble business world requires one kind of performance, parenting another, and so forth. Even Paul wrote, "I have become all things to all men, that I might by all means save some" (1 Corinthians 9:22).

Yes, but Paul was talking about our identifying with all people, as Christ did, in order to bring them the gospel. Paul never wavered from his walk or his true identity in Christ. Therefore we want to follow Paul's model and be strong enough to be faithful, and flexible enough to be useful. God isn't picking on us, far from it. In fact, He calls on us to be faithful because it is for our best good. "And now little children, abide in Him, that when He appears, we may have confidence and not be ashamed before Him at His coming" (1 John 2:28).

We can't escape this biblical message, foreign as it sounds to the vast majority today who never give a thought to His return. The message is that our lives should be shaped by the certainty that we are living between His first appearance and His final one. In the interim, we are visitors to this world but citizens of heaven. He will return here that He may return us there, and the point is that we should not be making ourselves at home in this world, with its ways. The consistency we want is one attuned to the ways of the spiritual world—the reality of Christ.

## The Marks of Our Consistency

"And now, little children, abide in Him" (1 John 2:28*a*), John writes as an affectionate father to his family. He refers to his readers as "little children" five times in this one chapter. He is the apostle of love, and he embodies that virtue in all his writing. In his gospel, we know him as "the disciple that Jesus loved" (John 13:23; 19:26; 20:2; 21:7; 21:20). He tells us in this letter that "God is love" (1 John 4:8). He even knows a loving way to describe the idea of consistency: the beautiful word *abiding*.

*Abide* is found eighty-two times in the King James Version of the Bible and very seldom in our daily language. When we speak of abiding, it is usually in some legalistic sense: a law-*abiding* citizen; one who *abides* by the rules. In John's discourse, the word means so much more than toeing the line. The Greek translates it as "to continue, to stay in a relationship, to remain, to be consistent." When we abide in Christ, we remain consistent in our relationship with Him. We believe His truth, we obey His Spirit, and we stay steadfast in our love for Him and for His children.

J. Hudson Taylor, the pioneer missionary to China, had been working far too hard, pushing himself to the breaking point. His friends feared he was nearing a breakdown. Fellow missionary John McCarthy sent him a letter in which he shared his personal discovery about the joy of abiding in Christ, based on John 15. McCarthy wrote that abiding does not mean striving or struggling but simply trusting

Christ to provide the necessary power. This had been a helpful insight for him, and he shared it in his letter of encouragement. He reminded Taylor that Christ is "the only power for service; the only ground for unchanging joy."

As Hudson Taylor read this letter at his mission station at Chinkiang on Saturday, September 4, 1869, his own eyes were opened. "As I read," he recalled, "I saw it all. I looked to Jesus; and when I saw, oh how the joy flowed!" To his sister in England, he wrote: "As to work, mine was never so plentiful, so responsible, or so difficult; but the weight and strain are all gone. The last month or more has been perhaps the happiest of my life; and I long to tell you a little of what the Lord has done for my soul . . . the Spirit of God revealed the truth of our oneness with Jesus as I had never known it before."

McCarthy had written: "But how to get faith strengthened? Not by striving after faith, but by resting on the Faithful One."[3] That is, *abiding*.

Most of us find ourselves to be sprinters in life rather than marathon runners. We're capable of bursts of speed and productivity, but we can't sustain the effort. Marathon runners have something to teach us about consistency. They find just the right zone of energy exertion, and they abide there physically. It's the same way with abiding in Christ. Many of us go from peak to valley, dedication to dryness, and we struggle with the sustained walk of faith. If we charted our spiritual walk, it would look like the recent stock market—wildly varying. We want that walk to be represented by a line, straight and unwavering as possible, climbing to higher values—what Eugene Peterson has called it in a book titled *A Long Obedience in the Same Direction*.[4] That's the life of godly consistency.

In a *Leadership Journal* cartoon, the pastor is speaking to his congregation: "We have a special gift for a lady that hasn't missed a service in forty-five years. Eleanor Smith! Where is Eleanor sitting? Eleanor? Eleanor . . ."[5] Oops!

I'll admit to hearing a speaker at some event, who informed us that she hadn't missed her morning appointment with God in more than four years. My natural human impulse was one of immediate resentment because I knew I lacked such perfect consistency.

Not long ago, I came across this prayer: "Dear Lord, so far today I am doing all right. I have not gossiped, lost my temper, been greedy, grumpy, nasty, selfish, or self-indulgent. I have not whined, complained, or cursed. I have yet to charge a penny on my credit card. Now, as I prepare to rise from bed this morning, I'll need your help more than ever."

That's someone who feels like many of us: intimidated on the way to the starting line. We've charged into diet plans, certain that nothing could stop us. We've begun fitness campaigns, keep-the-house-clean initiatives, and countless strategies for getting up early for devotions, for the rest of our lives. But the best-laid plans fall apart; sad and dejected, we quietly begin setting our goals much lower, so we won't shame ourselves again. We settle for a life of sporadic progress, fits and starts.

All the while God's Spirit whispers in our ear, "Don't condemn yourself! God's grace covers you. But you need not give up. There is unlimited power in trusting your heavenly Father and moving forward with each new day." He wants us to enjoy a consistent walk. We'll find out how to do that by following this wonderful word *abide* through the New Testament. Each usage gives us another piece of the puzzle in assembling the total picture of consistency.

# Consistently Christ-like

Listen to John's words: "He who says he abides in Him ought himself also to walk just as He walked" (1 John 2:6).

If your goal is consistency—defined in this chapter as abiding in Christ—then the key is to follow the Leader. Jesus shows us the way through His own life. We are called *Christians*, "Christ-Ones," and by that definition we want to live as He lived.

Again we feel intimidated—who can live up to the name of Jesus? I've read that Alexander the Great heard that a man in his army shared his name (all but the "Great" portion of it). Whereas the general was wildly courageous and visionary, the other guy might as well have been known as Alexander the Wimp. The leader called the soldier to his quarters, looked him straight in the eyes, and said, "You call yourself Alexander? Then either change your character or change your name."

If we determine to practice the discipline of abiding, we will discover that it isn't accomplished through some rote formula or by adhering to the steps of a self-help book. The only way to become like Christ is to humbly accept Him as both Savior and Lord and allow the Holy Spirit to begin His program of renovation within us.

An old missionary friend told me that his strategy for a consistent walk was to spend time every day meditating on the passion, death, burial, and resurrection of Christ. While he does other things during his devotional time, he always ends up immersing himself in the awesome, love-driven sacrifice of the Savior. He told me that when he began to follow this discipline, it changed his life.

So if you want a consistent walk, begin with consistent focus on Jesus and how He pursued life. A sermon here and a Bible study lesson there will never implant within your heart all that you need to know. You must develop a personal passion to know Jesus Christ as only the Scriptures can help you know Him.

Just as the character in Nathaniel Hawthorne's "The Great Stone Face" stared for years at the semblance of a face on the cleft a rock and in time took on those features himself, so you, if you look continually on the face of Christ, will become consistently like Him.

## Consistently Caring

John says, "He who loves his brother abides in the light, and there is no cause for stumbling in him" (1 John 2:10). This is one of John's favorite themes. In his written letters, he is consistently telling us that love is the proof of our being in Christ.

John tells us that we know we've passed from death to life by the way we love one another, and where there is love, there is Christ. As Christians, loving is what we do. Have you ever been among genuine, serious Christians and watched how they treat each other? Nonbelievers don't quite understand; it all seems very strange and unnatural to them. But we understand. We know that when we give our hearts to Christ, He gives us hearts for others. We can then love in a way that would never have been possible without Him.

As far as John is concerned, the full command of Christ is this: believe on the Son; love one another (1 John 3:23). Then he gives us that lovely verse that so many of us have memorized: "Beloved, let us love one another, for love is of God; and everyone who loves is born of God and knows God. He who does not love does not know God, for God is love" (4:7–8). Could anything be clearer? God is all about love, and anyone without love hasn't been in His presence lately, plain and simple.

Finally, John comes at the same message from the opposite direction. Loving God and hating others, he says, is a contradiction in terms. It's impossible to love an invisible God when we can't manage to love a visible brother (v. 20). In other words, if you are Christian, here is the test: love the people you know—really love them. That's what real Christians do. Anything else is simply playing religious games.

For most of us modern Christ-followers, hate is not the issue. The opposite of love is not hate but apathy. Apathy is oblivious to the needs of others. You may know about the thousands of Ukrainian children in orphanages, many of whom have been abandoned by parents who were unable to care for them. Maryna was a Tufts University doctoral student who found out that the care these children were receiving was insufficient. The children got the necessities, but no focused love; as many as fifteen different caregivers would be in and out of their lives in a week. These helpers were trained to avoid bonding with the children because they had to keep moving; there were just too many children for individual relationships.

This sad arrangement guaranteed poor cognitive and emotional development for the orphans. Maryna felt compelled to find a solution. So she started a "Big Sister" orphanage program, designed to provide every child with a university student to talk and play with him or her for five days of the week for one whole year. The difference to the children was profound. Maryna saw a need, felt compassion, and then did something about it.[6]

Mark Richt, the football coach I mentioned earlier, also felt moved by God to do something. He and his Bible group were studying James 1:27, a verse that says "pure and undefiled religion" includes caring for widows and orphans. He realized he couldn't read that verse and just walk away from its implications. Though the Richts had their own children, they traveled to Ukraine and studied pictures of the orphans. "It just seemed like God was prodding us," Katharyn Richt said. They came across the picture of a child born with a terrible facial deformity and learned that no one was likely to adopt such a child. The Richts felt God tugging at their hearts. This would be their new daughter. Finally, they came home with two new adopted children, and the Richts have a large, happy family that has become a wonderful testimony to the power of Christ's love.[7]

## Consistently Confident

"I have written to you, young men, because you are strong, and the word of God abides in you" (1 John 2:14).

You've noticed the subtitle of this section, and you're wondering what that verse has to do with becoming confident—and what confidence has to do with consistency. The truth is that as the Word of God permeates our lives, as we reflect daily on the nature of Christ and come to know Him in an intimate way, we begin to feel an inner strength we never knew before. And strength always produces confidence.

I've seen this in my life and in many believers who discipline themselves in God's Word. Its truth and its power begin to radiate from their personalities. The Scriptures are sprinkled through their talk as the Holy Spirit calls up verses from their memories to apply to every conversation, every new situation. You'll notice that Paul is constantly quoting the Old Testament. Do you think he kept a copy nearby, on the ship, in the tent, or inside the prison cell he was occupying, or do you think he kept the Word of God engraved in his heart? Notice how Jesus answered every temptation from the devil with the written

Word of God. These men, and those who have followed their lead, have continued in the Word until it continued in them. As you do the same, strength and confidence will characterize everything you do.

Professors from the Universities of Toronto and York recently announced that they had identified a connection between faith and anxiety. They had investigated whether a belief in God impacted personal stress. What they discovered through their studies was that the brains of spiritually driven people are calmer in the face of uncertainty. The scholars held a firm conclusion that those with a belief in God had 33 percent less brain response to anxiety; those with an outright certainty of God's existence demonstrated 45 percent less anxiety than atheists. Finally it was concluded that religious people are more effective in decision making. Knowing God builds strength, confidence, and a calm approach.[8]

## Consistently Compliant

We must be hearers of the Word, but we must also be doers of it. As nice as it is to know we will do better in dealing with anxiety, there is a far richer benefit: "He who does the will of God abides forever" (1 John 2:17). Yes, that's a promise. If you live as God wants you to, then you will enjoy eternal life in His presence.

Who would you say is the most submissive and compliant person you've ever heard about? Jesus may not be the first name that came to your mind, but He is the correct answer. There was nothing passive or hesitant about Him, but every moment of His life was lived in full obedience to God. Even when He faced the unimaginable prospect of arrest, torture, and crucifixion, He affirmed God's will and submitted to it. Here is how obedient He was: "He humbled Himself and became obedient to the point of death, even the death of the cross" (Philippians 2:8).

Jesus said: "My food is to do the will of Him who sent Me, and to finish His work'" (John 4:34). Again: "I do not seek My own will but the will of the Father who sent Me" (5:30). Jesus is the ultimate model of obedience and submission to God's will.

What that will is, of course, is the great question for many people. They seem to believe God has hidden it from them, and it's up to them to go look for it under every leaf. The will of God for your life is spelled out in Scripture. There's no magic formula; you won't discover His will by placing your Bible under your pillow at night. But as you develop a consistent pattern of reading God's Word and meditating on it, you will begin to sense the reality of God's will at work in your life!

The name of the college you should attend or the person you should marry will not be contained in any verse. But you will find many specific directives to get you serving the Lord, and the specific answers will be revealed as you are consumed by the work of God rather than your own self-interests. The Bible will show you what to do; the question is, are you are willing to do it?

## Consistently Consistent

I've saved the best for last. How about being "consistently consistent"?

John says, "Therefore let that abide in you which you heard from the beginning. If what you heard from the beginning abides in you, you will also abide in the Son and in the Father" (1 John 2:24). Only as the Word abides in you, will you abide in Christ.

Did you notice that the word *abide* appears three times in that one verse? Substitute it with the word *continue*, and read it again. You'll get the point. If we continue with the basics of the Word, we will continue with God.

So many of us began with a deep devotion to Christ, but we took detours from the narrow path of obedience. We are all prone to wander. Abiding is not about never missing your appointment with God. It is more about finding your way back when you stray. As the old song says, "pick yourself up, dust yourself off, and start all over again."[9]

Amy Carmichael was a product of a wealthy Irish home with every advantage. But Amy's parents had no intention of sheltering their children from the needs of others less fortunate. The whole family got involved in mission and ministry projects, serving the poor and hungry. Amy's father was generous with his resources in a way that made an impression on his offspring.

Sitting in a fashionable teahouse in Belfast one day, Amy looked out the window to see a small girl, barefoot and dressed in rags. As the rain came down, the little girl was pressing her nose against the window, gazing hungrily at the cookies and pastries on display. The image would not leave Amy's mind. That afternoon, she wrote on a scrap of paper:

> When I grow up and money have
> I know what I will do;
> I'll build a great and lovely place
> For little girls like you.

But then hard times came for Amy and her family. When she was seventeen, her father died. Rather than give into the bitterness of her loss, Amy began an outreach in the slums of Belfast. As many as five hundred poor factory girls were helped by this mission. It was just the beginning of what God would do with Amy Carmichael. She went to India as a missionary, and there she fulfilled her old pledge and built a lovely home in honor of the little poor girl in Belfast. She established what we know today as the Dohnavur Fellowship to save children from the human trafficking that was so prevalent in that region.

Amy Carmichael never came home again. She spent her remaining thirty-five years in India, serving Christ with love and boundless energy. She created a lovely home for one thousand children who might have become slaves or prostitutes. And even though Amy herself became an invalid, she kept on keeping on. From the physical pain that was always with her, she had one prayer request: "Ask for me one thing . . . ask for selflessness, power to help, console, lift the edges of the burdens if I can't lift the whole. Ask for love that forgets all but others."[10]

Amy Carmichael is a hard act for us to follow. That's a high level of consistency and submission. But we don't have to match that standard today; we can start right where we are. We do not need to go to India or even Belfast to be obedient to God. He will let us know what He requires, and He will give us the desire and the talent to do whatever that is. What He does expect is for us to begin to be consistently consistent as we follow Him.

## The Motive for Our Consistency

Here is our motivation for walking consistently with Christ: "When He appears . . . at His coming" (1 John 2:28). I heard about a woman who had a firm understanding of this point. A preacher friend of mine was in line at a big store. The woman was ahead of him, and she was holding up progress with a request that was out of the ordinary. The previous night, the store had charged her for one pencil sharpener. She had bought two; now she was returning to pay for the other one.

The cashier couldn't figure out how to handle a day-old correction. The manager, equally nonplussed, pleaded with the woman to simply keep both sharpeners with no additional payment. It really wasn't worth the trouble of refiguring. My pastor friend, possibly sensing a great sermon illustration, followed the woman out of the store and asked her why she was so meticulously honest. She replied, "The way things are going in this world, the Rapture is going to happen any day, and I didn't want to be caught with a stolen pencil sharpener."

We chuckle over that one merely because her point of view is so foreign to most of us. At any given moment there are probably fifty subjects closer to the top of our minds than the return of Christ. If it didn't happen yesterday, we believe that means it won't happen today—though in reality, of course, His return is that much more likely. Do you want to be caught with a stolen pencil sharpener? A shoddy job performance? Arguing with your spouse, cheating on your income taxes, inactive at church?

My friend Charles Swindoll worked in a machine shop while he was a college student. Every day when the whistle blew at the end of the shift, the other workers would hustle around to get their lunch pails and their clothes. By 5:15 or so, they'd be walking out the door. There was only one fellow who was way ahead of the pack. It seemed as if he was on his way to the parking lot thirty seconds after the whistle, lunch pail in hand, coat over his shoulder. One day, Swindoll asked him, "How do you get out so fast?"

The man replied, "Listen, boy . . . I stay ready to keep from gettin' ready."[11]

It's not a bad strategy. Christ is going to return, and we need to *stay* ready so we won't have to *get* ready. Keep your house in order and you won't have to put it in order. Keep your marriage from breaking so it won't have to be fixed. And stay on the path of consistent faith so you don't have to find your way back to it. The fact is that when the time comes, "getting ready" will not be an option.

Needless to say, the biggest question of all is whether you have accepted Christ as your Savior. If you have any doubts at all about that, stop right now and turn to the back of this book for a few words about how to surrender your life to him (see pages 233–235). The most important issue of your life, by an infinite margin, is your eternal destination. If you haven't settled it, don't you think it's about time?

## The Measure of Our Consistency

So how do we measure consistency? John says we will know we're on the right track because "we may have confidence and not be ashamed before Him and at His coming" (1 John 2:28).

That verse speaks of a bold commitment, and one that may occasionally require courage. When eight hundred buses in England, Scotland, and Wales carried those wide atheistic banners reading, *There's Probably No God. Now Stop Worrying and Enjoy Your Life*, some agreed with the message, some ignored it, but Ron Heather, a sixty-two-year-old bus driver, was horrified as he read the words plastered on his assigned bus. He knew that he just could not drive a bus bearing that message.

Heather took a stand and refused to drive the bus. Since there were no alternate buses he could drive, he simply went home. If it came to quitting his job, he was ready for that, too, even in the economic realities of 2009. He would not support the mocking of his faith.

Heather didn't know what to expect when he returned to work the next day. His supervisors told him he could drive a bus that didn't bear such a banner. And the result was this: Heather's story, told all over the world, is having an influence vastly broader than that of a few buses bearing cynical messages. His courage and consistency are inspiring others to be bold in the workplace.[12] Here is what John would say about that: "You are of God, little children, and have overcome them, because He who is in you is greater than he who is in the world" (1 John 4:4).

When Jesus comes, we will either be assured or ashamed. The Bible teaches that we will give an account of all the things we have done. That fact should cause us to be taking a pre-inventory of those activities right now. Some ask, "What would Jesus do?" Another question to ask is, "Would I be assured or ashamed if He returned right now?"

Our first event after Jesus returns will be an appearance before the judgment seat of Christ. Please understand that we will not be judged for sin. All of that was handled at the cross! But the Bible does say that " . . . we must all appear before the judgment seat of Christ, that each one may receive the things done in the body, according to what he has done, whether good or bad" (2 Corinthians 5:10). Our sins may be forgiven, but our work will not be forgotten!

## Will We Be Assured?

How can we be assured and not ashamed? First, our confidence is the result of our productivity. John quotes Jesus as saying to us, "Abide in Me, and I in you. As the branch cannot bear fruit of itself, unless it abides in the vine, neither can you, unless you abide in Me" (John 15:4). If we are abiding in Christ, we are bearing fruit. When we see God at work in our lives, we become confident in His power.

Our confidence also comes from our prayerfulness. Jesus continues, "If you abide in Me, and My words abide in you, you will ask what you desire, and it shall be done for you" (v. 7). Abiding in Christ puts us on the right wavelength with God's will, and we tend to ask for things in tune to what He wants. As we watch Him work in us through prayer, our confidence in Him grows and matures and when we stand before Him on that day, we will be assured.

The Bible says that five different crowns will be presented at the judgment seat of Christ. We won't walk around in heaven wearing these crowns, as if there could be pride or boasting in heaven; instead, we will lay them at the feet of our Savior in an act of worship. I'm convinced that the most coveted prize will be hearing our Lord say, "Well done, good and faithful servant. Enter into the joy of your Lord."

## Will We Be Ashamed?

How will it be possible to enter the gates of heaven and be ashamed? Believe it or not, this will occur for many people. Some Christians who have been unfaithful to God will be in heaven. The precious blood of Christ was shed as much for their sins as for the most fruitful and productive of saints. But these will be Christians who have accepted the gift without ever prizing it. Now, standing before the throne, they will see everything clearly. They will know their foolishness and feel shame, even in the midst of salvation. The Lord will say, "My precious child, I bled for you on the cross. I gave all that I had, and what did you do with My gift?" What answer other than remorseful silence can follow?

It is after this, according to the Bible, that God will wipe away every tear, and we will all enter into His joy and perfection. I don't want to begin eternity in a brief instant of self-humiliation. I'm sure you don't either.

So I'm going to stay ready to keep from getting ready. When I rise from my bed each morning, I'm going to ask the Lord to strengthen me, so that my eyes will remain focused on that eternal prize. I'm going to work with all my heart here on earth, but in spirit, my bags will be packed. I'm going to keep short accounts, holding no grudges, having no unfinished business in my personal relationships. And I'm going to understand to the best of my ability exactly what God wants me to do each day and do it with all my heart and soul.

Both of our sons loved football and excelled as quarterbacks. One of them is currently a scout in the NFL. As a guest at his training camp, I've observed the team's preparation for the season. I was especially curious to discover how a quarterback develops consistency. It turns out that the secret is *reps*—short for repetition. A starting quarterback receives all the reps in daily practice. He throws the ball in each drill, working on every route and every play from his team's playbook. Over and over he repeats the precise steps of his footwork, the reading of the defense, and the mechanics of his release. In the end, he has a kind of "body memory" that is close to perfection for executing the attack strategy of a professional team. His movement is smooth, fluid, and confident.

My own sport was basketball. I spent endless hours in the gym, all for the purpose of being an accurate shooter from every angle. A friend would stand under the hoop and toss the ball back after each shot, and I would work on shooting from the left, from the right, from the free throw line, and everywhere else until each shot became part of my DNA. When I got into a game, my body took over and knew exactly what to do, precisely how much "touch" to put on a shot from any position. Reps made the difference.

Here are the reps that will guide you toward perfect execution of the Christian life. The first drill is to study your Bible reflectively each day. The second is to be a person of prayer—regular and disciplined. Do these things over and over, for every situation. There will be days you don't feel like doing these things, just as the quarterback, aching from yesterday's scrimmage, isn't too keen on today's drills. But those hard-nosed decisions to be consistent will separate you from the luke-warm faith crowd. They will cause you to experience Christ in ways you never could have anticipated.

Read, pray, serve, repeat. Do this every day, and on that wondrous day when Christ returns, you will stand before Him without shame. Having walked consistently in this life, you will walk in boundless joy into the perfect consistency that is called heaven.

But before you get there, your consistency in Christ may well be tested in ways you can't imagine today. Indeed, the Bible says that a one-world government, ruled by a man with delusions of deity, will dictate economic, political, and religious policy for the nations. And that everyone on earth will be required to swear loyalty to him upon pain of death for refusing.

If you are a Christian, you won't be on earth during the seven years when the antichrist ruler is fully in charge. But you and I may well be alive when the world begins to experience the birth pangs of his arrival—intense, increasingly frequent, and painful probes into the freedom of our spiritual life. They will start small—like officials say-ing you can't hold a Bible study in your home—and grow larger. Now, not then, is the time to decide whether you are going to live consis-tently for Christ, regardless of the cost.

The only way to be strong enough on the day it happens to you is to put in your spiritual reps daily. You can't get in shape for the most important contest of your life on the morning of the big game. You must live consistently today in order to pass the test tomorrow.

# NINE

# Stay Committed

HE TOLD HIS FAMILY HE WAS GOING BACK TO THE OFFICE. HE drove to the parking lot of the company where he had made his fortune and stepped out into the early darkness of the frigid January evening. Instead of heading to the entrance of the familiar building, he climbed up the embankment, down the other side, and threw himself under the 5:30 train as it sped past his plant. He was seventy-four years old. He reportedly left a note for his family saying, "I'm sorry."[1]

There were many such stories in the newspapers early this year. This one happened to be about the great German drug manufacturer, Adolf Merckle. He was one of the richest men in the world, a billionaire more than nine times over. He lived a quiet life with a wonderful wife and four loving children. Despite their enormous wealth, they reportedly lived quite modestly.[2] As a young man, Merckle inherited his family's chemical business and developed it into one of the world's greatest pharmaceutical companies—Merck & Co.

He seemed to have a Midas-like intuition when it came to business dealings. He grew his family's small chemical/pharmaceutical manufacturing business from eighty employees in 1967 to nearly one hundred thousand in 2008. That year Merckle was the fifth-richest man in Germany, and Forbes ranked him in the top 20 percent of the world's richest.[3]

He was "a symbol of Germany's industrious spirit,"[4] with one notable deviation: a few years ago he began to take greater risks in the stock market. In an interview shortly before his death, he blamed the whole thing on "'a chain reaction' that broke the financial model that had worked 'superbly' before the crisis."[5] We will never know what caused the foundation of his confidence to crumble. But he was not alone in his descent into despair.

A day or two after Merckle's death, *Wall Street Journal* recorded the apparent suicide of the fifty-two-year-old real estate auction tycoon, Steven Good. In his red Jaguar, parked in a wildlife preserve near Chicago, he took his life with a single shot.[6] He left no note.

Then, in the week following that incident, a desperate money manager, who was also an amateur aerial acrobat, faked his own death in an airplane accident. With the controls set on autopilot, Marcus Schrenker, thirty-eight, bailed out over Alabama and left the plane to crash. He then drove his previously stashed motorcycle to a KOA campgrounds in Florida, where he was discovered three days later, unconscious and with a wrist slashed in a failed suicide attempt. In a statement before his trial began recently, he is quoted as saying that he had "snapped" and "it all came crashing down around me."[7] Now it's federal prison bars that are crashing around him.

Frayed nerves will snap. Chain reactions will sidetrack superb financial models, financial and emotional foundations will crumble, and irrational decisions will continue to plague today's society.

I'm not reassured by western political leaders who tell us prosperity is just around the corner. Hopefully, the economy will perk up in the immediate future, but one Wall Street guru warned: "The credit markets are in a shambles, the banking system is hanging by a thread, and the consumer is out of gas. Traders are clinging to the slim hope that the worst is over, but they could be mistaken. There's probably another leg down, and it will be more vicious than the last."[8]

You and I and our spouses and children—each man, woman, and child in America—currently owe thirty-seven thousand dollars per person in national debt, and it's getting worse by the day. A columnist in my home state of California stated the obvious when he wrote, "The severe economic downturn has exposed the state's finances as a delicate house of cards just waiting to collapse."[9] He could have been talking about the entire world economic system. Americans have transferred vast amounts of wealth to Middle Eastern oil producers and, in the process, borrowed over a trillion dollars from the People's Republic of China.

Many people see their jobs hanging by a thread and their own finances teetering like a house of cards. A Charlotte newspaper just reported that paramedics recently responded to eighty-one suicide attempts in eighteen days. It's no accident, said mental health authorities, that the upturn in attempted suicides coincided with the downturn of the economy, which included spikes in the city's unemployment and home foreclosure rates. "I can't believe it's not related to the economy," said one doctor.[10]

Where do people turn when times are tough? One school of thought says they go to church. As we mentioned in a previous chapter, there's evidence to support that. After the 9/11 terrorist attacks and other crises, church parking lots have needed extra spaces. But for every action there is an equal and opposite reaction. "Economic turbulence might give" gamblers, partygoers, drinkers, and smokers "more reason to indulge," says Thomas Anderson in *Kiplinger's Personal Finance* February 2008 issue, making "so-called sin stocks . . . a safe bet."

Isn't it intriguing? A crisis is really a fork in the road. You have two choices, a high road and a low one. Jesus used this kind of language when He said there was a broad way on which most people travel while His own path is a narrow one walked by few (Matthew 7:13–14). During trial and tragedy, some shake their fists at the heavens and say that this proves there is no God. Others come precisely to the opposite conclusion, saying they never found God to be so real or His comfort so encouraging. Testing reveals character—it is true of individuals, it is true of churches, and it is true of nations.

Without question, these are fearful days. Billionaire investment guru Warren Buffett has observed, "I have never seen Americans more fearful. It takes five minutes to become fearful, much more to regain confidence." He adds a profound statement, "The [financial] system does not work without confidence."[11]

Meanwhile, we find that stimulus plans, bailouts, and whatever else that is tried or not tried begins another contentious debate. The stakes are simply so high, and there is so little consensus about the way forward, that we find bickering within and among nations. The current president of the European Parliament called our emergency stimulus program "a way to hell." Furthermore, he said, it will "undermine the stability of the global financial market."[12]

We see all these things and recognize, once again, the signs of a civilization edging toward its final climax. The more chaotic things become, the easier it is for us to gravitate toward some social extreme—a path of least resistance, whether it's despair, anger, or simply closing our eyes and pretending that everything is fine.

An alternate suggestion: what about sitting down, reflecting on the sovereignty of Almighty God, and reminding ourselves that nothing takes Him by surprise? He is in no way confined by the limits of the moment. He rules from outside the realm of time, which is simply one more element of His complex sovereignty. He foresaw this moment at the foundation of the world, and it has its proper place in His great plan. It is woven, along with everything else, into the infinitely fine tapestry of His will and work.

Knowing that fact brings profound peace. If the world believed it, people wouldn't turn to whiskey, gambling, and narcotics. There would be less of a frenzy these days, and that would be good for everybody. People would understand that the true destiny of creation is in good hands, and believers would surge forward with new determination to seize the day for His glory. These are the times in which the hope of our Lord shines most brightly through the world's murky fog. Our destiny is decided: we will be reclaimed by the returning Christ to spend eternity in His presence. For now, we have the exciting task of seeing how many people we can bring along with us on that journey.

## Hurry Up and Wait

James, the most practical of New Testament writers, tells us, "Therefore be patient, brethren, until the coming of the Lord. See how the farmer waits for the precious fruit of the earth, waiting patiently for it until it receives the early and latter rain. You also be patient. Establish your hearts, for the coming of the Lord is at hand" (James 5:7–8).

As we await the Lord's return, therefore, we are to be patient. That ability comes from strengthening the foundation of our faith. The stronger our convictions, the better we'll handle challenging times.

There is a direct correspondence between the strength of one's faith and the depth of his patience.

Patience can be one of the most elusive virtues, even for the hopeful. It's certainly not one of our nation's best attributes. During the Reagan administration, Richard Nixon was interviewed about the subject of peace in the world. He was asked whether the nation was better off than it had been one year previously. Nixon replied, "As Americans, we have many great strengths, but one of our weaknesses is impatience. The Russians think in terms of decades, the Chinese in terms of centuries. Americans think in terms of years, and months, and days . . ."[13]

Someone said that patience has a bitter taste, but a sweet aftertaste. I wonder if any of us would labor with the steadfastness of some of the great Christian missionaries of the past—or have the commitment of their boards and overseers who hung in there with them. When the gospel was brought to Western Africa by missionaries, fourteen years passed before a single convert came to faith. It required ten years in Eastern Africa and sixteen years in Tahiti to win the first soul. William Carey is considered the father of the modern missions movement, yet it took him seven years to convert his first Hindu.[14] Adoniram Judson, America's first missionary, labored six years before he baptized the first Burmese believer.[15] More patient than his supporting churches, he once wrote home: "Beg the churches to have patience, success is as certain as the promise of a faithful God can make it."[16]

In all of those places the aftertaste of patience was sweet because workers for Christ—and their sponsors—knew how to wait upon the Lord and trust His timetable. Difficult? Absolutely. But patience is God's classroom for instructing us in faith and obedience. If we didn't have so much to learn, perhaps we wouldn't have so long to wait. We want to do well in this course of instruction. Let's learn what the Word of God has to teach us about waiting, trusting, and hoping.

## The Instruction of Patience

I like the way J. I. Packer describes our daily business: "living out the belief that God orders everything for the spiritual good of his children. Patience does not just grin and bear things, stoic-like, but accepts them cheerfully as therapeutic workouts planned by a heavenly trainer who is resolved to get you up to full fitness."[17]

That kind of believer understands that God is in control even when something unpleasant occurs. He accepts it as one more obscure, multisided piece of the jigsaw puzzle of his life—for which he has no box cover pattern. He trusts the One who sees the finished project and seeks to develop trust-based patience. Puritan Thomas Watson wrote, "There are no sins God's people are more subject to than unbelief and impatience; they are ready, either to faint through unbelief, or to fret through impatience."[18]

If you think back over your life, you're bound to realize that while a doctor needs bright light to do his surgery, God likes to work in the dark. We don't learn character when life is cruising along—only when it demands us to reach within ourselves and find new patience, new faith in God, and new resources to overcome the obstacles.

Perhaps your family is coping with difficult times at present. What if you viewed this as a time of revelation from God, an occasion for learning to trust Him, and a stepping-stone to good things in the future? That's how God has always worked, so why would this occasion be any different? If you and your family were to begin the coming week with that attitude firmly entrenched in your collective soul, giving thanks to God all the way, how much better would your week feel?

If you were to thumb through my Bible, you would find all kinds of markings and quick notes. I write these things down as they occur to me because they might be helpful next time I come to the same passage. I've noted that the word *patience* (or a synonym for it) is found seven times in James chapter five. It's remarkable how this idea keeps coming to the top. I've italicized them in this list:

- "Be *patient* . . . until the coming of the Lord" (James 5:7).
- "The farmer *waits* for the precious fruit of the earth, *waiting patiently* for it . . ." (v. 7).
- "You also be *patient* . . ." (v. 8).
- "Take the prophets, who spoke in the name of the Lord, as an example of *suffering* and *patience*" (v. 10).
- "Indeed we count them blessed who *endure*. You have heard of the *perseverance* of Job . . ." (v. 11).

*Patience. Waiting. Suffering. Endurance. Perseverance.* These are not the ingredients of popular preaching or reading these days. We're addicted to happy thoughts and synthetic optimism—sweet little lies though they may be. Back in the real world, life is filled with waiting and enduring.

Like many of us, the apostle Paul was not the type of man who enjoyed delay. He was visionary and ambitious—a whirlwind of kinetic energy who was evangelizing nonbelievers, mentoring young believers, and shepherding whole congregations all at the same time. Yet he was also a man who knew and trusted his Lord well enough to know how to trust God's schedule. As he wrote letters from political confinement, he might have been expected to rage in frustration against the Roman obstacles that hindered all the things he wanted to do for God. What we find is just the opposite. He wrote his friends at Philippi, "My chains are in Christ" (Philippians 1:13). He recounted how he was able to share the gospel with the palace guard, and how his correspondents had grown bolder in their faith because of his experiences. A letter of anguish for anyone else becomes an epistle of joy for Paul. As long as he knew God was doing something—and when is God not doing something?—he was able to find contentment.

In 1 Corinthians, Paul gives us the greatest paragraphs on love that were ever written, and patience finds its way into the mix. What is the very first attribute of godly love in his list? "Love is patient, love is kind. It does not envy, it does not boast, it is not proud" (1 Corinthians 13:4 NIV). Then, when we check Galatians 5:22 for the fruit of the Spirit—the crucial qualities that develop in us as we grow—we find patience (*longsuffering* in a few translations) in a prominent place, just after the immortal triad of love, joy, and peace. Paul obviously had a high regard for the kind of quality that must not have come easy to a vigorous, eager evangelist.

If patience, longsuffering, and perseverance are so critically important, why then are they so difficult for us? I believe the reason is that this pattern of faithful response can only be learned through tribulation. Paul again: "And not only that, but we also glory in tribulations, knowing that tribulation produces perseverance; and perseverance, character; and character, hope" (Romans 5:3–4).

When I begin a new day, tribulation is generally not on my list of requests to God: "Lord, can you really hit me with something nerve-racking today? My character needs a good test!" I wouldn't expect anyone to include that request in his or her prayer time. Yet in a sense, it would make sense to do so, if Christian maturity is our goal. Tribulation teaches us to hang in there, and hanging in there develops character in us. And that, Paul tells us, produces something incredibly wonderful: *hope*. And when we say *hope*, we're not talking about a mild desire for something to happen, as in, "I hope it doesn't rain today." We're talking about a solid, foundationally positive outlook on life; an absolute persuasion that God has already won any conceivable battle that this day might concoct, and therefore we can smile confidently *no matter what*. Don't you think we need hope like that in times like these?

Again, don't feel compelled to pray for tribulation tomorrow. It's provided free of charge. Trials are coming to a circumstance near you whether you look for them or not. They enter the door without knocking, regardless of any padlock. This is because the world is fallen and also because God wants you to grow. That's why James stands with Paul in telling us to embrace the quality of patience; to look for it in ourselves during tough times, and to depend upon it to inspire us.

## But What's the Big Delay?

James was writing to believers who were suffering deeply. It was not easy to be a Christian in the first century. Many believers thought the only positive outcome for them would be for Christ to return as soon as possible; there was certainly nothing in this life to increase their hope. James was telling them, "Just be patient! If Christ delays, it is for good reason—He's not ready to give up on this world just yet, so neither should you or I be."

So true. Our Lord Jesus Christ is "the Alpha and the Omega, the Beginning and the End . . . the First and the Last" (Revelation 1: 8, 11).

He knows the end from the beginning, and sometimes delays occur in life because God still has work to do, circumstances to line up, unfinished business to complete. It's likely to be something wonderful. These are times to learn the discipline of waiting upon the Lord, having patience in His timing, and resting in the fact that His plan is a perfect one. [19]

I'm talking to more and more people who are fervently praying for Christ to return and stop the madness. They repeat the plea that is found in the final words of Scripture, "Even so, come, Lord Jesus!" (Revelation 22:20). According to the Pew Research Center, more than three-quarters of American Christians now believe in the second coming of Christ, and 20 percent feel fairly certain He will return in their lifetime.[20] Those are truly remarkable figures. We have to be pleased that so many understand that Christ will come back, and that this sorry world is not all that we have. Still, we can't get into the business of backseat driving with God. James understands that, and reminds us to be patient and let Him take the wheel.

Have you ever gotten frustrated on the freeway, when traffic came to a standstill? It always seems to happen when we need to be somewhere. We stew. We fume. We think, *What's the big delay here? This is ridiculous!* Then, ever so often, we reach the point of bottleneck and spot the ambulance and the stretchers. We sigh. We hush. We know something tragic has happened here, and we'd have waited more patiently if only we could have seen the big picture from above.

I've been an impatient patient in a few waiting rooms, haven't you? We flip restlessly through magazines and wait for a nurse to open the door and say those words, "The doctor will see you now." We are patients without patience. The word *patience* comes from a Latin word meaning "one who endures" or "one who suffers." At the doctor's office, we're required to wait with a calm attitude, and that's the biblical meaning of the word. Delays don't occur because someone—in heaven or on earth—is trying to irritate us personally. There are very good reasons in most cases; as far as heaven goes, in *all* cases.

A past presidential First Lady—and I mean our literal *first* First Lady—offers us an example of patience. Martha Washington wrote a friend in December of 1789, confessing that she would much rather be at home at Mount Vernon, playing with her four grandchildren, than serving as a symbolic presence in the nation's new capital in New York City. Yet "I am still determined to be cheerful and happy," she wrote, "in whatever situation I may be; for I have . . . learned from experience that the greater part of our happiness or misery depends upon our dispositions, and not upon our circumstances. We carry the seeds of the one or the other about with us, in our minds, wheresoever we go."[21]

That is a fragrant attitude, one pleasing to God. It gives evidence of the kind of maturity God wants to grow in all of us as we set our hearts on eternal things rather than superficial circumstances.

## The Illustration of Patience

James, who is always good with word pictures, now gives us a visual reference for patience. He turns to the agricultural world: "See how the farmer waits for the precious fruit of the earth, waiting patiently for it until it receives the early and the latter rain" (James 5:7).

James and his brother Jude both had backgrounds in farming, so that vocation provided a naturally rich field of analogy. In a farming culture, the "precious fruit of the earth" is an apt description of the importance of the soil and what originated from it. If you didn't farm well, you didn't eat. We also need to understand that there were no irrigation systems in first century Hebrew farming. The "early rain" started the growth cycle; the "latter rain" provided moisture to mature the harvest.

As I write these words, we are in the third year of drought in California. Central Valley farmers have learned they will receive no allocation of water this year. When this happens, there is no harvest. The life in the seed remains dormant. Here is what would happen with proper irrigation: Water, lots of water, would be absorbed to activate the process of growth. As the seed grows larger it eventually bursts from its confining walls. The tip of the root emerges, the seed is anchored, and the new plant absorbs water and nutrients directly from the surrounding soil.[22]

In a post-agricultural society such as ours, we don't understand these things intuitively; James did. As a farmer, he knew that nothing transpired without the water. And he could do nothing about that water because it fell from the heavens. His job was merely to cultivate the soil, plant the seed, and, if rain fell by the grace of God, to bring in the harvest. Patience is instinctive for farmers since they can't bring the rain they need from the clouds. As we await the return of Jesus, the analogy is crystal clear. Our job is simply to till the soil, to nurture each other, to make good use of the "early rain" (when Christ came to earth the first time), and to prepare for the "latter rain" when He will come to bring the harvest.

We smile when we think of first century impatience for the return of Christ. They'd been waiting for three decades, whereas we've been waiting for two hundred decades—two millennia. If we were farmers, we would say that the clouds had closed up forever, and that the rain would never fall again. It's been a while. So what is the evidence of His return? I'd like to suggest that we view the issue from this angle. How long did people wait for the first coming of Christ? We believe Genesis

3:15 offers the first mention of the coming Redeemer. In the second chapter of Luke, the prophecy comes to fruition. How long in between? No matter how you date the first pages of Genesis, it was a very long time. Two thousand years have passed since Christ promised His return, but that's less than half the number of years between Genesis and Luke. According to Jewish tradition we are in the year 5769; subtract 2009 and the result would be nearly four thousand years between Adam and the birth of Christ.

Alfred Edersheim, the Jewish historian and Hebrew scholar, describes the ancient rabbinic conversations on the delay of the Messiah's appearance. Some rabbis believed the Messiah was waiting for Israel to repent. Others felt that He was the One who would come and call for that repentance. According to the Talmud, there were rabbis who believed the Messiah would appear exactly four thousand years after the creation of the earth. Isn't that intriguing? Jesus Christ fit that estimate—He came during that very time frame. Rabbis were limited in what they could do. They could crunch the numbers on their calendars, they could peruse the words of the old prophets, they could hope and dream, but in the end, all they could do was wait. Edersheim writes, "One by one, all the terms had passed, and as despair settled on the heart of Israel, it came to be generally thought that the time of Messiah's Advent could not be known beforehand."[23]

So much for getting ahead of God.

## Heaven Standard Time

From the rabbinical perspective, the Messiah was delaying His appearance. God saw things differently. We find His own perspective in the book of Galatians: "But when the fullness of the time had

come, God sent forth his Son, born of a woman, born under the law"
(Galatians 4:4). That phrase "the fullness of the time" means God's
chronology. Only He knows when time is "full" of all the elements He
wants to have in place. Jesus came to earth the first time, for example,
when the Romans had built roads and connected a vast empire; when
an ideal language, perfect for explaining the gospel, united that
empire; when the Jews had established synagogues all over the
Mediterranean region to become "seed walls" for that gospel to burst
forth; and when all the Hebrew prophecies concerning His coming
had been uttered, so that the prophets had fallen silent. We can now
see just how precisely God selected His timetable for sending His Son
the first time. Is there any reason to believe that the time of His second coming will be any less precise?

For most people, the problem is not intellectual but spiritual. Even
in the apostle Peter's time, people simply did not want to accept any
possibility of Christ's coming; many were comfortably ensconced in
their sin. Peter wrote: "Scoffers will come in the last days, walking
according to their own lusts, and saying, 'Where is the promise of His
coming? For since the fathers fell asleep, all things are just like they
were from the beginning of creation'" (2 Peter 3:3–4).

Kevin Miller says that he knows an executive coach who asks the
following question to CEOs: "What are you pretending not to know?"
Miller writes:

> This is the same question Peter is asking of the people who think there's
> never going to be a Second Coming—who think that there's never
> going to be a final judgment or an end to the world. Peter says: You can
> tell yourself whatever you want, but the thought that there's never
> going to be an "end of the world" is not coming from an objective,

impartial evaluation of ideas. It's coming from your deep, unacknowledged desire to do whatever you want to and get away with it.[24]

Peter suggests that we never forget one fact: "That with the Lord one day is as a thousand years, and a thousand years is as one day. The Lord is not slack concerning His promise, as some count slackness, but is longsuffering toward us, not willing that any should perish but that all should come to repentance" (2 Peter 3:8–9).

Translation: God sets His watch to a time zone not accessible to us. Once again we need to remember that He is the one who created time, like everything else, and He uses it for his own purposes. He is not within it, wondering what's around the next bend, as we are; He is outside of it, in the eternal "now." He *made* the next bend.

The Puritan Stephen Charnock wrote: "He is not a temporary, but an eternal God . . . He is the dwelling place of His people in all generations . . . If he had a beginning, he might have an end, and so all our happiness, hope, and being would expire with Him . . . When we say God is eternal, we exclude from Him all possibility of beginning and ending, all flux and change."[25]

I like the little story about the foolishness of quantifying God's timing. A little boy asked God, "How long is a second in heaven?" God said, "One million years." The boy asked, "How much is a penny in heaven?" God answered, "One million dollars." The boy said, "Could I have a penny?" To which God answered, "In just a second."

## The Why of the Wait

God has His timetable. From our perspective, He waits. And what is He waiting for? In particular, for us to share the news about Him.

There is someone who needs to hear about Christ at this very moment, someone within your sphere of acquaintances. There are countries and peoples who are on the verge of hearing the good news or on the edge of a true revival. As Peter said, He is not willing that any should perish, and like the captain who won't push the lifeboat away until it is absolutely filled with people to save, God waits for the biggest throng that can be ushered into His heaven.

Jesus spelled it out for us: "And this gospel of the kingdom will be preached in all the world as a witness to all the nations, and then the end will come" (Matthew 24:14). The Great Commission and the return of Christ are intertwined in that way. If you want to see His return, go and tell others about Him.

Robert Ingersoll may well have been one of the most famous atheists of all time. Not only did he have no faith, but he had no hesitancy in telling others that they shouldn't either. He was a bit like those of our own era who blame Christians and their belief in God for nearly every crime or tragedy that has ever happened. In his traveling lectures, Ingersoll ridiculed everyone who believed in God. Part of his routine was to take out his pocket watch, open it, and say, "Almighty God, I'll give you five minutes to strike me dead for everything I've said." Then for three hundred seconds, he would wait for God to do something to him as he stared at the watch. When the time expired, he would say, "That proves there is no God," and he'd put away his timepiece.

When an evangelist by the name of Joseph Parker heard about it, he asked, "Did the gentleman believe that he could exhaust the patience of an eternal God in five minutes?"[26]

Abraham must have wondered when God was finally going to send the child that was promised, one who would be the firstborn of a new nation; God kept his promise in the fullness of time. David, hiding in

caves for a decade, must have wondered when God would finally fulfill His promise, given in David's boyhood, to put the shepherd on the
throne. God came through in due time. And the disciples must have
wondered when God was going to reach down into the machinery of
Roman cruelty and rescue Jesus from the torture, mockery, and execution that befell Him. When Jesus died on that cross, God seemed to
be out of time. On Sunday morning, in the fullness of time, God carried out the plan He'd conceived before the foundations of the earth.
Is there any reason to be impatient with our God?

I pray for things, not knowing when He will answer. I long for His
coming, having no inside knowledge of when He will appear. I want
to see the end of our local drought, the recovery of our economy, or
any number of other things that may seem delayed. But I know this:
*delay* is not a word found in God's vocabulary. Never yet has He been
too late or too early by even the flicker of an eyelash. He is not slack
regarding His promises, and we'll understand it better by and by. It's
the divine prerogative to schedule and the human prerogative to wait
in faithful patience.

## The Implications of Patience

Finally, we explore the implications of patience. In James 5:8, we learn
that we are to "establish our hearts." What exactly is an established
heart?

The phrase here means "make your heart firm." One New Testament
paraphrase says, "You must put iron into your hearts" (Charles Bray
Williams). The New English Bible calls upon us to be "stouthearted."

James is talking about taking the initiative to strengthen ourselves
from the inside—to gird up the soul. In other words, we are to develop

confidence as we wait. His imagery is all about bracing some object of support so that it will not give way, like checking the load-bearing pillars to make sure they'll support the roof. We don't want our faith to weaken as God tarries, or to give in to those mockers who are described by Peter. When faith is challenged, it needs to be buttressed. Therefore James is saying, "Don't just sit there—pump up your faith, so that you can stand firm."

Linda Derby of Tulsa, Oklahoma, learned that her daughter-in-law, a young missionary wife with twin boys, had been diagnosed with breast cancer. Linda waited breathlessly for every bit of news—first, the good news that would send her spirits soaring, then the bad, which would send her into the depths of depression. It felt terrible to be so helplessly concerned for her daughter-in-law. Finally Linda realized that she couldn't sustain the emotional roller coaster. She retreated to the confines of her own room, where she spent time in serious prayer. Linda told God she was going to let Him be God. She needed to acknowledge that He was in control of everything, even during a season of fear and anxiety.[27] From the moment she committed it all to His sovereign purpose, her anxiety began to melt away.

Linda's example is a model for the attitude that we should accept. It's not that we should settle for a sad and passive resignation to destiny. God doesn't want us shrugging complacently and saying, "It is what it is." I'm talking about real hope in the face of uncertainty. The patience God wants to build in us is dynamic and vibrant, not a bland and apathetic submission. We base our perspective on the fact that a loving God is in charge of this, His universe, and patience means being steadfast in our faith even when life is difficult. In Him we can have confident patience, strength, and endurance.

It's been said that patience is "doing something else in the meantime." And that "something else" we do is to find how to profit from the very trials we're waiting through.[28]

How many blessings are never received because we lack patience? Quite often we fail to see that trials are opportunities in disguise. We are to "establish our hearts" by claiming the promises of Scripture and waiting for Christ to either return or to redeem our faith through fruitfulness.

## When the Son Sets You Free

Novelist Herman Wouk has written of a meeting he had with David Ben-Gurion, Israel's first president. Ben-Gurion urged him to move to the newly established nation. This was 1955, and *fedayeen* terrorists were still bringing regular bloodshed to the countryside. Ben-Gurion had left office and had begun his memoirs by this time. He invited Wouk and his wife for a visit to his home, where they talked for hours. At the end of the visit, he renewed his invitation to come live in Israel. "Here you will be free," he said.

The Wouks had arrived with an escort manning a mounted machine-gun, on the alert for terrorists. "Free?" Wouk asked. "With your roads impassable after sundown?"

"I did not say safe," replied the old man. "I said *free*."[29]

What we want is courage dependent on earthly security; what we need is courage based on heavenly security. We want comfort, but He gives something better: *freedom*. Because our destiny is settled, because this world is in the hands of God, we can be free from anxiety if we only have the faith. We can be free from the emotional tyranny of circumstances. Present discomfort that yields eternal joy is a formula we can receive with hearts of gratitude.

I've mentioned my inability to avoid getting lost en route to any-where you can name. Naturally I had a GPS system installed in my car. Great—that solved half the problem. You have to promise not to program the system while driving, and that's good because I can't get myself further lost while I'm parked and staring at the dashboard. But now I have to know how to put the addresses into the system—which is even harder than finding where I want to go. Where do I get a GPS to help me from getting lost in the instructions to my GPS? All right, go ahead and laugh, I'm technologically challenged too. But there's hope. My new leased car came with OnStar. I had no idea that this was a good thing until the day when I pushed the little OnStar button. Immediately I heard a nice, clear, female voice—and she knew my name! "Good morning, Dr. Jeremiah. How can I help you?"

Well, I wanted to get to a football game to see my grandson play. I'd been to that field before, but it was when his father was playing there. I gave the location and the kind voice said, "Just a moment." It was less than a moment before I was hearing, "I have downloaded the directions into your GPS system, and you'll be verbally guided from where you are to where you're headed." Then a second clear feminine voice began telling me *exactly* where to turn. Not only that, but exactly *when*—as if she were in the car with me! She'd say, "Take that right turn in fifty feet."

I know you've probably been there and done that, and it's no big deal for you. But my jaw was dropping. I felt this was a miracle on the level of Moses and the burning bush. I was driving through neighborhoods that were foreign to me, and I was cruising, confidently courageous! My anxiety was completely gone because I knew I could trust the voice to lead me to my destination.

Don't you wish there was a GPS for life? In a way, there is. God not only knows where you are with better-than-satellite precision, but He knows the trials ahead on your path. He knows the turns that will bless your life and those turns that will cause you heartache. Growing in Christ is the increasing ability to receive that signal—to know His still, small voice that is clear enough to those who trust Him. When you realize He is leading you, the anxiety just drains out of your life. It is replaced by the kind of patience that all these Bible writers describe. Then, what will you do with all that extra energy that you used to put into nail-biting and fretting? You'll find yourself using it to minister to others.

It's really a simple matter of obedience. I realize that we all have friends and family who are "fainting through unbelief or fretting through impatience," who are jobless, who aren't sure what is happening in the world. You can be the GPS for those people who are moving through strange new places in their lives. You can come alongside them and say, "Let me walk with you. Let me be a kind voice in your life." Can't you see how a time like this can be a wonderful opportunity for those of us who know and love the Lord?

For me, the Bible is the best GPS for my life. I thumb through its pages and hear a chorus of voices offering affirmation even though these people have been through far more anxiety than I could imagine. From the Old Testament book of Deuteronomy comes the word of Moses, who has endured forty years of wilderness, with whining in surround-sound. Moses says: "Be strong and of good courage, do not fear nor be afraid of them; for the Lord your God, He is the One who goes with you. He will not leave you nor forsake you" (Deuteronomy 31:6).

David, who has dealt with the darker nights of the soul, confides, "I would have lost heart unless I had believed that I would see the goodness of the LORD in the land of the living. Wait on the LORD; be of good courage, and He shall strengthen your heart; wait, I say, on the Lord!" (Psalm 27:13–14).

Isaiah, having wept for a wayward nation, adds, "The work of righteousness will be peace, and the effect of righteousness, quietness and assurance forever" (Isaiah 32:17).

Paul is quick to contribute: "We have such trust through Christ toward God" (2 Corinthians 3:4). He adds, "our sufficiency is from God." (v.5). Our confidence comes from Him!

From Hebrews we hear directions for the most important turn: "Therefore do not cast away your confidence, which has great reward" (Hebrews 10:35).

When the whole world is hanging by a thread—and when you yourself wonder if you're near the end of your rope—hold on to the confidence of the Lord, don't cast it away in the time of trial. Confidence is a longer word for faith, and that is the quiet spirit of the soul in a child of God. We will not despair. We will not give in to anger, and we will not cut the corners on our faithful obedience. When the going gets tough, the tough just pray harder—harder still as they see the day approaching.

# TEN

# Stay Convinced

I'VE THOUGHT LONG AND HARD ABOUT WORLD CONDITIONS, BUT I was still taken back by the headline of a recent opinion column by the Israeli journalist, Eitan Haber. It blared: *World War III has started!* Haber was writing about the success of North Korea's nuclear program, and he warned that the test missile fired recently by the North Koreans landed squarely in the prime minister's office in Jerusalem.[1]

The world is quickly reaching a point of no return, Haber suggested, especially when it comes to the Middle East. Experts believe the Iran–North Korean nuclear axis is now even stronger than when it was when it was formed in 2007. North Korea appears ready to supply nuclear weapons in exchange for subsidized oil from a nuclearizing Iran that is threatening to destroy Israel.[2]

With rogue states like Iran and North Korea grabbing the headlines, it's easy to forget that somewhere in the world right now there's a nuclear weapon already waiting to go off: maybe in a bunker in Pakistan, an armory in India, a silo in Israel, or stashed away in an Afghan cave. Perhaps below ground in Russia or on a firing range in

China. God forbid it's sitting in a suitcase on the docks of New York City.

Depending on who you believe, about twenty-five thousand nukes are scattered around the world.[3] The top Russian defense expert under Yeltsin revealed that nearly 40 percent of so-called suitcase bombs were unaccounted for.[4] Israel itself is believed to possess numerous nuclear weapons.

Elizabeth Zolotukhina, editor of the Case Studies Working Group with the Project on National Security Reform, recently warned that purveyors of nuclear materials are communicating with customers using sophisticated new methods not readily apparent to Western intelligent officials. The nuclear black market, she warned, is becoming more professional by the day, and is surprisingly strong and resilient.[5]

*National Defense Magazine* recently ran a chilling article entitled, "7 Deadly Myths About Weapons of Terror," warning that smuggled nukes cannot be easily detected at US ports. Our ability to spot small amounts of nuclear components is "over-hyped," said the report.[6]

All it takes is one explosion, and history will never recover.

It's a horrific thought, but what if a nuclear explosion occurred somewhere in the world tomorrow? What would people do? Where would people turn? What if a gathering of world leaders were attacked by terrorists? These are apocalyptic questions, but we're living in apocalyptic times. I'm not an alarmist, but sometimes I do feel alarmed.

And then I remember Romans 13:11, a verse with a clarion call from the Lord to be ready for the return of Christ. Here we find a clear strategy for living proactively as appalling things transpire around us. No weapon on earth can blast this verse out of the Bible; rather, these words tell us how to respond internally and intentionally to the times in which we're living.

Let me express to you the importance of this verse to me. The volume preceding this one, *What in the World Is Going On?*, has been the best-selling title of all my books. I've been asked to sign many copies, and on every occasion, after signing my name, I've written *Romans 13:11* on the flyleaf in hopes that the book's owner will turn to that verse and be compelled by its truth.

In this book, you'll notice that the conversation, like a boomerang, always comes back around to Christ's return. Now we have a chapter in which that subject is fully front and center. As I was deep in God's Word, researching the topic of what in the world we should do, I found that the Bible itself comes back to this topic over and over. In good times or bad times, God wants us to be alert concerning this issue, and never to fall asleep like negligent sentries on the tower of the fort. As we see our culture in decline, we know we are at war with the enemy; we need to be more vigilant than ever.

Read and reflect on Paul's words for us:

And do this, knowing the time, that now it is high time to awaken out of sleep; for now our salvation is nearer than when we first believed. The night is far spent, the day is at hand. Therefore let us cast off the works of darkness, and let us put on the armor of light. Let us walk properly, as in the day, not in revelry and drunkenness, not in lewdness and lust, not in strife and envy. But put on the Lord Jesus Christ, and make no provision for the flesh, to fulfill its lusts. (Romans 13:11–14)

In words terse and blunt, you might say that Paul's message is, *Live like you were dying.* That phrase was Tim McGraw's choice from the title song of one of his albums. In part, the lyrics are:

I loved deeper, and I spoke sweeter,
I gave forgiveness I'd been denying.
Someday I hope you get to live
Like you were dying.[7]

Meanwhile, Carnegie Mellon University Professor Randy Pausch was invited to be a speaker in an ongoing series asking thoughtful lecturers to assume they were giving their last presentation—to lecture as if they were dying. As it turned out, this was really the case with Pausch, who would be a victim of pancreatic cancer at forty-seven. He delivered an unforgettable talk that became a book with more than ten million readers, *The Last Lecture*.[8]

The country singer and the university professor hit a common chord: the importance of living on purpose, of moving through life with a sense of urgency based on something higher than the pursuit of pleasure. How much more should this apply to those of us who follow Christ?

If the church seems to be snoring through the fire alarm, it's not the first time. Listen to a few critical blasts from the past:

- "It has been a year of very limited spiritual fruitage, and great destitution; the church has fallen asleep."—Charles Brown, Midwestern evangelist[9]
- "I am sure I need not unroll a page of history and ask you to glance your eye down it except for a second; for again and again you will see it has occurred that the church has fallen asleep, and her ministers have become . . . destitute of zeal, having no ardent passion."—Charles Haddon Spurgeon[10]
- "It is not correct to say that the Church 'fell asleep' in

the last century, simply because it had never been awake."
—Henry Richard[11]

- "What is the present condition of the evangelical church?
  The bulk of Christians are asleep. I do not mean that the
  bulk of Christians who come to evangelical churches are
  not converted because if I meant that I would say they were
  dead and never had been born again. But I say they are
  asleep. It is possible to be morally asleep yet mentally,
  intellectually, physically and theologically alert. The present
  condition is that we are asleep."—A. W. Tozer[12]

In my last book, I quoted an observation by Vance Havner that
bears repeating: "The devil has chloroformed the atmosphere of this
age . . . . we need to take down our 'Do not disturb' signs, snap out of
our stupor, come out of our coma, and awake from our apathy."[13]

Tozer again: "God's alarm has been going off for years. Are we listening? Let's wake up—you and me!"[14] From the pages of Scripture,
written so long ago, that alarm has never ceased. It calls us to snap out
of the reverie of what to watch on TV tonight, where to find a good
pizza. We can almost hear the voice of Jesus in the garden at night,
imploring His disciples, "Watch and pray, lest you enter into temptation . . . Behold, the hour is at hand" (Matthew 26:40, 45).

Romans 13 offers four keys to resisting the seductiveness of this
world.

## We Are to Watch Vigilantly

First, Paul tells us that "now it is high time to awake out of sleep; for
now our salvation is nearer than when we first believed" (Romans

13:11). In the golden days of radio, the thriller program called *Lights Out* always began with a voice intoning, "It . . . is . . . *later . . . than . . . you . . . think*," pronouncing each word in synchronization with the chimes of a clock.

In a less sensationalistic manner, Paul is saying just that. The word for *time* here is *kairos*, which refers to the kind or quality of time; a season or an opportunity. This is not the same as *chronos*, which is actual, chronological time. Time is the theme of this passage, as evidenced by five references to the subject.

Throughout the Bible we are admonished to know the times and the seasons. In the Old Testament, a group was appointed for the specific purpose of discerning the times: "the sons of Issachar who had understanding of the times, to know what Israel ought to do" (1 Chronicles 12:32).

That crucial task, "understanding the present time," is Paul's theme here. The present time is the age of salvation that has come in the person of Jesus Christ. Paul consistently sets a dividing point between this age, which began with Christ's first coming, and the age to come, which will be ushered in when He comes again (1 Corinthians 1:20; 2:6, 8; 3:18; 2 Corinthians 4:4; Galatians 1:4, 14; Ephesians 1:21; 1 Timothy 6:19; Titus 2:12; Matthew 12:32; and Hebrews 6:5).

Reckoning with the future is always a part of wisdom. Many of us hire financial planners to help us prepare for the future and manage our money in a way that will provide security and (if we are believers) glorify God through our giving. In any time or season, it's always wise to factor the future into our plans. But now, all the wires have been tripped in God's warning system and we're on red alert. We must increase our watchfulness.

On one occasion Jesus scolded His critics: "You know how to

discern the face of the sky, but you cannot discern the signs of the times" (Matthew 16:3). In other words, they watched for rain or for the setting sun, but not for spiritual signals. Today's technology lets us consult seven-day weather forecasts with reasonable accuracy. Doctors can predict that certain diseases may occur, even before they are manifest. Some even spend their lives compiling data on stars many light years distant, and forecast the life cycle of those stars. But all the while, we are remarkably blind to the workings of the Holy Spirit in our very lives. We are hypnotized by the rhythm of life and culture, as if this moment has no bearing on eternal reality.

Some laugh at the very suggestion of spiritual barometric readings. As we have seen, Peter encountered these mockers: "Scoffers will come in the last days, walking according to their own lusts, and saying, 'Where is the promise of His coming? For since the fathers fell asleep, all things continue as they were from the beginning of creation'" (2 Peter 3:3–4).

You've heard this just as I have. With more than a little smugness, the skeptics smile and say, "That hysteria has always been with us. Every decade someone opens his Bible and declares that the End Times are upon us. Funny how those same prophecies are so flexible they work in every generation. And still no Rapture."

The same kind of skepticism was expressed on the eve of the stock market and mortgage meltdowns. To be sure, there were voices telling us there would be terrible economic consequences to the way we were conducting our business. But they were laughed off as "economic doom prophets." Talk to the Wall Street gurus today and you'll see them wince a bit before quoting, "Past performance . . . is not a predictor of future performance."[15] Some lessons have to be learned the hard way.

# The Imminence of Our Lord's Return

When we speak of the imminence of Christ's return, we're using the idea of time that Paul does—not chronological, but seasonal. We're not setting a date. We're speaking of the fact that all is in readiness, and there's no reason it couldn't happen today. Snow could be in the weather forecast, but no meteorologist would be able to tell you it would start falling on your yard at 3:15 in the afternoon. He could only tell you that it was imminent because all of the necessary conditions were in play for snow to arrive. With Christ, we're talking about prerequisites rather than precision.

I can identify with the frustration of Dr. Paul Kintner of Cornell University. He says his students "show a deep indifference" when he lectures about an event he and other reputable scientists at the US National Academy of Sciences deem imminent—a violent storm on the surface of the sun that "could conceivably be the worst natural disaster possible" on Earth—worse than even Hurricane Katrina. He adds, "It is terribly difficult to inspire people to prepare for a potential crisis that has never happened before and may not happen for decades to come."[16] Just because a highly probable event has not yet occurred is no guarantee that it will never happen.

Since NASA scientists are a pretty conservative group, if they are warning of a probable catastrophic geomagnetic storm occurring soon and without warning, there must be reason for concern.

One such solar storm, known as the Carrington Event, occurred in 1850, and it provides a cautionary note for us today. Just before daybreak on September 2 of that year, brilliant red, green, and purple auroras burst throughout the skies as far south as the tropics, which "produced enough light to rival the brightness of the sun itself."

Visually, the effect was awe-inspiring; pragmatically, there was chaos. The electric grid, such as it was at that time, was fried. Telegraph was the state of communication art at the time, and telegraph operators were shocked by flying sparks. Paper was set on fire and messages were sent even after machines were unplugged.

Scientists aren't comfortable with the implications of something like that happening in the context of today's technology. Everything from drinking water, fuel delivery, and ambient environmental controls like heating and cooling would be severely impacted. It is possible for sun storms to cause devastating results on Earth. NASA watches the skies for signs of supersolar flares that could create havoc throughout the world.[17]

Paul urges us to watch the skies for entirely different reasons. His idea of salvation, compared to our typical conception today, is like a widescreen HDTV picture compared to a wavy black-and-white one on a 1950s picture tube. We tend to simplistically think of salvation as a passing moment, the one when we accept Christ. Even then, we consider it to be a simple intellectual decision that affiliates us with a religion and serves as a simple ticket to heaven's gate—something to tuck away and forget about, like that life insurance policy or birth certificate.

Paul, on the other hand, uses a dynamic word for salvation that comes in three tenses—three dramatic dimensions. Past salvation is the moment when we say yes to Christ, are sealed by the Holy Spirit, and have our sins washed by the blood of Christ, with that debt declared paid in full, so that we are seated with Him in the heavenly places. And that's just the past part.

Present salvation is an ongoing growth process, as spiritual molecule by spiritual molecule we are conformed to the image of Christ through the redeeming work of the Holy Spirit. Through prayer and the Word, we learn to experience victory in Christ, issue by issue.

Then, most thrilling of all, there is a future salvation. That is the event Paul is describing in Romans 13 and elsewhere. There will be a day when we are finally freed from the presence of sin. As there can be no sin in heaven, no impurity in God's holy presence, it must finally be eliminated for good. We will see that happen, and I can't imagine how wonderful it will be.

This is threefold salvation. It began when I trusted Christ, and the penalty was removed. It continued as I began walking with the Lord, and more and more I learned how to be victorious over temptation and in trials. Salvation will be complete when Jesus takes me unto Himself in the future, when sin is judged and destroyed, and eternal life begins for us. And that day, Paul tells us, "is nearer than when we first believed."

No one could have a more prophetic name than me: *David Paul Jeremiah*. But I'm not a biblical prophet. Even so, reading this verse gets us all involved in prophecy. We are included in the whispers of heaven, telling us to stand by, something wonderful is in the wings . . . and objects in the biblical mirror are closer than they may appear.

## The Incentive of Our Lord's Return

Our love for Christ is incentive enough for us to await His return. But Paul gives us more. He tells us that in light of these expectations, we have work to do: "Knowing the time, that now it is high time to awake out of sleep" (Romans 13:11).

We define sleep as the suspension of consciousness. It can also mean allowing one's alertness, vigilance, or attentiveness to lie dormant—the human body doing absolutely nothing. We could use some of the same language to describe today's church—the Christian body doing absolutely nothing. At least this is true concerning the matter of His return. The catastrophic events in our present day world seem to have little or no impact on our individual or collective sense of urgency.

Charles Spurgeon preached to Victorian England about the same problem: "You can sleep, but you cannot induce the devil to close his eyes . . . The prince of the power of the air keeps his servants well up to their work . . . if we could, with a glance, see the activities of the servants of Satan, we would be astonished at our own sluggishness."[18]

Paul wants to astonish us out of our sluggishness with his words of urgency. And once he has our attention, he tells us what to do: "Owe no one anything except to love one another, for he who loves another has fulfilled the law" (Romans 13:8). He follows with a summary of the Ten Commandments (Exodus 20). You may remember that the first four commandments tell us how to love God; the final six tell us how to love people. Here in Romans, Paul is emphasizing the final commandments—the relational ones. He concludes, as Christ does in the gospels, that love is the grand summation of them all.

Love, in other words, takes care of the bill. If you have it, you will owe none of those debts Paul says to avoid because if you love your neighbor, you won't steal from him or lie to him. Love is the grand shortcut to fulfilling God's commandments. The Old Testament system works on the basis of detailed restrictions: *Thou shalt not.* The gospel, however, offers a streamlined and proactive way to live. We don't have to worry so much about what we should *not* do because we are busy with what we *should*, which is one simple thing: love those we would ordinarily not love. Simple, yes, but radical and foreign to this world. As the Scottish preacher Alexander Maclaren puts it, we become "a new thing . . . a community held together by love and not by geographical accidents or linguistic affinities, or the iron fetters of the conqueror."[19]

What does this have to do with the second coming of Christ? Love is an incentive for making right choices under duress. The next time you're stuck in traffic, think, *Do I want to be honking my horn and shaking my fist at the instant I'm suddenly looking into the eyes of my Lord?* Paul is saying, "Get your relationships in order. He could be here before you finish reading this sentence." One writer stated it well: With every passing day, we "pitch our moving tent a day's march nearer home."[20]

## We Are to War Valiantly

What else can we do? "The night is far spent, the day is at hand. Therefore let us cast off the works of darkness, and let us put on the armor of light" (Romans 13:12). Paul is about to make a rather aggressive point about the way you and I are to live our lives.

*Put Off Darkness.* When Paul tells us to *cast off* darkness, he chooses a decisive verb. It means to deliberately, purposefully, significantly, and permanently put aside the things of darkness. But what kind of darkness? He refers to the residue of the old, pre-Christian life; the difference between a child of God and the natural man, who is still walking in the shadow. By rights the old man should have no hold on us, but just the same, we fall into his patterns. We speak harsh words. We tell lies. We judge each other. We cannot stand each other's successes, and we often act like it is our duty to keep others in their place.

Paul is warning us that while Christ is accepted in a moment, sin remains our foe for a lifetime. We give in to the "little" temptations; we make a concession here, an exception there, and before we know it, we've conceded a great deal of authority to sin. We must put off darkness deliberately and purposefully, and do the same tomorrow and each day. Every victory of the redeemed will make us stronger while every concession draws us deeper into the slavery of sin.

Therefore, just as we are vigilant in watching for the return of Christ, like a guard on the wall, so must we be on constant guard against the encroachment of the old ways. We can't allow the devil to get his little toe into the door. The good news is that "the night is spent," as Paul poetically expresses it. "The day is at hand." The devil has played all his cards, and we have the victory of Christ on our side. As good soldiers, then, we buckle on the "armor of light" and prepare to make our stand.

*Put on the Light.* How do you put off the darkness of a room? That's easy—you flip a switch, and light makes darkness flee. There was no electricity in Paul's time, so he uses military language: "Put on the armor of light." This is the New Testament picture for walking in fellowship with God. "If we walk in the light as He is in the light, we have fellowship with one another" (1 John 1:7). Because we are saved, and indwelt by the Holy Spirit, we push back the assault of the rulers of darkness with the decisiveness of a great soldier.[21] In chaotic times, the battle rages wildly. More than ever we need to strap on that armor; more than ever we need to know our allies from our enemies. A soldier may stand on the wall, but he never sits on the fence.

About sitting on the fence: a new Barna research report suggests that three quarters of American Christians believe God is the "all powerful, all-knowing Creator of the Universe who rules the world today." So far, so good. The problems come when the subject turns to Jesus, Satan, and the Holy Spirit. Thirty-nine percent believe Jesus sinned during His time on earth, and 58 percent of Christians do not believe that the Holy Spirit is a living being. Strangely, nearly 60 percent don't believe Satan is real, while 64 percent believe that demons can affect us. Apparently demons are more believable to some people than the work of the living, indwelling Holy Spirit.

Consider also that one out of every three Christians believes the Bible and the Koran teach the same truths. We have to conclude that most of these have read neither book. Do you see now why we speak of the need for believers to wake up?[22]

I would say that the poll results suggest that we're not sitting on the fence at this point; we're helping the enemy tear down the fence entirely. Barna has concluded that American Christians tend to stretch the Bible to fit their everyday experiences. What we are called to do is to face our everyday experiences with the undiluted, uncompromised wisdom of the Word of God. We are soldiers, not defectors.

## We Are to Walk Virtuously

Now we are ready for Paul's third admonition as we watch vigilantly and war valiantly; we must also walk virtuously. "Let us walk properly, as in the day, not in revelry and drunkenness, not in lewdness and lust, not in strife and envy" (Romans 13:13). Paul often lists traits, good and bad. Again, this list is not an exhaustive one. But it's enough to give a good indication of someone who is not walking in the light. We have two checkpoints here:

- *We are to reject public sins of the night.* "Drunkenness and revelry" is Paul's first category, and it's not difficult to understand what kind of sin he means: disorderly social behavior. Thinking of warfare again, Paul may have envisioned the soldier who goes into the city on leave and abuses alcohol. The next day, he is worthless to the army. Paul's message: "You're in the army now. Don't disgrace the uniform."

- *We are to renounce private sins.* What about who we are when no one is looking? Paul warns us against "lewdness and lust, strife and envy." These are usually the most dangerous sins of all because they hide in the human heart. We can't be held accountable by others for what they can't see, but we can become useless to God. The self-centered person becomes concerned with ego more than Christ, and ego can be defined as Edging God Out. Paul wants us to be aware of sin in its daily and nightly manifestations, its assaults from the inside and the outside.

## We Are to Wait Victoriously

So far we've encountered a lot of soldierly discipline. Here's the payoff. All these things that Paul asks us to do are possible and positive. The strength and the strategy are both available to us—the strength through the Spirit, the strategy through the Word. Once we determine to live this way, we are happier, healthier, and far more productive.

But how do we get from where we are to where we want to be? Many Christians live in quiet defeat every day. Perhaps you would include yourself in that category. So many good people love the Lord, attend church regularly, and try to pray, all the while having a sense that there *must be more*. A. W. Tozer wrote about the spiritual craving people were feeling even in his time: "The hungry sheep look up, and are not fed. It is a solemn thing, and no small scandal in the Kingdom, to see God's children starving while actually seated at the Father's table."[23]

Maybe you're reading some of the chapters of this book while thinking, *Of course I would love to experience more of God, but I just don't ever seem to get there. My days are a series of small defeats, clusters of sin I can't overcome, and prayers that seem to bounce off the ceiling. Is there a way to get past the obstacles and live the kind of life you're describing?*

And the answer, as you might expect, is yes. Nobody has to live a disappointing Christian life. If you'll think about it, there are people we observe who are living in victory. We know it can be done because we've seen it—and we know that God is not partial in His dealings with men. This next section of Romans 13 gives us a genuine, hands-on strategy to live the kind of life we'd like to be living when Christ returns. Romans 13:14 has two calls to action. Read the verse again, and you'll see what they are: "Put on the Lord Jesus Christ, and make no provision for the flesh, to fulfill its lusts."

Yes, it's true that these steps are easier to talk through than walk through. How do you "put on Christ," and how do you "make no provision for the flesh"? Let's take them one at a time, and let me offer you an outlook that has helped me.

- *Putting on Christ.* Ray Stedman suggests this approach: "When I get up in the morning, I put on my clothes, intending them to be part of me all day, to go where I go and do what I do. They cover me and make me presentable to others. That is the purpose of clothes. In the same way, the apostle is saying to us, 'Put on Jesus Christ when you get up in the morning. Make Him a part of your life that day. Intend that he go with you everywhere you go, and that he act through you in everything you do. Call upon his resources. Live your life IN CHRIST.'"[24]

- *No Provision for Flesh.* What about the second warning? It concerns avoiding any temptation to gratify the desires of the flesh.

Harry Truman's biographer, David McCullough, recounts an example from Truman's life. The president was in the midst of talks with the USSR and Great Britain. The question at hand was what to do with postwar Germany, and there was great deal of anxiety and stress. After one really tough day, according to a Secret Service agent, Truman was ready to head back to his quarters. An Army public relations officer jauntily asked him for a ride. Truman, always the down-to-earth type, gave him a seat in the car. As a thank-you gesture, the stranger offered to get Truman anything he wanted from the city's thriving black market. He suggested a few of the products he dealt in: cigarettes, watches, whiskey, women—with a leering emphasis on that final one.

The smile was gone from President Truman's face. He replied, "Listen, son, I married my sweetheart. She doesn't run around on me, and I don't run around on her. I want that understood. Don't ever mention that kind of stuff to me again."

When they arrived at the yellow stucco house assigned for his use at the conference, Truman left the car with no further word to the now humbled officer.[25]

There's an old Native American saying that goes like this: "Call on God, but row away from the rocks." The idea is to put yourself in the best situation to succeed, and as far away as possible from the place of failure. Some people need to erase a few streets from their maps. Still others need to install software to protect their eyes from certain Internet destinations. When you're on a diet, you don't loiter at the ice cream parlor. That's what Paul means by making no provision for the flesh.

According to a *National Review Online* article, Americans rent eight hundred million pornographic videos and DVDs every year. A *vast majority* of men between the ages of eighteen to thirty-four frequent pornographic Web sites monthly. Among those addicted to pornography are a great number of people professing to be followers of Jesus Christ. We can only wonder if they've received the information that, according to research, pornography actually produces changes in the brains of users—changes that affect one's ability to give or receive genuine love.[26]

I find these facts extremely disheartening, even tragic. Don't you? So many children of God, blessed benefactors of the blood of Christ and the surpassing love of God, are choosing to hand themselves over to a new kind of slavery. We have the opportunity to walk in the light, but we wander off into dark alleys. We damage the precious minds God has given us, the very temples in which the Holy Spirit dwells.

The Bible tells us to run from four things: idolatry (1 Corinthians 10:14); youthful lusts (2 Timothy 2:22); materialism (1 Timothy 6:17) and sexual immorality: "Flee from sexual immorality. All other sins a man commits are outside his body, but he who sins sexually sins against his own body. Do you not know that your body is a temple of the Holy Spirit, who is in you, whom you have received from God? You are not your own; you were bought at a price. Therefore honor God with your body" (1 Corinthians 6:18–20 NIV).

Ray Stedman spells it out in language no one can misinterpret:

"'Flee immorality'—that is the advice everywhere in the Bible. Do not try to fight with it; do not try to overcome it; do not try to suppress it. Get away! These are subtle, powerful forces, and the widespread destruction we see in lives around us is simple testimony to the subtlety with which they can conquer us."[27]

The devil has a broad arsenal of weapons. But we are not helpless. We can strap on the armor of light (Ephesians 6), and Satan will flee. We can take simple steps to avoid the relentless temptations that are bearing down on us. Most of all, we can ask God to help us. The power of the cross is the most awesome force in the universe. Paul writes, "I have been crucified with Christ; it is no longer I who live, but Christ lives in me; and the life which I now live in the flesh I live by faith in the Son of God, who loved me and gave Himself for me" (Galatians 2:20).

Just knowing—*really* knowing—that Christ lives in you is half the battle. You can experience that power every single day. I'll never forget the first time I saw the film *The Passion of the Christ*. A group from our staff attended a premiere in Dallas. Like most people at that time, we had heard publicity and controversy about the film, and we had no idea what to expect. It was, of course, just a movie, and we'd seen any number of other movies about Jesus. In short, we were totally unprepared for the cinematic experience that was ours in that darkened church. I've spent much of my life studying the gospels, reading and praying and reflecting on the meaning of the Cross. But I had never seen it like this—not even close. We sat and watched a bloody, gory, graphic depiction of what the Lord endured for our sake.

Yes, we knew it was only a movie. We knew the blood was not real. None of that made any difference at all. God spoke to us in the very deep corners of our souls—places that hadn't before been touched in such an emotional way. It wasn't just the crucifixion, but the beatings, the spitting, and the pathetic mockery of Jesus. We were hearing the words in true Aramaic, as they were spoken two thousand years ago. I would never have thought any film could affect me so powerfully.

You may remember what movie theaters were like, all across our country, as the lights came on after that film—awed silence; stifled sobs. As we returned to California on the airplane, there was silence among us. We were each left to our private thoughts and reflections, processing what we had seen; talking to God about it. My own prayer was, "Lord, help me to live my life from this moment onward in such a way that I never do anything to hurt You or to break Your heart. Not after what You have done for me."

That's the power of the Cross, isn't it? It stands on that rock at Calvary, even today, casting its shadow across an entire planet, and across twenty centuries until it engulfs every one of us with its unquenchable power. To let ourselves experience that cross—to stand weeping before it with Mary and John and the centurion and millions of Christians through the ages—is to be radically and entirely changed from the inside out. To catch, even through a glass darkly, a fleeting glimpse of Christ and His incredible love for us, is to devote ourselves wholeheartedly to giving Him our lives in return.

In another movie from a few years ago, we cover a span of fifty years through a series of flashbacks. The four Ryan brothers have all bravely gone off to fight in World War II. When information surfaced that the other three brothers had died within days of one another, a senior official in Washington DC orders a special mission to bring Private James Ryan home from the front. Because Ryan's unit is listed as missing in action, it becomes a search mission, as well. Captain Miller assembles a seven-man rescue squad that succeeds in locating Ryan who refuses to leave his unit, despite the news of the death of his brothers. Most of the men on that mission lose their lives in the effort to save Ryan or in a subsequent battle between Ryan's unit and the enemy forces. As if holding Ryan responsible for the great sacrifice made on his behalf, the mortally wounded Captain Miller pulls the stunned private toward him and with his final breath says, "*James, earn* this—*earn* it!"

Then the scene flashes forward to the present where James Francis Ryan, now in his eighties, is seen paying homage at Captain Miller's grave at Omaha Beach in Normandy, France. Overcome with emotion and perhaps some guilt, he says to the grave marker, as if to Miller and the rest: "I hope . . . I've earned what all of you have done for me."[28]

We all know that no one could ever merit such a great sacrifice; no one could ever do enough to earn the incredible price of the gift of a rescued life. No gift is ever earned, especially the gift of life.

That is the truth about salvation as well; we can never earn it. There is zero mathematical possibility that a sinful life can ever, under any circumstances, make a good exchange for the one perfect and holy life that was ever lived; no way human blood can equate to the blood of God's Son. We can't earn it. But what we can do is to know what Christ has done in the past, to know He is with us right now, and to know that He is physically coming back soon. We know those things with our minds. But do we know them with our hearts? Or are we dozing?

A recent headline called the recent nuclear developments by North Korea and Iran a wake-up call to the world. Well, the world has had an endless series of wake-up calls over the past decade.

If we're not out of bed by now, we may be unconscious.

I believe Christians all over the world are wide awake and more aware of the times than we've ever been. As followers of Christ, we must be alert, watchful, and vigilant, with one eye on the headlines and the other on the eastern skies.

That's what Paul is shouting: "Awake! Awake! He's coming! Live every single moment for Him as if you knew this would be your last on earth and the sweet moment of reunion. Do nothing you wouldn't want to be doing when the Lord of the universe comes to claim His bride. The victory will be overwhelming—let's put on the armor of light and take our stand."

# One More Thing

Now that we've finished our journey through these chapters, I would ask you to consider two conditions, and whether either has changed.

1. The condition of the world. How has it changed?
2. The condition of your spirit. How has it changed?

During my writing and your reading, our country may have completely turned itself around. There might be peace on earth, a thriving business climate, and a fresh housing boom. Somehow I doubt it—but I won't say it's impossible. We can agree, at least, that it's a big world in the hands of a big God. Who knows what He has in store?

You—on the other hand—now that's a different question. If you have seriously interacted with the biblical truths in this book, I really believe that you have become a different person. My prayer would be that you are more hopeful, realizing that our Lord's return is certain, and I believe, very soon. I would also hope you would be more eager to dig in at church and begin encouraging people; to approach God in prayer with a revitalized eagerness to know His touch; and to let your joy in Christ shine as a light during a time of so much darkness.

These are the most challenging days I've seen in the span of my life, and I would guess it's the same for you. But my faith has not been shaken by so much as a molecule of a mustard seed. I love and trust the Lord of this universe more than ever. The more wayward our society becomes, the darker our culture grows, the more attractive to me is the life and love of Jesus. More than anything in this world, I want others to see in Him what I see. Don't you agree with me? Never before have I felt such an urgency to get the Word out and to see spiritual revival among us.

If we're agreed on that point, let's cast aside our fear of the world out there and get to work. Let's go *light it up*. We need to walk through its streets, find the lonely and the frightened and the downtrodden, and tell them the good news their souls are yearning to hear. You ask what on earth should we do? Along with the ten specific action points I've suggested, I want to remind you of this absolutely critical one: *Share your faith*. There is such a hunger for it out there that you're going to be shocked to see that the world is more prepared than ever to hear about a God of hope.

Imagine the following scenario coming to pass: There is a great commotion in the streets of the city. From the heavens comes a sound of a thunderous fanfare, a blinding light envelops everything, and Christ is revealed in all His glory as the King of creation. He gathers all His children to His side, and when He comes to you, your hands are interlocked with those of a brand-new believer you've just that moment led to the Lord. In the absolute final second of this epoch, your friend's eternal destination has been sealed—not a half-second too soon. And imagine that this friend is one of many you've arranged to take with you to the home that Jesus has been preparing for us.

Let's make it happen just like that. We need only decide that we love Christ that much. Are you ready to get to work? Where on earth should we start?

## What About *After* Earth?

What on earth should we do to live confidently in these chaotic days? In this book we've answered that question. We must be about our Father's business. As the day approaches, that business is more urgent than ever.

But let me propose another question; this one is personal. Actually, it's the same question I asked the listeners of our radio program *Turning Point* the day Chaplain Brad Borders heard it. *What's going to happen on the day you die? Have you made any plans for life after your life on earth is done?* God has certainly made plans for you, and He has sent you an engraved invitation. That invitation came in human form, as His only begotten Son, Jesus Christ. I hope and pray that you've accepted the invitation, that you've made Christ your Savior for eternity and your master for right now. But I want you to be certain about this issue.

You see, one of the symptoms of our troubled times is a tangled mess of confusion and misinformation on the things that really matter. People have a lot of ideas about heaven and salvation, and many of these ideas don't come from God's inspired Word. Therefore let's take a careful look at what's involved in identifying with Christ and having the assurance of salvation.

The Bible tells us that every one of us is a sinner. What that means is that all of us "miss the mark" of the perfection that God requires.

Every day, in many ways, we fail to live up to God's standard. Since He is holy and perfect, there can be no sin in His presence. Therefore, when it comes to being in heaven—the spiritual domain of His presence—we have a big problem. Our sin would make us ineligible to go there. Not only that, but we would have earned the penalty of death, which sin assures.

Our sin creates a barrier between God and His children. It would be insurmountable if God hadn't acted out of His love and compassion for our predicament. He sent His perfect Son, Jesus Christ, to this world. Jesus lived a life that showed us exactly how we should be living. Then, though He was completely without sin, He died on the cross, taking the punishment we had earned. You see, as He suffered and died, He voluntarily took all of our sin upon Himself. A perfect man took the punishment that sinful people had earned so that those people could be declared sinless and worthy to stand in God's presence someday.

That forgiveness begins immediately, on the sole condition that you accept His gift through faith. There is nothing you can do to earn that salvation; only accept it and identify with Christ. Then there is nothing you can do to lose it. The second you say yes to Christ, your sins are fully forgiven. The Holy Spirit enters your life, and from that moment on, He serves as your counselor and encourager. He will help to mold you to be more like Christ.

What, then, must you do to be saved? Simply pray to God and ask Him to forgive you of all your sins. Ask Christ to become your Lord and master, and then make a commitment to serve Him for the rest of your life. When you pray, you can use your own words—God knows your heart and simply asks you to be sincere. But you might say something like this: "Lord, I am a sinner. I own up to the fact that

I can never please You through my own efforts. Every day of my life I miss the mark. But I know that Your Son, Jesus Christ, died for me, in all His perfection, to pay the price of my sins. I accept His gift. I acknowledge His sacrifice on my behalf. And from this moment on, I identify with Him and will follow Him wholeheartedly, finding and doing His will for my life."

What will it feel like? Perhaps not much at all—not at first. This isn't about emotions, but about an act of your will. Though the moment may be very quiet, heaven will be rejoicing, and God will see you clothed in the perfection of Christ. You will be His child. Then, as you begin to read your Bible every day (the gospel of John is a great place to start), you will grow as a believer. Spend daily time in prayer, and find a church where the gospel is preached, the Bible is believed, and where the people are kind and caring.

We also want to be certain that you get off to the best possible start in following your Lord and Savior. If you need guidance or have questions, let us know at *Turning Point Ministries*:

P.O. Box 3838
San Diego, CA 92163

If you prayed to accept Christ, welcome to the family! You have begun a joyful life that will culminate in the wonderful reunion we've been describing, when Christ comes to take His children home. What a day of rejoicing that will be.

# Notes

## Introduction: Knowing the Signs

1. Fred R. Shapiro, ed., *Yale Book of Quotations* (New Haven, CT: Yale University Press, 2006), 206.

2. Renae Merle, "Wall Street's Final '08 Toll: $6.9 Trillion Wiped Out." *Washington Post*, 1 January 2009, www.washingtonpost.com /wp-dyn/content/article/2008/12/31/AR2008123101083.html (accessed 26 June 2009).

3. Luisa Kroll, Matthew Miller and Tatiana Serafin, "The World's Billionaires," *Forbes*, 11 March 2009, www.forbes.com/2009/03/11 /worlds-richest-people-billionaires-2009-billionaires-intro.html (accessed 26 June 2009).

4. Emily Kaiser, "Update 2- US 2008 household wealth fell $11.2 trillion," *Reuters*, 12 March 2009, www.reuters.com/article /marketsNews/idUSN1237085520090312 (accessed 26 June 2009).

5. "Economic News Release," *Bureau of Labor Statistics*, 5 June 2009, Al Jazeera, www.bls.gov/news.release/empsit.nr0.htm (accessed 26 June 2009).

6. Dan Levy, "Foreclosure Filings in U.S. Jumped 30% in February" (Update 3), *Bloomberg.com*, 12 March 2009, www.bloomberg.com /apps/news?pid=20601103&sid=aUzNMbJ3CIII&refer=news (accessed 27 June 2009).

7. Jeannine Aversa, "Forecasters see higher U.S. unemployment this year; Canadian jobless rate set to rise," Associated Press, 23 February 2009, humantimes.com/articleaction/printnow/59007 (accessed 27 June 2009).

8. "A look at economic developments around the globe," Associated Press Archives, 12 March 2009. The complete article can be purchased via e-mail at ap@newsbank.com.

9. Simon Hooper, "Putin: Financial crisis is 'perfect storm,'" *CNN .com/world business*, 28 January 2009, cnn.com/2009 /BUSINESS/01/28/davos.wef.wedsnesday.wrap/index.html (27 June 2009).

10. "U.S. protests harassing of Navy ship by Chinese," Associated Press, *MSMBC.com*, 11 June 2009; www.msnbc.msn.com /id/29596179 (accessed 11 June 2009); and "North Korea warned over nuclear move," One-Minute World News, *BBC.com*, 24 September 2008, news.bbc.co.uk/2/hi/asia-pacific/7634190.stm (accessed 27 June 2009).

11. Eric Talmadge and Anne Gearan, "US officials: North Korea may launch new missiles," Associated Press, 29 May 2009, www.google .com/hostednews/ap/article /ALeqM5iURO8fOyWVOA0ytFlaAGuC9F7R9wD98G52L00 (accessed 27 June 2009).

12. Ibid., Hooper.

13. "Recent Earthquakes in California and Nevada: Index Map of Recent Earthquakes in California-Nevada," 18 May 2009, quake .usgs.gov/recenteqs (accessed 17 June 2009).

14. "Earthquake Fact and Statistics: Number of Earthquakes Worldwide for 2000–2009," neic.usgs.gov/neis/eqlists/eqstats.html (accessed 2 July 2009).

## *Chapter 1: Stay Calm*

1. Based on personal conversations with friends in Beijing (RJM).

2. Marianne Bray, "Beijing to Shoot Down Olympic Rain," *CNN*, 9 June 2006, www.cnn.com/2006/WORLD/asiapcf/06/05/china.rain /index.html (accessed 27 June 2009).

3. Leonard David, "U.S. Military Wants to Own the Weather," Space .com, 31 October 2005;www.Space.com/scienceastronomy/051031 _Mystery_Monday.html (accessed 1 July 2009).

4. Quoted in *Weather Warfare: the Military's Plan to Draft Mother*

*Nature* by Jerry E. Smith (Kempton, IL: Adventures Unlimited Press, 2006), i.

5. Michel Chossedovsky, "Weather Warfare," *The Ecologist*, 22 May 2008, globalresearch.ca/articles/haarpecologist.pdf (accessed 27 June 2009).

6. Pam Belluck, "Recession Anxiety Seeps Into Everyday Lives," *New York Times*, 9 April 2009, page A1; Steven Reinberg, "Anti-Anxiety Medications Online," *Anti-anxiety Medications.org*, 10 June 2008, www.antianxietymedications.org/15-million-americans-suffer -from-social-anxiety-disorder.html (accessed 27 June 2009).

7. Paul Tournier, *A Place for You*, (New York: Harper and Row, 1968), 9.

8. Hyde Flippo, "Ludwig II: The Swan King and His Castles," *The German Way & More.com*, www.german-way.com/ludwig.html (accessed 27 June 2009).

9. C. S. Lewis, *The Problem of Pain*, The Complete C.S. Lewis Signature Classics (New York: HarperOne, 2002), 639–640.

10. "Part 2: Down but Not Out," *Time*, 2 December 1991, www.time .com/time/magazine/article/0,9171,974392,00.html?iid=chix-sphere (accessed 27 June 2009).

11. *General MacArthur Speeches and Reports 1908–1964*, Edward T. Imparato, ed. (Nashville, TN: Turner Publishing Company, 2000), 126.

12. William Barclay, *The Gospel of John, Vol. 2*, (Philadelphia, PA: Westminster Press, 1975), 157.

13. "Summary of Key Findings and Statistics on Religion in America," *Report 1: Religious Alliliation*, *Pew Research Center Publications*, 23 June 2008, religions.pewforum.org/reports (accessed 16 June 2009), and "Many Americans Say Other Faiths Can Lead to Eternal Life," *Pew Research Center Publications*, 18 December 2008, pewresearch.org/pubs/1062/many-americans-say-other-faiths-can -lead-to-eternal-life (accessed 27 June 2009).

14. Christianity Today Poll, 27 March 2009, www.christianitytoday .com/ct/features/poll.html (accessed 27 March 2009).

15. Ruthanna Metzger, "It's Not in the Book!" *Eternal Perspective Ministries*, www.epm.org/artman2/publish/salvation/It_s_Not_in _the_Book.shtml (accessed 27 June 2009).

16. Mark Twain, editorial in *Hartford Courant*, 1897. See also Ralph Keyes, *The Quote Verifier* (New York: Macmillan, 2006), 243.

## Chapter 2: Stay Compassionate

1. "An All-Star True Story, The Ami Ortiz 'Uvdah Interview' Channel 8 (Israel)," 2 March 2009. Transcript at www.amiortiz.com /(accessed 9 June 2009).

2. Ibid., Ami Ortiz.com, "Leah's Updates."

3. "Starbucks Customers Pay It Forward 109 Times," *KCRA.com*, Sacramento, CA, 24 November 2008, www.kcra.com/cnn -news/18052349/detail.html (accessed 28 June 2009).

4. "To Benjamin Webb," *The Writings of Benjamin Franklin*: 1783–1788, ed., Albert Henry Smyth (New York: The Macmillan Company, 1907), 197.

5. Philip Yancey, "A Surefire Investment," *Christianity Today.com*, 3 February 2009, www.christianitytoday.com/ct/2009/january/29.80 .html (accessed 28 June 2009).

6. Shannon Ethridge, "Why Didn't He Hate Me?" *Campus Life IGNITE*, February 2008, www.christianitytoday.com /cl/2008/001/10.44.html (accessed 27 June 2009).

7. Henry Wadsworth Longfellow, *The Prose Works of Henry Wadsworth Longfellow* (New York: Houghton, Mifflin and Company, 1890), 405.

8. Henri J. M. Nouwen, *The Way of the Heart* (New York: Harper One, 1991), 34.

9. Paul L. Maier, *Eusebius: The Church History* (Grand Rapids: Kregel, 1999), 269.

10. C. S. Lewis, *Mere Christianity* in The Complete C.S. Lewis Signature Classics (New York: HarperOne, 2002), 110–111.

11. From Joel C. Rosenberg, *Inside the Revolution* (Carol Stream, IL: Tyndale, 2009), 363–368.

12. *Christian History & Biography Magazine*, Issue 82, Spring 2004, 13.

13. Roy Anthony Borges, "Love Your Enemies: One Prisoner's Story of Risky Obedience," *Discipleship Journal*, Issue 107, 42–43.

## Chapter 3: Stay Constructive

1. Cathy Lynn Crossman, "An inaugural first: Obama acknowledges 'non-believers,'" *USA Today,* 22 January 2009, www.usatoday.com /news/religion/2009-01-20-obama-non-believers_N.htm (accessed 27 June 2009).

2. Stephen Ambrose, *Citizen Soldiers: The U. S. Army from the Normandy Beaches to the Bulge to the Surrender of Germany* (New York: Simon & Schuster, 1998), 471–472.

3. Eugene H. Peterson, *The Message: The New Testament in Contemporary Language* (Colorado Springs, CO: Navpress, 1993), 2171.

4. "Kurt Vonnegut's Rules for Writing a Poem." *Improv Encyclopedia. org,* improvencyclopedia.org/references/Kurt_Vonnegut's_Rules _for_Writing_a_Poem.html (accessed 28 June 2009).

5. Erwin Raphael McManus, *An Unstoppable Force: Daring to Become the Church God Had in Mind* (Loveland, CO: Group Publishing, 2000), 29–31.

6. Nicole Johnson, *The Invisible Woman: When Only God Sees* (Thomas Nelson, 2005), 31, 41, passim.

7. Jonathan Edwards, *The Works of Jonathan Edwards, Vol. I,* www *.ccel.org*/ccel/edwards/works1.ix.iv.html?highlight=mysticism #highlight (accessed 28 June 2009).

8. "Survey Describes the Spiritual Gifts That Christians Say They Have," *Barna.org*, 9 February 2009, www.barna.org/barna-update /article/12-faithspirituality/211-survey-describes-the-spiritual -gifts-that-christians-say-they-have (accessed 28 June 2009).

9. Dr. Robert McNeish, "Lessons from Geese," Northminster Presbyterian Church, Reisterstown, MD, 1972, suewidemark.com /lessonsgeese.htm (accessed 28 June 2009).

## Chapter 4: Stay Challenged

1. Compiled from www.vt.edu/remember/biographies/liviu_librescu .html and "Holocaust survivor sacrificed himself to save students," www.abc.net.au/news/newsitems/200704/s1899900.htm (accessed 28 June 2009).

2. Geoffrey T. Bull, *When Iron Gates Yield* (London: Pickering & Inglis, 1976), 199–223.

3. Madeleine Brand and Howard Berkes, "China Celebrates Opening of Summer Olympics," *NPR.org*, 8 August 2008, www.npr.org /templates/story/story.php?storyId=93420251 (accessed 28 June 2009).

4. R. C. Sproul, *Knowing Scripture* (Downers Grove, IL: InterVarsity Press, 2009), 31.

5. Louis A. Barbieri, Jr., *First and Second Peter* (Chicago, IL: Moody Press, 1998), 97.

6. Sabina Wurmbrand, transcribed by her granddaughter, Andrea Wurmbrand, "In God's Beauty Parlor," transcript members.cox .net/wurmbrand/godsbeautyparlor.html (accessed 28 June 2009) . See also Todd Nettleton, "Sabina Wurmbrand," *Banner of Truth Trust*, "In The News," www.banneroftruth.org/pages /news/2000/08/sabina_wurmbrand.php (accessed 28 June 2009).

## Chapter 5: Stay Connected

1. "Google search finds missing child,"*BBC.Com*/News, 9 January 2009, news.bbc.co.uk/2/hi/technology/7820984.stm (accessed 28 June 2009). See also George Barnes and Danielle Williamson, "Athol woman and granddaughter found in Virginia," *Telegram & Gazette Staff* (Worcester, MA), 7 January 2009, www.telegram.com /article/20090107/NEWS/901070289/1116 (accessed 28 June 2009).

2. Steven Johnson, "How Twitter Will Change the Way We Live," *Time*, 5 June 2009, www.time.com/time/business /article/0,8599,1902604,00.html (accessed 28 June 2009).

3. Ibid., Schaffner.

4. Michael Paulson, "Here's the church, but where are the people?" *The Boston Globe*, *boston.com*, 15 June 2008, www.boston.com /news/local/articles/2008/06/15/heres_the_church_but_where _are_the_people/ (accessed 28 June 2009).

5. "Southern Baptists and Catholics join US church decline trend," *Ekklesia, News Brief*, 2 March 2009, www.ekklesia.co.uk/node/8828 (accessed 28 June 2009).

6. Robert D. Putnam, *Bowling Alone: The Collapse and Revival of American Community* (New York: Simon and Schuster, 2001), 72.

7. Charles Colson, *Being the Body* (Nashville: Thomas Nelson, 2003), 19.

8. Paul Vitello, "Bad Times Draw Bigger Crowds to Churches," *New York Times.com*, 14 December 2008, www.nytimes .com/2008/12/14/nyregion/14churches.html (accessed 28 June 2009).

9. Leonard Sweet, *11: Indispensable Relationships You Can't Be Without*, (Colorado Springs, CO: David C. Cook, 2008), 23.

10. Ed Bahler and Bill Coucenour, "Created to Connect," *Your Church*, January/February 2009, 56.

11. Personal Lecture Notes: "The Trinity," Dr. Russell Moore, Southern Seminary.

12. Nina Ellison, *Mama John: The Lifelong Missionary Service of Mary Saunders* (Birmingham, AL: New Hope, 1996), 8.

13. Joel C. Rosenberg, *Inside the Revolution* (Carol Stream, IL: Tyndale House, 2009), 417.

14. Dave Anderson, "At Last, Jackson Is 'The Straw That Stirs the Drink,'" *New York Times on the Web*, 30 June 1980, www.nytimes .com/specials/baseball/yankees/nyy-rotb-jackson.html (accessed 28 June 2009).

15. Alvin J. Schmidt, *How Christianity Changed the World* (Grand Rapids: Zondervan, 2001, 2004), 157–158.

16. Phillip Yancey, *Reaching for the Invisible God*, (Grand Rapids, MI: Zondervan Publishing, 2000), 170.

17. Ted W. Engstrom, *The Fine Art of Friendship* (Nashville: Thomas Nelson, 1985), 131–132.

18. Clive Anderson, *Travel with CH Spurgeon: In the Footsteps of the Prince of Preachers* (Epson, Surry UK: Day One Publications, 2002), 16.

19. Robert J. Morgan, *Nelson's Complete Book of Stories, Illustrations and Quotes* (Nashville: Thomas Nelson, 2000), 127.

20. "Go to Church," *The Lutheran Pioneer*, May 1907 (St. Louis: Evangelical Lutheran Synodical Conference, May 1907).

## Chapter 6: Stay Centered

1. Raja Abdulrahim and Jessica Garrison, "Friends speak up for L.A. journalists held by N. Korea," *Los Angeles Times*, 11 June 2009, www.latimes.com/news/local/la-me-korea-ling-lee11 -2009jun11,0,7875895.story (accessed 28 June 2009).

2. Jae-Soon Chang and Kwang-tae Kim, "NKorea steps up rhetoric amid nuclear crisis," Associated Press, Yahoo! News, 9 June 2009, www.news.yahoo.com/s/ap/20090609/ap_on_re_as/as_koreas _nuclear (accessed 1 July 2009).

3. "Fax Threaten VOM Project," *PersecutionBlog.com*, 11 June 2009, www.persecutionblog.com/ (accessed 28 June 2009).

4. "World Watch 2009," *Open Doors.org.*, January 2009, www .opendoorsusa.org/content/view/432/ (accessed 28 June 2009).

5. "North Korean Christians Question Regime's Claims," *ReligionNewsBlog.com*, 27 April 2009, www.religionnewsblog .com/23425 (accessed 28 June 2009).

6. Ibid.

7. James Hill and Jaime Hennessey, "Kevin Everett: 'He Is a Tiger,'" *ABC News.com*, 31 January 2008, abcnews.go.com/Health /story?id=4216671&page=1 (accessed 28 June 2009).

8. R. G. Bratcher and E. A. Nida, *A Handbook on Paul's Letters to the Colossians and to Philemon*. Originally published as *A Translator's Handbook on Paul's Letters to the Colossians and to Philemon: Helps for Translators*. UBS handbook series (74) (New York: United Bible Societies, 1977).

9. John Phillips, *Exploring Colossians and Philemon: An Expository Commentary* (Grand Rapids: Kregel Publications, 2002),159, 163.

10. Vance Havner, *Vance Havner Quotebook*, Denis J. Hester, comp. (Grand Rapids: Baker Book House, 1986), 29.

11. *The Ante Nicene Fathers, Volume 1: Apostolic Fathers*, "The Epistle of Mathetes to Diognetus," chapter 2.

12. "Oath of Allegiance for Naturalized Citizens," *About.com*, immigration.about.com/od/uscitizenship/a/AllegianceOath.htm (accessed 28 June 2009).

13. Ibid., Bratcher.

14. Bob Laurent, *Watchman Nee: Man of Suffering* (Uhrichsville, OH: Barbour Publishing, Inc, u.d.), 67–68.

15. Charles Spurgeon, "Death and Its Sentence Abolished," 15 January 1899, www.spurgeon.org/sermons/2605.htm (accessed 28 June 2009).

16. Charles Swindoll, *The Tale of the Tardy Oxcart* (Nashville, TN: Word, 1998), 77.

17. John Ortberg, *Faith and Doubt* (Grand Rapids, MI: Zondervan, 2008), 84–85.

18. Robert J. Morgan, *From This Verse* (Nashville: Thomas Nelson, 1998), installment for July 4. See also Richard S. Greene, "Where Will the Money Come From?" *Decision Magazine*, May 1997, 32–33.

19. Geoffrey Thomas, *Reading the Bible* (Carlisle, PA: The Banner of Truth Trust, 1995), 10.

20. Rebecca K. Grosenbach, "A Holy Pursuit," *Inside Story*, Navigators. org, March 2009, www.navigators.org/us/view/one-to-one _mr/2009/mar09/items/inside-story (accessed 28 June2009).

21. Jerry Bridges, *Trusting God* (Colorado Springs, CO: NavPress, 2008) 7, 14, 16.

22. Helen H. Lemmel, "Turn Your Eyes upon Jesus,"1922, *Cyberhymnal.org*, www.cyberhymnal.org/htm/t/u/turnyour.htm (accessed 28 June 2009).

23. Randy Alcorn, *The Treasure Principle* (Sisters, OR: Multnomah Press, 2001), 42–43.

24. Ibid.

25. Viktor E. Frankl, *Man's Searching for Meaning* (Boston: Beacon Press, 1992), 48–52.

26. G. Campbell Morgan, "The Fixed Heart in the Day of Frightfulness" in *The Shadow of Grace—The Life and Meditations of G. Campbell Morgan,* Richard Morgan, Howard Morgan and John Morgan, comp. and ed. (Grand Rapids, MI: Baker Books, 2007), 76.

## Chapter 7: Stay Confident

1. See video of the 29 September 2008 interview www.youtube.com /watch?v=PHH2JItePlc&feature=PlayList&p=0AD448945A54A8B

9&playnext=1&playnext_from=PL&index=9. Transcribed by the author (accessed 28 June 2009).

2. Stephen Thompson, "Is There A God?" *A. V. Club.com*, 9 October 2002, www.avclub.com/articles/is-there-a-god,1413/ (accessed 28 June 2009).

3. Dan Gilgoff, "Bobby Jindal's Come-to-Jesus Writings," *U.S. News. com,* 24 February 2009, www.usnews.com/blogs/god-and -country/2009/2/24/bobby-jindals-come-to-jesus-writings.html (accessed 28 June 2009).

4. Winne Hu, "In a New Generation of College Students, Many Opt for the Life Examined," *New York Times*, 6 April 2008, www .nytimes.com/2008/04/06/education/06philosophy.html (accessed 28 June 2009).

5. Beth Moore, *Voice of the Faithful* (Nashville, TN: Thomas Nelson, 2005), 39–40.

6. "Titanic Memorandum", National Archives and Record Administration: American Originals, www.archives.gov/exhibits /american_originals/titanic.html (accessed 28 June 2009).

7. Thomas Watson, "A Body of Divinity," *Puritanism Today*, puritanismtoday.wordpress.com/theologians-preaching-and%20 -%20preachers/ (accessed 28 June 2009).

8. Told by M. R. De Haan, MD, quoted at www.preceptaustin .org/2_timothy_42.htm (accessed 28 June 2009).

9. Rob Suggs, *It Came from Beneath the Pew* (Downers Grove, IL: InterVarsity Press, 1989).

10. J. Sidlow Baxter, *The Master Theme of the Bible, Part One: The Doctrine of the Lamb* (Wheaton: Tyndale House Publishers, Inc., 1985), 19.

11. Arthur T. Pierson, *Many Infallible Proofs: The Evidences of Christianity, Volume One* (Grand Rapids: Zondervan Publishing House, 1886), 90.

12. Jill Morgan, *A Man of the Word: Life of G. Campbell Morgan* (Grand Rapids: Baker, 1972), 38–41.

13. Henry F. Schaefer III, *Science and Christianity: Conflict or Coherence?* (Athens, GA: The University of Georgia Press, 2003), passim.

14. John Steinbeck, *Travels with Charley* (New York: Penguin Classics, 1997), 60–61.
15. R. Kent Hughes, *Luke* (Wheaton, IL: Crossway Books, 1998), 145–149.
16. Amy Carmichael, *Edges of His Ways* (Fort Washington, PA: Christian Literature Crusade, 1998), 41.
17. Corrie Ten Boom with Elizabeth and John Sherrill, *The Hiding Place* (New York: Bantam Books, 1974), 130, 134–135.
18. Ibid., 194.

## Chapter 8: Stay Consistent

1. "Couple: County Trying to Stop Home Bible Studies," *10 News. com*: San Diego News, www.10news.com/news/19562217/detail .html (accessed 28 June 2009).
2. Rob Suggs, *Top Dawg: Mark Richt and the Revival of Georgia Football* (Nashville: Thomas Nelson, 2008), 5.
3. V. Raymond Edman, *They Found the Secret* (Grand Rapids: Zondervan, 1960), Chapter 1.
4. Eugene Peterson, *A Long Obedience in the Same Direction: Discipleship in an Instant Society* (Downers Grove, IL: InterVarsity Press, 1980).
5. Cartoonist Rob Portlock in *Leadership*, Vol. 13, no. 3.
6. Marjorie Howard, "Consistently Caring," *Tufts Journal,* January 2008, tuftsjournal.tufts.edu/archive/2008/january/corner/index .shtml (accessed 1 July 2009).
7. Danielle Bean, "Amazing Adoption Story," *Faith and Family Live!* 13 November 2008, view video at www.faithandfamilylive.com /blog/amazing_adoption_story (accessed 28 June 2009).
8. Omar El Akkad, "This Is Your Brain on Religion," (Toronto) *Globe and Mail,* 5 March 2009. The complete article may be purchased at GlobeandMail.com. See also Jenny Green, "Religious brains more calm in face of anxiety: study," *Calgary Herald.com*, Canwest News Service, 4 March 2009, www.calgaryherald.com/Life/Religious+bra ins+more+calm+face+anxiety+study/1354346/story.html (accessed 28 June 2009).

9. Dorothy Fields, "Pick Yourself Up," (© 1936) at lyricsplayground .com/alpha/songs/p/pickyourselfup.shtml (accessed 1 July 2009).

10. Frank Houghton, *Amy Carmichael of Dohnavur* (London: S.P.C.K. 1959, distributed by Christian Literature Crusade, Fort Washington, PA, 1959), 115, 357, and passim.

11. Charles Swindoll, *Rise and Shine* (Portland, OR: Multnomah Press, 1989), 169. See also Martin Hodgson, "Christian driver refuses to board bus carrying atheist slogan," The Guardian, 17 January 2009, www.guardian.co.uk/world/2009/jan/17/atheist-bus -campaign (accessed 29 June 2009).

12. "Man refuses to drive 'no God' bus," *BBC News/UK*, 16 January 2009, news.bbc.co.uk/2/hi/uk_news/england/hampshire/7832647 .stm (accessed 28 June 2009).

## Chapter 9: Stay Committed

1. Duncan Greenberg and Tatiana Serafin, "Up in Smoke," *Forbes. com*, 30 March 2009, www.forbes.com/forbes/2009/0330/076-up -in-smoke.html (accessed 28 June 2009).

2. Ibid.

3. Carter Doughtery, "Town Mourns Typical Businessman Who Took Atypical Risks," *New York Times.com*: World Business, www .nytimes.com/2009/01/13/business/worldbusiness/13merckle .html?_r=1&ref=business (accessed 28 June 2009).

4. William Boston, "Financial Casualty: Why Merckle Killed Himself," *Time*, 6 January 2009, www.time.com/time/business /article/0,8599,1870007,00.html (accessed 28 June 2009).

5. Ibid., Doughtery.

6. Timothy Martin and Kevin Helliker, "Real-Estate Executive Found Dead in Apparent Suicide," *Wall Street Journal*, 7 January 2009, online.wsj.com/article/SB123127267562558295.html (accessed 28 June 2009).

7. "Sale ordered of Marcus Schrenker's home, plane," Associated Press, Noblesville, Indiana, *The Herald Bulletin*, 2 June 2009, www .theheraldbulletin.com/local/local_story_153205807.html /resources_printstory (accessed 28 June 2009).

8. Mike Whitney, "Financial Markets and Economic Crash, the Next Leg Down Will Be Worse," *Market Oracle.com*, 26 May 2009, www.marketoracle.co.uk/index.php?name=News&file=article&sid=10904 (accessed 28 June 2009).

9. John Horgan, "The California dream is on life support," *San Mateo County Times*, 26 May 2009, Inside Bay Area.com, www.insidebayarea.com/sanmateocountytimes/localnews/ci_12453299 (accessed 28 June 2009).

10. Karen Garloch, "Economic hard times may be fueling rise in suicide attempts," *Charlotte Observer*, 27 May 2009, www.charlotteobserver.com/597/story/747127.html?storylink=omni_popular (accessed 28 June 2009).

11. "Buffett Says Five Years for Economy to Recover," *Sydney Morning Herald*, 19 March 2009, www.midasletter.com/news/09031906_Buffett-says-five-years-for-economy-to-recover.php (accessed 28 June 2009).

12. Steven Erlanger and Stephen Castle, "European Leader Assails American Stimulus Plan," *New York Times.com*, 25 March 2009, www.nytimes.com/2009/03/26/world/europe/26czech.html (accessed 28 June 2009).

13. Robert J. Morgan, *Nelson's Complete Book of Stories, Illustrations & Quotes* (Nashville, TN: Thomas Nelson, 2000), 600–601.

14. "William Carey: Father of modern Protestant missions," *Christianity Today.com*, Christian History, 8 August 2008, www.christianitytoday.com/ch/131christians/missionaries/carey.html (accessed 28 June 2009).

15. Eugene Myers Harrison, "Adoniram Judson," www.reformedreader.org/rbb/judson/ajbio.htm (accessed 28 June 2009).

16. Robert Stuart MacArthur, *Quick Truths in Quaint Texts: Second Series* (Philadelphia: American Baptist Publication Society, 1870), 172.

17. Don Aycock, *Living by the Fruit of the Spirit* (Grand Rapids, MI: Kregel Publications, 1999), 54.

18. Hamilton Smith, ed., *Gleanings from the Past, Vol.3* (London: Central Bible Truth Depot, 1915), www.stempublishing.com/authors/smith/WATSON.html (accessed 28 June 2009).

19. Robert J. Morgan, *Moments for Families with Prodigals* (Colorado Springs: NavPress, 2003), 101.

20. "When Will Jesus Return?" *Pew Research Center Publications*, 9 April 2009, pewresearch.org/pubs/1187/poll-christians-jesus -second-coming-timing (accessed 28 June 2009).

21. Charles Wentworth Upham, *George Washington, The Life of General Washington: First President of the United States, Vol. II,* (London: National Illustrated Library, 1852), 181.

22. "Seed Germination," *Washington State University*, gardening.wsu .edu/library/vege004/vege004.htm (accessed 28 June 2009).

23. Alfred Edersheim, *The Life and Times of Jesus the Messiah* (Hendrickson Publishers, Inc., 1993) 119–120.

24. Kevin Miller, "The End of the World As We Know It," *Preaching Today*, www.preachingtoday.com/sermons/sermons /endoftheworldasweknowit.html (accessed 28 June 2009).

25. Stephen Charnock, *The Existence and Attributes of God* (Grand Rapids: Baker Books, 1996; originally published in 1853), 278, 279, 281.

26. David Dunlap, "Eternity of God," *Bible & Life Bible Teaching Newsletter,* 1 January 2000, www. peter.sff.home.insightbb.com /bibleandlife_2000_1.htm (accessed 1 July 2009).

27. Linda Derby, *Life's Sticky Wicks* (working title/unpublished manuscript), 20.

28. W. E. Sangster, *The Pure in Heart,* cited in William Sykes, ed., *The Eternal Vision—The Ultimate Collection of Spiritual Quotations* (Peabody, MA: Hendrickson Publishers, Inc., 2002), 315.

29. *Perfect Illustrations for Every Topic and Occasion, Preaching Today. com* (Wheaton, IL: Tyndale House Publishers, 2002), 97.

## Chapter 10: Stay Convinced

1. Eiten Haber, "World War III has started," *Ynet News Opinion*, Ynetnews.com, 27 May 2009, www.ynetnews.com /articles/0,7340,L-3722339,00.html (accessed 28 June 2009).

2. Con Coughlin, "N. Korea helping Iran with nuclear testing," Telegraph.co.uk, 25 January 2007, www.telegraph.co.uk/news

/worldnews/1540429/N-Korea-helping-Iran-with-nuclear-testing
.html (accessed 28 June 2009).

3. Sandra I. Erwin and Stew Magnuson, "7 Deadly Myths About
   Weapons of Terror," *National Defense Magazine,* June 2009, www
   .nationaldefensemagazine.org/ARCHIVE/2009/JUNE/
   Pages/7Deadly.aspx (accessed 2 June 2009).

4. "Former Russian official says 100 portable bombs missing," AP,
   *Lubbock Avalanche-Journal,* 5 September 1997, www
   .lubbockonline.com/news/090597/LA0759.htm (accessed 2 June
   2009). And Richard Miniter, *Disinformation* (Washington, DC:
   Regnery Publishing, 2005), especially "Myth #17: Suitcase Nukes
   are a Real Threat," 135ff.

5. Elizabeth Zolotukhini, "The Loose Russian Nukes,"GlobalSecurity
   .org, Sitrep Situation, 19 May 2009, sitrep.globalsecurity.org/articles
   /090519345-the-loose-russian-nukes.htm (accessed 28 June 2009).

6. Ibid., "7 Deadly Myths About Weapons of Terror."

7. "Live Like You Were Dying", words and music by James Timothy
   Nichols and Craig Michael Wiseman. © 2004 Warner-Tamerlane
   Publishing and Big Loud Shirt. ASCAP/BMI. All rights reserved.

8. *ABC News.go.com,* abcnews.go.com/GMA/LastLecture (accessed 28
   June 2009).

9. "The Iowa Band," en.wikipedia.org/wiki/Iowa_Band (accessed 10
   April 2009).

10. Charles Spurgeon, "A Bright Light in Deep Shades," *The
    Metropolitan Tabernacle Pulpit, Vol. XVIII* (London: Passmore &
    Alabaster, 1873), 270.

11. Henry Richard, *Letters and Essays on Wales* (1884) Internet
    Archive/Texts, www.archive.org/stream/lettersessaysonw00richiala
    /lettersessaysonw00richiala_djvu.txt (accessed 28 June 2009).

12. A. W. Tozer (1897–1963), "Causes of a Dozing Church," *Tozer
    Devotional: Rut, Rot or Revival,* www.cmalliance.org/devotions
    /tozer/tozer.jsp?id=328 (accessed 28 June 2009).

13. Vance Havner, *In Times Like These* (Old Tappan, NJ: Fleming H,
    Revell Company, 1969), 29, as quoted in David Jeremiah, *What in
    the World Is Going On?* (Nashville: Thomas Nelson, 2008), 232.

14. Ibid., Tozer.

15. Larry E. Swedroe, *What Wall Street Doesn't Want You to Know: How You Can Build Real Wealth* (New York: Macmillan, 2004), 11.

16. Michael Brooks, "Space storm alert: 90 seconds from catastrophe," *New Scientist.com*, 23 March 2009, www.newscientist.com/article /mg20127001.300-space-storm-alert-90-seconds-from -catastrophe.html?full=true (accessed 28 June 2009).

17. "A Super Solar Flare," *NASA*, Science, NASA.gov, 6 May 2008, science.nasa.gov/headlines/y2008/06may_carringtonflare.htm (accessed 28 June 2009).

18. Charles Haddon Spurgeon, *The Metropolitan Tabernacle Pulpit: Sermons Preached and Revised, "Wake Up! Wake Up!"* (London: Passmore & Alabaster, 1879), 657.

19. Alexander Maclaren, *The Gospel According to St. John* (New York: A. C. Armstrong and Son, 1908), 228.

20. James Montgomery, "Forever with the Lord", *Poet's Portfolio*, 1835, Cyberhymnal.com. www.nethymnal.org/htm/f/w/fwithlor.htm (accessed 28 June 2009).

21. John Phillips, *Experiencing Romans*, (Chicago: Moody Press, 1969), 231.

22. "Most America Christians Do Not Believe that Satan or the Holy Spirit Exist," *Barna Research Group Update*, 13 April 2009, www .barna.org/barna-update/article/12-faithspirituality/260-most -american-christians-do-not-believe-that-satan-or-the-holy-spirit -exis (accessed 28 June 2009).

23. A. W. Tozer, *The Pursuit of the Holy* (Rockville, MD: 2008), front matter.

24. Ray Stedman, *From Guilt to Glory,* Volume 21 (Waco, TX: Word, 1978), 136.

25. David McCullough, *Truman* (New York: Simon & Schuster, 1992), 435.

26. Mona Charen, "'Tis the Season for Porn," *National Review Online*, 19 December 2008, article.nationalreview.com/?q=ZDkxN2NmO DI1NjE0OTNiZTI4MTNiMDRkZGY4MjI4Mzc= (accessed 28 June 2009).

27. Ray Stedman, *Expository Studies in I Corinthians: The Deep Things of God* (Waco, TX: Words Books, 1981), 130–131.

28. "Memorable Quotes for Saving Private Ryan," www.imdb.com /title/tt0120815/quotes (accessed 28 June 2009).

# Escape the Coming Night

No one can deny that the world is in trouble. Tragedy stalks our streets. Violence and bloodshed fill the news. Today's political debates spotlight the deep and bitter divisions in a society that often seem to be coming apart at the seams. How do we explain so much chaos? How do we live with such turmoil? Is there any hope for peace in our time?

Dr. David Jeremiah's dramatic narrative on the Book of Revelation answers these and many more challenging questions, guiding the reader on an electrifying tour of a world careening headlong into climactic times. His perceptive analysis of what many have called "the most ignored and most misunderstood book in the Bible" proves that we are living in the very times described by St. John the Apostle in his amazing prophecies.

*Escape the Coming Night* is a penetrating look at the prophetic time machine that is in the book of Revelation and a vivid reminder of how, in the face of coming darkness, we should live today.

### Resources Available:

**Book**

**Study Guide (Volumes 1 - 4)**

**CD Audio Albums  (Volumes 1 - 4)**
43 messsages

**For pricing information and to order**
***Escape the Coming Night,* contact us at**
**www.DavidJeremiah.org or call (800) 947-1993.**

# Until Christ Returns

Drawing from the Olivet Discourse in the book of Matthew, *Until Christ Returns* outlines priorities for believers in an era of heightened stress and confusion. The Shepherd has spoken! Some of His words comfort; others rebuke. Though heaven and earth pass away, not one of His words ever will. This is no time for the church to panic, to become distracted, to be confused by prophetic rabbit trails, or to miss priceless opportunities. In fact, these may be the best days to proclaim Christ since the first century. Learn more about the opportunities we have as Christians in this series by Dr. Jeremiah, *Until Christ Returns.*

## Resources Available:

Book

Study Guide

CD Audio Album
25 messsages

For pricing information and to order
*Until Christ Returns,* contact us at
www.DavidJeremiah.org or call (800) 947-1993.

# INCORPORATE THESE CORRELATING
# STUDY MATERIALS
## BY AUTHOR DR. DAVID JEREMIAH

### STUDY GUIDE

This 128-page study guide correlates with the *Living with Confidence in a Chaotic World* messages by Dr. David Jeremiah. Each lesson provides an outline, overview, and application study questions for each chapter.

### AUDIO MESSAGE ALBUM
10 AUDIO MESSAGES

The material found in this book originated from messages preached by Dr. David Jeremiah at Shadow Mountain Community Church where he serves as Senior Pastor. These ten messages are conveniently packaged in one audio album.

### DVD MESSAGE PRESENTATIONS
10 DVD MESSAGES

Watch Dr. Jeremiah deliver the ten *Living with Confidence in a Chaotic World* original messages in the special DVD collection.

### SMALL GROUP STUDY CURRICULUM

The *Living with Confidence in a Chaotic World* DVD-Based Small Group Kit will take your small group or Sunday school class through ten weeks of Dr. Jeremiah's teaching for living with certain hope in our uncertain times.

ORDER THESE *LIVING WITH CONFIDENCE IN A CHAOTIC WORLD* RESOURCE PRODUCTS FROM DAVIDJEREMIAH.ORG

# OTHER TITLES
## BY DR. DAVID JEREMIAH

### CAPTURED BY GRACE  *A NEW YORK TIMES* BEST-SELLER!

By following the dramatic story of the "Amazing Grace" hymnwriter, John Newton, and the apostle Paul's own encounter with the God of grace, David Jeremiah helps readers understand the liberating power of permanent forgiveness and mercy.

### LIFE WIDE OPEN

In this energizing book, Dr. David Jeremiah opens our eyes to how we can live a life that exudes an attitude of hope and enthusiasm . . . a life of passion . . . a LIFE WIDE OPEN! *Life Wide Open* offers a vision, both spiritual and practical, of what our life can be when we allow the power of passion to permeate our souls.

### SIGNS OF LIFE  *A NEW YORK TIMES* BEST-SELLER!

How does the world recognize us as God's ambassadors? In *Signs of Life* you will take a journey that will lead you to a fuller understanding of the marks that identify you as a Christian, signs that will advertise your faith and impact souls for eternity.

### MY HEART'S DESIRE

How would you answer a pollster who appeared at your church asking for a definition of worship? Is it really a sin to worship without sacrifice? When you finish studying *My Heart's Desire*, you'll have not just an answer, but the biblical answer to that all-important question.

## SEARCHING FOR HEAVEN ON EARTH

Join Dr. Jeremiah as he traces Solomon's path through the futility of:

• The search for wisdom and knowledge
• Wild living and the pursuit of pleasure
• Burying oneself in work
• Acquiring as much wealth as possible

Dr. Jeremiah takes readers on a discovery to find out what really matters in life, the secret to enjoying "heaven on earth."

## WHEN YOUR WORLD FALLS APART

*When Your World Falls Apart* recounts Dr. Jeremiah's battle against cancer and the real-life stories of others who have struggled with tragedy. Highlighting ten Psalms of encouragement, each chapter is a beacon of light in those moments when life seems hopeless.

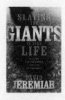

## SLAYING THE GIANTS IN YOUR LIFE

Loneliness. Discouragement. Worry. Anger. Procrastination. Doubt. Fear. Guilt. Temptation. Resentment. Failure. Jealousy. Have these giants infiltrated your life? Do you need the tools to slay these daunting foes? With practical appeal and personal warmth, Dr. Jeremiah's book, *Slaying the Giants in Your Life* will become your very own giant-slaying manual.

## TURNING POINTS & SANCTUARY

These 365-day devotionals by Dr. Jeremiah will equip you to live with God's perspective. These topically arranged devotionals enable you to relate biblical truths to the reality of everyday living—every day of the year. Perfect for yourself or your next gift-giving occasion, *Turning Points* and *Sanctuary* are beautifully packaged with a padded cover, original artwork throughout, and a ribbon page marker.

# STAY CONNECTED
## TO THE TEACHING OF DR. DAVID JEREMIAH

Take advantage of two great ways to let Dr. David Jeremiah give you spiritual direction everyday! Both are absolutely FREE!

---

## *TURNING POINTS* MAGAZINE AND DEVOTIONAL

Receive Dr. David Jeremiah's monthly magazine, *Turning Points* each month:

- Monthly Study Focus
- 48 pages of life-changing reading
- Relevant Articles
- Special Features
- Humor Section
- Family Section
- Daily devotional readings for each day of the month
- Bible study resource offers
- Live Event Schedule
- Radio & Television Information

## YOUR DAILY TURNING POINT E-DEVOTIONAL

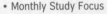

Start your day off right!  Find words of inspiration and spiritual motivation waiting for you on your computer every morning! You can receive a daily e-devotion communication from David Jeremiah that will strengthen your walk with God and encourage you to live the authentic Christian life.

Sign up for these two **free** services by visiting us online at www.DavidJeremiah.org and clicking on **MAGAZINE** to sign up for your monthly copy of *Turning Points* and your Daily Turning Point.

# ⬆ MAXIMUM CHURCH

## READY! SET! GROWTH!

LET DR. JEREMIAH'S MAXIMUM CHURCH TAKE YOUR CHURCH THERE.

With a united vision to strengthen the Body of Christ and reach the community, your church can experience spiritual and fiscal growth through creative and compelling campaigns.

With over forty years of ministry experience, founder Dr. David Jeremiah now shares his passion for pulpit teaching and church leadership by offering solid Bible teaching campaigns designed to stimulate the spiritual and fiscal growth of local churches. Maximum Church campaigns are created for full-spectrum ministry including preaching, teaching, drama, small group Bible curriculum, and suggested Sunday school material—all supported by electronic, print, and audio visual files.

## SIGNS OF LIFE

Lead your church to become one of Christ-like influence in your community as you take the five Life Signs discussed in this book and apply them to the lives of your congregation.

This campaign is based on Dr. David Jeremiah's best-selling book *Signs of Life*.

## CAPTURED BY GRACE

Based on the best-selling book *Captured by Grace* by David Jeremiah, this ministry growth campaign will help your church and community discover the depths of God's unrelenting love and grace.

For more information on Maximum Church,
VISIT WWW.MAXIMUMCHURCH.COM